"REMARKABLE BIOGRAPHY . . . In adopting a personal, reflective, biographical mode, Ms. Lane has joined other feminist scholars who are currently experimenting with innovative ways of telling the tales of women's lives. . . . This unusual plan works exceedingly well."
—*New York Times Book Review*

"THIS STUDY IS THE BEST SO FAR, primarily because Ms. Lane is critical as well as sympathetic. . . . The result clarifies Gilman's contributions, particularly her originality in seeing, and exploring, the extent to which our concepts of gender and gender roles derive from our cultural rather than our biological inheritance."
—*The New Yorker*

"A WOMAN'S COURAGEOUS—AND DEFIANT—PUBLIC AND PRIVATE LIFE . . . Lane diligently reviews Gilman's extensive writings to explain her contribution to feminism and social theory, and lets us hear her candid, even passionate, voice through her letters."
—*Kirkus Reviews*

"ENGROSSING . . . A MAJOR WORK."   —*Publishers Weekly*

ANN J. LANE is a professor of history and director of the Women's Studies Program at the University of Virginia. In addition to editing *The Charlotte Perkins Gilman Reader,* she rediscovered Gilman's novel, *Herland.* Her other books include *The Brownsville Affair: National Outrage and Black Reaction* and *Mary Ritter Beard: A Sourcebook.* She also edited and wrote the introduction for *The Debate Over "Slavery": Stanley Elkins and His Critics.* She lives in Charlottesville, Virginia.

"AN IDEAL INTRODUCTION TO THE LIFE AND WORK OF THIS EXTRAORDINARY WOMAN." —*Newsday*

"Richly researched and well-written biography . . . Lane's choice of an encircling mode of storytelling rather than a linear one is an important act of feminist scholarship." —*The Nation*

"THIS IS A FASCINATING BIOGRAPHY of a complex early twentieth-century woman, informed by the voice of an astute historian. . . . Lane provides the first convincing interpretation of the 'fit' between Charlotte Perkins Gilman's personal and professional life." —Joan Jacobs Brumberg, author of *Fasting Girls*

"A CHALLENGING INTERPRETATION which illuminates the connection between Gilman's life and work and elevates her stature as a feminist theoretician." —Gerda Lerner, *The Creation of Patriarchy*

TO
Herland
AND BEYOND

The life and work of
Charlotte Perkins Gilman

ANN J. LANE

A MERIDIAN BOOK

MERIDIAN
Published by the Penguin Group
Penguin Books USA Inc., 375 Hudson Street, New York, New York 10014, U.S.A.
Penguin Books Ltd, 27 Wrights Lane, London W8 5TZ, England
Penguin Books Australia Ltd, Ringwood, Victoria, Australia
Penguin Books Canada Ltd, 10 Alcorn Avenue, Toronto, Ontario, Canada M4V 3B2
Penguin Books (N.Z.) Ltd, 182-190 Wairau Road, Auckland 10, New Zealand

Penguin Books Ltd, Registered Offices: Harmondsworth, Middlesex, England

Published by Meridian, an imprint of New American Library, a division of Penguin Books USA Inc.
This is an authorized reprint of a hardcover edition published by Pantheon Books.

First Meridian Printing, November, 1991
10 9 8 7 6 5 4 3 2 1

The permission acknowledgments may be found on page 399.

 REGISTERED TRADEMARK—MARCA REGISTRADA

LIBRARY OF CONGRESS CATALOGING-IN-PUBLICATION DATA

Lane, Ann J., 1931-
    To Herland and beyond : the life and work of Charlotte Perkins
Gilman / Ann J. Lane
        p.   cm.
    Originally published: New York : Pantheon Books, c1990.
    Includes bibliographical references and index.
    ISBN 0-452-01080-2
    1. Gilman, Charlotte Perkins, 1860-1935.   2. Authors,
American—19th century—Biography.   3. Authors, American—20th
century—Biography.   4. Feminism and literature—United States.
5. Feminists—United States—Biography.   I. Title.
PS1744.G57Z74   1991
818'.409—dc20
    [B]   91-26893
                                                                                 CIP

Printed in the United States of America
Original hardcover designed by Jenny Vandeventer

For my daughters
Leslie Nuchow
and
Joni Lane

and to the memory of
Janet James
and
Warren Susman

CONTENTS

LIST OF ILLUSTRATIONS

PREFACE

This is the story of my Charlotte. The shape of the personality and the life of Charlotte Perkins Gilman as I present it conforms to what is known about her. The record provides the boundaries, but it does not offer the portrait. The portrait is essentially mine, a product of our dialogue these last years, the dialogue between Charlotte and me. I think others who know her work and her life will recognize her on these pages. I like to think she would recognize herself, smile, and nod with recognition at a design that is familiar but one she could not herself make, because she did not have the distance or the desire for introspection, both of which are required.

When I began to write, I did not know what kind of biography it would turn out to be. I had some idea what I wanted to accomplish but not how to do it. That sense came with the writing. What is important to know about Gilman is both the way she created her life and the significance of the work she left behind, and it became clear that the format of this book should reflect this dual concern: I needed to be sufficiently respectful of her work not simply to fit it into a chronological narrative. At a certain point in the book I stop following the flow of events and turn to assessing the work in order to convey a sense of the full contours of the intellectual legacy, without which the significance of Charlotte Gilman's life cannot be understood. Thus, there are two dialogues embedded in this study, that between author and subject and that between the subject's life and her work.

Biographers make many choices about how to present the life they are exploring, about what is to be of primary concern: the details of the life? the public career? the cultural context? I have chosen the life itself as my subject, not just the life in general, but the way in which Charlotte's inner life developed. And the way I understand her inner growth is through the major relationships that gave form to her personality. Charlotte made this task easy by writing so much about herself, even if her angle of vision was inevitably very different from mine.

The book is thus structured around the central relationships in Charlotte Gilman's life. It begins with her father and mother, includes three close and intimate women friends, two husbands, and the neurologist who treated her, and concludes with her daughter. Through these relationships one can see the struggles, the setbacks, the gains, the patterns of Charlotte's life. The approach I have used is not strictly chronological: just as a life process is not a smooth movement from place to place but a complex and multilayered progression, so too is my examination of her life and the relationships that characterize it. I return to given themes or aspects of relationships many times, reassessing their significance and implications, much as one does with one's own life. How much easier and more fruitful it is to assess someone else's life in this manner. The advantage of knowing as we start how it all turns out carries with it a danger that must be avoided—that of seeing inevitability in a process that is finished. But the benefits are greater, for it is possible to make sense of, to see a pattern in, to understand a response to, events and people that it would have been almost impossible to comprehend while the process was going on. If I have fulfilled my intention in this book, the reader will move along with me, making connections, filling in the spaces in the narrative, and while I care a great deal about persuading you, I also care about having you participate actively in the process of discovery. Thus, there is another dialogue: that between the reader and me. What do I want the reader to see, to know? How Charlotte's contemporaries saw her? How she is viewed today? How I see her? How she saw herself? A prior question remains unspoken but significant: what can we know and what can't we know about the life of another? Biography as a form is enormously valuable in helping us understand the ways in which social relations and social issues are embodied in the life of a given individual, and I have tried to deal with all of the questions I posed above, some more intensively than others.

"What would happen if one woman told the truth about her life," was a question the poet Muriel Rukeyser posed. And her answer? "The world would split open." Charlotte Gilman told us a great deal about herself to accomplish just that. Nobody, in fact, wrote more about her than she herself did, and I was both grateful for and burdened by the extraordinary outpouring of words that came in the form of diaries, letters, essays published and unpublished, an unpublished autobiography written when she was nineteen, and a published autobiography written in her mature years. There are obvious dangers to a biographer in having accessible such detailed and extensive sources of information, but the value of such rich resources is greater. Still, the reader should be alerted that much of my information on such central figures as Charlotte's mother, Mary Perkins, and Houghton Gilman comes filtered through Charlotte's pen.

Charlotte's autobiography provides wonderful material for a biographer. I have come to believe that Charlotte's self-portraits are emotionally true. The issues to be sorted out by a biographer have more to do with time than truth. Do her self-portraits reflect how she remembered herself at the time of a given event, or was this how, at age sixty-six or seventy-five—the two points at which she worked on her published autobiography—she assessed her earlier life, or how she had actually been? It is the dialogue between past and present that causes mischief for the biographer in reading her subject's autobiography. In Charlotte Gilman's situation, she largely restrained her impulse to reshape her story by relying greatly on diaries and letters. She went over those materials with care as she was preparing her autobiography. As a result, there is some, but not considerable, inconsistency between her view of herself as she lived her life and her view as she looked back upon it years later.

The casual relationship to the rules of spelling and grammar evidenced in Charlotte Gilman's writings reflects both her limited formal education and her later articulated belief that such rules were not especially important. Rather than clutter the text with endless [sic] notations, I have chosen to reproduce her language as she wrote it and alert the reader as to what I have done. I revert to the use of [*sic*] in the writings of others, where appropriate.

I was initially drawn to Gilman by the power and originality of her ideas. But as I prepared two different collections of her writing for publication, I found myself increasingly caught up in the way she lived her life, the way she was in the world, particularly how she managed her terrifying and unending fear of insanity and the gnawing poverty that always plagued her. She became of great importance to me, and I hope she will to the reader as well, both because of who she was and what she said.

A.J.L.

Hamilton, N.Y., 1989

ACKNOWLEDGMENTS

This book had its beginning when I was at The Mary Ingraham Bunting Institute of Radcliffe College preparing an edition of *Herland* for publication. I continued to ruminate on the idea of a biography of Gilman while I put together a collection of her fiction as a continuing part of the project. I begin these acknowledgments with the Bunting Institute because that place and the people in it and the people who directed it, especially Marion Kilson and Mary Anderson, provided the kind of nourishing intellectual and human environment I had until then never encountered. Grants from the National Endowment for the Humanities and the Ford Foundation provided the resources for me to continue at that institution while I worked on this book. A senior faculty leave from Colgate University made it possible for me to devote an essential final semester, free of teaching and administrative duties, to completing the manuscript. Special thanks go to the staff of the Arthur and Elizabeth Schlesinger Library of Radcliffe College, home of most of the Gilman papers, for the generous and unstinting help and creative support I received from everyone associated with that library, but particularly the Director, Patricia King; the Manuscripts Librarian, Eva Mosley; and the Books and Periodicals Librarian, Barbara Haber.

I very much appreciate the warm welcome and enthusiastic cooperation I received from members of Charlotte Gilman's family: her daughter, the late Katharine Stetson Chamberlin; her grandchildren, Dorothy Stetson Chamberlin and Walter Chamberlin; her nephew, Thomas Gardiner Perkins, and his wife, Jean Devareau.

Over a period of time many friends and colleagues have helped me by discussing my ideas, facilitating my giving public lectures on Gilman, directing me to new material, sharing their own work, or reading drafts of chapters or the entire completed manuscript, and I wish to thank Polly Wynn Allen, Ben Barker Benfield, Jeffrey Berman, Bea Chorover, Daniel Borus, Joan Jacobs Brumberg, Nancy Cott, Faye Dudden, Linda Gordon, Carol Hurd Green, Eugenia Kaledin, Linda Kerber, Gerda Lerner, Helena Lewis, Rolando Lopez, Dewey Mosby, Ruth Perry, Joan Rothschild, Claire Sprague, Warren Susman, Marilyn Thie, and Irving Zola. For the several years I lived in the Boston area, I was part of a very special biography group made up of five feminist scholars—Joyce Antler, Janet James, Barbara Sicherman, Susan Ware, and me—all of us writing biographies of women. Each month we met, the five writers and the five subjects, to talk, to argue, to challenge, to applaud, to celebrate, and I cherish no personal, intellectual, or professional experience more than I do those monthly gatherings. Stephanie Siegel and Katharine Feely, two former students, did resourceful work as research assistants. I am indebted to the many bright and lively students in my classes at Colgate over the years who helped me think through my ideas about Gilman. Mary Smith Keys typed the manuscript more than once, with endless patience tracked down photographs and bibliographical references, and most of all gave me valuable feedback at every stage.

When I learned I was to lose Tom Engelhardt as my editor, I was initially crushed because Tom and I had worked closely and well on two volumes of Gilman's writing, and he had already seen me through the early stages of this manuscript. But Helena Franklin was a superb successor. Rarely does an author have the good fortune to have an editor as committed, as wise, as judicious, and as attentive as Helena, and I very much appreciate and acknowledge how much I benefitted from the help I received from her.

My children came of age in the company of Charlotte Perkins Gilman, and I like to think that, however much they had to share my time with her, they gained much from that experience.

To *Herland* And Beyond

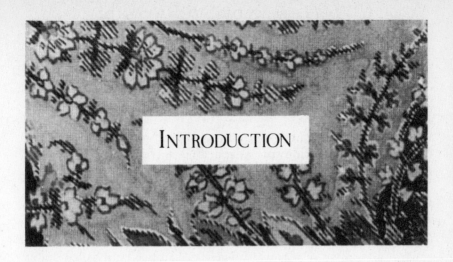

INTRODUCTION

T he story of Charlotte Perkins Gilman is that of a woman seeking
to create a life in which an autonomous sense of self, intimate
relationships, and emotional stability could all be sustained. Given
the many difficulties she faced throughout much of her life, her
ultimate achievement of these goals was extraordinary. Her childhood was filled with neglect and rejection, her father having abandoned his family shortly after her birth. Her young womanhood
was blighted by a disastrous marriage that triggered a severe nervous
breakdown, the first of many depressions that plagued her throughout her life. Her decision to divorce her husband and send their
young daughter to live with him and his second wife aroused public
vilification directed at her. And all her life she was poor.

Charlotte could not undo the past, but she learned to live with
it, to live around it, and to learn from it. She survived—no, more,
she soared, in a world that conspired to deny her flight. She ultimately accomplished much of what she set out to do: create a loving
and sustained intimate relationship with a partner and leave behind
a legacy of a lifetime of valuable work.

In the first decades of this century, Charlotte Perkins Gilman
was recognized internationally as a major theorist and social commentator. Even today, more than four decades after her death, her
work stands as a major theoretical contribution to feminist thought.
She offered a perspective on major issues of gender with which we
still grapple: the origins of women's subjugation; the struggle to

achieve both autonomy and intimacy in human relationships; the central role of work as a definition of self; new strategies for rearing and educating future generations to create a humane and nurturing environment.

Her written output was prodigious. In 1898 the first and best known of her nonfiction studies appeared. Its full title is *Women and Economics: The Economic Relation Between Men and Women as a Factor in Social Evolution*. It is not a catchy title, but it is an accurate one. Her second nonfiction book, *Concerning Children*, appeared in 1900. Although her earlier works, a collection of poems called *In This Our World*, published in 1893, and the story "The Yellow Wallpaper," as well as *Women and Economics*, had been published under the name Charlotte Perkins Stetson, in 1900 she assumed the name of Gilman, reflecting her second marriage. In 1903 *The Home: Its Work and Influence* was published, and in 1904 she published what she considered her most important book, *Human Work*.

From November 1909 through December 1916, Gilman published a monthly magazine called the *Forerunner*. She wrote every line of every issue of the thirty-two-page magazine. The Charlton Company, which she and her husband formed specifically to publish books by Gilman, brought out one nonfiction book and three novels that had originally appeared in the *Forerunner*. The novel *Herland*, which had been serialized in 1915, was not published separately until much later, in 1979. *His Religion and Hers: A Study of the Faith of Our Fathers and the Work of Our Mothers* appeared in 1923, and in 1935, a few months after her death, her autobiography, *The Living of Charlotte Perkins Gilman*, was published. Her books were widely reviewed and her name was internationally known, but she made her living primarily as a lecturer and not as an author.

Although she is best known in our time as the author of *Herland* and the short story "The Yellow Wallpaper," it was *Women and Economics* that established her immediate international reputation. It is often said, though it is not true, that she rewrote and rewrote that work in her subsequent books. It is true that much of what she wrote flowed from it, was built on it, and expanded and developed earlier ideas. *Women and Economics* itself was built on almost ten years of evolving ideas that were the basis of her early lectures in California.[1] Hers was a mind constantly in motion, but there is a pattern to the motion, a pattern that emerges with an overview of her vast numbers of books and articles. What appears to be endless repetition is usually not that, although her hasty writing would have much benefitted from the careful editing and rewriting she had neither the time nor the desire to do.

She was a formidable analyst of history and culture who created an extensive and complex social theory that combined socialism and feminism. (The word "feminist" was not current in her early years, and when it came into use in her later years, she repudiated it. The world was "masculinist," she said, and she, as a humanist, wished to bring about a just and fair balance. It is in today's language that I call her a feminist.) She envisioned a humane social order built upon what she saw as the female values of life-giving and nurturance. She constructed an analysis to explain human behavior past and present, and she created utopian fiction to outline her vision of the future. Her world-view encompassed history, sociology, philosophy, and ethics in an effort to understand the past in order to alter the present. All that was needed to make things change, she felt, was the will to do it. She believed the will itself could be changed, by education, which to Gilman was embodied in her lecturing and in her writing.

What we think of as "masculine" traits, she said, are human traits that men have usurped as their own and to which women have been denied access. One sex has monopolized virtually all human activities, and then called them male. Male dominance has been extended to virtually all areas, even language.

Women's subordination, she said, began with recorded history and is located in women's economic dependence on men. When, in that distant past, men appropriated women's work, forcing women to depend on men for survival, half the human race was thereby demeaned. At one time in human history, she argued, this involuntary female sacrifice was necessary for progress, because male traits of aggressiveness, combativeness, and competition were essential for continued growth. But civilization now requires the restoration of the original balance to include female qualities of cooperation and nurturance. Women's subordination will only end, Gilman wrote, when women lead the struggle for their own autonomy, thereby freeing men as well as themselves, because men suffer from the distortions that come from dominance, just as women are scarred by the subjugation imposed upon them.

Hers was an organic view of society, and she argued that our humanity is created only by our serving as part of a collective enterprise, not indulging our individual, privatized needs. Society is one living thing; we cannot ignore poison in one part of it and think we can escape because it is a long way off. She wrote about ethics, which she defined as the awareness of collective rights and duties. She wrote about mothering, which she saw as central to developing a new spirit of community, although she was irreverent in assessing what we now call the institution of motherhood. She wrote about the home, the prison for the private servant called the wife-mother. She wrote about work, which she argued was the most important activity in defining a sense of self, because what we do has greater impact on us than what is done to us. She believed that the work traditionally assigned to women—rearing children and nurturing men—was important, as important as the public work of men, but that it was demeaned by being carried out in an inadequate and destructive way: privately and in isolation and by automatic assignment to all females, rather than socially and collectively by those most gifted for parenting.

It is what she called "primitive selfishness" that she sought to replace with a humane sense of collectivity and community. We concentrate on "our" children and do not care about all our children, she argued, without understanding that unless we care for all we are neglecting our own. She applied this same concept to all aspects of social relations, including work, home, family, marriage, art, and politics, in an effort to forge a new idea about how better to live our lives. She took the prevailing belief in evolution, the process of growth and change, and constructed a full-scale historical and sociological analysis of men and women in history and society. Men and women are more alike than different, she asserted, and she then proceeded to examine why this similarity has been minimized and how to stop it from being so in the future.

Gilman's reputation during her lifetime as a major theorist and social commentator is easy to document because so many influential people wrote and talked about her significance. Her words, written and spoken, were sought by reformers and radicals, newspaper editors, teachers, and writers. When H. G. Wells came to the United States in 1904, the one person he asked to see was Charlotte Perkins

Gilman, although within two years he was exasperated by her criticism of him and said so. "The best brains and the best profile of any woman in America," said William Dean Howells; he was a very early supporter of Gilman's and remained a devoted one throughout her life. Lester Ward described himself as having roughly blocked out from the slab the statue which Gilman then refined with a fine-point chisel. While in England she was sought out by George Bernard Shaw, with whom she sparred, the Webbs, and others in Fabian circles, and she was known and respected by reformers in the new social sciences in America. In a letter to Florence Kelley, Jane Addams described *Women and Economics* as the "first real substantial contribution made by a woman to the science of economics." Florence Kelley agreed. Zona Gale, a prominent author, said she believed that next to Jane Addams, no one had as much influence as Gilman on her contemporaries. Gale described her as "a social force and a shaper of policies." Alice Stone Blackwell saw Gilman as "one of the great sources of mental stimulus and ethical inspiration, not only in the United States, but widely through Europe." The world is "still a hundred miles behind most of your ideas," she wrote to her. In 1924, Rebecca West described her as "the greatest woman in the world today." Gilman had a long-term correspondence with E. A. Ross, who included her in a chapter in his autobiography entitled *Celebrities I Have Known*. When she traveled to England, Alfred Wallace arranged lectures for her.

Theodore Dreiser, as editor of the *Delineator*, wrote to her asking if they might meet. Carrie Chapman Catt, asked to name the twelve most outstanding women of her generation, named Gilman first. Albion Small, chair of the department of sociology at the University of Chicago, having just founded the *American Journal of Sociology* and the American Sociological Society, wrote to Gilman about her contributions to the new journal.

Gilman's correspondence files over several decades are filled with letters from many parts of the world, from New Zealand, Denmark, Rumania, Italy, and Japan, fan letters from readers describing the impact her work had on them, descriptions of reading circles founded to study her works systematically, communications from those who were inspired by her lectures, her poetry, her essays. In 1930, upon the tenth anniversary of the passage of the suffrage amendment, the National League of Women Voters issued a book honoring four major women thinkers, and the first was Charlotte Perkins Gilman.

Not all of her books were extensively reviewed, and even those that were, such as *Women and Economics*, were received with enthusiasm and respect but not serious examination. The *New York Times* in a lengthy review in November 1898, mostly a summary, said *Women and Economics* was written "in a temperate and admirable spirit" and offered radical suggestions for change that "deserve consideration," but the author of the review argued that "like many theoretic measures of reform," Charlotte Stetson's "presuppose an exceptionally high ideal of human conduct," making one wonder how much of *Women and Economics* he had read. The *Nation* of June 8, 1899, and the *London Daily Chronicle*, among other respected journals, favorably compared *Women and Economics* to John Stuart Mill's *On Liberty*, a comparison that was often made. The book received attention in places as widely divergent in point of view as the *Manchester Chronicle*, the *Boston Evening Transcript*, the *Survey*, the *Nationalist Magazine* and *Lucifer, the Light-Bearer*, the journal of the sexual radical movement. The *Survey*, conceding that "a great many people are going to be very angry"—which they were, and are—spoke of Gilman's "restless, progressive, belligerent, unafraid and iconoclastic spirit." The prestigious English feminist journal the *Englishwoman's Review*, in October 1899, referred to *Women and Economics* as a contribution comparable to that of Mary Astell's *Defence of Women*, which closed the seventeenth century, and Mary Wollstonecraft's *Vindication of the Rights of Woman*, which closed the eighteenth. All three writers, said the reviewer, are "earnest, fearless women of original thought."

With the appearance in 1966 of a new edition of this first book, with a lengthy introduction by Carl Degler asserting anew Gilman's deservedly prominent place, her reputation as a sociologist and social critic has re-emerged. But it is still inadequate, for she is still seen as a commentator concerned only with issues of women's emancipation and women's social role. Her scope and creative imagination are as yet unappreciated even by today's admirers and supporters. A careful reading of the full body of her work demonstrates the immense breadth of her vision and the enormously ambitious character of the project she set for herself. Perhaps her brilliance does not place her in the tiny first rank of world thinkers, that handful of geniuses who have, by their ideas, appreciably moved the world in a new direction. But then the entire notion of first and second rank is itself a limiting one. Charlotte Gilman tried to comprehend the full range of human history and culture, and she employed a variety of then new and daring ideas and techniques. What she produced was an awesome and extraordinarily complex picture of past, present, and future. It is in many ways a flawed vision, but the flaws do not render it useless or unworthy of more than passing interest. The issues she addressed, the ways she saw the world, and her analysis of how it got to where it is and how to get it to where it should be, remain vital and important.

If one could choose a time in which to be born, especially if one had plans to be an ambitious and unconventional woman, then 1860, the year of Charlotte's birth, would have been a better choice than most. At first glance one might question what advantage there was for a woman to grow up in a time described by Mark Twain as "the Gilded Age" or "the Great Barbecue," for the unprecedented opportunities to accumulate wealth and power that emerged in the last decades of the nineteenth century did not extend to women. The image of the millionaire, or "robber baron," an appropriate symbol for the spectacular transformation of the nation between the Civil War and 1900, was without question a symbol of masculine power. Between the time Charlotte was born and the end of the century, the physical and corporate organization of industrial capitalism was essentially created. The expansion of the productive capacity of the American economy was awe-inspiring. A national economy was forged, a network of five transcontinental railroad systems was built, the land was peopled by westward expansion, creating the permanent borders of the nation. Incredibly rich mineral resources were exploited. The future seemed to have limitless possibilities. But by the end of the century the process of monopolization was under way, and investment bankers increasingly began to control industries; fewer and fewer individuals were thus able to control more and more of the American economy and American politics.

The process of accumulating immense wealth and new forms of power had great costs. Masses of immigrants were attracted by the promises of industrial development and great cities grew dramatically. The country did not cope well with the changes. If America produced more millionaires than anywhere else, it also produced slums, class inequities, cyclical depressions, social unrest, and rural and urban suffering. During Gilman's lifetime, then, there was both historic growth and chronic instability. Since its founding, America had been characterized by class inequities, but in the post–Civil War period, the disparities polarized the nation in new and frightening ways. The heartland of the country was settled, the frontier was declared at an end, but this reality also meant that remnants of once-great Indian tribes were forced onto reservations and agriculture became chronically depressed. Great cities rose in which enormous wealth was produced, but the impoverished, exploited working populations suffered hideously.

It was an age dominated by business and soon dominated by a business morality, qualitatively different from what had preceded it. Corruption became so widespread that even "good" men accepted it as part of the rights of officeholding. Traditional language was inadequate to describe new business and political activities. Traditional politics and law were unable to function. There was no politics in politics, as Lord Bryce said of the American system, only plundering and brokering. Politics evolved into a system of manipulation and deals. It was a world in which only success counted, in which the central goal was wealth, and there is never enough wealth if that is the primary goal. The earlier vision of a good society was fading. The problem was not a handful of powerful, evil men who built an industrial empire but saw no need to contribute to the public welfare. The problem, as viewed by many, was that the moral center of the nation was in jeopardy. The discrepancies between the old ideals and the new realities were hard to comprehend, and perhaps most people never did understand the full significance of the new capitalist world that was unfolding.

Why, then, is this a good time for Charlotte to have been born? Because as the preindustrial code of morality and sense of community seemed to be eroding, voices of dissent began to be heard. This was a time of great intellectual speculation and creativity in American thought. It was a period, in the words of Perry Miller, in which the American mind "was intensively active—in which the issues of national consciousness were, for better or worse, and for a long time to come, discovered and refined."[2] It was a time when ideas were important and valued.

The central struggles raged over interpretations of Charles Darwin's *On the Origin of Species* as they applied to human society. The English theorist Herbert Spencer was the most popular interpreter of Darwin in America. In fact, his first book, *Social Statics*, published in 1851, eight years before Darwin's great work appeared, set out the doctrines that were later called Social Darwinism (although Darwin was himself not a Social Darwinist). Spencer claimed that efforts to alter social development were a violation of the immutable laws of nature. Darwin asserted that nature had established its own mechanism for development, which he called natural selection. Darwin's ideas thus could be used to corroborate the body of thought already developing that applied the principles of science, especially biology, to social analysis. Those known as Social Darwinists asserted, as Darwin did not, that the same laws that governed nature also governed society, and their social science model was understandably modeled on the natural sciences. The primary reason Spencer appealed to so many Americans was that the economic theory that flowed from his ideas was one of a self-regulating order. The competitive system worked most efficiently if left alone. To Spencer and his followers, the competitive capitalist economy of post–Civil War America was the highest stage in the evolution of social systems.

Many and varied voices of protest were raised against this doctrine by broad coalitions involving Populists, liberals, socialists, muckrackers, and Knights of Labor. Reformers and radicals proliferated: William Dean Howells, Henry Demarest Lloyd, John P. Altgeld, Jane Addams, Ignatius Donnelly, Florence Kelley, Edward Bellamy, and hundreds, thousands, of others. Most of these social critics saw themselves also as Social Darwinists, but felt that within the Darwinian universe it was possible to create a just world.

The two philosophies, both Darwinian but opposed to each other, were articulated in this country by William Graham Sumner and Lester Ward. Sumner, who derived many of his ideas from Spencer but remained quite independent, shared with Spencer the belief that only the fittest individuals should survive in the struggle against nature and against other humans, and that the state must be kept from interfering in the struggle. Lester Ward argued that evolution had created the very instruments by which humans could control their own future. The intervention of government, which was to Sumner a violation of natural law, was to Ward the purpose of human existence.

The effort by many late-nineteenth-century thinkers to develop social science on the model of natural science was later challenged by such critics as Max Weber, Emile Durkheim, Sigmund Freud, and Thorstein Veblen, some of whose works Gilman read or was familiar with. They rejected the notion that social and psychological theory could be constructed on the model of physics or biology. Twentieth-century critics who followed them, such as John Dewey, Charles Beard, Mary Beard, and James Harvey Robinson, emphasized empirical, interdisciplinary, and historical approaches to problems of social analysis.

By the early years of the twentieth century some of America's most powerful corporations and financial institutions recognized the need for and the possibility of stabilizing and rationalizing the existing system. The earlier competitive struggle, with its attendant ideology of laissez-faire, was becoming outmoded. There was also a real concern that the Socialist movement, although not especially well organized or ideologically sophisticated, posed some danger with its appealing alternative vision of a collective social order.

The industrial expansion that was responsible for the growth of many social evils was also responsible for providing the leisure for many who attacked those evils. The coalition that emerged at the turn of the century and lasted through the outbreak of World War I was called the Progressive movement, and it was composed of urban middle-class reformers and some segments of the earlier forces of agrarian discontent; it was a somewhat more respectable, narrower version of the coalition that had existed in the last decades of the nineteenth century. Both groups of reformers, the loose conglomerate in the late nineteenth century and the somewhat tighter coalition in the twentieth, were trying to establish a coherent universe free of the arbitrary power of the big capitalists, on the one hand, and of the dangerous possibilities they considered inherent in the activities of the mass of workers, on the other. Many thousands of activists publicized and exposed social and political evils, wrote legislation to correct them, and then lobbied to get the legislation passed and enforced. Between 1910 and 1914, Congress and state and local legislatures enacted a significant part of the Progressive program. Teachers, writers, artists, ministers, and educated middle-class homemakers fought for and often succeeded in bringing about reforms of child labor, sweatshop conditions, public health, factory conditions, and slum living. The direct primary, the direct election of senators, women's suffrage, an income tax, a strengthened inheritance tax system, the formal dissolution of some giant businesses, and the beginning of the regulation of others all occurred during these years. The federal government instituted conservation measures, pure food and drug acts, and aid to children in the labor market. These years marked the beginnings of a modern welfare state.

Those representing the liberal corporate state during this period came to believe that the federal government was a valuable ally in intervening in economic issues to assure stability and reduce irresponsible business activity.[3] It was during this period that the ideological precepts of laissez-faire, derived from the Darwinian notion of survival of the fittest, were replaced by a belief in a responsible, publicly regulated social order in which all classes would benefit from an economy that continued to expand in an orderly fashion.

To the honest reformers in this period, responsibility meant an obligation to the underprivileged. To the corporate executive, it meant responsibility to the maintenance of the existing order. These two visions converged during the Progressive period. Liberalism thus was not in opposition to a corporate political economy. The corporate model could be supported by middle-class social reformers, because it envisioned a politics that most of them could accept. All that was required was that these reformers, permitted to tinker in any way they wished to make society work more justly and more sensibly, ultimately accept the basic tenets of a capitalist social system.[4]

In the last years of the nineteenth century another constituency emerged, a new and sizable group of women whose vocational and educational options had been greatly expanded by the strenuous efforts of their feminist mothers and grandmothers.[5] These were extraordinary women, partly because they were quite conscious of their special, privileged positions. They were the first generation of women to make informed but still highly unusual choices about their lives. These women lived in a culture that still defined woman's natural domain as home, her natural vocation as the care of husband and children, but they were freer than their predecessors had been to reject that limiting role. To this community of women, access to higher education was enormously important. They wrote and spoke often of the significant part college life had played in their subsequent careers and personal lives. The critical intelligentsia of the nation was being recreated during this time, and for the first time women were active agents in that formation. By the time the Civil War ended, women had access to eight state universities and several liberal arts colleges. After the Civil War, the major women's colleges were founded, including the Seven Sisters. John Adams did not heed the sage advice of his wife, Abigail, to "remember the ladies," but a bit more than one hundred years later, comparable "ladies" were making it impossible for anyone to forget them. These women, seeing themselves as different and special, sought ways of working that expressed their energy, their sense of service, and their pioneering spirit.

Much has been written by the historian Barbara Sicherman about the impressive record of social reform left by this first generation of college women.[6] In the words of Jane Addams describing herself, they were "a special generation of women," who were imbued with the sense that their special privilege obliged them to use their gifts in the service of humanity. They shared with men of their time an optimistic belief in progress and a genuine confidence that their activities could bring about change. But there were important ways in which their gender provided a different perspective. Most of them seemed to believe, for example, that they had to choose between career and marriage, and men did not have to make that choice.

The then-widespread fear that the new option of college for women carried with it dangers to the future of marriage and the stability of the birth rate did have some basis in reality. Many college-educated women remained unmarried, with estimates ranging from 25 to 60 percent. Many such career women devised new and interesting ways of living in community with other women, some in settlement houses, some in women's colleges, some in smaller, less structured communal arrangements. This new sense of gender solidarity was possible where women in significant numbers had options that allowed them self-supporting lives.

Not only did fewer college-educated women marry than those less educated, but among the college-educated group there were more divorces, fewer children, and more marriages that produced no children than among the non-college-educated group. Given the absence of satisfactory birth-control technology, career and family decisions carried delicate and complicated ramifications.

Women had traditionally staffed the informal agencies of social welfare as volunteers. Now their descendants entered the paid work force, but with similar social concerns. Some members of this post–Civil War generation went beyond elementary-school teaching, which was the central career available to middle-class women until this time, into professions that had previously been largely closed to them, professions such as law, medicine, business, and educational administration, albeit in relatively small numbers. Such women also created new professions to suit their social service goals; prominent among these achievements was the creation of the settlement houses, which, unlike their English counterparts, were established and sustained primarily by women.

Women of this generation had values and attitudes shaped by the nineteenth century, but many of them, like Gilman, lived well into the twentieth and continued their activities through their long lives. Their concern with exploitative working conditions, unemployment, inadequate housing, insufficient medical care for the poor, and child labor continued into the Progressive period in the years before World War I. Women sought influence and achieved leadership roles in the social-justice wing of the Progressive movement. Although all of these women strongly advocated women's suffrage, they achieved an impressive amount of power and importance at local and national levels even before the suffrage amendment was passed.

These women seemed to sustain throughout their lives the radical and reform vision that had informed their thought and action in their youth, whereas many of the male reformers appeared more likely to succumb to the desire for respectability and public acceptance, which meant that they often repudiated their reformist notions in their later years. Antiwar reformers, male and female, for example, split on the issue of supporting American involvement in World War I, but far more of the well-known women reformers persisted in an antiwar stance, despite its dangers to their careers, their status, and their physical safety. Perhaps the reason lies in the marginality of women radicals and activists, who had already lost their claim to social acceptance by engaging in public activity itself. The peace movement provides the most dramatic example of such division along gender lines, but it was not the only reform activity clung to with greater tenacity by the women in the various coalitions.

The women's movement, even if one can claim it remained "purer" and less susceptible to mitigating pressures when compared with male-directed movements, had nevertheless undergone its own dilution by the early years of the twentieth century. In the early nineteenth century, Frances Wright and her followers—very few, to be sure—had articulated a program that extended democracy beyond boundaries of sex, color, and class and that was rooted in a commitment to reason. That belief in rationality was replaced toward midcentury by a moral and religious fervor that eventually created the first women's movement. This movement, growing from abolitionism, continued to address the rights and needs of all oppressed classes. The vision of this generation of feminists, like that of Wright's, was of a new social order that linked women's reform to changes of a larger and more encompassing quality. But while the new generation of women reformers maintained a belief in a widened and deepened democracy, it made compromises concerning race, class, and traditional institutions. In the decades following the Civil War, this tendency continued as the women's movement became more obviously two movements, one for black women and one for white. Black women turned their attention primarily to issues of race that united them with black men. White women's reform activity focused on temperance, social purity, and suppression of vice as a way of envisioning a social movement to forge a new sense of female self-reliance. These late-nineteenth-century moral reformers felt a keen sense of betrayal as they watched the larger society move recklessly and ruthlessly into a viciously competitive laissez-faire capitalist mode. Their belief in the power of female solidarity when combined with a broad coalition began to falter as their efforts for grand reform failed. The model of moral reform as all-encompassing shifted even more in the early twentieth century as the Progressive era defined itself as centrally concerned with middle-class, urban social issues. The women reformers occupied the social-justice wing of the Progressive movement, they continued to speak in terms of expanded democracy and natural rights, but the revolutionary implications were gone, as they accepted permanent inequality and accommodated to a competitive social system. Their new sisterhood, moreover, embraced only white women. The racism that pervaded the cultural life of the nation permeated the women's movement too.

Attitudes toward people of different ethnic, religious, and racial backgrounds have shaped the American experience from the first European settlements. So pervasive have racist and ethnocentric assumptions been in our culture and so embedded are racial ideologies in our institutions that it is difficult to recognize how pernicious and insidious their impact has been. The belief that certain groups possess specific qualities, that all members of these groups share these qualities and that environmental change would not appreciably alter them, challenges another just as deeply held belief that each individual has a natural right to be judged by her or his own abilities, that caste, class, all cultural legacies, can be refashioned, rejected, or redefined. Both views, antithetical views, have been upheld as part of our national ethos.

As post–Civil War America was transformed into a modern industrial state, nativism, racism, and anti-Semitism revived in a new and virulent form. The long-held belief that the United States would escape the violent class antagonism and fearful social unrest that accompanied the growth of capitalism in Europe was shattered. It was easier to blame the foreigners, the African-Americans, the Jews, for the political corruption, the violent strikes, the erosion of traditional ways of doing things, than to understand that these marginal groups were themselves victimized by the industrializing process, and then to determine how to alter the process.

The ideologies that pervaded the intellectual and political climate, and that were shared by many, even most, of the social scientists of the period, asserted that the new immigrants from southeastern Europe as well as African-Americans were racially inferior. These ideologies claimed legitimacy through Social Darwinism, that is, through the claim that superior races evolved naturally through evolutionary law, that the progress achieved through the defeat of the weak by the strong applied to the struggle between racial groups as well as among species. The concept of a racial group, as it developed during these last years of the last century, considered mental, moral, and cultural capacities as part of the inherited racial legacy. What was seen as uniquely American entrepreneurial genius was identified with the racial background of the settlers in the seventeenth and eighteenth centuries. Some American theorists and many popularizers had long insisted that the political talent that produced democracy could be traced to the tribal council of the ancient Teutons. The Anglo-Saxons came from Teutonic stock, and so the cult of the Anglo-Saxon took root.

The notion of a superior race meshed with the expansionism of the 1890s and became a useful justification for imperialist expansion. The belief that European colonists were superior to indigenous Native American populations had operated in earlier expansionist movements, but by the 1890s, Social Darwinist theory was being used to support the argument. The application of its principles gave what appeared to be the sanction of nature and science to the belief in the dominance of "superior races." To the traditional fears of Catholic plots and cultural and political dilution was added the notion that the national bloodstream might be polluted by alien strains.

Most social commentators, social scientists, scientific "experts," those who created the conventional wisdom of the time, shared racist assumptions of some sort.[7] The liberals assumed that the cultural atmosphere in this nation would soon raise these inferior groups to the high moral plane of Anglo-Saxons, or more accurately, white, Protestant, middle-class Americans. The conservatives were less hopeful about rapid change and believed that the supposedly inferior qualities of these demeaned groups would be difficult to change and impossible to assimilate.

The debate that had raged in scientific circles concerning human origins was ended with the publication of *On the Origin of Species*, which demonstrated common ancestors for all humans. And while few social scientists any longer denied a common ancestry to all people in the evolution of the human species, many continued to insist that different roads to development over long periods of time had created differences that were in effect permanent.

Charlotte Gilman was in many ways the product of this extraordinary period of intellectual and political ferment—of its contributions but also, as we shall see, of its limitations. Still, her own limitations, serious as they were, should not mar the importance, the boldness, the power of the way she learned to manage her life and of the body of work she left behind. At the turn of the century, Charlotte Perkins Gilman was recognized as a major theorist, an enormously influential and able social critic, essayist, writer of fiction and verse, and lecturer. Hers was a name widely known in much of the Western world. The repercussions of her work are still felt today, not only in feminist circles, where she is once more a celebrated figure, but also in our society in general, where she remains largely unknown.

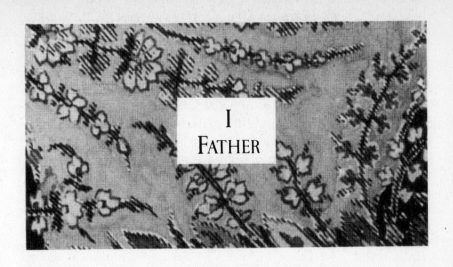

I
FATHER

She was born Charlotte Anna Perkins on July 3, 1860, in Hartford, Connecticut, the third child her mother gave birth to in the first three years of marriage. Both her parents came from prominent families that could trace their lineage back several generations in America, and before, but Charlotte's father was a Beecher and that was special and significant.

The Beechers were probably the most famous family in America. The first Beecher in America, John Beecher, landed in Boston Harbor in 1637, seventeen years after the *Mayflower* arrived. The first nationally known Beecher, several generations later, was Lyman Beecher, who, as zealot and evangelist, set out to regenerate society through his Christian teaching, and who lived to be almost ninety. He married three times and fathered twelve surviving children, which made him, said Theodore Parker, "the father of more brains than any other man in America."[1] Among those children were Harriet Beecher Stowe, author of *Uncle Tom's Cabin*; Henry Ward Beecher, pastor of the Plymouth Church of Brooklyn; Isabella Beecher Hooker, an outstanding suffragist; and Catharine Beecher, an educator and author of *A Treatise on Domestic Economy*.

Lyman Beecher, the family patriarch, Charlotte's great-grandfather, was still living when she was born. Then eighty-five years old, he had witnessed enormous changes in his lifetime, which began on the eve of the American Revolution and ended in the middle of the Civil War. But it was the spiritual, not the military,

21

life of his country that drew him, and he was unhappy with its direction. He despised and dreaded the growing secularism that denied the Calvinist heritage of his New England ancestors, and he struggled against the changes that enveloped him and threatened the moral fiber of his world.

As a young man he had been a sophomore at Yale when its new president, Timothy Dwight, was appointed. Dwight remained a major influence in Lyman Beecher's life. Dwight had been brought to Yale in the hope that he would be able to infuse the spirit of Calvinism into the hearts of Yale students, who, it was thought, were devoting more time to enjoying worldly pleasures than to struggling against sin. Such dangers did not jeopardize Lyman's spiritual life, for in his junior year he underwent a religious "conversion," an experience of affirming the Calvinist religion to which he already belonged, and this meant that he had demonstrated his probable membership in the community of the elect. Calvinists believed that since Adam's fall, all people were born depraved and wicked, and that to alleviate this condition, God had sent His son, Jesus, to die for the sins of men. Only those few who underwent an experience of "conversion" might be among the elect and thus permitted to enter heaven. These doctrines formed an essential part of the system of beliefs that shaped the life and spirit of Lyman Beecher. At his graduation from Yale, he joined with fourteen others from his class to study for the ministry; the remaining fifteen graduates entered the law.

After a year at the Yale Divinity School, Lyman Beecher began his career, his mission, in which he saw himself as called upon to fight the infidel, wherever discovered and however defined. His attacks were later directed at various times against heretics, Unitarians, Catholics, duellers, alcoholics, and other examples of the socially and morally depraved. He believed that the Second Coming was imminent, that Jesus was soon to return to the earth to rule, and that he, Lyman Beecher, had been chosen by God to help prepare for the event. His life's work took him from the Presbyterian church at East Hampton, Long Island, to a more affluent ministry in Litchfield, Connecticut, to Boston, and then to the Lane Theological Seminary in Cincinnati, to which he went as president at the age of fifty-six, resigning a substantial and comfortable church position to help run a "little struggling divinity school in a pioneering city."[2] It was his misfortune to head the seminary when the antislavery foment among the student body caused dissension with the committee of trustees. As a result, in 1834 Theodore Weld, a leader of the graduating class, and the rest of the forty-man senior class withdrew from the school to find a more congenial home at Oberlin College.

At some point in his religious life, Lyman Beecher began to move away from the belief that the fall of Adam doomed mankind. He embraced a more ameliorative doctrine, called immediate repentance, which held that people could and must repent of their sins by their own will and thereby achieve salvation. Beecher was never able successfully to reconcile these opposing notions, neither of which he could entirely reject or wholly accept: on the one hand the belief in foreordination or predestination, that our lives are foreordained by God, and on the other, the doctrine of free will and thus of human responsibility and accountability.

Lyman Beecher was surely not alone in being tormented by questions of the relationship between God's power and human will, but he was vocal about it, and his straying from orthodox doctrine led to a heresy trial in 1835. Although he was acquitted, he was regarded by the orthodox as dangerous, despite his commitment to defending the church in a changing world and the authority of the minister as the voice of God.

Beecher sought to capture the essence of the spirit of the past in a framework acceptable and meaningful to his present. He was in many ways a characteristic American reformer, one who speaks with passion and intensity in the language of change but essentially in order to conserve. He was willing to bend a fundamental doctrine in the larger interest of defending the church itself. The orthodox may have seen him as an enemy, but he saw himself as truer to the spirit of the faith than they. He recognized the flaws in the doctrine of foreordination. It could lead to a sense of fatalism and skepticism. It was no longer appropriate as it had been to earlier generations that had accepted without question the authority of the church. So he shifted his allegiance from one doctrine and sought another that placed responsibility directly on human actions. It was heresy, but it was heresy in behalf of the faith.

In his private life, Lyman Beecher early on sought a wife to share what was to be a demanding and difficult life. "I had sworn inwardly never to marry a weak woman," he said; his wife "must have sense, must possess strength to lean upon."[3] Such an extraordinary woman was Roxanna Foote, who gave birth to eight children—Catharine, William, Edward, Mary, George, Harriet, Charles, and Henry—and who ran a boarding as well as day school to supplement her husband's meager income. Roxanna contracted consumption and died in 1816. The following year Beecher married Harriet Portner, the daughter of a successful physician, a woman known not for her strength but for her beauty and culture. There were four more children: Frederick, Isabella, Thomas, and James, before she died and was followed, in 1836, by Lyman Beecher's third wife, Mrs. Lydia Jackson, who bore no children.

All of the Beecher children—all but one—were driven to question, to examine, to analyze, and then to communicate publicly the results of their investigations. All Beecher's sons became ministers. Each of them grappled as had their father, some with more success than others, with the moral problems they inherited from him, that is, how to understand and vindicate God's ways to man.

All but one of the Beecher women struggled with the same issues. Though banned from the ministry, they were "virtually ministers," says one family biographer,[4] for they found outlets as educators or writers or activists. Catharine Esther Beecher used her educational work and her extensive body of writing to persuade her generation that the home was the "nation's moral center"[5] and the women in it the bearers of moral superiority. Catharine Beecher was known to virtually every home in America as the woman who defined "a new role for women within the household" and who idealized the very idea of domesticity with maternal self-sacrifice at the core. Her sister, Harriet Beecher Stowe, was also a household name because of her writings. Harriet Stowe's pulpit was the novel. The one that established her fortune was *Uncle Tom's Cabin*, but all of her sizable output of fiction examined some moral issue or other, usually in a domestic setting. For Stowe, too, in the center of a busy household overflowing with children, the home and the family were the centers from which virtue and morality emanated. Isabella Beecher Hooker, a suffragist and activist for women's rights, was Lyman Beecher's fourth and youngest daughter, a founder in 1868 of the New England Suffrage Association and a decades-long activist on behalf of a federal suffrage amendment.

All the Beechers saw the home as a metaphor for human connectedness. The men, as ministers, were concerned with God the Father and His bond to His flock, the family of man. The women, through their work and through the experience of their lives, defined the family and its hierarchy as the basic social and moral unit. While it is true that nineteenth-century Americans in general evolved a similar notion of the central place of home and family in the unity of the nation and as its moral center, the Beechers, as a family, embodied in their persons and in their public voice the reality itself. They were, in a sense, The Family.

"The only purely private Beecher," Lyman Beecher Stowe later wrote,[6] was Charlotte's grandmother Mary, Lyman and Roxanna's fourth child. She taught for a short while in her sister Catharine's Hartford Female Seminary, then married Thomas C. Perkins, and thereafter devoted her energies to rearing a family as a comfortable, upper-middle-class matron in Hartford, dying in 1900 at the age of ninety-five. She had four children: Frederick, Emily, Charles, and Katherine. Emily married the noted author and Unitarian clergyman Edward Everett Hale. Katherine married William C. Gilman, a Hartford lawyer like her father. Among their children was George Houghton Gilman, who in 1900 would become Charlotte Anna Perkins's second husband. Frederick was to be her father.

Having important male relatives may have been exciting for a girl born in the nineteenth century. Having important female relatives was considerably more useful if one grew up seeking models, for there were not so many available. Harriet and Catharine and Isabella were little Charlotte's great-aunts, "world-servers," as she called them.[7] Her grandmother may have been the one private Beecher of that generation, but Charlotte could find her inspiration among the other women of the family.

Lyman Beecher's private daughter, Mary Perkins, chose to spend her life's energies protected from public view. The pressures she probably felt within her family to excel in the world did not reverberate in the larger culture, where being a well-bred woman meant staying within the domestic sphere. It was her sisters who were defined as breaking traditional bonds; she, an anomaly in her Beecher family, behaved appropriately by the world's standards.

Mary's oldest child, Frederick Beecher Perkins, born in 1826, did not fare well. The tensions he suffered as a Beecher, and ulti-

Frederick Beecher Perkins, 1862

mately as a failed Beecher, seem never to have been satisfactorily resolved. Not all of the Beecher clan could have the impact on their society that their family name seemed to demand. The Beecher name was a hard yardstick for the less gifted or less driven to measure themselves by.

Frederick never quite found himself, and in the process of looking he caused a good deal of unhappiness to many close to him. He grew to adulthood in Hartford; he attended but did not graduate from Yale University, because he lost his temper, which he did often, and assaulted one of his professors. He did graduate from a school which prepared its students to be teachers, the Connecticut Normal School, in 1852, and he taught for a while in Greenwich, Connecticut, but soon fell away from that occupation. He studied law but did not practice it. His younger brother, Charles, joined their father in his Hartford law practice, but Frederick ultimately found his vocation in the world of literature and letters. His passion for books led him to read them, write them, edit them, and, as librarian, classify them. Before he married her mother, their daughter Charlotte later wrote, he was familiar with nine languages.[8] He worked as editor on a variety of reputable journals, including the *Independent* and the *Outlook*. He published dozens of short stories, essays, political satires, and tracts, but he never made a living from his writings. For a time, in 1874, he served as assistant director of the Boston Public Library, and in 1880 he moved to California as director of the San Francisco Public Library. In his last years he returned to the East, where he died in 1899.

As a librarian, he was instrumental in implementing the decimal system of classification. His reference book, *The Best Reading: hints on the selection of books, on the formation of libraries, public and private; on the courses of reading, etc.*, went through several successful editions and for a long time was a standard in its field. He was author of several other collections, bibliographies, essays, and addresses. Under the pseudonym of Pharaoh Budlong, he published a number of tales, sketches, and satirical pieces, including *President Greeley, President Hoffman and the resurrection of the ring: A history of the next 4 years by Pharaoh Budlong (pseud.)*, as well as a piece on the Perkins Family of Connecticut.

A man of some literary and intellectual gifts, inspired with bursts of passion for justice and reform, a man of courage and substantial physical prowess, he was, ultimately, unable to put his strengths together into a well-ordered and satisfying life. He was talented but undisciplined, erratic, and unfocused. He had good impulses but not much staying power.

As a young man, Frederick had loved a "pretty and charming damsel" named Frankie Johnson, but the engagement was broken by his mother, Mary Perkins.[9] Miss Johnson thereupon married Frederick's uncle James, the youngest child of Lyman and Harriet Beecher. When he was just past thirty years of age, Frederick finally married twenty-nine-year-old Mary Fitch Westcott, a distant cousin from Providence, Rhode Island. They soon had three children: Thomas Henry, born March 15, 1858, who died one month later; Thomas Adie, born May 9, 1859; and Charlotte Anna.

Soon after Charlotte's birth the doctor reportedly said that if Mary Perkins had another baby she might die, with the result that Frederick Perkins left home. Whether the doctor's announcement was a reality, and if it was a reality, whether it was the primary reason for Frederick's departure, is not clear. "What I do know," said Charlotte, "is that my childhood had no father." Frederick did periodically visit his family, and a fourth child was born to Mary and Frederick in January 1866 but died the following September.

Frederick Perkins was remembered by his daughter as an occasional visitor. "Once he brought me some black Hamburg grapes. . . . There was a game of chess at which I beat him, or thought I did," when she was about nine; "one punishment, half-hearted and never repeated, at the same age; and a visit some two years later, when . . . he brought my twelve-year old brother a gun," she wrote in her autobiography. "These are the sum of my memories of my father in childish years."[10]

She elsewhere described a visit to her father in February 1876, when she was fifteen years old. At the time of the event she wrote in her diary the following entry: "Saw father. Had a nice long talk. Called me 'my child.' So nice."[11] Many years later she wrote about their relationship during that time, describing a visit to him, probably in early 1876. "I kissed my father in the Boston Public Library—not having seen him in years!" And what did he do? He left her "sitting there and being treated as a mere caller—I am about fifteen—and he put me away from him and said I must not do that sort of thing there. I made a little vow, to the effect that if ever my father wanted to kiss me he should ask for it."[12] Is she describing the same event, in one case commenting on it at the time, in the other evoking it twenty-two years later, and if so, which description is the more accurate? At the time there was no mention of hostile or rejecting behavior on her father's part, although Charlotte's pleasure at simply being called "my child" is painful for the reader and must have been so for her. Did her anger well up years later in retrospect, or did she withhold her feelings at fifteen and release them at a safer distance at thirty-seven?

Whatever her acknowledged feelings about her father as she was growing up, Charlotte had little contact with him. Commenting upon a visit she made to her father and stepmother when she was an adult, Charlotte said that "it was literally the first time I had ever been in my father's house since infancy, and at that it was only a boarding-house, kept by my step-mother."

As a young woman not yet twenty, Charlotte Perkins had sketched out an autobiography in which she recalled a time when the family moved to her grandfather's house and her father promised to pay board and keep them there for no more than three months, but they stayed for nine and he did not pay. From 1863 to 1873 he deposited his wife and children with assorted relatives or, occasionally, installed them in rented homes, and then in either case, as we have seen, left them for long periods of time. So they lived in Apponaug, Rhode Island; in Hartford, Connecticut; in Rehoboth, Massachusetts; and in Providence, Rhode Island. By the time Mary Perkins finally decided to divorce her husband, in 1873, years after an estrangement was acknowledged, the family had been forced to move nineteen times in eighteen years, fourteen times from one city to another.

When Frederick Beecher Perkins left his family, he took the value of his Beecher connection with him. While Charlotte, with her mother and older brother, Thomas, lived with Beechers on and off, here and there, they were regarded in the family as poor relations, charity relatives. Indeed, when Mary Perkins, a pathetic figure of an abandoned and rejected wife, finally determined to divorce her husband, the Beecher relatives turned against her, which makes one question the sincerity of the hospitality they had earlier offered. Charlotte never had the benefit of the rich cultural life of the Beecher kin, never had a sense of belonging solidly with them. Her family did not protect her or house her, except grudgingly and with a sense of shame, and it did not provide her with the education she needed, yearned for, and never got, the education she would presumably have had growing up in her father's company. She was marginal to her own family.

In certain ways Charlotte spent her life engaged in the debate begun by her older Beecher relatives. For just as they sought to locate the strength and power of community within the family and within the church, with mother at the helm in the household and preacher at the pulpit in church, so Charlotte's work too dealt centrally with home, work, children, and ethics. However, she consistently repudiated religious institutions and dogma and rejected the home as a limiting place for women. What was a shrine to her aunts Catharine and Harriet was a prison to Charlotte. She may have found inspiration in the fact of their public lives, but she challenged the very premises that shaped their beliefs. Her experience with family, parental love, and security provided no positive model. Still, she was grateful for her Beecher inheritance of "wit and the gift of words," along with the "urge to social service."[13]

Charlotte also inherited from her father and his Beecher kin an impulse to express one's private thoughts and feelings through public discourse, when it was difficult to do so directly.

In 1877, when Charlotte was seventeen, Frederick selected five of his stories previously written and rejected by editors, grouped them under the title of the first story, "Devil-Puzzlers," and persuaded G. P. Putnam and Sons to publish them as a book. It is impossible not to read that collection in the way it surely was intended: as a rambling, quasi-autobiographical mockery of himself, his family, and his traditions. It is as close to the "Confessions of a Sinner" as Frederick Perkins ever wrote. Like several Beechers before him and his daughter after, he took to the public arena to examine himself, translating his personal concerns into social terms.

The first story, "Devil-Puzzlers," is a Faustian tale of timid, ordinary Dr. Hicok, who has traded his soul to the devil in exchange for twenty years of bliss. Proof of the bargain is apparent in his successful wooing of his jewel of a wife. A lively and graceful creature, she had

> thick, fine, long black hair, pencilled delicate eyebrows, little pink ears . . . great astonished brown eyes . . . a little rosebud of a mouth, and a figure so extremely beautiful that nobody believed she did not pad. . . . furthermore she was good, with the innocent unconscious goodness of a sweet little child; and of all feminine charms . . . she possessed . . . a lovely voice.[14]

Frederick Perkins's description of his ideal woman could stand as the explicit model of everything Charlotte Perkins would later characterize as insulting and degrading in the male notion of womanhood.

Dr. Hicok has one hope. If he can outwit the devil in at least one of three questions, he is saved. The appointed day of reckoning arrives and so does the devil. The first question Dr. Hicok asks is: "Reconcile the fore-knowledge and the fore-ordination of God with the free will of man," the question that had tormented Grandfather Lyman and led to his heresy trial. The devil answers correctly: "The reconciliation is your own conscience, doctor! Do what you know to be right, and you will find that there is nothing to reconcile." Thereby Frederick eliminated the need for church and organized religion, and neatly abolished the calling of his uncles and grandfather.

The second question: "Reconcile the development theory, connection of natural selection and sexual selection, with the responsible immortality of the soul," or simply, reconcile science and theology. Again the devil answers correctly. There is nothing to reconcile because there is no connection between them. "You can't state any inconsistency between a yard measure and a fifty-six-pound weight." Thereby Frederick ridiculed the entire substance and legitimacy of theological debate.

The final question is innocently posed by the beautiful wife, and it is her question that stumps the devil, and her husband as well. Twirling a bonnet made of some flimsy, gauzy fabric, she asks, "Which is the front side?" Thereby does Frederick put all serious debate in its place, that is, as mere frippery, or less than frippery, because the devil and the learned doctor both are baffled by the mundane. So Frederick Perkins dismissed his learned relatives and ridiculed their frivolous seriousness. The devil take them all! (Charlotte Perkins wrote a good deal about foolish finery, particularly bonnets and feathers and plumes, perched ludicrously on the head of a woman. To Frederick Perkins that bonnet was reality. To Charlotte Perkins it was the embodiment of the demeaned female, the product of male vanity.)

In the second story, "The Man-Ufactory," Frederick attacked his male relatives more directly. Frederick's sometime fictional alter ego, Pharaoh Budlong, has a new business. He makes talking robots. As the story opens, Budlong tells us that he is "filling an order for assorted ministers." He has placed in one room two dozen finished—or, he suggests, ordained—ministers, "an extraordinary exhibition" of astonishingly lifelike preaching folk. There is even "a tall, gaunt spectre with large frame, harsh features, and rather coarse garments . . . swinging his fists, and vociferating an exhortation which seemed suitable for a camp-meeting." A model, perhaps, of Grandfather Lyman? As for the morality of passing off one of these items as the authentic person, the question, we are told, is not one of right or wrong, but whether the invention is a real discovery. It is the truth of science, not the truth of religion, that is affirmed. However one may interpret Frederick's feelings for his esteemed relatives, reverence and respect are not in evidence here.

In the third piece in the collection, a reminiscence called "Childhood: A Study," Frederick evokes a lonely and isolated childhood. The isolation was largely self-imposed, he suggests, because he early developed a habit of resisting what others wanted of him. Even as a child he lacked an "instinctive desire" for the good will of others and sought instead to live out his own life for himself, "fully and freely, not so as to infringe upon the rights of others, but not stinting or . . . amputating myself."[15] Is he here searching for some reasonable explanation for his neglect of his children and for discarding responsibility for a young and dependent wife? Is he trying to understand the conflict he felt between the needs of a life lived "fully and freely" and the limits of adult responsibility?

The sense of home and family he evokes is contradictory. There was, first, the ceaseless wandering from place to place. "I can count twenty houses where I remember to have lived. The Wandering Jew is a parable for a tenant housekeeper that 'moves' every spring; and I might be his son. Cursed be moving!" he says in words almost identical to his daughter's later description of her own childhood. The physical instability of his early living arrangements has made it impossible for him to dredge up a sense of "dignity or beauty or quiet or distinctiveness" when he ruminates on the idea of home. Direct references to his parents are few. He speaks once of the two of them, mother and father, as "alike inflexible in hygiene and morality." Yet having just described a lonely childhood and stern and rigid parents, he then refers to the "pure, calm, quiet, bright, loving, intelligent, refined atmosphere of my home," adding that for such pleasures did "God establish the family."[16] The contradiction between the joyless reality and the fantasy home, both described in the same piece, is startling. What he reproduced for his own children was the childhood he had had, one of loneliness, isolation, and inaccessible parents, not the dream.

The fourth story, "The Compensation Office," is a parable

about a way station where compensation is granted to people in great need, so long as their need is not self-imposed and therefore within their power to alter. A lonely woman enters, protesting that her children are growing away from her and that her husband neglects her. The Compensation merchant is unsympathetic. He criticizes her for turning away from her family. She protests that it was not possible to keep love alive in her heart "when I was left alone for years by the man who had promised to love and cherish me." She asks, "How could I help becoming cold and distant myself, when the only human being who was bound to love me, left me alone." But the Compensation merchant insists that her suffering is a product of her unwillingness to perform her expected domestic duties. So much for the plight of Mary Perkins.

The next customer, a young man of letters, a dilettante, bears a startling resemblance to Frederick himself. He can find no purpose in living. The work he has tried—and he has worked at law, at teaching, at editing—has given him no sustaining joy. "I am only a literary vagabond now," he sighs. This man is also turned away by the Compensation merchant because he has never sought, he is told, as all men must, to understand that however much he may want to follow his pleasures only, he must also labor at that which may not be always beautiful but is essential.

Frederick Beecher has now spoken to his grandfather, his uncles, his parents, his wife, and himself. In the final story he addresses his children. In "My Forenoon with the Baby," Frederic, a young bachelor, has volunteered to take charge of his Aunt Fanny's sleeping infant. The first half-hour passes pleasurably while young Frederic sits by the window and reads from the writings of Lyman Beecher's early mentor, Timothy Dwight. Then the child awakes and cries. Frederic tries everything to soothe the howling child, even reading to him from the Reverend Mr. Dwight's words. The baby continues to cry. "I had no idea there was so much noise in anything. This was evidently a diabolic energy," he says. At some point, he confesses, "my long-tried patience utterly failed . . . I felt myself [in] absolute opposition to this terrific child; [with] positive anger and spite, not entirely unmingled with fear." Aunt Fanny propitiously returns, and the baby smiles.

Young Frederic then asks, "What's the use of a baby?" And Frederic's answer:

A baby is providentially provided as an "awful example" for the warning of maids and bachelors, as terrific consequences universally follow great follies. It is the delerium tremens of matrimony. If you don't want to have it, let the causes alone.[17]

And so ends the story, with a cheer to Mother Ann Lee, whom Frederic describes as "the only true prophet," whose church he is about to join. Among the Shakers, founded by Mother Ann Lee, there are no babies because there are no "great follies." The Shakers are celibate.

Did seventeen-year-old Charlotte read her father's collection? She probably did, and if so, one wonders how she felt about a father, an absent father, whose description of children is as unfortunate products of the "delerium tremens of matrimony."

Still, Charlotte Perkins missed her father all her life. She longed for him and she was angry with him, although she rarely permitted that anger to appear directly. The few surviving letters from her childhood, written to her father, generally implore, but occasionally burst out. She learned that the one successful strategy for maintaining contact was to ask him for reading lists, for intellectual guidance, and so she did. He responded as if he were supervising a student's research project. She asked for a list of books to read, and he answered that it would be easier if he had a catalogue and could check names off for her. He advised her to try Grote's *Greece* and then Mommsen's *Rome*, and to be sure to read Hildreth's *United States* "and remember the principal dates and occurrences."[18]

He remained, despite all her overtures, a distant and ungiving figure, and she never forgave him, although he became, in several important ways, the model for her own later behavior. In her middle years, when she began to write fiction, she portrayed fathers, almost without exception, as explosive, tyrannical, self-centered, suffocating, arrogant, and unloving. "The word Father, in the sense of love, care, one to go to in trouble, means nothing to me," she said about Frederick.[19] At his death she was able to find pity: "What a sad dark life the poor man led." But her yearning for him never entirely ended. After her death in 1935, her daughter, Katharine Stetson Chamberlin, wrote to the company that was about to publish Charlotte's autobiography, *The Living of Charlotte Perkins Gilman*, inquiring about a missing photograph: "The last words Mama ever wrote were those pencilled ones on the margin of my letter saying she wanted her father's picture in the book."[20]

II
MOTHER

Life did not work out the way it was supposed to for Mary Ann Fitch Westcott. She followed all the rules and behaved in all the appropriate ways, as taught by her mother and by their world. She was blessed with all the assets required for success—matrimonial success, which was the measure for young women—for she was beautiful, musically gifted, properly educated, and "femininely attractive in the highest degree." Yet her life was described by her daughter as "one of the most painfully thwarted I have ever known," and it became the model for Charlotte of precisely the kind of life women must learn to reject.

Charlotte could trace her mother's family almost as far back as she could her father's, back to Stukely Westcott who accompanied Roger Williams when he settled Providence Plantation, with hints that farther back the Stukelys could be traced to English gentry. The original American Stukely Westcott was a Baptist in the days when being one "took some courage," wrote Charlotte, and Mary's father, Henry Westcott, Charlotte's grandfather, was a Unitarian when "being a Unitarian took even more." However prominent the Rhode Island Stukelys were and however courageously the male family members asserted their religions independence, what mattered to Charlotte, and before her to her mother Mary, was the immediate family constellation in which she grew.

Little is known about Mary's family. Henry Westcott, her father, was a widower with a daughter of four when he married fifteen-year-old Clarissa Fitch Perkins. She was herself, although a bride, but "a small child," who wore a "little dress" with a "tiny Empire waistlet and short sleeves, mere shoulder-bits," a dress which was "deeply embroidered" and had lace insets, the fine and careful work of "those slim fingers."[1] By seventeen Clarissa had borne a child who died, and at eighteen there was another, Mary Fitch Westcott, a child so frail that the doctor was certain she too could not survive. Charlotte described her mother as the "darling of an elderly father and a juvenile mother, petted, cossetted and indulged," but one wonders what kind of experience Mary had of being loved, considering the rejecting mother she herself became. Perhaps her father was too distant and her mother too young to provide her with the genuine nurturing she needed; we do not know. Despite Mary's description of her father as filled with "tenderness and benevolence," the one illustration Charlotte offered of these qualities is a description of how he would start for home with a basket of groceries and give away most of the food to the needy before he ever reached home, an indication of benevolence to others that his family might feel indicated neglect of and indifference to them.

Mary began her adolescence in much the same way her mother had, with great success in the arena of wooing and courtship—that is, of being wooed and courted. Her "adventures and sorrows," as her daughter described her entrance into womanly sexuality, began when she was still a schoolgirl of fifteen; her first suitor sought permission from her mother, herself only thirty-three, to court the young girl. Thereafter came a flood of lovers. Unlike her mother, Mary did not marry quickly. Perhaps the model her mother offered of early motherhood was not enticing. Perhaps Mary wished to sustain as long as possible the gay and pleasurable life of the wooed and desired girl-woman, free of adult responsibility. There were engagements, "made, broken and renewed, and re-broken."

In time Mary met Frederick Beecher Perkins of Hartford, Connecticut, her mother's second cousin, and they became engaged. That engagement, too, was broken, until "finally, at the extreme old maidenhood of twenty-nine, she married him" on May 21, 1857.[2] Frederick, as we have seen earlier, married his distant cousin Mary only after his first chosen had married another. It was not an auspicious beginning for the couple.

With marriage Mary Perkins began the re-enactment of a woman's story through most of time, one pregnancy after another, three in three years, and then Frederick Perkins left home, perhaps to try to live his life "fully and freely." Mary Fitch Westcott had had many adult years before she married and bore children, but she seems not to have used that time to develop skills or resources that would enable her to face life with independence or self-confidence. Hers had likely been a busy life before marriage, filled with social events, visits with friends and family, pleasurable activities designed to fill the hours and days and then years until she assumed an adult role, which for most women meant marriage and motherhood. But she probably had had little serious preparation for these roles. Young women of Mary's class commonly entered marriage with minimal housekeeping skills, no more than they could gain by observing their own mothers, and with little knowledge of children, except as haphazardly obtained through involvement with younger siblings and cousins. While young men were expected to be readying themselves for their careers, young women devoted themselves to the business of marrying well.

In any case, Mary Perkins had every reason to expect to be supported and taken care of by a loyal husband as she devoted her own life to rearing children and heading a household. But after years of attention and adoration from male admirers, she suddenly found herself an abandoned wife, alone with two infants. A woman whose only place was in the home found herself without a home of her own, living briefly and awkwardly in the homes of others. Yet to the husband who left her, she was, said her daughter, "absolutely loyal as a spaniel which no ill treatment can alienate." She did not complain but packed up her children and her bits of furniture and moved on to the next place: to her parents, to Frederick's parents, aunts, cousins, to various houses where she was installed by a husband who then fled, leaving behind debts and humiliation. During the occasional times when mother and children lived alone in a home, the monthly rent was always a worry. If marriage was the only acceptable career for a woman, then rejection by a husband spelled failure at her life's work. It was undoubtedly difficult for a woman like Mary Westcott Perkins to turn against even a rejecting husband; her tendency would be to blame herself.

After thirteen years of a marriage of this kind, Mary Perkins divorced her husband. She was perplexed to find herself greeted with anger and resentment by Frederick Perkins and others in his family. Mary was so obviously the abandoned, discarded wife and Frederick so clearly the injuring party that one can only read the family's disapproval of her decision to divorce as at least in part a product of impatience with her dependence on their charity. Pity, pushed too far, comes perilously close to contempt, and besides, she had so long conspired with Frederick to present as much of a united front as possible under the difficult circumstances that her sudden reversal may have been seen as a betrayal of their marriage.

"Divorced or not she loved him till her death, at sixty-three," wrote Charlotte Gilman. "That's where I get my implacable temper," she commented,[3] but she surely learned a good deal more than that from observing her parents and their marriage. She also learned that the world is not a safe place inhabited by people who can be trusted. She learned that the risks in loving a man are great, that the cost a woman suffers for not keeping a man's love is enormous and permanent, and that the burdens of motherhood are severe. It is not clear at what point in her life Charlotte was told of the doctor's warning to her mother of the danger of another pregnancy, but if that information was communicated to her as a young child, she also learned of the looming dangers of sexuality. The results of this sexuality were death, apparently, or desertion, and Charlotte perhaps saw herself as additionally responsible for this last, because it was her birth that occasioned her father's flight.

Although Mary Perkins was "loyal as a spaniel" in her devotion to her absent husband even after their divorce, she did have to raise her children, who were ever-present. In her description of her mother's manner of child-rearing, Charlotte expresses barely concealed anger, usually in the form of self-pitying pathos. We learn from Charlotte's autobiography that Mary Perkins had a natural affinity for babies, but that she "increasingly lost touch" with her children as they grew out of infancy into childhood and beyond. We are told that, despite her "sublime devotion to duty," she relied upon "unflinching severity of discipline," inappropriate to growing youngsters of vastly different temperaments from hers. Charlotte elaborated on her mother's advanced notions of kindergarten techniques and her mastery of the latest medical information on child-rearing. But there is a sense of strain in the favorable descriptions, as if Charlotte were dredging up isolated memories to fashion a positive model of motherly affection. On the same page she simultaneously evokes very different memories, ones that are chilling to read, in spite of, or perhaps because of, the daughter's need to justify the maternal rejection as she is exposing it.

> Having suffered so deeply in her own list of early love affairs, and still suffering for lack of a husband's love, she heroically determined that her baby daughter should not so suffer if she could help it. Her method was to deny the child all expression of affection as far as possible, so that she should not be used to it or long for it.

Years later Mary Perkins told her adult daughter, "I used to put away your little hand from my cheek when you were a nursing baby." She would not allow her daughter to caress her, nor did she caress the child, unless she was asleep. Charlotte, having discovered this secret, did her best to stay awake, even sticking herself with pins to keep from dropping off, so as to "rapturously" feel her mother's kisses.

Immediately following this disclosure of maternal rejection, Charlotte concluded:

> If love, devotion to duty, sublime self-sacrifice were enough in child-culture, mothers would achieve better results; but there is another requisite too often lacking—knowledge. Yet all the best she had, the best she knew, my mother gave, at any cost to herself.[4]

Charlotte's description of her mother's behavior bears little relation to the conclusions she draws from that behavior; in fact, it suggests quite the opposite. Although she calls it heroic, her mother's treatment of her seems hideously cold and rejecting. "To deny the child all expression of affection as far as possible" is a horrendously rejecting and punishing way to treat a child who has already lost a father. It is so punishing that Charlotte, in her elderly years, could not even construct the sentence with herself in it except by indirection: "the child" was, after all, Charlotte, but she objectified the situation, pushing it away from herself, from little needy, frightened

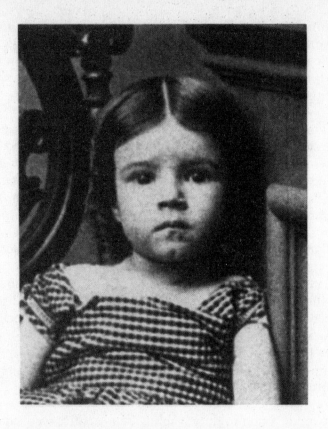

Charlotte Perkins, age two to four

Charlotte; she turned herself into "the child." She was honest enough to include it in her published memoirs, insightful enough to know its importance, but its implications, the pain it entailed, seem to have been so awful to evoke that she needed to remove direct reference to herself by name from that paragraph. Charlotte tries to soften the blow, to offer an explanation, to understand her mother's needs, for after all, Mary suffered "her own list of early love affairs" and still was "suffering for lack of a husband's love." These are observations that can have meaning, if at all, only to the adult Charlotte, looking back, trying to understand, perhaps trying to forgive.

However, Charlotte described herself as not very good at forgiveness. As a child she thought to avoid a whipping from her mother by humbling herself and confessing to some crime and begging forgiveness. Her mother forgave her, she said, but whipped her just the same. That gave her, said Charlotte, a "moral 'set-back' in the matter of forgiveness."[5]

It is certainly odd that Charlotte concluded that her mother had quantities of love, devotion, and "sublime" self-sacrifice, but what she lacked was—knowledge. Charlotte has actually described a mother who, on the contrary, was armed with knowledge—all the latest information from doctors and educators—but who lacked love and devotion.

"Absolutely loyal as a spaniel" is a phrase that suggests a good deal of anger at a mother who loved a rejecting husband but could not love a needy child. Charlotte later told how sickened she was by the devotion her mother displayed toward the fleeing Frederick, whose locks of hair and nail parings Mary Perkins saved for years after the divorce. But she seems never to have made the connection between Mary's abandonment as a wife and the anger she displaced onto her children. Charlotte in some fashion must have known of her mother's inability to manage her own life, however, and this recognition of weakness must surely have fed into the daughter's resentment at her mother's use of maternal authority to control her.

However much compassion and sympathy Charlotte was able to call upon in her adult years for her mother's sorrows, her memoirs indicate that throughout her life she continued to feel considerable resentment towards her, a resentment always expressed, like her anger at her father, indirectly. Characters patterned after Mary in Charlotte's fiction are invariably treated with contempt, and while her mother was with her many years later in California, slowly dying of cancer, Charlotte wrote:

Mother sinks wavering downward. . . . [But] her being here has served me well—made me seem a live human creature to the others, and so made my words better weighed.[6]

Such an unfeeling sentiment surely came from untapped, unrecognized rage. Years after her mother's death, Charlotte expressed surprise at Mary's decision to have herself cremated. "I should not have expected it of her. Such a clean, sweet, natural redistribution

41

of things," observed Charlotte, unable even after her mother's death to grant her any wholly unambiguous praise.[7]

Charlotte's relations with her brother Thomas also seem never to have been satisfying. They did not seek solace in each other's company, and no doubt competed for the attention of their parents. Charlotte remembers her father bringing his son a gift, a gun, but nothing for her. There are indications that Mary may have favored Thomas, or that Charlotte believed she did. Perhaps Mary resented more the child who was the cause of her husband's desertion—and a girl-child at that. In any case, when Charlotte is describing Mary's coldness she refers to it in relation to herself alone, using the pronoun "she" or the words "the child," whereas when she is referring to Mary's good qualities as a mother, she speaks of "the children," sometimes meaning Charlotte and Thomas, sometimes meaning children in general. In a letter to her father, written when Charlotte was eleven or twelve, she says, "I wish you would write to me often. Willie Judd and Howard Lord write to Thomas and he to them, but nobody writes to me but you." A forlorn little girl sees her older brother getting what she needs.

Thomas was a mean tease; he, the older brother, the only male in her early life, provided no refuge, no place of safety. His "continual teasing" caused her "to cultivate a black and bitter temper, rebelling at the injustice of it, steadily resenting what I could not escape."[8] To her diary, Charlotte confided that Thomas was "just unbearable."[9] When Charlotte was a young woman, in deep emotional distress, she tried to retaliate with an unexpected visit to her brother, which she described as a product of the grudge she still bore "for the teasing which had embittered my childish years"[10]— surely a curious way to view an unexpected visit from a sister.

Thomas undoubtedly had his own grudges. He never developed "singleness of purpose, retentive memory of detail relating to the purposes in view, strength of conviction, and bravery of action," which he described as his younger sister's characteristics.[11] Thomas Perkins recalled his childhood as a time when he held a "secret consciousness of having to 'step lively' to keep up with my sister mentally," and it was to that he attributed "the unkind teasing I visited upon her."

The literary critic Ellen Moers suggests that the "rough-and-tumble sexuality of the nursery loomed large for sisters," and that the play between brothers and sisters was the only heterosexual world Victorian girls were permitted to explore. "Women authors of Gothic fantasies," she says, "testify that the physical teasing that they received from their brothers—the pinching, mauling, and scratching we dismiss as the most unimportant of children's games—took on outsize proportions," exacerbated by the limited physical experiences of any kind permitted to middle-class girls.[12] To Charlotte, those memories were outsize negative.

By contrast, she remembers a little boy, when she was seven, Harry by name, who was a "dark, handsome boy, and polite to me—a new experience."[13] Another long-cherished happy memory was a visit to Uncle Edward Hale in Roxbury, then an elegant Boston suburb. She and Thomas went down one Christmas, for their father was boarding with his sister then and "she wished to keep alive his interest (if any) in his children." Here Charlotte saw, as she never had before, "how lovely family life could be." There was no "teasing and ridicule," only "courtesy and kindness." When a younger child interrupted his older brother's chess game, she observed that his intrusion was received with affection, not rejection. "It was quite a revelation to me," wrote Charlotte. She and Thomas played together, "but tenderness—never. Never from any one, and I did want it."[14] Although Charlotte later described this Christmas event as a "pleasure well remembered," it seems to have released as much pain as pleasure through the contrast of "how lovely family life could be" with how unlovely hers really was.

Still, the limited contact with a father, the daily connection with a mother who was severe in her ideas about children's obedience and punishment and who was too enveloped in her own misery to embrace her children, even literally, forced an extraordinary dependence of brother and sister on each other. In their early years they played together a good deal, so much so that Thomas remembers they "were rather independent of others."[15] The frequent moves from home to home and a consequent sense of isolation from a community of other children no doubt strengthened the inevitable dependence on one another, whatever their sibling struggles. But their relationship, their connection, could not possibly have withstood the pressures put upon it. It could not make up for all the other losses. Their neediness could not be satisfied by each other. Nor would they have dared to express or acknowledge openly whatever hostility they felt, for their mutual dependence was about all they had to be sure of. Between children so close in age—only fourteen months apart—there would have been intense rivalry in the most caring of homes.

Thomas and Charlotte reached adulthood afflicted with the same sibling tensions that had characterized their childhood. In 1878 Thomas flunked out of MIT for the second time, this time for good. "Failed again," wrote Charlotte in her diary about her brother's academic fiasco. "I wonder if he will ever amount to anything."[16] The following year Thomas left for Nevada to work as a railroad surveyor, a job secured by his uncle Edward Hale.

At the age of twenty-three Charlotte wrote a letter to her brother which mercifully she seems not to have sent, for an unfinished version remains in her diary of 1883—although of course she might have sent another. The letter begins with a series of bossy but concerned instructions on health and nutrition, written to a brother who was presumably ill. She endorses good food, much exercise, lots of sleep, comfortable and few garments, and no tea or coffee, a regimen she undertook for herself, she tells him, from the time she was fifteen.

Then comes the outburst: "I seem to be singularly barren of natural affection. 'Brother' brings no answering thrill to my heart. Perhaps because we had so little genuine loving intercourse when we were together. Fun we had in plenty, and a large fund of common intelligence, but I can never remember any companionship or beautiful ideas."

Charlotte and Thomas's relationship did not improve thereafter. Thomas Perkins had many gifts and unusual intelligence, but he was never able to support himself and his family, nor did he ever achieve much gratification or success in whatever work he undertook. He tried mining, farming, and writing, but in the end, Charlotte, with the help of her second husband, supported him and his family throughout much of his mature life. He spiced what must have been painful letters asking for additional money (she sent a regular check), for an occasional operation for his wife or braces for his son's teeth, with a few swipes at the younger sister who took care of him. He made a point of telling her that he rarely read her books. He planned, he told her, to send one of his articles (he wrote many and most were rejected by editors) to a Hearst magazine (Charlotte refused to write for Hearst), where he could make some real money instead of the few cents she would earn publishing in a "dinky magazine."[17] In their adult correspondence he assumes the posture of an elderly, ailing father, uneasy about his dependence on an affluent child, probably the least uncomfortable stance he could manage, particularly since he knew how difficult it was for Charlotte to spare any money from her own small income. His letters rely upon exaggerated language and flamboyant rhetoric to establish what is supposed to pass for closeness, but it is really a poor substitute for the brotherly affection he apparently did not much feel.

Still, Charlotte's childhood memories were not of unrelieved misery or alienation from her larger family. One of her earliest recollections—Charlotte was about five at the time—was of a splendid visit from Great-Aunt Catharine Beecher to the Perkins family in Apponaug, Rhode Island. Later, when they moved to a "square old house" in Hartford, where Mary Perkins ran a school for her children and a few others, they were, said Charlotte in her memoirs, "most lovingly entertained by my father's aunts, Charlotte and Anna Perkins, for both of whom I was named."[18] Remembered too was the visit, also in Hartford, to the "new big house of Aunt Harriet Stowe," purchased by her after her great success with *Uncle Tom's Cabin*.

Other memories, of a tall, narrow four-story boardinghouse, evoke the "varied mischief of two lively-minded youngsters without sufficient occupation," despite all of mother's "conscientious severity." Two special varieties of mischief stand out. Thomas and Charlotte would roll their hoops in muddy puddles, "accidentally" run into the "voluminous crinolines of the period," and then diffuse the wrath of the victims with their innocent, wide-eyed apologies. The second devilish memory involved a detested landlady, Mrs. Swift, whom the two imps mercilessly tormented. One "crowning outrage" was Charlotte's alone. Standing at the top of the three-story winding staircase, little Charlotte noticed Mrs. Swift leaning over on the ground floor: "She had the beginning of a bald spot on the crown of her head." "It was just too tempting" and she spat right down, hitting her target. That occasioned the only whipping she ever got from her father, who happened to call that evening, when her furious mother insisted on paternal punishment with a small whip she had at hand.[19]

One of the ways Charlotte learned to cope with the largely cheerless and lonely reality of her life was by resorting to fantasy. Her refuge in the imagination evolved, she suggested, early in her life. In the fall of 1870 Mary Perkins and her two young children moved to the country near Rehoboth, Massachusetts. Frederick Perkins was probably contributing to the support of his family during this period, enabling them to live alone. "Healthy but barren" is Charlotte's description of the life that began when she was ten and ended three years later. There were few playmates and no formal schooling, "though mother still gave us lessons." Thomas planted a garden, took charge of the hens, and hunted, activities that for some reason Charlotte did not share. Instead, she turned inward, creating and embellishing an extended interior life. "It speaks volumes for the lack of happiness in my own actual life that I should so industriously construct it in imagination," she later wrote.

The fantasy world that flourished within Charlotte was shaped, as she described it, in opposition to the reality her mother provided. "Under mother's careful regimen," she and Thomas, as young children, had an early supper and then either read themselves or were read to by their mother. But a "painfully early bed hour stopped the story," leaving the eager children with an appetite whetted but not satisfied, and "off we went, dumbly, but with inward rebellion." Unable to sleep because of the story's excitement, Charlotte tells us that she "learned the joy of brain building." Only through her creative imagination could the "stern restrictions, drab routine, unbending discipline" be escaped. And so "the dream world grew apace,"[20] and little Charlotte imagined herself a fairy princess with enormous powers of magic.

When Charlotte was somewhere between the ages of ten and eleven, she put together a collection of imaginative pieces under the splendid title of:

Poetess
Literary and Artistic Vurks
of the
Princess Charlotte

One of the stories, entitled "Prince Cherry," describes a good king's weak son who was presented with a gold ring that would prick him when he behaved wrongly. At the point when Prince Cherry, who had been good for a long time, began to slip, Princess Charlotte left the story unfinished. Another conventional tale with a punitive moral describes the disobedient offspring of Mr. and Mrs. Rabbit who was caught in a trap set by some boys (the word "boys" is circled in the original), and served as a warning "to all future children allways to obey their parents."[21]

Two other short stories deal with bad sons. In the first a three-year-old male child afflicted with a club foot tore up his mother's garden, kicked his nurse, and tortured his cat until "his father was so angry with him that he did not know what to do with him." In the second, a widow with two children had a dutiful daughter, Jenny, and a three-year-old son who passed his time "squealing, squalling, scratching, and bawling" until his unhappy mother was driven from 1,600 homes because none of the neighbors was able to sleep.

If the first story about goodness coming from within was left unfinished, the second about disobedience culminated in destruction, and the two others described unmanageable and hateful sons who caused rage in their parents, then the most elaborate and the longest of the tales—running some fifteen pages—rings true as a statement of the fantasies of a little girl not yet eleven years old, whose power brings the most wonderful of happy endings: love and acceptance from her father, the king.

Entitled "A Fairy Story," it describes the woes of good king Ezephon and his "beautiful and only daughter whose name was Araphenia." The king once reigned over the whole planet, but his subjects drove him to a small city. Princess Araphenia tried to comfort him "but he had to much else to think about to pay much attention to her." And poor Araphenia was lonely "as she had no one to talk to but her mother and the servants." And then one day another princess, Elmondine, from another planet, appeared before her. Elmondine asked Araphenia if she would not like to "be disguised like a young warrior and be yourself the leader of the army," and Araphenia was overjoyed. Elmondine kept her promise. Soon the army closed in around Araphenia, now a warrior. "The men fell like grass before a scythe mowed down by her invincible sword." When she disclosed her true identity to her parents, her father promised her anything in his power and "her mother said she would give her permission to do anything he thought fit." Her request was to be given permission by her parents to leave them, to spend time with Elmondine in her foreign home. The request granted, she appeared at Elmondine's immense palace, but when shown to her bedroom, a gorgeous chamber, she chose to sleep with Elmondine. Elmondine then told Araphenia her story. Her life, she said, was without difficulty and so to express gratitude for her blessings, she frequently visited our planet to help deserving people, Araphenia learned. Searching for a person in distress, she heard a "low cry, down in the middle of a thick wood, in your country it is called The Forest of Dark Deed." The cry came "from an almost inpenetrable thicket." Elmondine discovered "an unprotected female at the hands of twelve ruffians. They were in the act of forcing her into the mouth of a deep dark cavern." Elmondine thereupon cut off the heads of six of the villains, thus frightening away the remaining six. The terrified lady then told her of how a baron had fallen in love with her, but when she refused to marry him he sent the ruffians to take her to the forest, "where the witch who dwelt there would soon put an end to her." At this point, the story breaks off.

Fragments of "A Dream," recorded but undated, describe Charlotte wandering alone in a forest, entering a "dark frowning mouth of a huge cavern," where she sees a "deep black pool." Spotting an old decayed log "gently rising and falling with the motion of the sable waters," she decided to risk her fate "on this fragile support." To her horror and dismay she felt the "log move under me with an undulating motion that told me but too plainly that I had trusted myself on the back of a gigantic sea-serpent." The creature began to sink, "and I knew no more." End of "A Dream."

Recognizing the dangers inherent in making too much of a few fragments of stories from the childhood of a woman long dead, it is still tempting to ruminate a bit on these imaginative pieces. In this period in her life, as she was entering puberty, Charlotte was trying to resolve the problems that troubled her: concerns as to who she was and what she was to become, anxieties about growing up and inevitably separating from parents, a normal process made somewhat problematic by her own unsettled and unsatisfactory relations with her mother and father.

"Prince Cherry" was left unfinished at the point when the young prince, abandoned by his good father, begins to slip from goodness and thereby incurs the wrath of the good fairy. Mr. and Mrs. Rabbit warn their children of the danger from boys, and the one who does not listen suffers death. The other two fragments examine the misdeeds of sons. These short pieces seem to stand as vehicles for anger by a sister at her brother, anger at the good father and the good white-clad lady of magic who cannot produce a good son, an inept father who cannot handle his son and an unhappy mother who is victimized by her ill-behaved male child.

The perils of coming adolescence are described by young Charlotte in symbolic language with her frightening descriptions of caverns in "A Fairy Tale" and "A Dream." Nameless terrors are also hidden in the almost impenetrable forest into which innocent young girls are forced. In the "Dream" sequence Charlotte, writing in the first person, seeks refuge on an old decayed log, an aged and therefore presumably safe object, only to discover from the "undulating motion" that it is a "gigantic sea-serpent."

It was in the lengthy tale "A Fairy Story" that Charlotte gave in to her creative, imaginative needs and spun out a wondrous and magical world where virtue and strength triumph, courageous and powerful daughters are rewarded by their good but helpless king-fathers, and women join together to create a power larger than each commands alone. Also in this story a nameless young woman is saved from a marriage she does not want, spared from death at the hands of a wicked witch. The well-meaning but ineffectual king is saved by his lonely daughter—lonely because she has had only her mother to talk to—who is transformed into a male warrior armed with a sword and who, after the bloodshed is over, resumes her female attire to join forces with another princess from another world. It is magic that empowers Araphenia, but it is magic given her by another woman, not her mother.

If fairy tales offer children fantasies in symbolic form which help them to cope with their struggle for self-realization, as Bruno Bettelheim suggests,[22] then Charlotte created such a fairy tale for herself, one in which she confronts basic human predicaments and triumphs over them. In this extended story the young daughter's wish to be given permission to leave home is granted, the separation from parents thereby made possible and painless. In these imaginative stories, Charlotte has incorporated ways of coping with despair, danger, sexuality, and separation, and she has found ways of establishing a world of hope and success with the support of a powerful woman who befriends her.

The reality of adolescence for Charlotte Perkins was another matter; it was certain to be very difficult. Puberty was in general seen as a perilous time in late-nineteenth-century America. The conventional wisdom, supported by medical opinion, saw adolescence in females as a particularly dangerous phase when young girls were prone to extremes of excitement. Mothers were urged to teach their daughters patience, modesty, self-control, and moderation. The always uncertain balance in human beings between body and mind, nature and civilization, was seen as considerably more uncertain in young women than in young men. A woman's body was viewed as a delicate machine that was vulnerable to extremes of activity, especially mental activity.

The risk in adolescence, the risk of taking one's love and one's need to love into the world outside, undoubtedly frightened Charlotte's contemporaries, as it continues to frighten young people today, but it probably aroused extreme apprehension in Charlotte. The ability to struggle for and achieve independence must rest upon a sense of trust in others, which ordinarily has its roots in deep attachment to an early adult nurturing figure who gave dependable and consistent care. Such a consistent, loving, trustworthy figure Charlotte did not have.

During this transitional period from girlhood to womanhood, Charlotte's job was to separate herself from her parents, taking along into adulthood aspects of each while leaving much else behind. It is a stressful time of choosing and selecting and examining, confronting and accommodating, rejecting and accepting, finding and refining an adult sense of self. This process must have been made all the harder for Charlotte because the options represented by her parents were so unappealing. The private world of women, as exemplified by her mother, was stultifying and ungenerous and restrictive. The public world of men, as exemplified by her father, was free but unkind, involving flight from responsibility and duty to loved and dependent ones.

Charlotte's immediate family traumas only added to the anxieties she had at this time. In the fall of 1873, when Charlotte had just turned thirteen, the family left their rural life and moved to Providence, where Charlotte's great-grandmother Perkins, although well past eighty, cared for her bedridden daughter, Grandmother Westcott. They were both elderly and ill, and first Great-Grandmother Perkins died, in December, leaving Mary Perkins to care for her mother, who died the following March. In the same period Thomas contracted typhoid fever and was for a time dangerously ill. Fantasies of adolescent sexuality that enveloped Charlotte at this moment in her life ran directly into terror of the deaths of mothers, her mother's mother and hers before that, and perhaps of the death another pregnancy might have meant for her own mother. Charlotte's grandmother had married soon after puberty, her mother was wooed at the same time in her life. Puberty was the beginning of the time to make choices about one's life, and all the choices must have seemed frightening, laden as they were with heavy risks and responsibilities.

Several months after they moved to Providence, the Perkins family moved again in June 1873, after the death of Mary Perkins's mother, to another Providence home, this time to a cooperative housekeeping group headed by Dr. and Mrs. Stevens, friends from Rehoboth. The group also included a Mrs. Isham and her two sons, with whom they had lived in Hartford, and a Mr. Wellman, of Cambridge, Massachusetts. The two-and-a-half years spent in this community were traumatic for Charlotte, although it is not clear how much this had to do with the group and its complexities and how much with the difficulties of being thirteen-to-fifteen years of age.

In Charlotte's memory, the group is to blame for her miseries. "Cooperative housekeeping is inherently doomed," she later insisted, and was exasperated at any confusion of cooperative housekeeping with her doctrine of professionalized housekeeping. The families, all of whom were followers of the ideas of the eighteenth-century Swedish mystic Emanuel Swedenborg—including Mary, who promptly adopted these beliefs—were "immersed in the mystic doctrine of 'Correspondence,' according to which everything in the

Bible means something else." Charlotte remembers "endless discussion of proofless themes," at the end of which she and Thomas developed a "severe distaste for anything smacking of the esoteric or occult." Mrs. Stevens, who looms as a major villain, was also a spiritualist.

Soon after the Perkins family joined the community, a friend of Mary Perkins's with a "pre-Freudian mind," Charlotte later said—probably Mrs. Stevens—became concerned at what she felt Charlotte's inner life might become, and persuaded her mother to order Charlotte to relinquish her fantasy world. Perhaps Mary Perkins and her friend feared that Charlotte's fantasies would keep her from coping with reality, not understanding that quite the opposite is true, that the fantasies of childhood provide the child with the skills and confidence to face adulthood. Such fears were common then, if seldom voiced in so extreme a manner. It was a devastating moment for Charlotte.

> Just thirteen. This had been my chief happiness for five years. It was by far the largest, most active part of my mind. I was called upon to close off the main building as it were and live in the "L." No one could tell if I did it or not, it was an inner fortress, open only to me.[23]

Fanny Burney, Jane Austen, George Sand, many women authors have described the value of their rich fantasy life in developing their imaginations and providing them with a release that the outside world did not. Said Mary Shelley of her castles in the air, her waking dreams: "I accounted for them to nobody; they were my refuge when annoyed—my dearest pleasures when free." The Brontë virgins, says Ellen Moers, "loved with brute passion, committed adultery and incest, bore illegitimate children . . . murdered, revenged, conquered and died unrepentant in their imaginary kingdoms."[24]

But Charlotte Perkins, on the edge of adolescence, obeyed her mother's orders. "Obedience was Right, the thing had to be done, and I did it. Night after night to shut the door on happiness, and hold it shut. Never, when dear, bright, glittering dreams pushed hard, to let them in."

In this same turbulent moment in her life, Charlotte's mother had "put upon me," she said, "two more prohibitions." She was to read no novels and to have no intimate friends, or so Charlotte recalled in her autobiography. Such remembered prohibitions were probably an exaggerated version of her mother's rules. Charlotte did read one forbidden work, *The Wandering Jew*. This was, she later claimed, "a signal piece of disobedience—the only one I recall in those years."[25] Charlotte would have us believe that it was the only disobedient act in her new obedient stage, although we know there had been many earlier instances of disobedience.

Did she obey or did she just say she did? Why did she obey? Was the obedience a sacrifice or did it reflect Charlotte's own sense of danger? Did she follow her mother's orders because they conformed to her needs? It seems likely to me that at a time of extraordinary stress, confronted with all the turbulent changes of adolescence and living in a household haunted by sickness and death, Charlotte did indeed choose to do as her mother ordered. It was not just her mother's wishes she was obeying, it seems fairly clear, but her own, flowing from her own fear of where adolescent imaginings and steps toward independence might lead. Neither of her parents, after all, had instilled in her the kind of hopefulness and self-confidence that would permit her to strike out on her own emotionally, to take the risks that come with growing up. In accepting her mother's prohibition on fantasy, with its underlying message that her inner life was dangerous, she must have suffered a kind of estrangement from self that could only further diminish her self-confidence. Fearful of separating from her mother, fearful of trying to survive on her own, fearful of confronting the dependency she felt on her rejecting parents, she handed to her mother power over herself. She was not yet ready to begin her journey alone.

In this way the "stern restrictions" and "unbending discipline" that Charlotte had bitterly resented at an earlier age now apparently became a refuge, a source of security, and the once-mischievous child became a rigorously obedient teenager. Still, she must have continued to feel some resentment, and thus blamed her mother for the loss of her inner life.

As for Mary, we can only guess at the fears that Charlotte's budding womanhood inspired in her and that in turn inspired the unusual strictures she imposed on her daughter. Those fears, a sense of peril and danger, were characteristic of the period, but were doubtless exacerbated by Mary Perkins's own personal crises. Mary

MANCHESTER'S | PROV., R. I.

Charlotte, age about fourteen

may have clung to Charlotte, fearful for her daughter as she entered her teens, just as, on Charlotte's side, her mother apparently became the dumping ground for her own hostile and frightened feelings, a state common enough in girls as they begin the separation process from mothers. Ordinarily this tension moves ultimately into a positive and balanced resolution. That resolution, that coming to terms with the struggles of adulthood as worked out in the relationship between mother and daughter, seems never to have occurred in Charlotte's life.

At the age of thirteen, Charlotte was an obedient daughter. But at fifteen, she began her journey to autonomy. The event in Charlotte's fifteenth year that embodied the first major challenge to mother's authority not surprisingly involved the detested Mrs. Stevens. According to Charlotte's recollection, Mrs. Stevens was seen by young Charlotte eating a bunch of grapes that were community property; although Charlotte did not directly accuse her, Mrs. Stevens insisted that her psychic powers enabled her to know that Charlotte thought her consumption of community food improper. Mary Perkins, "being greatly under this woman's influence," recounted Charlotte, accepted Mrs. Stevens's version and insisted that her daughter apologize to the older woman, or, said the indignant mother, "You must leave me." Charlotte, provoked into disobedience by a charge that was untrue, insisted that she would neither apologize nor leave. "And what are you going to do about it?" she asked, taunting a mother who insisted on absolute obedience. Mary struck her daughter. "I did not care in the least," Charlotte remembered, because "I was realizing with an immense illumination that neither she, nor any one, could *make* me do anything. . . . I was born."[26] This confrontation with her mother became "one of the major events of a lifetime," responsible for "opening an entire new world," wrote Charlotte Perkins.

Charlotte was a strong-willed girl, who no doubt had communicated to those around her her disapproval of Mrs. Stevens in general, if not specifically during the grape-eating episode. Perhaps she disliked Mrs. Stevens partly because of her mother's attachment to her. Charlotte felt that she got little enough of her mother's attention and likely begrudged sharing it any with another female. Charlotte was angry at her mother, particularly during these years, and if she had difficulty expressing her anger directly, which she seems always to have had, then expressing dislike of Mrs. Stevens was a safer way to hurt her mother. The incident over the grapes might have relieved those feelings somewhat and allowed Charlotte to defy her mother's stifling authority. But Charlotte was now left in a quandary: what was she to do next? how was she to follow up her declaration of independence? She decided that her duty required that she obey her mother, who was surely wiser and would suffer deeply if she did not, until she was twenty-one. Then she would declare her freedom and leave, but until then she would try to live in peace.

In February 1876 the cooperative housekeeping group broke

up, and school ended at the same time. "We leave here Saturday," wrote sixteen-year-old Charlotte in her diary, "loaded with 'Stevenish' opprobrium. 'Fiddle de dee'!"[27] The Perkins family, mother and children, lived for a month with Mary's half-sister, Mrs. Caroline Robbins, on Vernon Street in Providence; another month was spent with a Rehoboth neighbor, a Mrs. Peck. Then the family settled for five years on the second floor of a two-family house on Manning Street in Providence. Frederick Perkins made frequent financial contributions during this period, although more than once, said Charlotte, "I saw mother without any money or any definite prospect of any." They had a small flat of four rooms, and one of the two on the top floor was Charlotte's bedroom. For much of that time Thomas was in and out of MIT, his father having agreed to pay his tuition.[28]

Thus, from age sixteen to twenty-one, Charlotte lived in one home, primarily with her mother alone. While she continued to try to be an obedient daughter, in this period she began the process of attempting to remake her life, reconciling its different strands so that she could be true at once to her father, her mother, and her developing self. In some fashion she understood that her mother's standards were impossible to meet and so, over the next few years, while outwardly adhering to them, she slowly evolved her own. These proved as rigid as her mother's. The adolescent girl tried to find integrity and specialness of self by vigorously and strenuously applying external standards to improve herself. Charlotte underwent years of retraining, self-training, to learn to speak only the truth, to be good and kind, to be strong and healthy, all achieved through painful self-denial.

In her autobiography Charlotte designates this critical period, her adolescence, with the title "Girlhood—if Any," and she begins the chapter with the statement "Sixteen, with a life to build." In the previous chapter she had explained at great length how at this time her philosophy of life, to which she would consistently adhere, took shape. As a young girl, she asserts, she studied and observed and learned that the first duty of life is "to find your real job and do it." The business of "mankind," she went on, is "to carry out the evolution of the human race, according to the laws of nature, adding the conscious direction, the telic force, proper to our kind— we are the only creatures that can assist evolution; that we could replenish our individual powers by application to the reservoir; and the best way to get more power was to use what one had." This thinking is straight from the evolutionary school of thought as developed by Lester Ward, who was later to become a friend, supporter, and admirer of Charlotte's. Even if we discard, as I think we should, the claim that Ward's philosophy was hers first as an adolescent and attribute her overblown notions to a desire to use her autobiography to preach, it is nevertheless clear that during this period she was indeed seeking to find her real life's work and trying to decide whether it should be "female" or "male," mothering or career.

Looking back from the perspective of a life almost over, Charlotte saw herself during those years as engaged in a "cumulative effort toward a stronger, nobler character." To the age of sixteen or seventeen she perceived herself as having "no character to be specially proud of: impressionable, vacillating, sensitive, uncontrolled, often loafing and lazy." Not a bad description of an adolescent. She was determined, she remembers, to change herself into a disciplined, controlled person. So she set about a course of exercises to increase her will and determination, and she taught herself, painstakingly, to think before she spoke and to be concerned for others. In her autobiography she explains her method. She starts with the determination to change, and then she engages in countless repetitions so that the new trait ultimately becomes integrated into her personality. Each year after she turned sixteen, she would lay out one trait or two to be acquired. She remembers the satisfaction of accomplishment: "For eight years I did not do anything I thought wrong, and did, at any cost, what I thought right—which is not saying that all my decisions were correct." "Eight years" would take her from sixteen to twenty-four, when she married.

In fact, her life began to take a different shape from the time she was fourteen or fifteen. She began a new mode of living that included dress reform and health reform, especially strenuous physical exercise, fresh air, and cold baths. "Each day I ran a mile, not for speed but wind," she later wrote.[29] She also became a voracious reader. Reading, at that time considered primarily a female activity, was in Charlotte's case associated with her father. Choosing not to enter the world of boys and sexuality, which could be expected to end in marriage and motherhood, she selected instead the life of the mind, which she identified with him. In her mid-teens she wrote to him:

> *Dear father,*
> *How I want to have a nice long talk with you. Here I am fifteen years old, quite strong, moderately supplied by nature with members and such, instructed in the ordinary branches of study in a reasonable degree, with a taste for literature and art. . . . I don't approve of that ordinary mode of mending the broken fortunes of young ladies (?) in general, via advantageous matrimony, and the question is, in the words of a ranting, Methodist preacher whom I once heard, "What shall I do to be saved?" I have an inclination in the direction of authorship, but I have doubts as to whether I could make it <u>pay</u>. [A swipe at her father, perhaps, who never did make it pay.] I also have a learning on the side of art; but have the same misgivings . . . and more than all, de worse than all, I confess to the <u>heinous</u> crime of being <u>strongly</u> attracted to the <u>stage</u>!!!!!*

On a sheet of paper similar to the one used in this letter, perhaps a continuation of the same letter, Charlotte wrote of her unmanageable emotions: "I often feel hopelessly despairing at my total inability to work. It is the instability of character." She described herself as giving "vent to the most extraordinary series of roars and shrieks." What does she want from Frederick? "*Now!* I want a good strong dose of advice, though I can't depend sufficiently on my present shaky frame of mind to promise to follow it. . . . I remain your helpless daughter. . . ."

A problem that plagued Charlotte all these years and limited her program of self-improvement was inadequate and infrequent schooling. Charlotte and Thomas went to school only on and off. She attended school a total of four years, she said—not an uncommon situation for girls in her class, or more precisely declassed, position. She went to seven different schools, and her formal education ended when she was fifteen.

Just after the family had moved to Providence, when Charlotte was thirteen, a great-aunt in Hartford died, leaving half her property to Charlotte and Thomas. Mary Perkins was eventually able to raise enough money on the property to send both her children for a time to private schools, providing Charlotte, at the age of fourteen, with the most exciting formal education she ever experienced.

Charlotte's school was kept by a Mrs. Fielding and a Miss Chase. Her teachers, she said, were initially impressed with her intelligence but were soon disappointed in her performance because she did not flourish under the rigid routines that restricted her imagination. Her most successful subject was elocution, a skill she later used to earn her living. She loved more subjects than she excelled in, particularly poetry and calisthenics. It was at this school that the influence of Dr. Studley, a woman physician who taught hygiene, instantly converted Charlotte to a regime of cold baths, exercise, fresh air, and dress reform. Physical culture was a growing movement in late-nineteenth-century America. Charlotte became caught up in it and took pride in her flexible body. She might have been a good dancer, she mused, "but dancing was one of the many forbiddings of my youth."[30] Still, in a culture that valued frailty in women, Charlotte took delight and pleasure in her robust health and her strong body. (Later in life, when she turned to fiction, Charlotte Gilman frequently selected women physicians to play a crucial role in significant moments of conversion when young women, confused and troubled, seek advice from such role models.) Both Charlotte's impulse to read avidly and her lifelong concern for dress and health reform were thus inspired by the experiences she had in this school.

The one serious study that Charlotte years later said affected her deeply was physics, or natural philosophy, as it was then called. It is sadly apparent that Charlotte did not receive from her father or from her schooling the kind of encouragement that would have been so valuable at this moment for the further development of her intellectual and personal ambitions.

The emotional cost to Charlotte of her driven and conflicted adolescence was high. She said of herself that during these years she learned self-control and discipline. Someone else might say that during this period of emerging womanhood she learned to deny her emotions and her sexuality. At age seventeen she wrote in her diary: "Am going to try hard this winter to see if I cannot enjoy myself like other people." She was truly very hard on herself at that young age, trying desperately to force herself into a mold of perfection. She later described her life at the time as externally "meager, poverty-stricken, repressed," but said that inside there was much "earnest 'living' going on." It seems more valid to call what was going on inside denial rather than earnest living. It is not surprising, given her herculean efforts at self-suppression, that from age seventeen on Charlotte spoke in terms of great weariness and depression. At nineteen she admitted to her diary: "If it were not for mother I had just as lief 'go out' as not. As a tired child drops asleep, I could lay down my arms." Mother, who she claimed had been the cause of all her misery, is now cited as her reason for staying alive.

Much of Charlotte's time in these years of late adolescence was devoted to nursing her frequently ailing mother. Thomas, too, was not strong, suffering at one time from a prolonged bout of diphtheria. But then, cured, he went off to Nevada, while Charlotte remained with her mother. Mary Perkins was ill on and off for years, and Charlotte complained, at least to her diary: "I am no sort of good with invalids."[31] During these years many gloomy, morose feelings of futility and despair are unloaded in her precious journal.

These melancholy and cheerless feelings were exacerbated by continued friction with her mother, with continued problems flowing from Charlotte's ambivalent efforts to be a dutiful, obedient daughter. True, the two women shared some good times, such as their occasional practice of reading sentimental novels to each other, enjoying the emotions that would cause them to "weep and snivel consumedly."[32] More frequent are the outbursts from Charlotte against "a submission to a tutelage so exacting that even the letters I wrote were read, as well as those I received; an account was always demanded of where I had been, whom I had seen, and what they said—there was no unhandled life for me." Charlotte spat out in her early unpublished autobiography, written in January 1880, before she was twenty, that her mother "forbade practically every pleasure that was offered."[33] "Dance or not to dance? Charlotte versus mother," she had written four years earlier.[34] Mary's joyous youth did not flower into an adult life of happiness, and she evidently had resolved that her daughter was to have a different set of expectations.

Mother was so "rigorous in refusing all manner of invitations for me," complained Charlotte Gilman, looking back at herself in her late teens, and "I was denied so often," she went on, that she protected herself by denying herself beforehand, and thus, following the examples of Emerson, Socrates, Epictetus, and Marcus Aurelius, "I became a genuine stoic." But one deprivation was "so drastic," she recalls, that it dwarfed all previous and subsequent ones. When she was seventeen, one of her mother's cousins, ten years her senior, invited her to a students' concert at Brown. "Mother declined for me," not wishing to have her get involved with college students. "I made no complaint," she said, "being already inured to denial." But the same day another cousin, twenty years older than she, invited her to join him and his sisters in a box at the theater to see Edwin Booth in *Hamlet*. Again her mother refused, and why? For fear of hurting the first cousin's feelings should she accept an invitation from another. To her diary she confided:

> Oh dear! Oh dear! An invitation from Robert to a *College* concert and one from Edward to Booth in *Hamlet* & I couldn't accept either! Mother didn't think 'twas best. Oh dear! Oh dear!

Fifty years later Charlotte Gilman recalled that moment. "Something broke. . . . I have never since that day felt the sharp sting of disappointment, only a numb feeling. So deep was the effect of continuous denials and my own drastic training in endurance, that it was many years later before I learned to accept an offered pleasure naturally."[35]

However legitimate Charlotte's anger may have been at her mother's shackles, one senses that acceptance of her mother's rules still provided some protection from encountering the world of sexuality that she feared. In her autobiography Charlotte Gilman recounts an incident in her adolescence when a young man tried to kiss her and she primly lectured him on the need to retain purity, his and hers. Some time later he shot himself, she wrote starkly, without adding further details or explanation. The reference to the suicide is followed by further criticisms of Mary for being "rigorous in refusing all manner of invitations for me." What strikes the reader is the inevitable connection between dangerous events involving boys and a mother's irritating but nevertheless comforting restrictions.

Despite the strains and difficulties of her adolescent years, Charlotte does note in her diaries many pleasant events and occasions. It is hard to know how much weight to give these accounts, for, she wrote, "it was my definite aim that there should be nothing in my diary that might not be read by anyone." Moreover, in a novel she wrote in 1914, *Benigna Machiavelli*, she describes a young woman who keeps two diaries, one for her mother to read, one for herself—and we know that Mary Perkins did indeed frequently read her daughter's journals and letters. Still, Charlotte clearly did have some wonderful times in this period in her life. There were parties and sleigh rides and jolly visits and occasional events at the theater. Almost every night Charlotte played whist and chess, cribbage or backgammon, with a steady group of friends, many of them male. She regularly visited family and friends in Boston and Cambridge, where she "was far more popular than in Providence." There she met charming Harvard boys.[36] Thomas was in residence in Cambridge, and one wonders how Charlotte, who was ambitious, intelligent, and intellectual, felt while she was cavorting with Harvard and Brown boys, who then went back to their studies as she went home to an unstructured and undirected life, in which the day centered primarily around housework and the evening was spent playing chess and whist.

Each year she anticipated with great excitement her visits to Uncle Edward Hale's home in Boston, where she enjoyed a flurry of teas and parties and sleigh rides and "carousing with her kissing cousin Arthur Hale."[37] "I never was so courted and entertained and amused and done for in all my life," she wrote when she was twenty.[38] The return home after these annual joyful interludes, however, was difficult. "I am feeling very lonesome and unsatisfied just now," she wrote after one such visit had ended. "I am entirely deprived of any intercourse with the other sex, and it makes me one-sided and unhappy."[39]

Uncle Edward Everett Hale did more than supply a few pleasant weeks a year to his lonely niece. He also introduced her to several wealthy and prominent families, who befriended her. The Hazard family of Rhode Island often took her in. Mrs. Rowland Hazard II had her give lessons to her daughter and sometimes invited her to parties. A friendship developed between Charlotte and Caroline Hazard, who was four years older than Charlotte and who was later to become president of Wellesley College. Kate Bucklin, another valued friend, "used to take me to the theatre and buy me books," Charlotte recalled.[40] She went with Kate Bucklin on vacation to Maine on at least one occasion. Although Charlotte does not express any disgruntlement or wistfulness at having only occasional glimpses of a world out of her reach, it is hard to imagine that she did not sometimes have such feelings.

By the age of sixteen, her attendance at private school behind her, Charlotte was beginning to make a variety of efforts to develop skills that would provide her with some economic independence and some sense of purpose. She began doing watercolors, especially of flowers, and was able to sell a few. She painted advertising cards for Kendall's Soap Company, a venture into business with her cousin Robert Brown. Occasionally she gave private lessons or taught art classes. When her mother ran a small school out of their home, she assisted.

Although Charlotte was later to describe her artistic gifts as those of "no artist, but a skilled craftsman,"[41] she showed early signs of talent and interest in art. For a while, at the age of nineteen, at the urging of a friend of her mother's, she attended the newly opened Rhode Island School of Design. Mary Perkins objected but Frederick Perkins was "willing to pay the fees." Charlotte exacted from her mother the following whimsical but nonetheless telling commitment:

> I, Mary Perkins, do hereby agree . . . never to badger my beloved and obedient daughter on the subject of going to Art School, having given my *full* and *free* consent to her so doing.[42]

Somewhat later she joined "The Society for the Encouragement of Studies at Home," headed by Miss Tichnor of Boston, and studied, through correspondence courses, a variety of academic subjects. Charlotte's interest in art and her successful efforts at selling cards and watercolors do not constitute a commitment to an artistic career but suggest it was a possibility she considered at this time.

During these years she maintained her interest in physical fitness. She walked a good deal daily. She never wore corsets and wore only sensible shoes. In 1881 she persuaded a Dr. Brooks, who had taught calisthenics at a school she briefly attended, to open a woman's gymnasium. With Mrs. Hazard's patronage, she rounded up a group of girls, some of them from the "first families" of Providence. For three years, till her marriage, Charlotte went twice a week to the gymnasium and ran a mile a day. "I never was vain of my looks, nor of any professional achievement," she said, "but I am absurdly vain of my physical strength and agility."[43] The physical pleasure she found had to do with strengthening herself for her sense of self; it was divorced from any conscious concern with sexuality.

During her teens Charlotte had struggled, with great success, to internalize discipline and control so that these qualities became part of her and no longer simply an obedience to external maternal authority. The entire program of self-training, designed to alter her personality and strengthen her body, she saw as a preparation for some important work she was destined to do, although the exact nature was still uncertain.[44] By the age of twenty-one she was ready to declare her independence, as she had promised herself at fifteen that she would. She had her freedom, the long-awaited freedom from her mother. It was then that she declared her freedom from her father in characteristic style—in a letter.

Less than two months before her twenty-first birthday, she wrote to Frederick, describing herself as "well now, reasonably happy, and as busy as I want to be."

I am twenty-one this 3rd of July, have outgrown sundry imbecilities of which I wrote you at the age of fifteen; and am rapidly turning into an unattractive strongminded old maid. . . . I know of old that you are too busy to write letters even if you cared to, but I *should* like to know whether you wish me to write to you, for I am anything but desirous to intrude.

She ended the letter with these words: "Do you know—I think I should have liked you very much—as a casual acquaintance. Yours truly, C. A. Perkins."[45] Did she ever send the letter? Is the one in her papers the original, never sent, or a copy of a delivered communication?

The following year she wrote again to her father, although again it is unclear whether the original or a copy remains in her papers. Torn between mother and father, still seeking approval from one or the other, she wrote:

> I have wanted for very long to have some ones judgement set against my own which I could obey. . . . somehow I can't show things to mother. I can't be easily myself in her company. She always used to read my letters, written and received, and I never knew what it was to write a letter till I was twenty-one and rebelled. May I not take you for my invisible judge. Perhaps it wouldn't do though, for I hardly know you enough to tell that

and here the letter ends.[46]

The freedom that Charlotte declared for herself at twenty-one brought excitement and challenge, for the world was now hers to explore. It carried as well danger and fear and responsibility of making judgments for and by herself, though she did not see herself capable of making those judgments. She had her freedom, self-declared. Now she had to decide what to do with it.

III
MARTHA

The overriding problem Charlotte struggled with in her young womanhood was what to do with her life. Her search for identity and self-awareness took place in a context defined by the nineteenth century's notions of masculine and feminine, appropriate male and appropriate female behavior and emotions. It took her years of torment to come to terms, more or less, with the tension that resulted from the world's sharply polarized views of gender roles. The form through which she expressed her attempts to resolve that tension was the written word—in her diaries and journals, in her prolific letter-writing, and ultimately in her published work. The inner agonies were scrutinized on the page.

Throughout her life she used letter-writing to trusted and special friends as a device to explore issues with which she was then grappling. In the significant period around her twenty-first birthday she was primarily caught up with the tension between work and marriage, and the person with whom she shared these concerns was her beloved friend Martha Luther, "a gentle, intellectual girl" whom she had met when she was seventeen and Martha sixteen. As a young girl Charlotte had developed a deep and strong affection for Etta Talcott, a "pale, long-haired Sunday schoolish child." Then there was Harriet White, daughter of the despised Mrs. Stevens, for whom she "conceived my second devout affection."[1] But the most important female friendship she had in her early youth was with Martha. They hiked together, studied Latin and French together, exchanged short stories and poetry, but above all they talked and shared secrets. Soon after the death of a mutual friend, they established a "compact of mutual understanding," which involved, Charlotte wrote in her diary, their wearing similar "lovely little red bracelets with gold across," which was to be a "bond of armour."[2] They committed themselves always to be totally frank with each other and never to pretend. Martha Luther provided Charlotte Perkins her "first deep personal happiness."

In the spirit of the frankness to which they were pledged, Charlotte apprised her dear friend of a characteristic she called being "irregular in fervor," explaining that though for a time she would want to see her continually, "there would be spaces when affection seemed to wane," but that if Martha would be patient, "it would well up warmly again."[3] Was Charlotte preparing her first close friend for the withdrawal that she knew would accompany her depressions? Did she feel herself unworthy of Martha's love and was she therefore sabotaging it? Or did she select a friend who she sensed was incapable of assuming the emotional burdens she would place on her and was she already preparing herself for failure? All were patterns that would later appear in Charlotte's adult relationships.

Their intimacy reached a point of great intensity as Charlotte was approaching her twenty-first birthday, the moment of her self-declared freedom from maternal authority. The May before the July 3 birthday, Charlotte wrote in her diary:

> Martha comes. . . . I let her in unseen, she prowls up to my room, and we spend the afternoon in tranquil bliss. . . . She returns as invisibly as she came, at which I am exalted.[4]

Martha then went off for the summer and Charlotte was therefore free to express her feelings in a safe, comfortable, and familiar way, through her written words. During that "blessed summer of eighty-one," the summer she turned twenty-one, she was so happy about Martha that later, as a married woman of thirty, she wondered "if most people have as much happiness in all their lives as I had then."[5]

The correspondence with Martha that summer focused primarily on marriage and career, or more accurately, marriage or career. As we have seen, Charlotte began to identify with her father's world of books and public work in her mid-teens, but just after she passed her twenty-first birthday these matters took on an urgency they could not have had before. In her numerous letters to Martha, Charlotte posed the problem of choosing between the "masculine" model of public work and the "feminine" model of husband and children. It did not occur to her to imagine a marital arrangement that would permit her options beyond the traditional ones. Career meant no marriage, marriage meant no career. Male or female, public or private, active or passive, powerful or submissive, duty to the world or duty to the family.

The decision about her future course was tied up with her sense of self as woman and as person, and touched the deepest layers of her personality. Charlotte respected her own intelligence, her energy, and her commitment to the social good, whatever that meant precisely to her. She lived on the margin of the world of the educated and cultivated, peeking in at it but not herself able, because of her economic position, to share in it. She wanted to use her mind productively, but it had never been trained and she did not know quite what to do with it. She knew she had potential, but she did not know for what. Charlotte was working, in a limited way, as a commercial artist, and she had done some teaching in schools run by her mother, but it is not clear that these were the careers she was contemplating. At this point she was trying to decide in which direction to proceed, but there was no one near her—not father, mother, teachers—to help her assess and direct her future in ways that would be helpful to her and reflect her aspirations, vague as they were.

The world in which she lived did not envisage the public sector as a legitimate place for a woman. As I indicated earlier, some women broke through those barriers, but they tended to be middle-class and upper-middle-class women who were educated in ways Charlotte was not and who, as a consequence, established friendships, developed skills, encountered role models to pattern themselves after, and created a female community that offered support. School connections were crucial for women of this generation. By 1880, 40,000 American women, more than one-third of the entire student population, were enrolled in institutions of higher learning.

In the last decades of the nineteenth century, large numbers of women also formed women's clubs and civic associations to participate in reform work of one kind or another. This women's club movement was made up of women much like Charlotte, though probably more secure in class position than she and many of them married, who became involved in associations concerned with temperance, labor reform, "social purity," and community health. There were others, from working-class backgrounds, who sought their voice in trade-union activity or radical politics. All together such women constituted a minority, especially at this time, although the numbers continued to grow enormously throughout the century and well into the next. Still, their behavior was considered inappropriate by the culture at large if it constituted the central focus of the woman's life and was channeled into a career. The preferred role for women was anchored in marriage. Some activity in church or community groups, raising funds for hospitals, playgrounds, or schools, did not challenge their domestic role; indeed, it was incorporated into it. But to make one's life in the public sphere, to support oneself with paid work, was not much more acceptable for respectable middle-class women in the early 1880s than it had been for their mothers.

There were some women in the nineteenth century who envisioned a life that combined marriage, motherhood, and career and who acted upon that determination. But they were not many, and by the last part of the century that still was hardly the model readily available. Charlotte's aunt Harriet Beecher Stowe had managed all three (though a writing career was perhaps the one most feasibly intertwined with family), but more such career women would have agreed with Louisa May Alcott when she said, in 1868, "I'd rather be a free spirit and paddle my own canoe." The effort and commitment and dedication required to seek and then to sustain a professional career usually meant a life without marriage and children. Those professional women who married frequently remained childless.

It was possible in the second half of the nineteenth century for a woman to aspire to the kind of career that had earlier been virtually unattainable—in medicine, social work, the university. However limited these options were, they now existed in larger numbers than before, and they permitted substantial numbers of women to imagine a profession and a reputation for themselves that were not dependent upon financial or professional connections through a husband or father. There were thus many practical reasons permitting women to think realistically that they did not have to marry in order to enjoy certain privileges and a certain degree of security. There were also practical reasons for not wanting to marry. Ineffective birth control meant for most married women either years dedicated to the rearing of children or dramatic accommodation in one's sexual life.

The emotional reasons for considering marriage and a career incompatible were more complex, and were in part responsible for the kinds of sentiments Charlotte expressed to friends and to herself in her regular anguished journal entries. It was assumed that at marriage the wife entered a relationship in which she was the lesser party. The male was expected to be older, taller, and smarter. His superiority was taken as an inherent part of the social contract between husband and wife, regardless of whether or not the husband chose to behave in an overtly dominant manner. Unless both man and woman were self-consciously aware of social constructions and were determined to eradicate them in their own relationship, an unexamined, deferential relationship was assumed, accepted without thought. Even couples prepared to deny the social definitions of marriage had, and still have, difficulties.

Henry James, Jr., described his mother's life in terms that embody the ideal of his time:

> She was patience, she was wisdom, she was exquisite maternity . . . one can feel, forever, the inextinguishable vibration of her devotion. It was a perfect mother's life—the life of a perfect wife. To bring her children into the world—to expend herself, for years, for their happiness and welfare—then, when they had reached a full maturity and were absorbed in the world and in their own interests—to lay herself down in ebbing strength and yield up her pure soul to the celestial power that had given her this divine commission.[6]

Many women could not imagine themselves filled with sufficient virtue, selflessness, and goodness to merit such a eulogy—perhaps Mrs. James among them. Young women like Charlotte Perkins were not at all sure they even wanted to try, finding such a portrait unappealing.

There were, thus, many understandable reservations a woman might have about marriage. Charlotte had additional reasons to see marriage as unappealing or impossible. Loving and being loved had a long history of uncertainty for her, and this history damaged her ability to imagine a safe and happy future of any kind.

However, there were also many factors pulling her toward a decision to seek to marry. The risks and difficulties of taking responsibility for one's own life loomed large. General social pressures for women to find their life's definition in marriage made it easy to take that route. For many young women the quality of obedience inculcated in them as girls carried over into their acceptance of the inevitability of marriage. The obedience her mother required of her rankled Charlotte for years, but she was not free of its power. However disillusioned about her own life Mary Perkins was, there was no sign that she ever encouraged her daughter to seek a different course. Mary spoke in her own voice but with the authority and force of conventional wisdom behind her. Her life as wife and mother was hardly a positive model for Charlotte, but Mary offered no alternative models for her daughter to explore. Marriage did not present itself to Charlotte as a grand path, but it appeared an acceptable one. It also promised a life of love, and Charlotte yearned for love.

As she approached adulthood Charlotte looked for some one or some ones in whom she could invest her trust, her longing for affection. Her very sense of herself was being tested at this critical moment. She wanted, somehow, to be a whole, separate, autonomous, independent human being and a woman, and she could not imagine the world in which she lived as embracing, even tolerating, both those visions simultaneously. Being twenty-one meant she had to make that choice; she had to decide which way to go. In personal terms it meant trying to determine where she was most likely to find the love, the respect, and the comfort that she needed both to give and to get.

The question as she saw it was whether to be a woman, that is, a wife and mother, and to devote one's life to private pursuits— or to be a person, cultivate public work, a public career, and relinquish the traditional female roles. She grappled with the choices and seemed to come down on the side of public work, "father-work," "humanness."

"I am really glad not to marry," she wrote to Martha late in July 1881. The decision was not easy to make nor easy to stick with. Less than a week later she wrote to Martha about a conversation she had had with her sometime male friend Sam Simmons, who had learned something new from her and who said so. "Now *that* is just what I want. To be the sort of woman, handsome, self-poised, well-read, keen-sighted, refreshing—who men will delight to talk with." She saw her hope in "gradually strengthening my now inconquerable desire for mental culture and exercise," in her "determination to drop my half-developed *functional* womanhood, and take the broad road of individuality apart from sex." Here it is again: one cannot be both human and woman.

She turned to Sam for advice in this crisis. He said to her, " 'Go ahead!' and I'm going," she told Martha. She was not as yet at all sure where to go, but at least she had decided what *not* to do. "*I have decided*. I'm *not* domestic and I don't want to be. Neither am I a genius in any special sense, but a *strong-minded* woman I will be. . . . What I want you see is to acquire sufficient *strength*, real literal *strength* of mind to be able to see clear and *kill* swiftly any recalcitrance of the part of my heart in after years." The letter ended with an exuberant Charlotte saying, "Yours with the first free breath I ever drew."

And to those friends and relatives who disapproved, she had only to say: "I *know* I am right, defy the world."[7]

Along with this declaration of autonomy came an acknowledgment of the fears that independence evoked. The momentary decision to reject the world of men and marriage made her value Martha all the more, made her need and depend on that love all the more. She wrote long daily letters to her friend, whose responses were not as frequent nor as detailed. To Martha she was able to expose some of her vulnerability as she probably had not to anyone before. She needed to be cuddled by her friend, she said. "Fancy me strong and unassailable to all the world beside, and then coming down and truckling to you like a half-fed amiable kitten."[8] Charlotte at this time could *not* fancy that one could be strong and independent and yet need to be cuddled and held and made to feel like an "amiable kitten." She was trapped in a polarized world where one was one or the other. Caught, she said, between the demands "of two opposing natures in myself," she was determined to "suppress the weaker one once and for all"; she did not yet know that the "two opposing natures" could, do, must inhabit the same place, the same body, at the same time, and that one is not the weaker, nor the stronger.

Letters from Martha were essential to Charlotte in this turbulent period. When an expected letter from Martha did not appear, Charlotte returned, she tells her, "to my work in the most dispirited way." Nor did Charlotte concern herself with "the Philistines" who might misconstrue her love. "If I am not ashamed of having sentiments I am not ashamed of admitting them, and shouldn't I love my little comfort when I haven't anything else to love?" she asked her friend,[9] acknowledging some discomfort at her declaration.

How to come to terms with men, what they did to her sense of self, were issues she continued to play off against daily interchanges. She entered into intellectual combat with Sam's brother, the formidable one, Jim. He put her down for her faulty Latin—hers was self-taught, his studied at Brown. They debated the meaning of the Biblical story of the prodigal son, and she was sufficiently combative to chase him away. And she was angry because he withheld from her what she wanted. "Once and only once did I detect a glimmer of what I want—equality, and some benefit on my side."[10]

Then later: "And truly I bethink me he has absented himself for good and all. I do not care. . . . If he couldn't understand me, couldn't see how much I cared for, respected, admired him—if he must needs be angry and feel hurt . . . why he had better go."

And did she mind? "I feel freer and better without his influence. . . . Last fall I should have wept. . . . *Now* I do not care."

The decision was made. "I do not want men friends just now, not until my head sitteth more firmly on my heart, not until brain exercise has enlarged and strengthened that organ, and I am sure enough of my ground to venture off it." The commitment to embrace a public at the expense of a private life had been made, but it lacked a sense of permanence. "My ambition . . . is but feeble yet, and I will carefully repress his futile character until he is strong enough to move mountains. [Note that she sees ambition as masculine.] So no gentlemen for me just now. I have friends enough, and one love."[11]

Later when Jim returned, Charlotte greeted him a different person. "You've no idea how different he seems to me now. I neither heroize nor fight him."[12]

Charlotte may have been content to have "friends enough, and one love," but the love was less content. Charlotte was sure that Martha would "make up to me for husband and children and all that I shall miss,"[13] but Martha was not certain that she wished to be assigned that role in her friend's heart. (All Martha's responses are surmises, inferred from Charlotte's letters, for we have Charlotte's correspondence but not Martha's.) "Little kitten, little kitten," said Charlotte to Martha, ". . . I love you this warm bright Sunday morning. . . . But you don't answer letters worth a cent. When I take pains and writes lotts of petty fings to 'moose my little girl, I like to have my little girl notice 'em."[14] And later: "I'm disappointed. That mean owdacious postman stalked straight by, and I have no letter from Marfa!"[15]

Feeling hurt and abandoned, she tried to assure Martha of her importance. "My one stay and support—my other self. . . . Are you convinced of your indispensability?" Several days later she tried to reassure a seemingly reluctant Martha that the deep love she felt for her was probably not permanent anyway. "It seems improbable to me," wrote Charlotte, "that two souls *could* be so perfectly matched as ours seem now. There must be places in each that we don't either of us know about yet—undiscovered countries where we may go together, and may not. . . . I don't dare hope for years and years. . . . Perhaps, as I grow older, my mother's constancy may take the place of my father's fickle fancy." Was Charlotte's fickle fancy really the issue, or Martha's? Charlotte's letters make one think it was her friend's inconstancy that caused the unease. The last phrase of that very letter seems to confirm it. Said Charlotte to Martha: "Yours in a *calm ordinary wellbehaved friendly* (not intimate) *masculine* way" (original emphasis).

If there is appropriate masculine and feminine behavior to cover all occasions, then if Charlotte aspired to do what men did, she must be masculine. Apparently Charlotte succumbed to some such painful confusion about locked-in roles assigned by gender; this belief, and her sense that others found her love for Martha inappropriate or suspect, surely added to her already strong sense of alienation from self.

Her genuine feelings of love for Martha continue to be a topic of Charlotte's ruminations. "The freedom of it! The deliciousness! . . . Never again will I admit that women are incapable of genuine friendship"—suggesting that she once did believe so.[16] The exploration of the new and exciting world of loving friendship with a woman continued to stimulate and satisfy Charlotte. "I think it highly probable (ahem)," she wrote two days later, "that you love me however I squirm, love the steady care around which I so variously revolve, love me and will love me—why in the name of heaven have we so confounded love with passion that it sounds to our century-tutored ears either wicked or absurd to name it between women? It is no longer friendship between us, it is love. Why I feel it in me to be the *friend* of thousands, but you—!"[17]

This was an exciting, if frightening, period for Charlotte. Her "one stay and support—my other self"—Martha—loomed as the major source of strength and comfort and therefore was the focus of her greatest fear of loss. "As for your heart—with its everlasting hungry little corners," she wrote to Martha at the end of July, "just dilute me and fill 'em up, and I will leak quietly away when an interloper appears."

And that was the fearful word—interloper, the man who might come and take Martha away. And he did. His name was Charles A. Lane and he did indeed that summer steal Martha's heart, but not without a spirited fight from Charlotte. She attempted a variety of strategies, probably herself unaware of the desperation in her moves. Cavalierly assigning Mr. Lane a frivolous place in Martha's affections, Charlotte could urge her friend to "go ahead and enjoy yourself *heartily*," assuring her that someday "such trivial incidents of youth will seem absurd." Even granting permission for Martha to marry, "marry all you please and be loved and cared for to your heart's content," Charlotte went on to assert her rights. "But be your home as charming as it may, I am to have a night *key*, as it were, and shall enjoy in you and yours all that I don't have myself."[18] Here Charlotte seems willing to settle for a marginal place in Martha's life, in order to give herself some sense of place and belonging. Later in the summer she challenged the intrusion of

Charles Lane more directly. Fighting for Martha's entire affection, as if sharing it were unimaginable, Charlotte projected the effect of a traditional male personality on Martha's life in the future. "Suppose you love that man as I think you do—fear you will. Suppose he's cold and proud enough to suppress his own feelings forever . . . is that sort of thing going to satisfy you? Can you live and grow on an *uncertain* consciousness of a grand man's love?" Charlotte conjured up Charles in the image of Jim Simmons, with a "keen powerful mentality" that would nevertheless "imperceptibly" warp Martha. She warned her friend: "Love can do great things, but could all the love under God make Jim Simmons change those religious views of his? Do you want to be dragged into things; persuaded, convinced, and converted before you come to it naturally . . . to have him pray *for* you, and not *with* you?"[19] The specific issue is not clear, but it is not necessary to know it in order to understand the quality of Charlotte's fears. She did not trust Charles's magnanimity. She saw Martha drawn to his grand virtues, his "clear logical mind," his "heroic image," but she did not see a man with generosity of heart.

In a truly morbid state of mind, Charlotte wrote out her fantasy: "We live in our big house. . . . You are to marry, of course, you would never be satisfied if you didn't, and after a certain period of unmerited, *his*, happiness, your young man is to drop off, die somehow, and lo! I will be all in all! Now isn't that a charming plan?"[20] A few days later Charlotte wrote: "Just open your big eyes, and tell him you are spoken for by a female in Providence, and can't marry just yet."[21]

As summer's end approached, Charlotte sighed at the "rather grievous" prospect of a new season of housework. More difficult, despite her recent birthday, was her project of learning to "keep my temper and be pleasant with Mother . . . & to learn to grow under adverse influences." That project was "as *hard* a thing as I can do, and hence desirable."[22] Charlotte's need to find the adverse desirable, for the sake of strength it called forth, helped her through rough times. One of the roughest was just ahead: the ultimate loss of Martha, who had announced her engagement. Charlotte's diary for the fall unfolds the pain. October 18: "Go to Martha's. All alone." October 27: "Martha there. . . . Verily I love the damsel." October 29: "Am closeted with Mrs. L[uther] and change my views a bit. Tell M. to go ahead. Kiss her." November 9: "Martha over. She hath a ring. I have a pain." November 13: "Go home with Mrs. Luther. Spar with the enemy." November 15: ". . . have my crucial struggle with my grief. Victory. Too utterly worn out to do anything in the evening but write down my 'state o' mind.' " November 16: "Walk in the dark sts . . . in dumb misery. Where is that victory?" More than a month later, on December 28, she wrote about a party that was "a grand jolly unmitigated success. But it fills a mighty little place."

In her papers there are two unfinished letters to Martha, written during the fall of 1881, without accompanying envelopes, perhaps revised and sent, perhaps never sent. In them Charlotte exposes her deep pain and profound sense of loss. The first one begins plaintively:

Will you come and see me again please?

I have lost outright the largest happiness I ever had, and it leaves a great empty place with a small pain in the middle.

I do not ask it to be real, I do not ask it to be lasting. I simply ask . . . that you play at being friends awhile because I am in trouble.

You would come if I had lost my eyesight and wanted you, you would come if I had lost my mother and wanted you; come now, for I am miserably unhappy, and I want you. [The words "more than any one" are crossed out.]

A few days later she begins with:

I'm better. I find that grief, properly utilized is as strong a force as any other passion. The hurt and the hunger are there for a long while yet, but the difference is in the attitude of reception.

Mental, moral, or physical pain is nothing to humanity as long as humanity *accepts* it. It is when nerves give way and muscles fail that torture brings confession; and important resistance is the worst sting of pain.

Wherefore I cover up my "empty sleeve" and trudge. Now you needn't laugh. One of my pet indulgences always was to nurse a sorrow and enjoy it. . . .

The little girl is very happy. And all the family, high and low . . . are well-pleased.

Wherein—I am

Finis

Martha Luther and Charles A. Lane were married on October 8, 1881.

It is impossible to read widely in the correspondence of most nineteenth-century women without stumbling across language similar to that used by Charlotte to Martha. Love relationships between women were so common in that century that there were specific terms used to describe them: "Boston marriage," "sentimental friendship," "the love of kindred spirits." Deep as these loving relationships were, there were far fewer that sought sexual expression than would be imagined today. Undoubtedly many, perhaps most, women of that time internalized the widely held belief that women did not have significant sexual passion, so the passion and love between women was often seen as spiritual. And if women were sexually aroused, they could deny it, for there was no obvious physical demonstration. Eroticism was viewed as that which existed between members of the opposite sex, or in certain perverse situations between men, and therefore what would today be labeled as erotic behavior and language were not seen that way in the past. Charlotte was aware that her love for Martha might be misunderstood, but she was not deterred from using endearments and professions of love that she would have withheld had she herself understood her relationship to Martha as erotic, although that element was clearly present on Charlotte's part. Those who lived in the past had a greater tolerance for the rich diversity and range of possibilities that encompass human relationships. Charlotte truly loved Martha and felt deeply her loss to Charles Lane. Sexuality was not the cutting edge of relationships for Charlotte and probably many others like her, and so her relationships with men and women had more in common with each other than they could have today with most people.

When Charlotte as an elderly woman described her feelings for Martha as "love, but not sex," she was undoubtedly speaking her truth. "With Martha I knew perfect happiness." Many years after

Martha's wedding, as Charlotte's first marriage was dissolving, she wrote to Martha that "through the first year or two of my marriage, in every depth of pain and loss and loneliness, *yours* was the name my heart cried—not his. I loved you better than any one, in those days when I had a heart to love and ache."

"Four years of satisfying happiness with Martha, then she married and moved away," she wrote in her autobiography. "In our perfect concord there was no Freudian taint, but peace of mind, understanding, comfort, deep affection—and I had no one else," was the way she assessed this important loving relationship. Martha's loss was, she said, "the keenest, the hardest, the most lasting pain I had yet known." Her year's diary ended with a record of a "year of steady work. . . . A year of surprising growth. . . . A year in which I knew the sweetness of a perfect friendship and have lost it forever." Why Charlotte believed that "a perfect friendship" could not survive the friend's marriage is not clear.

As she would henceforth throughout her life, Charlotte dealt with her grief by using it to advantage. She wrote it out and then she managed it by struggling to incorporate it as a form of character-building. "Grief is an emotion," she said. "It may be used as a spur to action—like anger, or love." She used it to develop her sense of self-discipline. "I am stronger, wiser and better than last year," she said of herself. "I have learned much of self-control. . . . Most of all I have learned what pain is, have learned the need of human sympathy by the unfilled want of it, and have gained the power to *give* it. . . . This year I attained my majority—may I never lose it."[24]

IV
WALTER

On January 1, 1882, midway between ages twenty-one and twenty-two, and after Martha's marriage, Charlotte reaffirmed in her journal her determination to remain unmarried:

> This is for me to hold to if, as I fore-fear, the force of passion should at any time cloud my reasons, and pervert or benumb my will.
>
> Now that my head is cool and clear, now before I give myself in any sense to another; let me write down my reasons for living single. . . .
>
> I am fonder of freedom than anything else . . . I like to have my own unaided will in all my surroundings . . . I like to select for myself, to provide for myself in every way. . . .
>
> The sense of individual strength and self-reliance is sweeter than trust to me.
>
> I like to be *able* and *free* to help any and every one, as I never could be if my time and thoughts were taken by that extended self—a family.
>
> . . . For reasons many and good, reasons of slow growth and careful consideration, more reasons than I now can remember; I decide to *Live*—alone.
>
> God help me!

A few days later, Charlotte met the young artist Charles Walter Stetson. On January 11, so her diary says, she attended a lecture of his on etching. The following day Charlotte went to "Mr. Stetson's studio," adding, to her journal, "I like him and his pictures." Two days later she again saw Mr. Stetson, with whom she has, as she called it, "a twilight tete-a-tete." She continued to find him likable, and significantly confided to her diary, "It's a new thing to me to be admired." On the following Sunday, Mr. Stetson called and they were left alone to have "a nice talk." She introduced herself "as fully as possible, and he does the same. We shake hands on it, and are in a fair way to be good friends."

Walter might have begun his introductions by saying that he was born Charles Walter Stetson on March 25, 1858, in Tiverton Four Corners, Rhode Island, the youngest of four children. His childhood had been, like Charlotte's, bleak and cheerless. His father, the Reverend Joshua A. Stetson, was a Baptist minister: a migrant pastor, he moved frequently from church to church. His mother, Rebecca Louisa Steere Stetson, chronically ill, led a life, he later wrote, that was "warped and embittered by poverty and dark struggle."[1] In 1869 the family moved to Providence, Rhode Island, and while their economic crises did not end, they lived, at least, in a settled place. By the time of this move, Joshua Stetson was in the business of selling herbal cures and patent medicines; he achieved little success with this venture.

Walter, as he was ordinarily called, decided while in high school that he wished to be an artist. How he settled on such an unusual career is not clear, especially since, as he said of his early years, "I had to my knowledge never seen any painting worth mentioning; surely none that had influenced me in any way; but I saw many fair engravings and of these I was very fond."[2] Soon after graduation from high school, he "began to understand what a painter's vocation really is," which meant that he rented a studio and began to paint, but soon had to give it up and return to his parents' home for a time. Most of his early paintings have been lost or destroyed, but based on his recollections of them, it seems that the penchant for color for which he was later best known was evident in his early work.

In those early years Walter railed against the entrepreneurial values that dominated Providence. Even "Raphael would be unknown in this stupid little town," he said.[3] He suffered from predictable bouts of despair and self-doubt. But by the time Charlotte met him, in 1882, when he was twenty-four years old, he was receiving some good reviews from art critics, several of his paintings had been accepted at exhibitions, and he had even met some wealthy and important patrons who were providing support, financial and professional.

However much their similar childhoods of loneliness and sadness drew them together initially, as Charlotte later suggested, surely she was not indifferent to Walter's physical appearance. Photographs taken of him as a very young man, and particularly photographs taken two years after he met Charlotte, show an extremely attractive man, seductive and provocative. Walter, wrapped in a cape, looks boldly into the camera, representing, not the stolid, solid virtues such as are reflected (misleadingly) in pictures of Charlotte's father, but the bohemian, the artist, the sexual man, the defier of convention. In choosing a life's work that challenged the prevailing business ethic of his time, Walter did defy convention.

He was bold and ardent enough to propose marriage less than three weeks after he met Charlotte. To "the one question in a woman's life," as she put it, her answer was no. But for the next two years Charlotte, with much the same inner dialogue as she had shared the previous summer with Martha Luther, was torn between conflicting needs, enduring a fierce internal struggle over what she was to do and who she was to become, over whether she should continue to see Walter or end their relationship. Each decision she came to, however much it negated the one before it and the one that was to come, was achieved with a sense of conviction and determination.

Walter was equally determined, but did not vacillate. He knew what he wanted. Unfortunately for the couple's future, his attitudes to women's place, marital relations, and male and female sexuality were already fixed and, for all his evident bohemianism, strikingly conventional.

Walter confided to his journal his view of Charlotte:

She was innocent, beautiful, frank. I grasped at her with the instincts of a drowning heart—was saved for the time. I loved all that I saw pure in her. . . . She was cleanliness to long

Charles Walter Stetson, age about twenty-six

for. Yes, I loved her purity of innocence, or perhaps, ignorance of the world. I told her so.[4]

However much Charlotte might have been pleased had she read
these words then, she was later in her life to condemn the cultural
demand that women be innocent and ignorant to satisfy a male
need.

Walter's conventional ideas about pure womanhood long preceded his encounter with Charlotte. "I admired them," he wrote
of his long-standing view of women, "reverenced them, considered
them something much nearer angels than ourselves. I believed them
as a whole to be pure."[5] Walter was not pure; he lusted, he sought
physical relief with women he would not marry and whom he
condemned. Like many men of his time, he yearned for a pure and
loving good woman to save him from sinful acts. He was repelled
by "four harlots" he sat near in a streetcar, but then entered Charlotte's home "and saw the utter cleanliness of my Love."[6] Later in
their courtship he asked Charlotte to return a copy of *Leaves of Grass*
to the friend who had offered it to her because, in his words, "I
did not want her to think all men such animals as Whitman described
them."[7]

Walter's relationship with Charlotte was not the first one he
had hoped would save him from his torments. He had "so short a
while ago" whispered "those three words to another," although
this was a secret from Charlotte. He had worshipped this other
woman "as a goddess," only to discover later that "for seven years
I had worshipped an idea which I deposited in her."[8] Walter, re-
peating his pattern, now sought a new object to worship in Charlotte, who was also to disappoint him. Nor was Charlotte to be
the last person with whom he repeated this behavior.

As Charlotte was not Walter's first love, neither was he her first
suitor. There were, in Charlotte's words, "various youths in Providence who came and went harmlessly." "I am puzzled," she wrote
years later, "by the diary's frequent mention of young men . . .
and my utter forgetfulness of any of them."[9] But Walter was different. In August, seven months after their initial meeting, she could
say, "I'm really getting fond of him." In October she met his parents
and expressed the hope that they liked her. A few weeks later Walter
signed the following agreement, which indicates, first, how serious

their relationship had become, and second, however playful the language, how important the issue of domesticity was for Charlotte:

> I hereby make my solemn oath that I shall never in future years expect of my wife any culinary or housekeeping proficiency. She shall never be required, whatever the emergency, to D U S T!

Signed by Charles Walter Stetson on October 22, 1882.

A November diary entry tells how "Walter joins me on Main St. & walks home with me. Mother asks him to stay to tea. . . . He does. Reads me a letter to Mrs. Creesons [actually Mrs. Cresson, a wealthy patron of Walter's]. I love him. Henrietta here to tea."[10]

In the period that followed Walter's initial marriage proposal, a proposal that was repeated regularly, Charlotte often tried to open her heart to Walter and lay bare her torments and reservations. Were she to marry, she explained, her thoughts, her acts, her whole life would be centered on husband and children. To do the work she needed to do, she must be free. If she were to allow herself to love Walter and consummate that love, she would be of no more use than other women. Walter replicated this conversation in his diary. He heard the words, he understood their meaning, but he seems not to have comprehended the seriousness with which Charlotte held these opinions and their importance to her. Her concerns in no way altered his plan to woo her and win her. Her initial response to Walter's proposal had been rhetorical and in a conventional mode: "O my Friend. My Friend! What can I say to thank you for your noble confidence?", she wrote to him. Having spoken with the extravagance and formality of the period, she then permitted herself some honest, if immodest, sentiments: "You are the first man I have met whom I recognize as an equal." A week later, the doubts about marriage surfacing, she confessed to Walter that "the more I think the more appalled I am at the gravity of the subject. . . . the fruit of my meditation thus far is this conclusion: That it is an open question which life I can work best at." If she accepts the path he offers, she says, then she could never try her own. She leans to the conclusion that she should withhold herself from marrying, for "to risk the loss of a few years possible happiness" is preferable to risking "the endurance of a lifetime's possible *pain*," which is how she sees marriage; not a reassuring sentiment to share with Walter. The next day, in another long letter, she returned to the same subject and the same inner conflict: "It is no easy thing to refuse one great work on the ground—self-assured and unproven—that I can do a greater." "I knew of course," she went on, "that the time would come when I must choose between two lives, but never did I dream that it would come so soon, and that the struggle would be so terrible." She told Walter how happy she was when they met, "with the simple joy of anticipated friendship." And then, in anguished tones: "Why did you? O why did you!. . . . if only you might have given me what I wanted and not this." Then she shrinks back from her own words: "Forgive me. I ought not to complain of being offered the crown of womanhood even if I may not wear it."

Walter listened, he read her words, and then he tried to find a strategy to defeat them. To be fair to him, it is also true that Charlotte's messages were ambivalent. Less than two weeks after she asked him, "Why did you? O why did you!" she wrote of how "depressed and pessimistic" she had been all winter, and of what he had done for her—"You are giving me back myself." The letter was accompanied by a poem that described the difficulty of the decision to renounce the prospect of such marital bliss and happiness.

During the same month, March 1882, Charlotte wrote to her friend Charlotte Hedge, "I have a Lover! Yes'm. Not an 'admirer' merely, but a real one. He is a young artist of rising reputation." With great pleasure she described how "he thinks me a queen among women, and I am rapidly giving him first place in my esteem," suggesting that it is his admiration for her that is winning her over. Still, she says that she is not cut out for marriage, although "I esteem it the crowning glory of my life that such a man . . . should think me worthy to be his wife."[11]

As her indecision and resistance continued, Walter, too, suffered. "The worst thing that I can record is that my sexual desires are almost overpowering," he wrote soon after their meeting. If only Charlotte would marry him: "Then would be combined true love and passionate desire as they should be."[12] Walter is torn, as Charlotte is torn, but differently, his conflicts focusing on a natural appetite and the strains of abiding by a Victorian code of morality. The portions of his diary that he did not later destroy portray a struggling and anguished young man, an impoverished, unknown artist flirting with wealthy female patrons, playful with and drawn to attractive young models, pondering past loves and present lusts, while pursuing a reluctant lover who talks and writes ceaselessly about her passion for him but her higher commitment to some untried mission. He did not, could not, take seriously Charlotte's conflicts, so involved was he in his own.

The romantic notions of late-nineteenth-century America had their attractions, and Charlotte often got caught up in the language and the idealized vision of love that they promoted. She never believed it entirely for very long, but then she was never free of it for very long either during this period. Another poem, dated September 8, 1882, catches her in one of her romantic moods.

He loves me. I am throned
Highest of earth in that great heart. . . .
O may that Power of Good
Who makes all Right and Beauty, fill my life,
That, as his wife,
I may grow fair and perfect in all ways
And be the crown and blessing of his days!

But the much-yearned-for romance did not forever cover the reality of fear and self-doubts. Another poem, April 1, 1883, focused on the fear of motherhood.

O God I wish to do
My highest and best in life!
Stop not for hinderance or strife:
Be Wise, and Strong, and True.
And can I also be a wife?
Bear children too———?

. . . .

Can I, who suffer from the wild worst
of two strong natures claiming each its due
And can not tell the greater of the two;

Who have two spirits ruling in my breast
Alternately, and know not which is quest
    And which the owner true;

Can I, thus driven, bring a child to light?

   With all her doubts and misgivings, Charlotte agreed in May of 1883 to marry Walter. In her diary she wrote of her decision this way:

Read part of Century. Nap. Retta calls for a few minutes. . . . Sup. Dress. Walter. I have promised to marry him. (Robert called) Happy.[13]

Her casual reference to her decision to marry covered a fiercely ambivalent and turbulent heart. What made her decide to accept his proposal after so many months, almost a year and a half, of refusal? She said she loved him. She wrote it in her diary, on November 3, 1883.

I, Charlotte A. Perkins, am at this time 23 years old and not content. I desire to know why not! What have I done so far to fulfill my duties as a member of the world? If I were dead tomorrow, what were lost? . . . I have promised to marry Charles Walter Stetson. I love him? Yes. And by love I mean that I want him more than anyone else on earth? That and more. . . . Now love is more than *wanting*. *Love* is the infinite desire to benefit, a longing to give not merely a hungry wish to take.

She said she was drawn to Walter because of his courage, his aspirations, his "bitter loneliness." She also wrote of "the natural force of sex-attraction between two lonely people, the influence of propinquity," as if it were circumstances more than Walter himself that accounted for her sexual feelings. Martha Luther had abandoned her by marrying, and Charlotte met Walter on the rebound, which may have contributed to her decision. Life with her mother was unsatisfying, and Walter's pursuit was flattering.

Marriage to Walter solved many problems for Charlotte, or so she may have thought. By taking refuge in what she called "that extended self, a family," she could repudiate responsibility for her own growth and development. If she was at all uncertain of her own abilities, marriage must have seemed an attractive prospect.

However, the reason Charlotte gave for accepting Walter's proposal when she did, after "a terrible two years" of vacillation, was that he had "met a keen personal disappointment."[14] The crisis in Walter's life that prompted Charlotte's change of heart was the rejection by the *Atlantic* of several sonnets he tried to place with the magazine. He had no talent for poetry, he was told, and he was crushed by the criticism. "My painting is of like sort, I suspect," he wrote to Charlotte. Is his whole life to be a failure? He told Charlotte to burn the sonnets he had previously sent to her, and then he burned almost one thousand pages of his journal.

The young lovers had been separated at this point for five weeks, Charlotte having made one of her many decisions to sever the relationship, because it made her feel, she said, "not a woman" but "maimed, warped, imperfect." When Walter appeared to be powerful and filled with confidence, Charlotte felt small and weak beside him. But when his vulnerability was exposed, when he was devastated by the critical review of his work, Charlotte reversed herself. He rushed to her side, showed her the letter of rejection, and in a broken voice she said she loved him and, he wrote, "promised or vowed rather to marry me."[15]

She commented in her autobiography: "After that, in spite of reactions and misgivings, I kept my word, but the period of courtship was by no means a happy one."[16]

The struggle over conflicting duties was the arena in which Charlotte played out her continuing ambivalence. Had she no lover, she said to herself, the world would claim her, but "having a lover it is my first duty to him."[17] Here, then, Charlotte accepted the contemporary notion of true womanhood as unselfish and self-denying; love itself is defined by these qualities. The world said that concern for one's own development was selfish and therefore unwomanly, and she accepted this notion. She relinquished herself to a "woman's passion of abnegation," although she did so with reluctance and ambivalence.

Walter, too, was expected to make sacrifices to uphold the notions of manhood to which he was committed. Walter "means to give up his art!" wailed Charlotte to her diary, "because he cannot make it 'pay,' and because he must have money to marry, and he must marry. Well————."[18] (It should be noted that Walter never did give up his art, although it never did pay.)

As the year that she and Walter were to marry began, she made the following entry in her diary for December 31, 1883:

1883–1884
Midnight————Morning
The clock rings 12
With no pride, with little hope, with uncertain occasional happiness, with no glad energy and living power; with no faith or nearly none, but still, thank God! with firm belief in what is right and wrong; I begin the new year.

Let me recognize fully that I do not look forward to happiness; that I have no decided hope of success. So long must I live . . .

Perhaps it was not meant for me to work as I intended. Perhaps I am not to be of use to others.

I am weak.

I anticipate a future of failure and suffering. Children sickly and unhappy. Husband miserable because of my distress; and I————!

I think sometimes that it *may* be the other way; bright and happy, but this comes oftenest; holds longest. . . .

Let me keep at least this ambition; to be good and a pleasure to *some* one, to some others, no matter what I feel myself. . . . And let me not forget to be grateful for what I have. Some strength, some purpose, some design, some progress; some esteem, respect—and affection.

And some Love. Which I can neither feel, see nor believe in when the darkness comes.

I mean this year to try hard for somewhat of my former force and courage. As I remember it was got by practice.

But O! God knows I am tired, tired, tired of life!

If I only could know that I was doing right————."

The following day Charlotte was distraught to learn that her friend Conway Brown had killed himself. He had been a "bright-faced boy of twenty or twenty-one, an only child, loved, cared for, the idol of his parents, with no known grief or trouble." He had spoken to her the previous summer of his suicidal depressions. "I can sympathize with him, mental misery is real; and in a season of physical depression might well grow unbearable," she added. Her way of coping was to work. "How needful to live so that in such times there is enough real work to look upon to pressure one's self-respect! *The only safety is within.*"[19] Seeking refuge in work in the public realm and finding strength within were, indeed, later to save her own life.

Despite the real misgivings and depression that seemed to surround Charlotte when she contemplated her marriage to Walter, these two years before her marriage were filled with a great deal of activity: studying French; running a Sunday Bible class; reading Darwin's *On the Descent of Man*, which the librarian said was ten times more popular than any other book, Mill's *On Liberty* and some Greek history; making regular and frequent visits to the gymnasium, where she took enormous pleasure in her strength (on March 24, 1883, she "carried a girl on *one arm* and hip—easily!"); doing much dreary, time-consuming housework; visiting and calling; sewing; spending much time with women friends and little time with Walter. "I joy to find my old book hunger growing on me again," she wrote to Grace Ellery Channing, the intimate woman friend who succeeded Martha Luther in her affections and who remained a friend throughout their lives. She was also tutoring a child an hour a day in writing. In spite of her reservations about the impending marriage, then, Charlotte was functioning actively and enthusiastically for much of the time, but only in those activities unconnected with Walter and their future together.

Shortly before the marriage took place, Charlotte wrote an extraordinarily revealing letter to Grace Channing. It is all the more remarkable because at this time, February 1884, their friendship, not as intimate as it would later become, had a quality of formality. "Walter likes you, which is agreeable," she wrote, "and you like Walter, which is balm to my soul."

Then a strange observation; strange even though we do not know the specific reference:

It is a constant source of shame to me that I should suffer under the adverse opinions of those about me concerning my lover. I know the opinions to be unfounded, ill-founded, unwise, unfair, ignorant, short-sighted, etc., etc., but for all that it does have an affect on me—fairly makes me think less of him!

Which being the case you can see what a comfort it is to have some person whose judgment has weight with me look favorably on the man of my—choice? *hardly, I had no choice, really, there was no other, the man of my acceptance, say* [my emphasis].

She goes on to say:

As to being *very* happy, as you hope, that is not my constant expectation. The whole thing seems to me far different from what it is to most women. Instead of being a goal—a duty—a hope, a long expected fate, a bewildering delight; it is a concession, a digression, a good thing and necessary perhaps as matters stand, but still a means, not an end. . . . It fills my mind much; but plans for teaching and writing and studying for *living* and helping, are more prominent and active.

And that is where I fear some sorrow; lest my other occupations rob my love of time and interest he may feel should be his and ours.

Well, he knows what to expect.[20]

For a woman contemplating an impending marriage, the letter is filled with feelings of misery and dread, but here at last Charlotte is trying to reconcile her two opposing natures by envisioning a life that would encompass both domestic life and public commitment. Her worries that her public concerns might take precedence over her private ones and the last phrase concerning Walter, that "he knows what to expect," suggest that some discussion had occurred between the two about Charlotte's interests, activities, and plans.

The low feelings did not disappear. On March 9 she wrote, "Am lachrymose. Heaven send that my forebodings of future pain for both be untrue." Two days later she says, "Am *miserable*. Write a piece of biography and some verses." Two weeks later: "Some housework and write to Walter. Letter from, it is his birthday and I had forgotten it! It was not for lack of thought of him," she tries to reassure herself. At the end of April she is down: "Go to Gym for last time at present. They are sorry to have me go. Walk home alone"[21]—although it is not clear why, as a married woman, she would find it so difficult to continue a practice she so much enjoyed as a single one. She would soon relinquish much of her art work on account of her marriage. It seems she chose to withdraw from work that in any way competed with his—and I suspect the decision was hers, not Walter's. She seems now unable to sustain the vision of combining marriage with her other interests, so depressed is she.

Throughout their troubled courtship, Walter failed to understand Charlotte and did not know how to respond to her. He loved her, as best he could. But they did not talk much to each other. They talked at each other, presenting arguments and counterarguments. Despite all his concern for her, love for her, tenderness for her, his overriding goal was to win. He saw her struggle for autonomy as selfishness and as a threat to his love, and her reluctance as a challenge.

He knew well what he wanted from her. Two months after they met he admitted to himself: "It is very much to have her look up to me as if I were superior. . . . That my love of her has conquered." The following week Charlotte had an accident at the gym. He found her "lying on the lounge in the sitting room looking a little like an invalid, but more womanly than ever." He took her hand, struggling not to kiss it because she did not wish it. "There was a piteous look in her face (Ah! how different from the triumphant conqueror's look of sometime ago!) which thrilled me."

Walter chose to ignore or misread signs of trouble in their relationship. Early on in their courtship Charlotte asked him if he would mind if she supported herself after their marriage. "It took me some minutes to answer," Walter said, that kind of question being unusual in 1882. "And the answer was that I should rather support her; besides if she bore to me, she would have little time to earn for herself; except by writing, in which case I should not object. Then she smiled."[22] Walter read the signs in this conversation as indicating that his proposal was "taking deep hold upon her," which it was, but he did not acknowledge this and all subsequent signs of impending conflict.

Walter was not untouched by Charlotte's uncertainties and frequent changes of mind and mood. She was hard to understand, he admitted, because she contradicted herself and "mostly because she does not understand herself." But like many lovers he assumed that all her problems would disappear when she gave herself up to him and to his love. When her overstated declarations of her intellectual superiority were followed by professions of abject worthlessness, instead of feeling concern at the extreme postures, he expressed delight that her "spirit is broken." What he saw was that "the false pride is melting before love rapidly." He noted that Mrs. Cresson, long involved in his career, felt that Charlotte would be a burden to him unless she could "give herself up—become as nothing for my sake." It had never occurred to Charlotte before that she might be a burden to Walter; she had only imagined the marriage as restricting *her* freedom. "It set her to thinking in a new direction," wrote Walter, "and the good effects are apparent already."

As the idea of marriage became increasingly a possibility to Charlotte, Walter noted that she underwent significant and surprising changes. "She wants to be treated more as a child now than as a woman. I could scarcely have foreseen so complete a subjugation of self—or rather abnegation. She is willing to do anything, go anywhere, so long as I am with her." When these moments of self-abnegation were followed, as they invariably were, with demands for separation or perhaps severance, Walter became stunned and angry at her unpredictable behavior.

In March of 1883, Walter commented that Charlotte was "not the strongly independent creature she was a year ago." A few days later he noted that Charlotte was "more like what is best in other women—more thoughtful, bland, gracious, humble, dependent." Occasionally, he admits, "the old fire comes" and she has "one of those spasms of wanting to make a name for herself in the world by doing good work; wanting to have people know her as Charlotte Perkins, not as the wife of me." Walter does not comprehend how such a "terrible mood came again to her." Charlotte even suggested a "wild theory" that they live separately and come together when "the erotic tendency was at a maximum." Naturally, Walter said he would not agree nor would he think much of any man who would.[23]

Walter was aware of the large social changes that were occurring around him and the new opportunities in the public sphere that women were seizing. He believed that such women would go into the world, be buffeted about, and then return home, having learned that freedom is false "which makes them rebel against ties of love and home." Walter saw himself patiently waiting and enduring until Charlotte's madness passed. But when a few days later she insisted on another separation, something went out of him, he said. He saw her unwillingness to make a commitment to him as "deep selfishness," and he chose not to examine the implications of her wavering for their future together. He did not seem to hear her when she said, "I am not ready to marry you. This suffering, these tears, are only premonitions."

It was this separation that was ended with Walter's rejected sonnets. Walter and Charlotte agreed to use the remaining time before their wedding to prepare themselves for their life together. Her responsibilities were to curb her ambition and learn the gentle ways of loving. "Women do not seem to understand what a man's life is. Even women's earnestness seems half play," Walter said in his journal, thus assigning her struggle for meaningful work to a place of inconsequence.

But the relapses continued. "It is," he said, "all her old ambitious 'freedom'-loving nature rising in rebellion against the 'weakness' of tenderness and love." He found incomprehensible her claim that the saddest day of her life was the day she knew he loved her. Nevertheless, his decision to marry her was unshaken. "I trust, perhaps foolishly, that marriage will cure her."[24]

The young couple planned to take over a small three-room apartment that constituted the entire second floor of the Perkins house on Manning and Ives streets in Providence. Concerning the decorating of their new home, the bride-to-be said to her artist husband, "Do it just as you choose, I have no tastes and no desires. I shall like whatever you do,"[25] further relinquishing an active role in their shared life.

And so the young couple married, with reservations, at least on the part of the bride, that easily matched the reservations with which her parents had entered their marriage. The ceremony was performed by Walter's father. Charlotte's father seems not to have attended the wedding, and of her mother she says, "mother declines to kiss me and merely says 'goodby.' "[26] But her doubts faded, for the moment anyway, as convention and romance took over. Charlotte's journal entry describing her wedding night reads like something out of *Godey's Lady's Book*.

> Friday, May 2nd, 1884
> My Wedding Day
>
> I install Walter in the parlor & dining room while I retire to the bed chamber. . . . The bed looks like a fairy bower with lace, white silk and flowers. Make myself a crown of white roses. Go to my husband. He meets me joyfully; we promise to be true to each other; and he puts on the ring and the crown. Then he lifts the crown, loosens the snood, unfastens the girdle and then—and then. O my God! I thank thee for this heavenly happiness! O make me one with thy great life that I may best fulfill my duties to my love! to my Husband! And if I am a mother—let it be according to Thy will! O guide me! teach me, help me do right!"

After a short weekend honeymoon, they settled into a quiet life together, the early days filled with discoveries of the pleasures and pains of shared life. The bride experimented with elegant cooking and other household chores, minimal enough in their tiny home. Her daily routines were much as they had been before marriage, only with more leisure and less physical activity. Instead of visits to the gym, there were long walks with Walter. In place of lively evenings of whist and chess with several friends, there were quiet evenings of reading aloud.

The first recorded squabble was portentous. After one week, she wrote in her diary: "Get a nice little dinner. I suggest he pay me for my services; and he much dislikes the idea. I am grieved at offending him. Mutual misery. Bed and cry."

A more perplexing entry in her diary the following month reads: "Am sad. Last night & this morning. Because I find myself too— affectionately expressive. I must keep more to myself and be asked— not borne with. Begin to make arrowpudding." What did she mean,

Charlotte Perkins Stetson, age about twenty-four

"too—affectionately expressive"? Ten days later she confided to her journal: "Get miserable over my old woe—conviction of being too outwardly expressive of affection." The following day she wrote that she is "still miserable and feel tired. . . . Am miserable some more but he persuades me to believe that he never tires of me."[27]

Perhaps the little girl tucked away inside the woman Charlotte, the little girl who was starving for touching and loving and caressing, expressed her sensual yearnings for the handsome artist, only to be told that she was "too—affectionately expressive," that she must wait to "be asked—not borne with." Walter acknowledged his sexual appetites and sought in marriage a place to satisfy them legitimately. Charlotte was an intense and passionate young woman, proud of her strong and flexible body, living in a culture that denied her the recognition of her own sexuality. The repressions of her early training evidently ran counter to her passionate nature and would have to be reconciled within the marriage, worked out in some way with her partner. Walter's conventional notions of proper womanhood would have made him find any signs of overt sexuality in Charlotte disturbing to his own sense of maleness. There was sure to be trouble between them. It is likely that for Charlotte, far more than for Walter, affection and sensuality would be intimately bound up with her sense of being loved and loving. Perhaps the problem between them was that she could never have enough affection, that Walter could never give the needy Charlotte enough to make up for all the losses of father, of mother, of brother, of Martha, of the hope of accomplishing something big and important. With his traditional values, it seems likely that he would not even know how to try.

Despite these difficulties, it appeared for a short time that Walter's prediction that the marriage would bring permanent change in Charlotte was accurate. "A marvelous impalpable change has come over her," he wrote in August of 1884, three months after their wedding. "She is as dainty and exquisitely gentle now as a woodland flower might be if it had a clear brain and quick senses. . . . She is everything a *perfect* wife should be."[28] Charlotte was probably trying desperately to be that perfect wife, to subdue all those untested ambitions, to hold down all those passions that threatened to erupt. Her diary recorded genuinely happy times, laughter, and contentment, and when Charlotte learned that she

was pregnant, she expressed some joy at the prospect of a baby.
But very soon the depressions that she had been experiencing periodically throughout the courtship increased and deepened, "the
not-wellness coming oftener and oftener."

Walter's reaction to her depression?

> A lover more tender, a husband more devoted, a woman
> could not ask. He helped in the housework more and more
> as my strength began to fail, for something was going wrong
> from the first. The steady cheerfulness, the strong, tireless
> spirit sank away. A sort of gray fog drifted across my mind,
> a cloud that grew and darkened.

Walter continued to care for his ailing wife, assuming that the illness
would end with the birth of their child.

A daughter, named Katharine Beecher, was born on March 23,
1885. Wrote Charlotte:

> Brief ecstasy. Long pain.
> Then years of joy again.
>
> Motherhood means giving.

But Charlotte found no joy in it. Instead, she fell into a deep depression. She had everything she was supposed to want—a loving and
concerned husband, a healthy and agreeable baby, and after the
Stetsons moved to larger quarters nearby, a lovely home, as well
as a new live-in German servant girl to lighten the burden of household chores. Yet, Charlotte says, "I lay all day on the lounge and
cried." She was too depressed to care for the baby, who was tended
first by a nurse and then by Charlotte's mother, who rushed home
from a visit to Thomas and moved in with them in order to look
after Katharine.

The next years must have been nothing less than a relentless
nightmare for Charlotte and her family, not only because her
depression persisted and deepened, but because of the peculiar bifurcation of her life. Outside, either literally out of the house or
engaged in work outside the domestic sphere, she rallied, became
almost exuberant with external stimulation. Inside, as wife and

mother, she wept unendingly, was forever fatigued, in constant need of nurturing by others, and unable to nurture her own child. Having a child apparently reopened old, never-healed wounds of neediness in herself, setting off her sense of herself as a child in need of mothering. Even Mary's return to tend her grandchild could have reawakened Charlotte's anger at her mother for having failed to give *her* the sort of mothering she had required as a child.

Charlotte could not give the love that motherhood demanded. "I would hold her close—that lovely child!—and instead of love and happiness, feel only pain. The tears ran down my breast. . . . Nothing was more utterly bitter than this, that even motherhood brought no joy," wrote Charlotte in her journal.[29]

"Every morning the same hopeless waking. . . . Retreat impossible, escape impossible," she confided to her diary in the summer of 1885.[30]

And she blamed herself. In her autobiography, she recalls thinking: "You did it yourself! You did it yourself! You had health and strength and hope and glorious work before you—and you threw it all away. You were called to serve humanity, and you cannot serve yourself. No good as a wife, no good as a mother, no good at anything. And you did it yourself!"[31]

The neediness and vulnerability that had so pleased Walter during their courtship became a drain as those qualities deepened in Charlotte and as she became unable to be the cheerful, contented housewife Walter expected his wife to be. "Sickness makes Charlotte clinging, dependent in disposition. I dare do nothing contrary to her request lest she take it as a signal of vanishing love." Months later, the situation little improved, Walter could exclaim: "I felt that I was sorry that I had married, for the first time distinctly. I would not marry if I had the chance again, knowing what I do now." He spent his time in housework and in trying to raise money by selling his paintings, but nothing cheered Charlotte. "I feel that I am becoming degraded to a mere instrument of money getting," he lamented.[32]

In the winter of 1885, under the advice of her doctor, Charlotte accepted an invitation from Grace Channing's family, who had moved to Pasadena in the hope of improving Grace's fragile health. The Channings feared Grace had tuberculosis. Charlotte traveled alone, without Walter or Katharine. "Feeble and hopeless I set forth," she wrote, "armed with tonics and sedatives. . . . From the moment the wheels began to turn, the train to move, I felt better." The trip was punctuated by renewed contacts with her brother Thomas, living in Utah, and her father, in San Francisco, neither of whom she had seen in years, and with neither of whom the visit was a success. Her family, the family she had never had and the home she had never had, waited for her in Pasadena with the Channings. Pasadena spoke to her hunger for nurturing and to her hunger for beauty: "Never before had my passion for beauty been satisfied. This place did not seem like earth, it was paradise."

In this congenial atmosphere she stayed the winter, recovering so well that she "was taken for a vigorous young girl," she said.[33] That winter Charlotte and Grace began to write plays together, a collaboration that was to continue for years and that cemented a friendship that would continue all their lives. They started with improvisations and completed a play before Charlotte left. She also began to paint again. Writing to Martha that she was to return East in two weeks, she said that she looked forward to this event with "both joy and dread. Joy to see my darlings again, and dread of further illness under family cares."[34]

Charlotte's fears were realized. With the return to "family cares" came hysteria, incompetence, impatience, lethargy, paralysis. On impatience, February 14, 1887: "Dr. Knight comes to see K: says her liver is not working right. . . . [K] makes herself disagreeable as usual." Irritation with Walter, February 15, 1887: "A financial crisis. No coal. No money. I tell Walter he *must* get it, or I will, and he does. Sit doleful a little, then manage to eat something, and get to work. . . . After supper Walter . . . fixes Valentine to send off. Then I try to make him design another card; but he won't work." Perhaps Charlotte was resentful at having sacrificed her identity, her future, for their marriage, while Walter did not fulfill his part of the bargain. After all, he had said during their courting days that he would give up his art to support his family, and now he was not willing to do what was necessary to make money from his artistic talents, at the same time that he denied her her wish to work. Perhaps this situation evoked memories of her father's behavior toward his family.

March 9, 1887: "Bad night again. . . . I give out completely in the morning, crying with weariness." A week later, on March 15: "Put K to sleep . . . have a crying fit."

Later that month, she described herself as "getting back to the edge of insanity again." The following day she commented that she "slept in the spare room last night and feel much better." The next day: "Try the spare room again, but Miss Kate howls for me in the night, won't let her father touch her." Is it Kate she is escaping by sleeping in the spare room, as she suggests, or is it Walter? On Sunday she observes: "Dismal, of course, being Sunday. But we get up very late, so there is less of it." Why is Sunday "of course" dismal; perhaps because the family is together? "Very tired and miserable." Occasionally she is soothed by the caring she seemed so desperately to need: "Walter gives me a warm bath and puts me to bed."[35] If only she could be, not have, a baby. As the spring continued, Charlotte's condition worsened.

Walter, too, suffered greatly in this pitiful marriage. "It is so terrible," he cried, "so hard to minister to. I find it less & less easy to bear, yet God knows I try and try persistently." The following day's entry: "She does not yet believe that I really am pained by her condition: she thinks me indifferent. Good God! how long must this last. I must *become* indifferent or lose all heart and hope."[36]

At the same time that such misery prevailed inside the home, Charlotte was able to find moments of respite and freedom outside. Back at the gym, she found great, temporary relief in the physical activities and the female company. In February of 1887 she scribbled in the margin of a journal entry filled with "Buy some jelly, cake pans . . . Mend clothes," an item that read "Letter from Miss Stone Blackwell asking me to manage a w[oman] suffrage column in Prov[idence] paper." The next day, again amidst the daily activities of the home, she slips in: "Write to Alice Stone Blackwell accepting offer."

Charlotte worked diligently on her column. The paper for which she was asked to contribute it was the *People*, a Providence, Rhode Island, weekly newspaper sponsored by the Knights of Labor of Rhode Island. By this time Charlotte had already published articles and poems in the paper. While she had little knowledge or appreciation of working-class struggles or radical politics, she had then, and continued to have thereafter, general prolabor sympathies

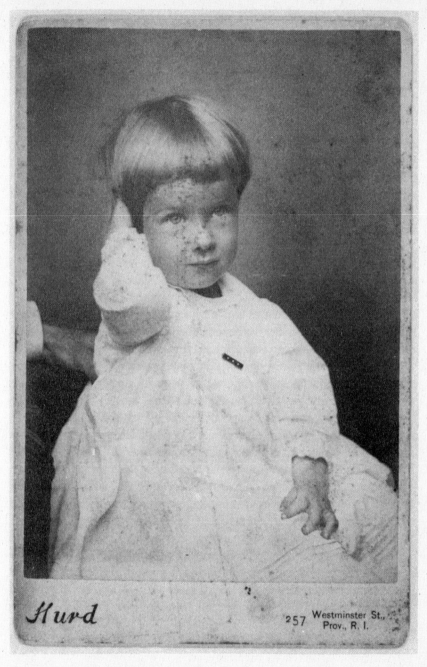

Hurd

257 Westminster St.,
Prov., R. I.

Katharine Stetson in 1887, age about two and a half

that flowed from her support of women's issues and from her own tenuous class position. In March 1887, the editor of *People* announced the appearance of Charlotte Stetson's suffrage column. Most of the columns that carried her by-line dealt with women caught in the tension between career and family, and discussed how women, like men, need work as well as love to sustain a rich life.

She also began to sell greeting cards as she had in her late teens, and to use the money to pay bills. "She likes to do it," Walter observed, without seeming to understand why she liked to. During these months of 1887 Charlotte tried to lift her spirits by more active socializing with friends. She set up a weekly whist game at her house, as she had done in her girlhood years. Walter said that he approved of these efforts, but then complained that she was up too late at night and talked too much with her old friend Jim Simmons, and that it had "not been good for her." Walter wanted Charlotte to be happy and cheerful, he said, but he seemed to resent all efforts that did not place him at the center of her attentions. He admitted that "Charlotte of late has been so absorbed in the woman question—suffrage, other wrongs, that she has tired me dreadfully with it. . . . But she is a dear sweet loving girl."[37]

She began to focus her reading on women's concerns, commenting in her journal how she got herself a new card from the public library and filled it "with books on Women."[38] That winter she began an intensified course of reading focused on women.

The *Woman's Journal*, the official organ of the American Woman Suffrage Association, which began publication in 1870, was edited by Alice Stone, Henry Blackwell, and Mary Livermore. A conservative publication within the women's movement, it attracted readers and contributors from the rapidly growing numbers of women in the club movement and in the professions. During this period Charlotte published several poems in the paper, as well as some drawings. Indeed, her first poem, "In Duty Bound," had been accepted for publication in the *Woman's Journal* in December 1883, the winter before her marriage. Three years later, now married, she published the following poem, "An Answer," which reflected the pain in her life:

A maid was asked in marriage. Wise as fair,
She gave her answer with deep thought and prayer.

Expecting in the holy name of wife
Great work, great pain, and greater joy in life.

Such work she found as brainless slaves might do;
By day and night, long labor, never through.

Such pain—no language can such pain reveal;
It had no limit but her power to feel.

Such joy life left in her sad soul's employ
Neither the hope nor memory of joy.

Helpless she died, with one despairing cry
"I thought it good! How could I tell the lie!"

And answered Nature, merciful and stern,
"I teach by killing. Let the others learn."

However energetic Charlotte was while engaged in public activities, she remained listless and depressed while involved in domestic chores. Walter suffered from the repercussions of the continuing depression, unable to comprehend its source or discover a solution. He decided that the reading course on women was too strenuous and persuaded Charlotte to drop the reading. But two weeks later she was back at it again, reading *The History of Womankind in Western Europe*, she said in her journal of February 1887 (probably referring to Thomas Wright's *Womankind in Western Europe from the Earliest Times to the Seventeenth Century*, published in London in 1869).

Slowly Charlotte began reaching out for a woman's community to help her cope with her inability to function at home. In March of 1887 she visited a Miss Brown, whom she liked "very much" and who "has had nervous prostration too." Miss Brown told her of a group of forty women who were ready to go to the polls to distribute ballots and agitate for suffrage. While Charlotte did not see her way clear to do that, "and am not able now, either," she was interested. She made her own small contribution by talking to the women at the gym about "our laws that they didn't know before. Stay late talking."

The next evening Charlotte had a hysterical outburst at home, reaching the level of "frenzy," as she called it, and Jim Simmons, having just arrived, was able to calm her in ways Walter could not. Walter, in a burst of jealous anger, rushed out, leaving Jim with Charlotte, who reported having a pleasant evening. Late that evening, after Jim had gone and Walter had returned, "Walter breaks down, and I soothe him and love him and get him to sleep."

Walter's poem to Charlotte in 1887, clinging to love as a refuge from their troubles, may have been meant as a reassuring gesture, but probably did not have such an effect.

What tho you grieve and feel your work undone!
What tho my life seems all distress!
Hold fast to Love—to Love, and all is won!
Thenceforth our days are pleasantness!

In spite of Charlotte's moments of electric energy and vitality— when she was at the gymnasium or when she was at work on her writing—the depression, the inability to mobilize her strength to care for home, husband, and child, dominated her existence and continued to pull her down further and further. Whatever the temporary respites she was able to achieve away from home, she continued in general to be in "a pitiful condition nervously," as she described herself.[39]

With the urging of mother and husband, Charlotte decided to use the one hundred dollars a friend of her mother's had given her in April of 1887, "to send me away to get well," to seek help from Dr. Silas Weir Mitchell, the noted specialist in nerve diseases. The last entries in her 1887 diary, written not in December as they were each year but in April, were for and to Walter:

I have kept a journal since I was fifteen, the only blanks being in these last years of sickness. . . . Now I am to go away for my health, and shall not try to take any responsibility with me, even this old friend. I am very sick with nervous prostration, and I think with some brain disease as well. No one can ever know what I have suffered in these last five years. Pain pain pain, till my mind has given way. O blind and cruel! Can *Love* hurt like this? You found me—you remember what. I leave you—O remember what, and learn to doubt your judgment—before it seeks to mould another life as it has mine. I asked you a few days before our marriage if you would take the responsibility entirely on yourself. You said yes. Bear it then.

The final entry on the last written page, April 19, 1887, read: "Snowed yesterday. . . . Take baby to Mary's. . . . Begin to write an account of myself for the doctor."

V
SILAS WEIR MITCHELL

So common were debilitating diseases of the nerves among women in Victorian America that one inevitably seeks clues hidden in the collective life of the nineteenth century. The frustrations many were forced to accept in a society that denied them any but the most limited range of options provided the battleground on which psychological and related physical ailments were fought.

The traditional manner in which people had previously lived was being smashed as capitalism in America moved into its industrial stage in midcentury. Women's lives were recreated, as were men's, but differently. The world was rapidly ending in which husband and wife shared a life of agricultural production, working at different jobs, but with the recognition of the essential interdependence of their labor. Production was moving out of the home, forcing men to follow, seeking work in the new public arena of factory and office. Women stayed behind; even those who worked outside the home generally felt their primary identification was tied to it and that their work in the public sphere would end with eventual marriage and children.

Among the working-class population, single women went off to work in factories or in private homes as domestic servants; married women earned money by taking in boarders, washing the clothes of the wealthy, or doing piecework sewing at home, and in general providing substantial economic value to their homes in various forms of unpaid labor. Middle-class and upper-class women found themselves locked into their homes, rather than driven out of them. They became "hostages to their homes," in Barbara Welter's words, caretakers of home, husband, and children, the anchor upon whose "voluntary" self-sacrifice the stability of the social order came to rest. The talents and skills of these women were not permitted to share in the production of goods or services required by the society at large. Their work was to minister to their private families. Not all women suffered in these circumstances; many accepted their life and enjoyed it, not finding its restrictions oppressive or suffocating. But rigid notions of proper behavior and activity for women denied the rights of many others whose needs and desires did not fit the ideal and who were granted no alternative. It is true that, as we have seen, increasing numbers of women sought alternative ways to shape their lives, but the total number of such women remained small.

The problem for women who were not comfortable with the prevailing ideal of femininity was that it not only defined options concerning activities and behavior but presumed also to take charge of women's psychological needs. The ideal woman was not only assigned a social role that locked her into her home, but she was also expected to like it, to be cheerful and gay, smiling and good-humored. Because myths that permeated the lives of most women told them both what they were supposed to do and what they were supposed to feel, it was difficult for women to acknowledge negative feelings about their prescribed role.

The outcome of being confined to such an explosive, closed psychological state was predictable: numbers of women struggled, often unsuccessfully, with intense inner turmoil and accelerating internal tension. Ambitious and imaginative women who found themselves with no outlets for their abilities, while in the larger culture opportunities proliferated for ambitious and imaginative men, suffered particularly.

Diaries, letters, and medical case studies detail the range of diseases that devastated numbers of women in the middle and upper classes from the antebellum period through the turn of the century. Descriptions of depression, spiritlessness, exhaustion, and hysteria fill the writings of many such women and their doctors. "I sometimes . . . wonder that I am alive," sadly wrote one, whose over-powering sense of futility and joylessness was shared by so many others.

In a world that admonished women to retain an exemplary pose of permanent cheer, one could credit such depressions as a form of rebellion, but if so, the rebellion damaged the rebel most seriously. For it came out of unexpressed anger, unfulfilled emotional needs, and unexamined feelings of guilt and inadequacy at not fulfilling the role that was being rejected.

Men, too, suffered similarly, for they were as rigidly locked into social roles and behavior as women were, though of a different sort. Men too broke down, many of them, perhaps as many as women; we have no way of being certain. We need not look further than Charlotte's own Beecher kin, beginning with the patriarch Lyman Beecher, who apparently suffered from what today would be called manic-depressive illness. He often fell into long periods of apathy and depression, or "the hypo" (hypochondria), as depression was then designated. At other times he displayed extraordinary energy, what seemed to others superhuman vitality. When on the verge of nervous and physical collapse, as he was periodically throughout his life, he threw himself into exhausting physical work, if he could. He used parallel bars and other gymnastic equipment in his back yard, and when the weather was too bad for outdoor activity, he shoveled sand from one side of his cellar to the other and back again. Earlier he had used farm labor to deal with his tendency to depression.

Many of his children suffered similarly. Mary, "the Lady," Charlotte's grandmother, the one who accepted her domestic role, was one of the few exceptions among the thirteen. James, the youngest, with a history of violence, suffered like his father from manic-depressive states, had a severe breakdown, and spent four years at Dr. Gleason's water-cure sanitarium before he shot himself. Thomas, again like his father, experienced enormous mood swings that went from exuberance to depression. Catharine suffered a severe breakdown in 1829 at the age of twenty-nine, and another in 1835. Years later, in an address to a graduating class, she described the experience as one where she "found the entire fountain of nervous energy exhausted . . . utter and irretrievable prostration. . . . I could not read a page or write a line, or even listen to conversation without distress."[1] (Her great-niece was to write startingly similar descriptions of herself years later.) For more than ten years Catharine went regularly to a sanitarium where she was treated with waters from a mineral spring thought to have healing qualities. She also underwent hypnosis to relieve pain she felt had psychological origins.[2]

Harriet, too, suffered some form of serious depression in her early twenties. She described it as being caused by the "constant habits of self-government which the rigid forms of our society demand. . . . My mind is exhausted and seems to be sinking into deadness," she wrote to a woman friend in 1832, when she was twenty-three years old. Another breakdown occurred when she was in her late thirties, leaving her feeble for a year and fearing permanent invalidism. After spending seven months in the same sanitarium where Catharine had stayed, Harriet returned home substantially improved. Only much later did she find real release in her writing. Although her brood of children continued to increase, she began writing furiously at night and discovered that she suffered no ill effects, physical or emotional. "In fact," her biographer says, "her health was better than it had been at any time since childhood,"[3] although it was only with the financial success of *Uncle Tom's Cabin* that she was able to relieve herself of the domestic responsibilities that were so burdensome.

I have dwelt upon the emotional history of Charlotte's famous Beecher relatives, not because the family was unique in its psychiatric background, but because it was not. Not *all* families were filled with members who regularly broke down, of course, but the phenomenon was common enough in middle- and upper-class households. We know more about the famous families because they are famous and probably not primarily because they were more prone to collapse, although the ambition that made them famous likely contributed to the strain that caused the collapse.

In the mid-1840s persons suffering from nervous diseases took the waters, as did Lyman Beecher's family. They drank and bathed in mineral springs that were naturally saline and contained calcium chloride and that were believed to cure a range of ailments from gout and rheumatism to anemia and liver problems. Whatever limitations were intrinsic to the water cure, it provided a place of rest and removal, if only temporarily, from the world's tensions. It also offered the presence of a largely female supportive community, since most of those who sought relief were women. The water cure was certainly preferable to leeches or drugs, both of which were common medical alternatives.

Although the water cure continued to be popular through the 1890s, later in the century other kinds of treatment began to appear for women's nervous diseases. There was, for instance, the Adams Nervine Asylum, founded in 1877 to treat nervous people who were not psychotic. The institution had facilities for thirty patients, all women, and provided, as did the water cure, prolonged rest and absence of responsibility. Other efforts at dealing with ailing women patients utilized the "Swedish movements," a set of exercises, or motorpathy, a kind of massage. Often used in conjunction with massage, or by itself, was the application of electric current to various parts of the body on the assumption, referred to as the theory of "galvanism," that there was a similarity between electrical and nervous power or energy. Medical practice rested on the belief that all mental disorders could be traced to diseases of the nervous system, as nerves were seen as the link between mind and body. Thus doctors could treat the presumed physical disorder to get at the mental one. Some doctors had their own theories about the cause of nervous diseases. Others had no idea what caused them, and simply experimented with a variety of techniques that would at least alleviate some of the symptoms and might offer some clue about their origin.

Men and women tried a variety of cures, some for both genders and some for only one. The choice of cure depended in part on the class to which they belonged and, therefore, the funds that were available. All of the cures were geared to preparing the patient to return to his or her place, men to men's work, women to women's work. The distribution of the work itself by sex seems never to have been questioned.

Charlotte Stetson's confrontation with the renowned and respected neurologist Dr. Silas Weir Mitchell was a crucial moment in her life, a moment she used to begin her liberation. At the time of their meeting, Mitchell was at the height of his powers and she was at her lowest.

Even before his new patient arrived at his sanitarium just outside

Philadelphia, Mitchell had formed certain assumptions about her. He found utterly useless the long letter she had written to him detailing her symptoms; that she should imagine her observations would be of any interest to him was but an indication of her "self-conceit," he advised her. He had already treated two Beecher women; "two women of your blood" was the way he put it. It was a bad start.

What manner of man did Charlotte Stetson encounter when she entered Mitchell's well-appointed office? He was a handsome, vigorous, urbane, self-confident man in his mid-forties, who that very year had been granted an honorary degree, his first of many, from Harvard University, and who was then elected to the presidency of the Philadelphia College of Physicians.

As a young man, just after his medical training, Mitchell had turned to the study of rattlesnake venom and related nerve injuries. During the Civil War that interest came to focus on human paralysis caused by wounds and bites, and this led him thereafter to an interest in paralysis that developed in the absence of any recognizable physical cause, and in the end to his lifelong work at the "boundary between physiology and psychology."[4] Mitchell remained a neurologist, that is, a "nerve doctor," who tried to cure patients who suffered from motor and sensory malfunctioning.

At the time Mitchell met Charlotte Stetson, he had an international reputation as a neurologist and as a research scientist who had made original contributions to the study of poisons and nerve diseases, although his reputation was greatest as a specialist in the nervous diseases of women. He had an enormously affluent medical practice. He was adored and venerated by hundreds of women patients who traveled from all over the world to undergo his treatment.

Mitchell had also begun publishing novels and poetry, and although at this time his major energies were engaged by his work as a pioneer psychologist and neurologist, toward the end of the century his literary work became his prime occupation. By the time of his death he was a prolific and immensely popular writer, not only of hundreds of articles and several books on medicine but also of some twelve novels, a controversial biography of George Washington (his unfavorable portrayal of Washington's mother as overbearing caused a stir), many successful children's stories, one of

Portrait of Dr. Silas Weir Mitchell, by Robert William Vonnoh (Courtesy of the College of Physicians of Philadelphia)

which went through twelve editions, and several volumes of verse.

A man of extraordinary versatility, he was viewed, and not just by Philadelphians, as a contemporary Ben Franklin. He was the father of two sons, both of whom achieved distinction in their own work. He married twice, his first wife dying young, and both marriages appear to have been successful. He was thought to be a genius, "an opinion Mitchell came to share," as one of his biographers put it.[5] If he was not a genius, as subsequent generations have come to acknowledge, he was indeed a formidable and overwhelming presence for a frightened and fragile Charlotte to face.

But he had not always been so self-assured. He had himself evolved from an emotional state startlingly close to that which he treated in his patients. Emotional traumas he had suffered early in his life and the control he achieved over them were at the root of the growing and seemingly flawless successes he went on to achieve in his maturity. He chose to work in the very area—nervous diseases—in which he had himself suffered as a young man. Weir Mitchell, son of an affluent Virginia doctor, described his early life as repressed, dominated by an extraordinary father for whom he had, he said, "a sort of veneration" and a mother for whom he felt "a passionate love." His father initially opposed his decision to become a doctor, saying he was "wanting in nearly all the qualities that go to make success in medicine." Weir persisted, and his father relented, but then insisted he become a surgeon. "Surgery was horrible to me," Weir admitted, but he went on to become a surgeon. He soon found it impossible to continue because he fainted regularly and developed a tremor in his hand. Unable to refuse his father's command, he seems to have developed physical disabilities that made surgery impossible. He did as a young man what Charlotte Stetson did as a young woman: he and she made it impossible to do what they did not want to do.

When the Civil War broke out he was appointed head of a hospital that handled nerve wounds and diseases, a splendid professional opportunity to establish a specialty that eventually made him famous. After the war he suffered the loss of wife and father, which set off a nervous breakdown. He went to Europe for a two-month recovery period. Three years later, in 1872, his mother died, and he suffered another breakdown. Then he married for a second time and thereby stepped from the gentry into the aristocracy of Philadelphia. Mary Cadwalader Mitchell devoted her impressive personal skills and family connections to providing a good home for him. From this time on "the sunshine of life," as a biographer said, began to shine on this previously depressed and unhappy man,[6] and his enormously successful career began.

In her interviews with Mitchell, Charlotte Stetson was told she was suffering from neurasthenia, or exhaustion of the nerves, a disease that was commonly held to be associated with the pressures of nineteenth-century American society. It was, in the words of another renowned doctor treating the illness, a "neurosis without organic basis." Neurasthenia, said George M. Beard, one of the most respected physicians of the period, is "impoverishment of nervous force."[7] At the time it was popularly compared to an overloaded electrical current and an overdrawn bank account, observes a twentieth-century historian of medicine. Most physicians of the period believed that each person possessed a certain amount of nervous energy, which was transmitted to different parts of the body. Neurasthenia was a result of a breakdown in the system, of the demand exceeding the supply. When the limited quantity of nervous energy was improperly used, there was, in the words of one neurologist of the time, a "partial or general nervous inefficiency, or perversion, of the nerves," affecting particular organs, different in men and women.[8]

Although many men were diagnosed as suffering from neurasthenia, Silas Weir Mitchell's attention was primarily addressed to its manifestation in women. In fact, one might say he moved from treating one marginal group, wounded men, to another precarious group, vulnerable women, that he spent his life testing his manhood as an endless demonstration that he could match his father's success. As a doctor, Silas Weir Mitchell sought groups to minister to who helped him define his own maleness. By controlling women patients who were weak and helpless, perhaps he could purge himself of those remaining fears of female weakness that had tied him to his revered mother.

In 1871 Mitchell examined neurasthenia in his book *Wear and Tear*. Three years later he wrote *Nurse and Patient* and *Camp Cure* on the same subject. He became famous for the treatment he developed and called the Rest Cure. During the 1870s he published an analysis and description of various aspects of his Rest Cure in several medical journal articles, but in 1877 it had its fullest examination in his little book *Fat and Blood*. Neurasthenia was developed, he argued, by the "wear and tear" of our overcivilized life. The foundation of his medical treatment was to improve nutrition and to restore energy by revitalizing the patient. He evolved rather than discovered the treatment, he said, by combining several standard medical procedures already in fashion.

The treatment subjected the patient to: 1) extended and total bed rest; 2) isolation from family and familiar surroundings; 3) overfeeding, especially with cream, on the assumption that increased body volume created new energy; 4) massage and often the use of electricity for "muscular excitation"[9] to compensate for the passive regimen to which the body was limited.

The purpose of the isolation from friends and family was to

disrupt old habits and cut off hurtful influences, but above all, Mitchell said, to separate "the invalid from some willing slave, a mother or a sister."[10] Isolated from the familiar, the patient was subject to total enforced rest. Mitchell's idea was to enforce that rest and isolation so severely that the patient was "surfeited with it and welcomed a firm order to do the things she once felt she could not do."

In Mitchell's view this treatment constituted "moral medication," necessary because women suffering from these diseases were, he felt, characterized by a kind of "moral degradation."[11] They had "lost the healthy mastery which every human being should retain over her emotions and wants." He also referred repeatedly in his writings to "the selfishness which a life of invalidism is apt to bring about." "If you tell the patient she is basely selfish she is probably amazed and wonders at your cruelty. To cure the case you must morally alter as well as physically amend, and nothing else will answer."[12] This "moral medication" commanded his women patients, Charlotte Stetson among them, to return to the work of women: care of home, husband, child.

Fat and Blood included detailed descriptions of the treatment and its effect on many women patients. The Rest Cure was not designed, said its creator, to satisfy "these thin-blooded emotional women, for whom a state of weak health has become a long and almost, I might say, a cherished habit."[13] A patient was restricted to bed, where initially she was not permitted to read, write, sew, converse, or feed herself. One nurse cared for her during her stay, which might last from six weeks to two months. At the beginning of the treatment the patient was forbidden to use her hands at all except to brush her teeth, nor was she allowed to move out of her bed or even in it by herself. The process of infantilization was presumed to "make the patients contented and tractable"—tractable like docile children, in the view of one modern critic.[14]

Enforced rest, enforced passivity, acceptance of the commands of male authority: Mitchell's treatment was an extreme version of the cultural norms that operated outside his sanitarium, just as, ironically, the incapacity of these women patients took the form of an exaggeration of the very qualities they had been taught to value.

Mitchell could not imagine a woman like Charlotte Stetson and therefore could not treat her properly. Able to see only what he was trained to see, as most of us are, he saw a woman shirking her duty and determined to get her back to it.

A few years before he met Charlotte Stetson he described hysteria "among women of the upper classes . . . caused by unhappy love affairs, losses of money, and the daily fret and weariness of lives, which passing out of maidenhood, lack those distinct purposes and aims which, in the lives of men, are like the steadying influences of the fly-wheel in an engine."[15] That a woman's life might have a "distinct purpose" like that which informed "the lives of men" was apparently beyond him. A rigid personality kept Mitchell from any imaginative leap beyond the norms of his culture; even in his later years, when the world had somewhat altered, Mitchell could not accommodate to change in customs or values.

In addressing Radcliffe's student body in 1890, he expressed his view that women in general often collapsed under the strain that higher education imposed on their physical and emotional state. "I no more want [women] to be preachers, lawyers, or platform orators, than I want men to be seamstresses or nurses of children," he told the women undergraduates.[16] His notion of a proper education was one that taught child care and domestic skills. Mitchell objected to any girl under the age of seventeen using her brain even moderately. To do so, he warned, would endanger her health, and her future would be "the shawl and the sofa."[17] Although there were many women and some men in 1890 who challenged the validity and sense of separate spheres for men and women, Mitchell was not among them.

The writer Owen Wister, an old and dear friend, described how Mitchell, to his death in 1914, "obstinately clung to his own view of traditional women. . . . The truth was his standard was extremely conventional; his ideal woman was the well-sheltered woman. . . . So those who loved him felt it wise to turn the conversation whenever it drifted dangerously in the direction of the New Woman."[18]

Mitchell's restrictive notion of proper womanhood, and the dangerous result his treatment might and did have on many women, still should not obscure the positive value of certain aspects of his Rest Cure. Its goal was to permit neurotics to function normally, and in order to accomplish such a goal, Mitchell had to assume that neuroses were treatable and curable and that the gulf between normal and abnormal behavior did not permanently divide people as was widely believed at the time. If he was not the first to "take psychiatry out of the madhouse [and bring] it into everyday life,"[19] he surely made an important contribution to that process. He took seriously the complaints of his patients. He knew their suffering was real, and he focused on relief. Cure was to be sought by a natural approach to medical practice, and Mitchell's practices have a ring of something that would today be called holistic medicine, for he was careful to stress the entire person, not one diseased portion.[20]

The torment that Charlotte Stetson suffered for years was made worse by the well-meant but damaging responses of loved friends and family. She herself could not understand why a healthy, energetic woman collapsed without cause—she never did understand—and surely those around her did not understand and therefore, however much they tried, could not genuinely sympathize with or comprehend her pain. Their wonderment, which always ended in gently urging her to try just once more, only made her more clearly aware that it was somehow her lack of will, her lack of character, that had permitted her to behave in a fashion often described as "lazy." Weir Mitchell told her she was not "lazy," she was sick. She was sick, but she could be well if, under his guidance, she created an atmosphere in which she could regain her health through her own efforts.

For many patients, the psychological value of receiving attention and acknowledgment that the ailment was legitimate in an environment that encouraged self-confidence was sufficient to restore some semblance of normal functioning. Mitchell's treatment did seem to "work" a good deal of the time, if the number of satisfied patients is evidence. An uncritical biographer maintains that "there is no doubt that Dr. Mitchell did not expect and did not forgive failure. Success might take a long time but come it *must*, otherwise he lost interest."[21]

Not just many women patients and their families but Freud as well was impressed with Mitchell's technique, stating that he was adding his own psychoanalytic therapy to "the Weir Mitchell rest cure."[22] Freud reviewed *Fat and Blood* and described Mitchell as the "highly original nerve specialist in Philadelphia." Years later, in 1895, in *Studies on Hysteria*, Freud again referred favorably to Mitchell and to the Rest Cure.[23]

Weir Mitchell—and Charlotte Stetson—lived in a world that had not yet learned to think psychologically, and it is very difficult for us today to recreate such a world. They had to seek motivation and understanding in the upper reaches of consciousness. Changes in behavior were sought as a product of retraining such as Mitchell attempted in his Rest Cure, retraining aimed at restoring to the enervated woman a sense of her capacity and a belief in her power to exert her will. Mitchell saw himself as permeating the listless bodies of his women patients and instilling them with his strength, releasing his power into them. Gilman later used the image of a muscle, relying as she always did on the physical body for strength, literally and metaphorically. The brain was a muscle, and emotions were a form of muscle; the more one flexed them and used them, the more control one achieved over them. Mitchell used an early form of behavior modification, a retooling of patients' skills to restore to them lost powers.

The idea of the unconscious that Freud later introduced, and particularly his emphasis on sexuality, were anathema to both Mitchell and Gilman, one of their few strongly shared beliefs. In the treatment of his patients, Mitchell showed no particular interest in sexual matters, and indeed rarely referred to sexuality at all in his writings on nervous diseases. One of the few references was to the danger of sexual excess, rather than of repression, as a contributing factor to some nervous diseases.[24] "Where did this filthy thing come from?" was Mitchell's response to the first, and probably last, book of Freud's he perused, just before he threw it in the fire.[25] Mitchell, and most of his colleagues who practiced therapy, rejected the new psychoanalytic doctrines of Freud as they were expounded by his followers in England and America. To have acknowledged the social and moral implications of Freudian doctrine would have required a profound revision in the values they had upheld their entire lives. In any case, at the time of Charlotte Stetson's treatment by Mitchell, Freud had not done his significant work.

Very little is known about the actual treatment Charlotte received in Mitchell's Philadelphia sanitarium. The final entry in her diary in 1887 was written in April, just before she set off to see

Mitchell. In her autobiography, she said she was put to bed in the sanitarium and kept there. "I was fed, bathed, rubbed. . . . After a month of this agreeable treatment, he sent me home."

Consistent with his conventional views of woman's role, Mitchell could in good conscience send Charlotte Stetson home with these instructions after pronouncing her "cured":

> Live as domestic a life as possible. Have your child with you all the time. . . . Lie down an hour after each meal. Have but two hours' intellectual life a day. And never touch pen, brush or pencil as long as you live.

This advice, which Charlotte quotes in her autobiography, was offered to a woman who was trained as a commercial artist and who was beginning to forge a career as a writer. And the consequences?

> I went home, followed those directions rigidly for months, and came perilously near to losing my mind.

Her description of the subsequent months makes it clear that she was indeed "perilously near to losing" her mind. "I made a rag baby," she said, "hung it on a doorknob and played with it. I would crawl into remote closets and under beds—to hide from the grinding pressure of that profound distress."[26]

Finally, in the fall of 1887, the unhappy couple agreed to separate—Walter very reluctantly—although they did in fact live together for another year before they were able fully to accept this decision. In September 1888, Charlotte, with barely any money, with no marketable skills with which to earn a living, in a mental state still not far from collapse, took her baby Katharine and went back to California, not to San Francisco where her father lived, but to Pasadena, to the warmth of the sun and to the warmth of the Channings. Walter followed the next year, hoping their life together was not over, but the reconciliation failed. Legal complications kept their divorce from becoming a reality for a long time, but with her flight to California—and it can only be seen as the desperate escape of a desperate woman—Charlotte Stetson began a new phase of her life.

Hurd   257   Westminster St., Prov. R. I.

"This is what my breakdown did": Charlotte at about thirty

"I decided to cast off Dr. Mitchell bodily, and do exactly what I pleased," wrote Charlotte to a friend in November 1887.[27] And she did; from that moment on she patterned a life for herself that repudiated his explicit instructions to her. Charlotte Stetson's rejection of a seemingly loving and loved husband and of the country's leading neurologist constitutes the first major act of defiance in her entire life, defiance against the accepted rules of her world, rules that determined how one behaved and to whom one deferred, rules that were imposed upon her with difficulty but that she nevertheless had accepted as her own.

As we have seen, Charlotte had expended enormous amounts of energy trying to do what was expected of her, first by her mother, then by her husband, and finally by her doctor. Now, for the first time, she was truly declaring her independence.

She struck for freedom when she fled from Weir Mitchell and Walter Stetson, but she had not the habit of introspection nor any respect for the value of wallowing in the deep recesses of one's mind, and so she never achieved much understanding of the tensions that led to her collapse. Even at the end of her life she continued to ask, as she did in her autobiography, "What is the psychology of it?" Admitting in her autobiography that "part of the ruin" was a product of her childhood, part was a result of her "rigid stoicism," but most was caused by her marriage, she asserted that had she enjoyed a "period of care and rest" in 1890, after she was "free," she might have made a full recovery and not suffered periodic nervous collapses and depressions all her life.[28] The solution she wished she could have sought was an entirely physical one—rest. These prescriptions from the perspective of her later years ran directly counter to what she actually did at the time: rejected orders to rest and stay passive and instead moved out on her own, taking responsibility for herself, asserting her sense of self against doctor, husband, mother, and, eventually, child. In fact, her observation that had she had a "period of care and rest" after her flight to Pasadena she might have made a full recovery is a sentiment that strangely echoes Mitchell's Rest Cure idea. She was free, but not entirely.

The struggle between Charlotte and Weir Mitchell also occurred in a literary arena. Neither one was known primarily as a writer of fiction, but both used that genre to examine characters and situations that came from their personal psychological experience. Charlotte wrote more than half-a-dozen novels and hundreds of short stories, but the one piece of fiction that stands as a brilliant psychological study is her most famous, "The Yellow Wallpaper," which she wrote in Pasadena in 1890 and which was published in the May 1891 issue of *New England Magazine*. In it, she critically portrays a Rest Cure similar to Mitchell's, and implicitly recommends a very different approach, thus, in effect, usurping the place of her former doctor.

In 1913 Gilman included in the *Forerunner* a brief statement entitled "Why I Wrote 'The Yellow Wallpaper.' " That statement and a few relevant pages in her autobiography published more than twenty years later represent her entire public expression on the matter of Mitchell. "For many years I suffered from a severe and continuous nervous breakdown tending to melancholia—and beyond," she said in 1913, probably the first time she made such a public admission. After suffering for about three years, she consulted, "in devout faith and some faint stir of hope," a noted specialist in nervous diseases (who remained unnamed). His advice, which she followed for three months after returning home, brought her "so near the borderline of utter mental ruin that I could see over." Casting aside his orders, and with the help "of a wise friend," she resumed work—"work, the normal life of every human being; work, which is joy and growth and service, without which one is a pauper and a parasite."

She was so "naturally moved to rejoicing by this narrow escape" that she decided to tell her story, but with a different end. The story describes, she said, the "inevitable result" of her doctor's treatment for those who stay with it, and that is "progressive insanity." She wrote the piece, she said, "to save people from being driven crazy."[29]

"The Yellow Wallpaper" is a study of a young mother's descent into madness, caused by a well-meaning but insidious husband-doctor who follows S. Weir Mitchell's Rest Cure. In the story John, the husband, takes his ailing wife, who is suffering from a nervous disease, to the country for the summer, along with their baby and the nurse.

John, as husband-doctor, embodies Mitchell's treatment, but

he lacks the neurologist's major strength of acknowledging the legitimacy and seriousness of his patient's illness.

> John is a physician, and *perhaps* (I would not say it to a living soul, of course, but this is dead paper and a great relief to my mind)—*perhaps* that is one reason I do not get well faster.
> You see, he does not believe I am sick! And what can one do?

Her husband is not alone in asserting that she is not really ill. Her brother, also a physician, confirms the diagnosis.

John rents a large, isolated, run-down home (analogous to his wife's psychological state of isolation and disintegration) to provide his ailing wife with "perfect rest." And so they move to "the nursery at the top of the house," a literal acting out of the infantilizing process. She had preferred a room downstairs, one that opened onto a piazza, but John pointed out that there was "not room for two beds and no near room for him if he took another." Thus her preference was for a room leading out, an escape, and a room without space for her loving, adoring John. In the converted nursery, the bed is nailed down and there are bars on the window. There is no escape.

John's treatment has a reminiscent ring:

> So I take phosphates or phosphites—whichever it is—and tonics, and air and exercise, and journeys, and am absolutely forbidden to "work" until I am well again.
> Personally I disagree with their ideas.
> Personally, I believe that congenial work, with excitement and change, would do me good.
> But what is one to do?

The young wife accepts the definition of herself as others see her. When John leaves "a schedule prescription for each hour in the day," she comments, "he takes all care from me, and so I feel basely ungrateful not to value it more." She observes that she gets "unreasonably angry with John sometimes," and maintains that "it is due to this nervous condition." She tells us that John "is very careful and loving, and hardly lets me stir without special direction"—

language remarkably similar to that which Charlotte Stetson used
to describe Walter.

She persists in believing that if she only could "write a little it
would relieve the press of ideas and rest me," but she finds herself,
as the weeks go on, too tired to write in secret and forbidden to
write publicly.

John ultimately threatens her. If she does not get well faster she
shall be sent to Weir Mitchell, and she is terrified of going. She had
a friend "who was in his hands once," and "she says he is just like
John and my brother, only more so!" This is the only reference to
Mitchell by name in the story. He is cast as someone even more
dangerous than her husband, whom by now we recognize as the
force leading her to her destruction. John calls her "his darling and
his comfort and all he had," but he will not listen to her pleadings
that he take her away. She is his "little girl," and he exerts the
power of father, husband, and doctor combined. "I am a doctor,
dear, and I know," he tells her.

As her condition deteriorates, the woman becomes obsessed
with and increasingly disgusted by the yellow wallpaper in her
bedroom. It has no predictable pattern. When she tries to follow
the "lame uncertain curves" in the paper, "they suddenly commit
suicide." Within the wallpaper there is a "strange, provoking, form-
less sort of figure that seems to skulk about," an ambiguous form
that threatens, frightens by its skulking. As the days pass, the shape
gets clearer. "And it is like a woman stooping down and creeping
about behind the pattern." It is frightening that she wishes to escape,
but John, who is so wise and loves her so, will not acknowledge
her need. At night the pattern in the paper becomes clearly bars,
like the bars on the windows, and the woman in the wallpaper
becomes plainly visible, imprisoned behind the bars at night, just
as the young woman imagining her feels imprisoned, just as the
author who created the young woman used to feel imprisoned. The
figure begins to "shake the pattern, just as if she wanted to get
out." Nighttime, of course, is also the time when John is present,
in the great immovable bed that is nailed down.

The young wife now wants John in another room because he
is so odd. She also wishes to keep for herself the secret of the woman
in the wall coming out at night. John, she now believes, only
pretends to be loving and kind.

As the story nears its grim conclusion, the young woman, in an effort to escape the barred windows, tries to move the bed, but it will not move; she has forgotten that the bed is nailed. She gets so angry that she bites a piece off one corner, hurting her teeth. She is now like the ravaging children who gnawed at the bedstead long before she occupied it. She is both child and mother. She is the child in the mother. Frantically she peels off the paper and sees "all those strangled heads and bulbous eyes and waddling fungus growths," imagery which brings to mind dead babies. She contemplates suicide, but decides it would be wrong and, in any case, confined as she is, impossible.

The remaining escape is another route to self-destruction. It is madness. She is now surrounded by creeping women, and she is one of them, but unlike the others, she will not stop her creeping at night to crawl back into the wall. And all this while John is at the door calling for an axe to break it down. She stops his forcible entry with her madness, for he enters the room and faints. She escapes by creeping over him.

"The Yellow Wallpaper" is an intensely personal examination of Gilman's private nightmare. Never again in her writing did she take such an emotional chance or engage in such introspection as she did in this story. After writing it, Charlotte did not for many years return to fiction, except for an occasional effort at collaboration with Grace Channing in writing drawing-room comedies. Perhaps the emotional truth and intensity of "The Yellow Wallpaper" drained her; perhaps it frightened her.

"The Yellow Wallpaper" thus stands apart from the entire body of her extensive fiction. It is, in my opinion, the only genuinely literary piece she ever created and it is also, of all her fiction, the most clearly, the most consciously autobiographical.

When Charlotte said that she wrote the piece to "save people from being driven crazy," perhaps one of the people she saved was herself, for in this story she seems to have let herself go, allowed her unconscious to help her creative art, and in so doing may have helped to purge the demons that terrified her. Although she cited a didactic reason for writing it, "The Yellow Wallpaper" is not a simple product of ideology, as most of her other fiction is. She did not just write about what she knew, using her experience to provide her with material, as Mitchell did. She used her experience to plumb her inner life by conjuring up the past and using it to help others through her words, and in so doing she achieved some control over both her illness and her past.

Charlotte permitted herself to touch emotions and dredge up deep-hidden fears in this semi-autobiographical, fictionalized story in ways she could not in her autobiography, in her letters, in her diaries, or in her time of treatment with Mitchell. The language and the imagery she used in the story allowed her to express buried fears, fear of her own baby, memories of childhood's blank walls, walls that did not encompass mother-love or father-love, fears of being strangled, devoured, violated by those who pretend to love and by those whom one is supposed to love and protect.

She recreated nightmares of her own childhood in which she is the child abandoned by a rejecting mother and an absent father. The young mother in the story has abandoned her baby to another, as Mary Perkins abandoned Charlotte by withholding needed expressions of love, and as Frederick literally abandoned her. The young mother in the story is imprisoned in the nursery, where she becomes a baby and recreates over and over again horrible, fantastic nightmares in which she faces the terror of all babies, dead or alive, and all mothers who deny and push away, just as the mother of little Charlotte pushed away her hand when it sought her mother's cheek.

The scarred and thwarted psyche of Charlotte Perkins, suffering from the fears that haunt an abandoned child, was driven further into trauma by a cultural voice, Walter Stetson's voice and particularly Silas Weir Mitchell's voice, commanding that she not seek relief in work; that she imprison herself everlastingly with a child whose terrifying demands she felt she could never satisfy; that she abide by a Victorian morality that denied her, as it had denied her mother, avenues to express feelings of rage and hostility; that she achieve mastery of self and womanly restraint but without being permitted to develop the tools and resources to achieve that mastery. Although Charlotte never explained to her own satisfaction the causes of her breakdown, in "The Yellow Wallpaper" she makes clear the context in which the mental collapse took form. She, Charlotte Stetson, found relief by externalizing, by writing about and creating a fictional person who, finding her desire to write aborted, went mad.

One suspects that "The Yellow Wallpaper," the work of fiction, is closer to the truth than Charlotte's seemingly accurate autobiography. For whatever reason, Charlotte publicly sustained a heroic vision of Walter Stetson. A few slightly bitter diary entries aside, Walter Stetson is consistently drawn in saintly terms. In her autobiography she speaks of his "unbroken devotion, his manifold cares and labors in tending a sick wife, his adoring pride in the best of babies."[30] In a diary entry from 1884, written as "the gray fog drifted across my mind" she said: "He has worked for me and for us both, waited on me in every tenderest way, played to me, read to me, done all for me as he always does. God be thanked for my husband."[31]

Why, then, if God is to be thanked for Walter, did she make John, the husband in "The Yellow Wallpaper," the villain? Is that the thanks Walter gets? Or is some kind of quasi-conscious anger finally surfacing, if only in fictional form? Charlotte describes in "The Yellow Wallpaper" how at night, dangerous night, the imprisoned figure creeps about in "that undulating wallpaper." And the yellow, the smoldering, repellent yellow, develops a smell as well. The woman in the story wakes up at night "to find it hanging over me." It is, she says, "the most enduring odor I ever met," and perhaps it is, even if Gilman did not recognize it, the dreaded smell of sex, a sensual smell, excretion of the night. The woman lies on her "great immovable bed—it is nailed down." John, the "loving" husband, imprisons her in a room with no escape, with bars on the windows, in a bed nailed down, trapped with a child, for the foul smell is also a smell, perhaps, of a child's feces, and the yellow wallpaper also embodies fear of babies. The woman sees a recurrent spot where "the pattern lolls like a broken neck and two bulbous eyes stare at you upside down." The spot becomes "impertinent," an odd word to use of a design. She gets angry with its impertinence and its "everlastingness," and what new mother has not felt some resentment at the "everlastingness" of the demands of a tiny infant?

The designs crawl sideways with those "absurd unblinking eyes," a familiar view to a mother nursing a child. "I never saw so much expression in an inanimate thing before, and we all know how much expression they have!"—though it is not clear who the "they" is supposed to be—inanimate, sleeping babies, who sleep like the dead, and then instantly are awake, crying, demanding, asserting their wants? She continues: "I used to lie awake as a child," entertained and terrorized by blanks walls and plain furniture. The woman sees frightening images of babies in the walls and immediately thinks, not of her baby on the floor below, but of herself as a child. The images are of a baby, the one she has and never sees, and the one she was, and she is frightened by them. It is her own baby and herself as baby that terrify her, perhaps pregnancy as a threat to the life of the mother, perhaps the insatiable needs of children that devour their mothers and from which mothers must protect themselves by withdrawing from their children, Mary Fitch Perkins from Charlotte, Charlotte Perkins Stetson from Katharine, the young woman in the story from her baby, both unnamed. Later in the story, when the wallpaper begins to move, the woman locked inside shakes the paper, anxious to get out, but she is in danger of being strangled by the many heads, upside down, with white eyes— again the image of babies strangling, devouring their mothers.

The children in the nursery have, at some time in the past, before memory, torn the room apart. It looks "as if it had been through the wars." The narrator says she "never saw such ravages as the children have made here," an acknowledgment of the damage that children can do, the power they have to destroy. "How those children did tear about here! This bedstead is fairly gnawed." Children again are likened to dangerous animals that tear and destroy.

The young wife, locked upstairs in the hideous room, has one comfort: "The baby is well and happy, and does not have to occupy this nursery with the horrid wallpaper." The mother has sacrificed for her baby, and the sacrifice will cost her her sanity; babies, and their insatiable needs, drive their mothers mad.

"The Yellow Wallpaper" was originally seen as a horror story. It has been reprinted as a horror story. Although it got its first feminist reading from Elaine R. Hedges in the Feminist Press edition of 1973 and has since won recognition as something of a feminist classic, awareness of its feminist dimension should supplement, not replace, an appreciation of its power as a story of horror. When it originally appeared, it elicited a good deal of response of all kinds. For example, an unnamed doctor published a letter arguing that the story could hardly "give pleasure to any reader," and indeed "must bring the keenest pain" to those whose lives have been touched "by this dread disease." For others, "whose lives have become a struggle against an heredity of mental derangement, such literature contains deadly peril," and one wonders, the good doctor concluded, whether "such stories [should] be allowed to pass without severest censure."[32]

After "The Yellow Wallpaper" appeared, Charlotte received a good deal of mail, much of it favorable, including a lengthy, congratulatory letter from a physician. Until "The Yellow Wallpaper," he said, "there has been no detailed account of incipient insanity." Presenting himself as a former opium addict who inspired trust in a drug-addict patient because, as the patient said, "Doctor, you've been there!" he asked of Charlotte a similar revelation: "Have you ever been—er—; but of course you haven't." She replied that she "had been as far as one could go and get back."[33]

Charlotte Stetson's description of her collapse is the description of a woman who hit bottom: holding a rag doll and weeping, sitting on the floor, being a baby rather than caring for one. In this state she accepted Silas Weir Mitchell's treatment. Mitchell became another version of a commanding, authoritative father-figure, but at least he was what a father-figure was conventionally supposed to be, at any rate in relation to his patients. With Mitchell, Charlotte finally got the attention she wanted from a father, and perhaps she was thus able to engage that male power, reject it, and move out on her own.

Frederick Douglass wrote in his autobiography how when he had a bad master he wanted a good master, but when he had a kind master he was able to see that he wanted none at all. A childhood spent deprived of both mother-love and father-love leads the child, whatever her age, to seek, desperately seek, parental engagement. When some authority in the clear role of an authoritative and authoritarian father intercedes, issues orders, commands, takes charge, then there is a force, a negative force, against which to rebel, a tyranny to reject. Freud's talking therapy later was to stress the value of free association and resistance in the treatment of neuroses. "The Yellow Wallpaper" was Charlotte's version of free association, a controlled version, and her rejection of Silas Weir Mitchell's power over her life is somewhat comparable to the crucial resistance in a therapeutic setting. She had transferred her need for a father to her doctor, rejected the father by rejecting the substitute, and then took an additional step by talking it out. Perhaps Weir Mitchell's ultimate contribution to Charlotte Stetson was that he allowed her to deny her father's power sufficiently to begin to heal herself. With her break from Weir Mitchell, and soon thereafter a break from Walter Stetson, Charlotte Anna Perkins Stetson began to build her life again.

VI
GRACE

Although Charlotte and Walter decided to separate in the fall of 1887, not long after Charlotte returned from Mitchell's Rest Cure, they did live together for another year before Charlotte left permanently for California with Katharine. During this year's time Charlotte and Walter came to terms with their decision, she with relief and he with resignation, and during this year's time Charlotte deepened and strengthened her friendship with Grace, who was to be an anchor in her life from this time on.

The juxtaposition of these two relationships, the one ending with Walter and the one developing with Grace, is reflected in a letter Charlotte wrote to her friend shortly after the decision to separate had been reached. Charlotte's emotional state during the year before the break was unsteady, with the characteristic ups and downs of anyone in such a situation, but her initial reaction to the estrangement was one of exuberant release:

> O I *am* so much better! . . . I laid plans for more sociability this winter, and am carrying them out.

"More sociability" meant, for example, playing whist every Tuesday evening with Sam Simmons and Edward Brown, as well as regular chess games, "mental exercise," she said.

And how did Charlotte account for her change in spirit?

I have given up trying to assimilate with Walter: have accepted my life as I did that with mother, as a thing to be endured and resisted, not a thing I must agree with. . . .

It is astonishing how my whole nature responds. The other life is impossible, that's all. What pleases me most is that when I leave Walter entirely out of my calculations, and make no attempt to fulfill my wifely duties toward him; why straightway his various excellences become visible again and he becomes a loved companion instead of a nightmare husband.

She concluded her letter with the words: "Dr. Mitchell be————!"[1] The end of "wifely duties" should be read as encompassing more than just a sexual relationship. She no longer thought of herself as tied to a partner in any fashion. She was free, she said, "to be myself," as if marriage, in its very essence, made being herself impossible.

In her published autobiography, Charlotte looked back to that fall of 1887: "In a moment of clear vision, we agreed to separate, to get a divorce. There was no quarrel, no blame . . . but it seemed plain that if I went crazy it would do my husband no good, and be a deadly injury to my child." In this way Charlotte used her depression to achieve what she wanted but did not have the language to ask for. "If I had been of the slightest use to him or to the child, I would have stuck it," she said. She constructed the sentence backwards. It was because she did not want to "stick it" that she made herself of no use "to him or to the child." Curiously, she blamed her illness for her decision to marry as well as to divorce, for she insisted that had she been stronger and wiser, "I should never have been persuaded into [marriage]."[2]

Charlotte had sought in marriage a feeling of security; instead of giving her an identity, the marriage had fragmented and mutilated even more her fragile sense of self. It had forced her to face again, this time as an adult woman, the old question of love and its place in her life; it threatened to reopen recognition of that early deprivation. Surely she felt in some deep-buried place that she never deserved that longed-for love, for if she had deserved it, if she had not been a bad girl who drove her father away and consequently made her mother's life bitter, then she would have had it. She was being punished for being unlovable.

Her marriage to Walter would once more demonstrate how little she deserved. To make certain of the outcome, she provoked the inevitable response. Making herself unable to take care of her child and her husband, demonstrating how incompetent a woman she was, she illustrated how undeserving she remained. She punished herself, but at the same time she punished her family, forced them to respond to her incapacities by taking over. She made Walter and Katharine suffer the absence of love that had its source in Mary and Frederick.

It is not likely that any marriage would have been successful for Charlotte Perkins at this time in her life. It is unlikely too, I believe, that marriage to Walter Stetson at any point in her life could have been satisfactory for her. Walter sought an essentially conventional relationship; he needed a woman who would hope to satisfy her dreams through satisfying his, a woman emotionally amenable to living in a deferential relationship where the husband was to be the center of attention. Looking back at the failed marriage, Walter confided to his diary that he had "offered her all I have," and wanted in return only "a mind to share my thoughts, to interest itself in my work, my success or my failure."[3] Charlotte was herself too vulnerable and too needy to be able to accept such a role at this point. Later, when she was more healed and more whole, she did not want such a relationship.

Perhaps Charlotte's later fiction offers a clue to the collapse of her marriage. Her fictional women must attain autonomy before they marry, or they find themselves in trouble. Some of the best short stories she wrote years later describe disastrous marriages that come about because the young, inexperienced woman is so flattered by attentions from a lover that she persuades herself that she loves him. In other fictional pieces women who have not attained self-confidence invariably seek out the wrong kind of man; they are drawn to the artful, attractive seducer, the man "practiced in the art of pleasing women," as Charlotte said. Until her fictional women achieve maturity they cannot distinguish genuine strength of character from the façade of strength that a scheming scoundrel may offer.

A present-day psychoanalyst, Alexandra Symonds, has described a certain type of woman patient whose portrait is startingly similar in key ways to that of Charlotte Stetson. These women, whom Symonds encountered over years of clinical practice, are capable, independent, and assertive until they marry, at which time they become excessively helpless and dependent. They seem to "shrivel up after getting married," becoming depressed and anxious and often suffering from psychosomatic problems. These women invariably portray their husbands as kind and helpful. On a conscious level they show no anger, rejecting even the normal tensions that inevitably exist between people living together. Instead, as is characteristic of a dependent personality, they rely upon a kind of helplessness; the "appeal of helplessness" was the way Karen Horney described this quality. The husbands go about their business unaware, as is the wife, of the enormous rage building up in her, a rage that takes the form of psychosomatic symptoms such as chronic headaches, insomnia, gastrointestinal pain, tension. Afraid of their own hostility, which they identify with almost any act of assertiveness, these women use enormous energy to control their feelings. "Ruthlessly they choke off their inner self" is the language Symonds uses to describe their response.

What is it about the state of marriage that triggers such reactions? All of these patients came from families where they had to control their feelings and shape a self-reliant personality at a young age. They grew up in environments that did not encourage or appreciate childlike interests. The early need to develop self-control and self-reliance gave these women, as adolescents, the illusion of strength. They were forced to repress the legitimate needs children have to be taken care of, and thus they repressed much of the child in themselves. Many of them remember themselves as fearless. But with marriage they could put down the tremendous burden they had been carrying so long and allow themselves to be that dependent little girl they had not had the chance to be at the appropriate age. Marriage became, because that is what marriage acceptably could be, their "declaration of dependence." Charlotte described what happened to her after her marriage as going from "proud strength to contemptible feebleness, from cheerful stoicism to a whimpering avoidance of any strain." Her "hand-made character," so carefully built and shaped, collapsed immediately after she and Walter wed.

Charlotte was a nineteenth-century version of Symonds's contemporary patients. Without a husband, without a man on whom she could focus her dependence, Charlotte perceived herself as a capable, independent person. Then all the self-confidence and self-reliance, the independence and assertiveness, melted with the decision, the reluctant decision, to marry Walter. Charlotte had been holding her breath for all those years, fearful of acknowledging those long-unsatisfied child-needs. With her marriage, she allowed herself to take that deep breath and dissolve into dependence, depression, collapse. Marriage was for her, in the words of Alfred Adler, a "sort of emergency exit out of life."[4]

In her later fiction Charlotte often examined and exposed the prevailing notion that marriage and motherhood bring ecstasy. In *What Diantha Did* and in many short stories she made it clear that women who had grand dreams of expanding their gifts and talents in the public world often found the narrow world of the home a nightmare. Her fiction ends simply and happily; the solutions are social and feasible, for when the external realities are altered, all problems disappear. In *What Diantha Did*, for example, Isabel Porne, a trained architect, hires a skilled surrogate so she can return to her work. The reality of Charlotte's own experience was much more complex and tangled, though ultimately she, too, sought her answer in an altered external environment, and if she never entirely resolved her inner conflicts, her self-designed therapy in certain ways worked well for her. While her estrangement from Walter was deepening, Charlotte turned to a woman for emotional sustenance, as she had done once before with Martha Luther. This time the woman was Grace Channing.

Charlotte and Grace had become friends when they were barely more than girls. Before she was out of her teens, Charlotte was a frequent visitor at the Providence home of the family of Dr. William F. Channing, who was the son of the famous Unitarian minister William Ellery Channing. In their home Charlotte found "broad, free-thinking scientific talk, earnest promotion of great causes—life"—all attractions that her own home lacked. In the Channing home there were also "two beautiful daughters, lifelong friends, one closer than a sister to this day," she later wrote.[5]

Grace's lineage was as impressive as Charlotte's own, including a signer of the Declaration of Independence as well as her famous grandfather. While Grace's father, William F. Channing, did not carry the family reputation to more stunning heights, he was a most satisfactory member of his clan: he provided a close and spirited family environment and he maintained the Channing affiliation with leading social and intellectual currents and personalities. Grace received from her Channing kin what Charlotte did not from her Beechers. Thus, the original pull of affection was, not surprisingly, to the family constellation rather than to any one member of it. The tone of intellectual excitement was set by the father.

Charlotte's friendship with one of the "two beautiful daughters" grew into love, in many different forms, and this love is captured in their correspondence of more than fifty years, although most of what remains is letters from Charlotte to Grace. (Everyone seemed to keep Charlotte's letters.) There is much to be learned from an examination of their relationship, much to be learned about the nature of intimacy and friendship in nineteenth-century America, and much to be understood about the nature of their deep affection that permitted it to change over time and thereby endure.

In the winter of 1885, deep in the depression that followed upon her marriage, we have seen that Charlotte did not simply seek out but fled in desperation to the Channing family in Pasadena, where they had moved in an effort to restore Grace's fragile health. After Charlotte returned home to Providence and again collapsed into depression, she found support from Grace's letters, which were filled with encouraging plans. Charlotte and Grace had been dear friends in Providence, but their intimacy had deepened in Pasadena. Grace was Charlotte's only girlhood friend who shared her literary aspirations, for Grace, too, wrote poetry and short stories. They were both creative, energetic, ambitious young women. Both lived on the edge of a great American family, although unlike Charlotte, Grace was solidly centered in her family, in the home of her childhood and in the Channing clan.

Grace too had ambitions for public life. As a very young woman she taught in one of the pioneering kindergartens in Providence. She wrote prolifically and persistently throughout her life, publishing a small body of stories and poems. Most of her creative work remains in manuscript form. The quantity of her output is remarkable. In her later years she worked for a time as a journalist and as a war correspondent. But Charlotte was the assertive, defiant one, Grace, self-effacing and reserved.

Despite that considerable difference in their personalities, or perhaps because of it, in the summer of 1888, after Charlotte's "Rest Cure" and just before she actually did leave Walter, Charlotte, age twenty-eight, and Grace, three years younger, spent several weeks together in Bristol, Rhode Island, where they rested and played and together wrote a play called "A Pretty Idiot." This collaborative piece is a frothy drawing-room comedy, a feminist one, that examines male and female foibles and male-female tensions.

In the play the heroine, Jean Churchill, embodies genuine womanly virtue as defined by Charlotte and Grace. She is intelligent, gifted, independent, beautiful, athletic, and witty. She mischievously provokes one of her two suitors by suggesting that his

ideal woman would be strong, free, self-reliant, independent—with both intellect and muscle, having a career of her own—ambitions—able to meet you on your own ground!

The suitor responds predictably:

Heaven forbid! You are describing a man!—Shall I tell you what my ideal really is?

And then he does: a woman of sweetness, gentleness, patience, amiability, but above all with the capacity for a great, absorbing, self-sacrificing, all-enduring love. She must also be cultivated and intellectual, although intellectual in a womanly way, "able to enter into every interest of her husband's life." Of course, she must be young and beautiful, "with that nameless, ineffable charm, that mysterious, subtle something which no man can explain—or withstand!"

The suitor is not put off but falls madly in love with the frivolous character Jean makes herself out to be. When he pronounces his love for her, proclaiming that he adores her "fresh and innocent youth," her "exquisite beauty," she is disgusted with him. He loves her for qualities that do not attest to her value or worth, mere superficial attributes. His love is "not compliment, but insult."

Jean expresses her disappointment in this suitor in a later conversation with her cousin and confidant, Jack: "I really thought he was going to be clever, brilliant, sensible—and he's turned out to

Grace Ellery Channing around 1888

be just a *man*!" Jack, who is supportive, kind, sensible, and unglamorous, knows and secretly loves the total woman: her strength, her intelligence, even her unbeautiful qualities of ego and stubbornness. It is her human, not uniquely female, qualities that Jack recognizes and loves in her.

The plot of "A Pretty Idiot" turns on the publication of an anonymous novel, *A Double Game*. The author is none other than our Jean, but her two leading suitors, recognizing each other in the book, are certain that the other is the author. It never occurs to either of them that Jean is the culprit. And it does not occur to Jean until the curtain is about to fall that she too has overlooked the obvious: the man she truly loves and who is worthy of her love is Jack.

Writing this play was undoubtedly a distraction for the two women and it provided a safe way for Charlotte to play with matters of marriage and courtship, but Charlotte and Grace, along with Walter, had work to do in dismantling the Stetson home. Charlotte returned from vacation on September 1 to make plans for the separation. Mary Perkins, who had returned to care for her ailing daughter, once more moved back to Utah to live with her son. Walter moved into his studio. On September 22, 1888, Charlotte shipped her belongings to California: "Weight—5750 lbs. . . . Total bill $213.96. . . . Then rest and hope and health and joy. . . . *Dead tired*." Two weeks later, on October 8, Charlotte, with Grace and Katharine, left for Pasadena. When her friends asked what she would do when she got to California, she answered, "I shall earn my own living."[6]

For the first time in her life Charlotte was striking out alone. With little money, a few friends, not much in the way of marketable skills, and the responsibility of caring for a child whom she had demonstrated no ability to mother, she set out to recreate her life. Despite several years in a mental state of near-collapse, with instructions from the leading neurologist of the day that indicated her struggle for independence would destroy her stability, she trusted herself enough to reject Mitchell, Walter, and her mother. She was able to cling to the firm belief that she had great gifts in her, if only she could so structure her life as to give them a chance to blossom.

In Pasadena, where she remained for more than two years before moving north to Oakland, Charlotte began to reconstruct her life. In this crucial Pasadena period, enormous changes occurred in both her personal relationships and her public work, changes that helped immeasurably to shape her future.

Southern California, particularly Los Angeles, was an astonishing place; its growth was spectacular even by American standards. Pasadena, some twelve miles away from Los Angeles, had a very different history, one of slow evolution, and it remained a refuge of sorts for its residents. It was a haven for health-seekers, for its climate was a major appeal in the days before it suffered from smog. Its rich cultural life, an interesting combination of its legacy from back East and its Spanish and Indian heritages, drew writers and artists to the community. Its reputation as an artistic and cultural enclave was undoubtedly of some importance in attracting families like the Channings.

The Channings had found a "little wood-and-paper four-room house" for Charlotte, for which she paid a monthly rent of ten dollars, and that is where she and Katharine lived. Pasadena was lush and gorgeous. Charlotte's little cottage was in an orange grove "rich with fragrant blossoms." Roses covered her roof, a lemon verbena bordered the front path. She bought a peck of white grapes for ten cents. For long hours she lay in a hammock under the roses, giving herself finally a chance to rest. She wrote when she could, and took care of herself and her child. She managed her life herself in ways she had been unable to do back home when surrounded by offers of help from husband and mother, offers which, however well-intentioned, only served to prevent her from taking charge for herself, of herself. During this time Charlotte eked out a meager living by giving art lessons, tutoring, and selling some writing. A friend staked her initially to one hundred dollars; for the rest she was on her own, Walter not being able to provide any support for their child, and Charlotte apparently not expecting any from him.

Walter unexpectedly arrived at Christmastime, hoping for a reconciliation. The Channings offered him a room in their home. Charlotte was becoming involved in a variety of activities, Walter wrote to his mother. "In fact," he said, "I think she is trying to do too much," without, it seems, a sense of irony at criticizing his wife for doing too much when just a few months before she had been able to do almost nothing.

It is astonishing how much Charlotte was able to do. During her first year living apart from Walter, despite his proximity, she wrote, she said "some thirty-three articles and twenty-three poems, besides ten more child-verses." There were weeks in her diary that were "absolutely blank"—the "drowned time" she called it—but what is striking about those first two years in Pasadena is not the lost time but the ability to perform and to produce during the other times. What is extraordinary is the difference between the good times and the bad, a difference that allowed Charlotte to perform in public in ways that belied the abject suffering she underwent out of sight.

When Charlotte arrived in Pasadena she was not yet thirty years old; she described herself as "heavily damaged but not dead." The "dark, feeble mind" terrified her, but she wrote in her diary that "it is intellectually conceivable that I may recover strength enough to do some part of my work." And then she proceeded to do so.[7]

She earned small amounts of money by lecturing on diverse subjects. She also made money, as we have seen, by giving lessons, but until Grace left Pasadena in the fall of 1890, the two also continued to work on plays together and then act in them. Charlotte joined a theater group, where she found herself usually cast in comic parts. She also accepted, with trepidation, an offer to complete the interior decorations on the new Pasadena Opera House, a project she carried out with great flair and pleasure. Virtually all of the poems she wrote in Pasadena were given away; a few sold for a small sum. She managed to sell several articles for slightly higher amounts, some even for ten dollars.

In this short recuperative period of two years or so in Pasadena she did not earn much from her words, written or spoken, but she wrote a considerable amount, including two excellent short pieces that brought her recognition: the story "The Yellow Wallpaper" and the poem "Similar Cases" (see Appendix). Writing the first, a psychological self-examination, freed her to write the second, a witty, satirical, playful slap at traditional thought and traditional thinkers. To read these two short works of hers one after the other gives one a sense of the range of emotions that bombarded her and the range of responses she was able to evoke.

Charlotte participating in an amateur theatrical

Publication of "Similar Cases" in the April 1890 issue of the *Nationalist* not only won for Charlotte some reputation in reform circles nationwide but also achieved for her the lasting admiration and support of William Dean Howells. Howells was an established novelist at the peak of his powers, but it was as editor and critic that he was particularly influential. It was during the 1870s that literary criticism became a reputable profession. Magazines had large readerships and their editors were important in creating and shaping tastes: Howells as editor of the *Atlantic Monthly*; R. W. Gilder of the *Century*; M. W. Curtis of *Harper's*; J. G. Holland of *Scribner's*. Liberal editors such as Howells did much to project the ideas of what came to be called literary realism, which challenged the predominance of romantic conventions.

Charlotte was delighted to have a fan letter from him after "Similar Cases" appeared. In it he said:

> I have been wishing ever since I first read it—and I have read it many times with unfailing joy—to thank you for your poem in the April *Nationalist*. We have had nothing since the Bigelow Papers half so good in a good cause as "Similar Cases." And just now I've read in the *Woman Journal* your "Women of Today." It is as good almost as the other & dreadfully true!

Although Charlotte privately admitted to Martha that Howells "never was a favorite of mine; His work . . . seems to me of small artistic value,"[8] his support was important and she knew it. His admiration and his help in promoting Charlotte never diminished, although he was not always, or even often, successful in his efforts. He had tried to place "The Yellow Wallpaper," sending it to a friend who had succeeded him as editor of *Atlantic Monthly*, but without success. The editor rejected the story, writing to the author as follows:

> *Dear Madam,*
> *Mr. Howells has handed me this story.*
> *I could not forgive myself if I made others as miserable as I have made myself!*
>
> > *Sincerely yours,*

A few years later Howells wrote Charlotte that her first book of poems, *In This Our World*, contained "the wittiest and wisest things that have been written this many a long day and year . . . you speak with a tongue like a two-edged sword. I rejoice in your gift." She finally met him in 1897, when she lectured to a Manhattan Single Tax Club, and wrote to Grace, "I was made very happy to really see him at last—and to have his approval again." In 1919 he wrote to ask permission to include "The Yellow Wallpaper" in his new collection, *The Great Modern American Stories,* so that he could "give the recognition to the supreme awfulness of your thing" in his introduction.

Howells explained the limited success he met with in promoting Charlotte in the letter cited above that spoke so highly of her poems. "I have my bourgeois moments," he said, "when I would have wished you for success's sake to have been less frank. But of course you know that you stand in your own way. (The thing can be done.)"[9]

Despite Howells's belief that Charlotte's uncompromising stance jeopardized her success and made his support ultimately ineffectual, he never withdrew his attention and respect. In a letter to Grace in 1929 she quoted excerpts from a letter she had received from an old friend of Howells, Oliver Herford:

> Howells, whom at one time I used to see every day (I almost had a latch key) was constantly quoting you and was the first who read "Similar Cases" to me—& he asserted in my presence that you had the best brains *and* the best profile of any woman in America, and Mrs. Howells added "or anywhere else"![10]

Charlotte's creativity and energy burgeoned in Pasadena as she began to develop a reputation as a writer and social critic, but simultaneously her personal relationships were turbulent. Walter had no doubt come to Pasadena in a vulnerable state, feeling shaken and perhaps guilty at his marriage's disastrous course and the recent split from Charlotte. That rejection must surely have hurt his pride, however much she insisted he was blameless. He was also no doubt astonished to find her, after only two months away from him, displaying the same vitality she had had when he first met her. It could not have made him feel very good, especially since Charlotte's reception at his arrival was not enthusiastic.

But if Charlotte did not seem to want him or need him, Grace did. It was Grace who extended herself to make him feel comfortable, to provide companionship when Charlotte was too busy. If Charlotte's breaking down and then healing alone had weakened his masculine self-confidence, then Grace's attentions and acceptance did much to strengthen it. It was Grace who ultimately proved to be the more suitable partner, for her self-effacing character fit Walter's needs more closely than Charlotte's tangled web of dependence and assertion. Grace was calm, predictable, accommodating. Grace's family was accepting and generous; perhaps their being famous didn't hurt either. Walter would never earn much money or achieve much prominence with his paintings. He was at this time a man in his late twenties with slim prospects for a future that, by late-nineteenth-century American standards, could be called a success. The Channings, like the Beechers, had a heritage of valuing artistic accomplishments, even if they were not crowned in the marketplace. In such surroundings he would feel less a failure. Finally, it is not impossible that Walter, rejected by his wife, was unconsciously striking out at her by appealing to her best friend for needed support. In any event, Walter had left Providence that Christmas in search of a wife, and a year later he returned there with plans to secure a new, more suitable one.

By the time Walter left Pasadena in January 1890 to rush to see his dying mother, not only had he and Charlotte finally separated, but he and Grace had established a new relationship, one which had an extraordinary impact on Charlotte, though not the impact one would have thought. Little is known about Walter and Grace's courtship. One can only conjecture how the scenario must have played itself out as these three closely connected people rearranged themselves in the course of that year.

We know very little of Grace's feelings during and after her courtship with Walter. We know that she had been the only friend of Charlotte's to approve of Walter during Charlotte's engagement. We can imagine that it must have been a strain to live in the same house with Walter and form a growing romantic bond with him while at the same time remaining Charlotte's closest friend and greatest support. Apparently, Grace never said a word about this difficult situation to Charlotte. Perhaps her very silence indicates how trying it was for her. The hidden, unexamined state of things could only have made the three of them intensely uncomfortable and probably made two of the three, Grace most of all, feel deceitful. It was not the way of any of them to talk directly.

What were Charlotte's feelings about Grace and Walter's growing involvement? Her continued correspondence with Martha Luther, now Lane, gives a few clues. In the spring of 1889, for instance,

Charlotte described Walter as "very happy," painting steadily but without any pecuniary gain, but "we think the prospect is good." She observed that Walter and Grace "are great friends, which gives me sincere delight."[11] Charlotte, drawn more and more into work, was genuinely pleased that Walter was freeing himself from her, discovering his own distractions. Her unwavering assertion that her feelings for Walter were dead and that his acceptance of that situation pleased her were probably true. She was preparing herself, healing herself, freeing herself from the bonds of a marriage she felt had almost destroyed her. At the same time she had no hostile feelings that she would acknowledge toward Walter. His moving away from her made her more comfortable. It was a time of reckoning for Charlotte, and Walter was not essential to the process. But Grace was. "Grace Channing saved what there is of me," Charlotte wrote to Martha. "Grace Channing pulled me out of living death, set me on my staggering feet, helped me to get work again, did more than I can say to make me live, and I love her, I think, as well as any one on earth."[12]

It is probably significant that during the year in Pasadena when Walter established an intimate relationship with Grace, Charlotte resumed a correspondence with Martha, a correspondence that had lagged in the years of their marriages. Did Charlotte, observing the friendship between the husband from whom she was alienated and the woman whom she needed and loved, feel left out, closed out from these two—just as she had felt closed out when Martha turned to the man who became her husband? If the dear friend, Grace, whom she counted on during this time, was with her and yet not with her, sympathizing with her estrangement from Walter and at the same time drawn to Walter, then how natural for Charlotte to seek out someone to whom she could turn. Charlotte undoubtedly felt much alone in this traumatic period when she was ending a marriage, putting her life together, and finding the friend she most needed not entirely available to her.

It is not surprising that to Martha she unburdened, perhaps even exaggerated, her emotional debilities: on August 15, 1899, she wrote that "the weakness of brain which has so devastated my life for the past five years still holds very largely." She told Martha that she was able to do considerable work of a certain kind but "ordinary labor" was out of her reach. The two things still impossible for her to do were "sewing and the writing of letters"—one representing the work of her mother, the other the attentuated connection with her father—although she refers to this inability to write letters in a letter. And then came words of love and loving memory:

> No one has ever taken your place heart's dearest. No one has ever given me the happiness that you did, the peace, the rest, the everpresent joy. I do not forget. Neither do I remember for the immediate past is still so vital a horror and all the antecedent years so lonely and dreary that I never look back if I can avoid it.[13]

No wonder she did not forget that happiness, for she had had nothing comparable since, and the sight of Walter and Grace's growing closeness must have caused her to seek some solace, some memory of when she too had been loved and not excluded.

A letter to Martha that Charlotte wrote the month Walter left Pasadena, engaged to Grace, ends with Charlotte's poignant cry:

> Goodnight dear. You were more comfort to me—more pure joy, than any one else ever was. Good night. Yes I did well to mourn you when you left me; but it was to be.

But it was when Grace returned East in the fall of 1890, at least in part to be near Walter that Charlotte truly suffered, writing to Martha in stark agony, "Grace has left me."[14]

As she did each December, Charlotte assessed the year's activity in her diary at the end of 1890. "A very quick but very hard year; cruelly hard since Grace went. A year of great growth and gain." Charlotte's survival rested on her incredible ability to take strength and energy from hardship. By the following December Charlotte had been informed of Walter and Grace's plans to marry. The loss, years before, of Martha was now repeated with Grace.

On December 3, Charlotte wrote an extraordinary, open letter to Grace. She began by complaining of her physical ailments, which she treated with swimming in hot water, tonics, and "a sleeping arrangement" to make her sleep more restful. Her debts had mounted, she said, "and I wish for the dear girl to hearten me up, straighten out my fuzzy brains, and lift things generally." But Grace was no longer available for such caretaking.

> Do you know I think I suffer more in giving you up than in Walter—for you were all joy to me. And it was not till things were well underway that that side of the arrangement dawned on me. I know I was gradually getting very near to you, and now that dreadful angel has come and swallowed you and I am nowhere! It is awful to be a man inside and not able to marry the woman you love! When Martha married it cracked my heart a good deal—your loss will finish it. . . .

> I think of you with a great howlin' selfish heartache. I want you—I love you—*I* need you *myself!* How's that for a "virtue"?

Grace had apparently some inkling of Charlotte's feelings, for in the same letter Charlotte referred to how "your clairvoyance has seen through my mask of joy," which suggests that this declaration of love is the first direct, outspoken statement of the kind that Charlotte had yet made to Grace.

Walter did not have any idea of her feelings, Charlotte went on, about "the new internal discoveries," and she would not tell him because "it would worry him seriously," and besides, "it is only a temporary matter."

Charlotte Gilman made no effort to destroy or withhold this letter. Indeed, as she approached her death, she carefully examined her papers, put them in order, and in appropriate places made annotations directed to an assumed reader.

It is a remarkable letter. It is a declaration of feeling, not a call to action or a statement of hope that Grace will do anything. It is the statement of love that matters. It is putting herself on record for the record, not with the expectation, hope, perhaps even desire of winning Grace. It is loss that Charlotte emphasizes in this letter, more than desire.

Why did Charlotte wait till marriage loomed, till she was faced with loss, to make her declarations of love, first to Martha and now to Grace? I think the impending loss inspired her to express feelings that she had never needed to give voice to before, when the intimacy was unchallenged and mutually satisfactory. Perhaps Charlotte was afraid to express such loving sentiments during the time she was in daily contact with Martha and Grace. And perhaps she felt love most intensely when she feared its loss, not an unlikely reaction from one who had spent her childhood yearning for unattainable love objects and thus had come to identify love with this feeling.

What sort of love, exactly, and what sort of loss was Charlotte confronting when she wrote her letter? She says that Walter will swallow up Grace and "I am nowhere." But Walter will not swallow Grace up simply by marrying her; marriage does not mean absorbing, swallowing, causing one to disappear, although Charlotte, on the basis of her own and her mother's experiences, may have felt that marriage did just that.

What marriage did was to threaten the intimacy of Charlotte's relationship to Grace and to remove her sexually from Charlotte. But there is every indication that however erotic the language Charlotte employed, whatever sexual feelings she may have had toward Grace were unacknowledged and unexplored. The letters of love that Charlotte wrote before to Martha and now to Grace seem to be the way she chose to declare her feelings. Letters were safer. Distance was protective.

What were those feelings, then? What did Charlotte mean when she said, "It is awful to be a man inside and not be able to marry the woman you love"? Were the "internal discoveries" truly new, and if so, how did she understand her love for Martha? Or when she said "new," did she mean only in regard to Grace?

It is important not to put labels on Charlotte. She loved Martha and Walter and Grace, and later others, in different ways and with different intensities. She did not reject or despise any feelings of love, any more than, in all probability, she acted on them in ways that such language might suggest to contemporary readers.

Charlotte's feelings for Grace suggest some confusion, some distress on her part, some sense that her expression of love is inappropriate or will not be well received. As Lillian Faderman has persuasively argued, in a pre-Freudian time before the sex drive was identified as a central one, love, passionate, enduring, genuine love, between women could be expressed with comfort because it was not assumed to have a sexual meaning.[15] Thus it was possible for Charlotte to have unrecognized sexual feelings for Grace and feel free to express them without fully realizing their erotic nature.

Charlotte was clearly not altogether unaware of the implications of her words, since she did not want to worry Walter about the "temporary state of things." She knew and she didn't know; she blurted out her feelings once to Grace and then never again.

The concept of being trapped in the wrong body, the phrase itself, has a long history. Transsexuals today, like their earlier counterparts, Faderman says, often feel they are "trapped in the wrong bodies." The assumption underlying such a concept must be that there is an appropriate, inherent masculine and feminine behavior, and thus a woman who loves a woman is a man. In Charlotte's case it also probably meant that because she wanted to do what men do—that is, not raise children and accept a domestic life but be a public person—she felt she was meant to be a man. Ultimately Charlotte came to believe that there was no "masculine" or "feminine" behavior, except for that directly linked to childbirth. But at this point in her life she was grappling, suffering, plagued by a world that locked people in by gender and provided no space for those who did not fit.

The declaration of love for Grace was never repeated, as far as I can tell. It did indeed prove to be a "temporary matter." And Grace's loss did not devastate Charlotte as Martha's had. Charlotte had learned from her experience with Martha; she did not reel back in agony and clutch in such a way as to drive her friend away. Instead, their relationship evolved into a lifelong mutual dependency between two remarkable women who loved and respected each other and who chose to ignore the inevitable tensions in their difficult situation. Rather than allowing Grace's marriage to estrange them, Charlotte used the connection to create a deeper bond between them. Indeed, in May of 1894, Charlotte took the then extraordinary step of sending Katharine to live with Grace and Walter, who had just married, a step which meant that Charlotte and Grace were bound together for the many years Katharine remained with them. Charlotte occasionally visited them, though throughout most of this time she was traveling or living many miles from them. Although the two longtime women friends were unable to spend much time together, they corresponded constantly, and Charlotte frequently reiterated her devotion to Grace and her gratitude to her for being the mother to Katharine that she herself could not be. For example, on October 13, 1898, she wrote to Grace:

There are few women on earth who could do what you have done. . . . Poor as my own surroundings have been for the child I should have kept her with me if I had not known that you were heavenly-wise with children; and must love Walter's child—be fond of mine—and be won by the darling herself. . . . I shall be grateful always for the beautiful fruit of her life with you.

This letter was written to Grace the year *Woman and Economics* appeared, a book Charlotte could not have written had she had the responsibility of rearing her child. She signed her letters to Grace "Always with love and gratitude" or "With love always dear Mother of my child." In another letter she wrote:

You dear great woman. . . . Some day we shall be largely together again, and you will like me better than you ever did before. I grow and grow and grow. . . . I am happier now, freer, stronger, broader, wiser, *gladder* than in twelve long years.[16]

In her relationship with Grace, Charlotte sought, and for the first time found, a person who gave her much if not all of what she asked. This time she chose more wisely and this time she asked more wisely. Grace Channing possessed the nurturing, caretaking qualities for which Charlotte yearned. Whatever tinge of resentment, anger, and hostility occasionally arose in Grace, she came through for Charlotte, as she did for Walter and her stepchild. Perhaps she did not come through for herself, but that is another story. And this time, unlike in the confrontation with Martha, Charlotte achieved a strategy that was feasible: she learned to share Grace with Walter and Katharine. If the arrangement was not what she would have most wanted, she was willing, finally, to compromise so as not to lose all. Such a change was a sign of growth in her.

The triangle—Charlotte, Walter, Grace—scandalized many of their generation because of the cordial relations that prevailed among them. Even today there are speculations as to the "real" meaning behind that friendship. I think the essential triangle was a different configuration: Charlotte, Grace, and Katharine, the two women and the girl-child they shared and who formed a deep bond between them, for with the gift of Katharine, Grace became not only a mother to the child but a mother to the mother as well. Indeed, one feels that all three of them, Grace, Katharine, and Walter, as a family, were Charlotte's people, that although she could not settle in with them or perhaps with anyone at that time, they helped satisfy somewhat her need for roots and family.

Seeing Walter in his new family setting was important for her, for that "glimpse of Walter . . . quite obliterates the wavering past and makes it recede still further into the fading distance." Grace functioned as an odd confidante, for she served as the sounding board for Charlotte's ruminations on her past marriage, and yet she also served as the present and future connection with that husband and the child they produced.

Even after Katharine grew up, Charlotte's deep love for Grace did not weaken; only the emphasis altered as Grace's mothering role declined. In 1929, when Charlotte was sixty-nine and Grace was sixty-six, Charlotte could still tell her:

> You've never done anything but shower around your un-selfish devotion, bottomless generosity, exquisite sympathy and understanding, with a background of sheer nobility and heroism, which I literally bow to . . . it is good for me to have someone to honestly look up to.

And shortly before her death in 1935, Charlotte wrote:

> It's been an honor to be your friend, dear Grace. And I have loved you a long time—some 56 or 57 years, isn't it?[17]

We all live simultaneously on many levels, but most of us manage to integrate different parts of our lives so that we live with a sense of wholeness, with a sense that we are the same person performing different roles. Charlotte's strategy for survival for many years was to compartmentalize, so that her private torments were closed off and put away to allow the public person to evolve. Such a strategy is not without cost, but for a long time it was the best Charlotte could manage. The struggling, suffering, frightened, groping, clutching, depressed young woman lived alongside but

Walter in 1892

apart from the increasingly successful, energetic, engaged lecturer, writer, and activist.

That bifurcated existence had been evident in her years with Walter, with the balance heavily on the side of depression and emotional instability. During their marriage Charlotte had managed to salvage some sense of her other self with small amounts of writing and public engagement. During these moments she was able to free herself from her sense of bondage to home and family, a bondage which was the catalyst for her depression and breakdown.

In California, in these two years in Pasadena, that same bifurcation existed, but the balance was shifting. The public Charlotte was gaining strength, power, and predominance. The private side of her personality, the side that was still feeble and fragile, was shrinking in importance; it was taking up less of her life. As she reduced the energy she put into her private self, she appeared to be healing, was in fact healing, although at cost. The cost was that she denied herself a rich, full private existence.

During the year Walter resided in Grace's home and their friendship grew into intimacy, Charlotte survived by distancing herself from them, seeking some solace in frequent letters to Martha, but primarily by focusing upon her work, her writing and her lecturing. She was lonely, confiding in her diary on the first day of 1891: "I watched the old year out and the new year in as before these many years—alone—writing a letter to Grace." She fled from intimacy, either by rejecting those who did want her, like Walter and Katharine, or by seeking out those, like Martha and Grace, who would not, but from now on in her work she would return to face the issues she avoided in her life.

By defining herself in the world of letters, she would take on her father's legacy. She followed his family pattern as well, leaving behind her mate and ultimately her child, as he had. But in the substance of her work, in the subject matter to which she addressed herself, she was from the first the female figure, infusing values of cooperation, caring, and concern, values she defined as maternal. "The Yellow Wallpaper" was the most personal and obviously autobiographical story she ever wrote, but everything she said and everything she wrote addressed concerns of women as she saw them and lived them.

It was through her work that Charlotte began to heal herself;

it was in her work that she was able to project herself whole. In Pasadena she first discovered and then learned to value her gifts for writing and lecturing. If she could not serve husband and child, she could serve the world. She could give herself—her intellect, her insights, her passion, her vitality, her wit—in a public forum. She would now take the experiences that tormented her and chained her and project them onto a public screen, there to look at them, expose them, examine their source and thereby put them to rest by understanding them.

To be sure, the work Charlotte produced during her two years in Pasadena was not from her isolation; on the contrary, she found personal salvation in an intellectual and political community, from which she received the sustenance her family and friends had not given her or which she could not take from them. "Charlotte has a long list of disciples among the young women," was the way Walter described some of her new friendships in a letter to his mother.[18] Finally, Charlotte began to find her sense of place and belonging: it was community as family.

The move to California afforded Charlotte not only a place of safety in which to hide but also a place of bustling reform activity, of intellectual and social ferment—of another kind of safety in which to find herself.

VII
ADELINE / DORA

H aving sought a period of warmth and protection in Pasadena, primarily from the Channings, Charlotte was now ready to leave behind the nurturing community she had found there to engage in a more stimulating, active, challenging, but risky life in Oakland and San Francisco. During occasional trips to speak at and attend meetings she had already had a taste of that life, and encountered two forces that would help to shape it—the Bellamyite socialism espoused by the Nationalist Club, and the friendship of Adeline E. Knapp. In 1890 she made the decision to move to Oakland, with Katharine, and she moved there the following year, in the early fall of 1891, to remain in the area till the summer of 1895.

In the course of these years in northern California, the subject of this chapter, Charlotte's life again changed significantly. Her reputation as a writer and lecturer grew substantially. She became a recognized person in the overlapping but distinct circles that espoused Bellamy Nationalism, social gospel, social purity, trade unionism, temperance, women's suffrage, and Populism.

In the private arena, the changes in her life were no less dramatic but considerably less successful. During this time Charlotte's mother came to live with her and subsequently died of cancer in her home. And during this time Charlotte was granted a divorce from Walter and entangled herself in a traumatic relationship with Adeline E. Knapp.

The exciting and politically engaged San Francisco area was the right place for Charlotte to be. The period of internal peace and smooth growth that the Civil War was expected to bring the nation had brought instead brutality and violence, dislocation and disruption, as industrial capitalism created changes that staggered the land. Those enormous changes spurred efforts for reform to cope with the social and human problems being created daily. A growing sense of national peril and a growing sense that change was necessary to meet that peril dominated the political climate.

Americans were feeling powerless in a new and frightening way. America had been settled and developed by people who were firmly convinced that they had the ability to alter profoundly the course of their own existence. That spirit, that feeling of control, was being jeopardized, indeed was collapsing in the wake of changes wrought by industrial development. People began to feel themselves helpless in a world that was unmanageable. Political corruption, monopoly power, and an international market were shattering an earlier dream in which individuals saw themselves as determining their own destinies. A division between employers and a growing proletariat led to efforts by one group to organize and efforts by the other to prevent organizing. Women found themselves divided as well—working-class women locked into hideously exploitative jobs and middle-class women locked into lonely and privatized existences. It was a world of fear and powerlessness, a new and alien world in which the democratic ethos seemed to be rapidly disappearing.

It was a world that in its externals reflected Charlotte Stetson's inner struggles; the fear and powerlessness in the public place had their counterparts in her private existence. By participating in reform efforts, she could hope to find some way to manage her own private demons and arm herself with a sense of personal achievement and personal power.

Such reform activities were on the rise again by the 1890s. The moral spirit that emerged before and during the Civil War had given way to a collapse of reform fervor after the war, exacerbated by the damaging effects of the Depression of 1873. By the late 1880s, however, reform movements began once more to stir, setting out to transform American society along cooperative lines. They all seemed to coalesce into a grand reform army made up of union leaders, middle-class reformers, Populists, suffrage activists, socialists, temperance advocates—all challenging the exploitative conditions created by industrial capitalism.

Even before these reform activities began to reappear, women in great numbers had been organizing their own associations, creating a loose-knit but nevertheless powerful movement of female solidarity. The women's clubs founded in the 1870s and 1880s sought to find a place for white middle-class women in the political and economic life of the country and to provide assistance to working-class women caught in the grip of a severely exploitative system. If Charlotte's generation was the first to have access to a college education, the preceding generation of women, then in their middle years, had been the first to be freed of an entire lifetime tied to child-rearing, thanks to smaller families, longer lives, and greater affluence. Their children were out of the home while they were still relatively young, they were surrounded by social and economic problems that seemed to challenge the very structure of the nation, and they set out to make changes. Women, primarily middle-class, by the many thousands joined hundreds of organizations—missionary societies, the Women's Educational and Industrial Union, the National Woman's Christian Temperance Union, women's suffrage associations, clubs for mutual instruction, municipal reform, and help to the needy. The formation of the International Council of Women, an umbrella organization for hundreds of local groups, testified to the major political force the women's movement had become.

When, a decade later, in the late 1880s, the male-led reform coalition, the "grand reform army" referred to above, began its new crusade, the women's movement, already well organized, entered into these new activities, but without losing its cohesiveness. Women, now well accustomed to organized reform activity, brought their skills, their ideas, and their commitment into the various socialist, agrarian, and trade-union movements and helped shape their activities and their ideologies.

The full range of reform activities was available in northern California, and indeed more accepted there than in many locations in the East. In California, as elsewhere in the nation, a generation of women activists enthusiastically embraced every aspect of the protest movements.

It was this exciting, intellectually and politically innovative atmosphere that Charlotte now entered. It was the Bellamyite Nationalist movement that she found most congenial. She had, in fact, begun her association with Nationalism before she moved north, and that association was probably one of the factors in her decision to leave Pasadena for the Bay Area.

Edward Bellamy's book *Looking Backward: 2000–1887* was one of the century's three best-selling novels. It articulated for the reform movement a utopian ethic, Nationalism. The book inspired a generation of American-born reformers to identify themselves with socialism, to call for cooperation to replace competition, and to identify socialism with Americanism and not with a foreign ideology associated with immigrants. Bellamy's ideas were especially acceptable because they advocated socialism achieved by peaceful, gradual, evolutionary change. Middle-class Americans could safely embrace Bellamy's ideas as espoused in *Looking Backward* because they repudiated the Marxist notion of class struggle and violent change, and spoke instead with a voice informed by the Christian ethic of cooperation based on love. "Nationalism has put a silk hat on socialism," said a contemporary account.[1] The goal of the movement was to eliminate injustices by a further extension of democracy, not by using the political system but by relying on moral suasion. A central tenet of Nationalism was that human nature was plastic, that it would change with changed circumstances, and that a collective society would produce better people.

One cannot easily discount Nationalism as mindlessly "utopian." Chaos, disruption, and violence were widespread enough in the United States so that many feared or cheered, depending upon where they stood, what seemed to be a coming revolutionary struggle. Alternative social visions, such as that embodied in Nationalism, were viewed not as academic exercises but as genuine alternatives for a world in trouble. Bellamy's work also addressed, as did "utopian" writers in general, questions of the relationship between men and women, marriage, child-rearing, love, and work, in a way that the Marxist socialist movement did not. For all the flaws in his projected model society, flaws easy to recognize today, Bellamy was the first popular novelist to identify economic independence with women's freedom. Women were to play a central role in his classless society, the Cooperative Commonwealth. Frances Willard, the temperance leader and prominent reformer, even insisted that Edward Bellamy must be Edwina, because only a "great-hearted, big-brained woman" could have written such a book.[2]

As individuals converted to Nationalism, they set up Nationalist clubs where they lived. The movement began in California, for example, with the formation of a reading circle in Oakland in 1889. Similar clubs were quickly formed in San Diego, Los Angeles, and San Francisco. By 1890 there were sixty Bellamy clubs in California with a membership of more than three thousand. Not surprisingly, large numbers of these Bellamyites were women.

Nationalism was the road Charlotte used to make her way to public recognition. As we have seen, her poem "Similar Cases" first appeared in the *Nationalist*, which was the official journal of the Bellamy movement. She served as an officer in the Nationalist Club in Oakland and her first lecture was delivered to a Nationalist club.

If Nationalism was the organization that made her known, lecturing was the method. Initially she wrote out her lectures, but ultimately she was confident enough and the material was familiar enough for her to speak even without notes. In January 1892, within two years of her first public lecture, she attempted to deliver one from memory. She commented after in her diary: "Do not make a success of it, nor enjoy it, but mean to try again." She did try again, many times, until she had perfected the style and learned to enjoy it. Of the written lectures, some sixty remain. The major themes that were to appear later in her first and most famous book, *Women and Economics*, and in her subsequent works are already clearly defined in this early period,[3] essentially 1890 and 1891, at the end of her time in Pasadena and at the very beginning of her San Francisco years. During this period she worked out a group of lectures that dealt with Nationalism—"Nationalism and the Arts," "Nationalism and Religion," "Nationalism and the Virtues," "Nationalism and Love," and "Why We Want Nationalism" were among the titles. Nationalism's belief that human beings were creators of their own destiny clearly spoke to the experiences of her own life. Her overriding concern, expressed in these lectures and in her subsequent writings, was the need to improve the group, the community, the human race; and such improvement could be accomplished by the application of reason to the environment.

In addition to delivering individual lectures, in the fall of 1891 in Oakland Charlotte began a practice that she continued throughout her life—running a series of lectures that formed a mini-class. She offered a series of twelve classes that ran through the winter of 1892. Subjects, themes, and analyses that would later figure prominently in her books first appeared in these early lectures and in her early writings. Among these themes were: the need for women to be independent economically and the catastrophic effect their economic dependence had always had; the superior quality of collective enterprise; and the belief that seemingly unalterable problems were resolvable by community effort. The assumption on which all these lectures were based was that all our sufferings are preventable if we apply our human intelligence to their resolution, because human beings are capable of reshaping their social environments; unlike all other creatures, human beings are not simply passive agents of evolution but are capable of controlling the evolutionary process.

Charlotte began to see her role in life as that of propagandist, inspirer-of-new-thought. As she said later in her utopian novels, all that was necessary to make changes was the determination to do it. She was less concerned with blueprints for bringing about change than with showing the world the way to go. Once persuaded, she felt the world would know how to make the changes it sought.

By the end of her active career, Charlotte had lectured on more than two hundred topics having to do with men, women, children, labor, work, education, socialism, dress, myths, ethics, municipal reform, evolution, women in government, principles of sociology, feminism, art, literature, beauty, women's suffrage, and virtue. Most of the lectures became journal articles, and most of those were incorporated into her books. She often used her lecture series as a forum to help her develop her ideas systematically, which allowed her very quickly to put her words together into book-length essays.

During her years in Oakland, Charlotte made great professional strides in another new direction. Early in the summer of 1894, with two acquaintances, Paul Tyner and Helen Campbell, she took over the running of the *Impress*, which had been the journal of the Pacific Coast Women's Press Association, and turned it into a journal,

Charlotte said, "for both men and women of wide aims and views." Appointed by the PCWPA, Charlotte became editor; Tyner, publisher; and Campbell, associate editor. The three not only worked together but lived together while they published the weekly paper. Their management lasted only five months, but during that time Charlotte wrote articles, poems, editorials, and reviews of all kinds, foreshadowing the kind of journalism she later undertook when she published her own magazine, the *Forerunner*. Helen Campbell, considerably older than Charlotte, was already a nationally known lecturer and author in the same reform network. Her central concern was the home economics movement, which at that time dealt with issues of public health and safety, encompassing a much broader conception of home economics than that which later evolved.

However, Charlotte believed that her greatest literary triumph during this period was unquestionably not her management of the *Impress* but the publication of *In This Our World*, her first book of poetry, in 1893. Printed initially by two of her Socialist friends, she said, with funds raised by them from private subscribers, the book enhanced appreciably her budding reputation. It soon had an English edition, also in cloth, in 1895, and a new enlarged American edition that same year. In Oakland, Charlotte's writing, lecturing, and reform work kept her in a whirl of activity, and her reputation grew steadily.

The Trades and Labor Union of Alameda County, in September 1892, presented her with a gold medal for her essay *The Labor Movement*, published in pamphlet form. A second edition appeared in 1895, and an English edition, published by T. Fisher Unwin, appeared in 1896. She was at this time a member of the Oakland Federal Labor Union Number 5761 of the A.F. of L. She was also a member of the executive board of the newly formed Woman's Congress Association of the Pacific Coast, which had been formed to interest women "in matters which tend to improve moral and social conditions." She participated actively in its first convention, held in 1894, on the theme "Woman, and the Affairs of the World as They Affect and Are Affected by Her." The second annual weeklong event, held in 1895, had as its theme "The Home." Charlotte shared a panel with Robert Jordan, president of Stanford University, who discussed "The Woman of Pessimism and the Woman of Evolution," and Susan B. Anthony, who addressed the question "Shall

We Cooperate?" Charlotte spoke on the subject of "Organization in Home Industry." She had come a long way in a short time.

Charlotte's frenetic public activity in Oakland, her increasingly valued and important public work, existed alongside a traumatic private life characterized by a destructive personal relationship. It was as if her unconscious still felt fears voiced years before to Martha, fears that a rich and satisfying private love would distract from one's public mission. Perhaps Charlotte needed to prove to herself that she was capable of the world-work she saw as the measure of one's value before she could trust and respect herself and then find others who would value her. Till that time came, and it did not come for years, and it did not come until she had survived a long period of separation from all entangling alliances and demonstrated her ability to be alone, till that time came she found herself in one unsatisfactory relationship after another. While so desperate to be loved, she could not find an appropriate partner. When the desperation lessened, when she learned to be alone and to take care of herself, take charge of her own needs, then she was, "miraculously," able to find the personal happiness she had so long sought.

In the meantime, there was Adeline Knapp, soon affectionately called Delle, and, much later, in *The Living of Charlotte Perkins Gilman*, referred to as Dora. She was a reporter whose job took her alone around the world. Such women reporters were ordinarily literate and adventurous but likely not well-bred or cultivated, perhaps not even college-educated, for such a position was on the edge of respectability. We know very little about Delle, but it seems clear that she did not have family connections, she was not an intellectual, she was not involved in the reform network.

The two women were introduced to each other on May 11, 1891, just after Charlotte had lectured to the Woman's Club in Oakland, although she still lived in Pasadena. Charlotte was visiting the San Francisco area on a lecture tour following her successful participation in the annual PCWPA convention earlier in March, and was to remain there till mid-June. In her diary Charlotte reported that she had met and liked her. "Miss Knapp, newspaper woman," called the following day, then two days later on May 14, then again on May 17 when they, along with Kate, spent the day together. They became daily companions. Charlotte was going down again into a periodic low but she now had Miss Knapp to help her. June 2, she wrote, "was a wretched night—only made bearable by Miss Knapp's tender helpfulness. She is a dear woman." Two days later she confided to her journal that "we two happy together. She spends the night."

It is possible, but not certain, that Charlotte and Delle were lovers. Charlotte was a very physical person. She needed physical demonstrations, not necessarily sexual, of the affection she craved. For example, a later entry in her diary notes that a woman physician and friend, Dr. Gleason, whom she had been seeing a good deal professionally and personally, "sleeps with me." On and off she had also slept with Kate. On these occasions she seems to have needed special comforting. Years later, she wrote of a kindly patron with whom she was staying while traveling on the lecture circuit. When Mrs. Rogall came into her room to turn on the radiator, "I took her into bed for a good hug," she said. But the relationship with Delle was different, to be sure.

Years later, in 1899, Charlotte wrote to the man soon to be her husband of her special friendship with Delle. Is it meaningful that she changes the subject to Delle in her letter to her future husband just after she describes taking Mrs. Rogall "into bed for a good hug—and hurriedly plucking your letter from my bosom and secreting it under my bolster." For those words are immediately followed by: "A thought occurs to me goodness knows why! Adeline Knapp has (I suppose she has) letters of mine most fully owning the really passionate love I had for her. I loved her, trusted her, wrote her as freely as I wrote to you. I told you that I loved her that way. You ought to know that there is a possibility of such letters being dragged out some day."[4] She returned to the subject later in the letter:

> I am not sorry for nor ashamed of my life. . . . I see no reason, looking back, to regret one step. . . . But you must consider the disagreeable practical possibilities like this. Fancy San Francisco papers with a Profound Sensation in Literary Articles! Revelations of a Peculiar Past! Mrs. Stetson's Love Affair with a Woman. Is this Friendship! and so on. Dear Heart. *Am* I a woman you ought to marry? Are you willing to give such a mother to your son—or Daughters? Are you

sure you have understood when I told you "all"? Don't be afraid for me dear. I am not afraid to face the rest of life alone. I have always been alone in the past—and I have never been able fully to feel that the home joys were meant for me.

After she and Delle became intimate friends, which they seem to have done almost immediately, Charlotte had someone to look after her. Within ten days of being introduced, Charlotte "feels better—thanks to Miss Knapp" (May 21, 1891). She now discussed all her busy activities with Delle, who was barely on the periphery of this world. She made Delle a confidante and trusted intimate instantly.

When Charlotte returned home to Pasadena, she and Miss Knapp exchanged at least daily letters until Delle arrived in person in mid-July for a visit. Charlotte greeted her with two sonnets written for her, "To the Conquered" and "To the Conqueror." Charlotte had much to teach her "Delight," as she referred to Delle. They discussed Nationalism, she taught her chess. Charlotte read Ibsen's *Ghosts* to her one evening.[5]

At the end of the summer Delle sent her fifty dollars "to come with," and by mid-September Charlotte and Kate moved to Oakland. Within a short time Charlotte had borrowed one hundred dollars from Delle, the largest of the small debts she had incurred. It was Delle who presented her with her next year's diary, for 1892, as well as the one for the year following, and this gift was traditionally given Charlotte by the central person in her life.

In the fall of 1891, just after the relationship between Charlotte and Delle had reached a deep intensity, Mary Perkins left her son's home to live with Charlotte. Charlotte, her daughter, her mother, and her new friend all moved into two rooms of a boardinghouse; Mary Perkins with her grandchild Kate in one room, Delle and Charlotte in another. Charlotte was lecturing, writing, trying to float a class in "domestic sociology,"[6] devoting hours to a deepening friendship with Delle, and juggling the management of her daughter and mother.

The budding of a new and serious relationship with a loving friend under the scrutiny of her mother must have provided an extraordinarily difficult environment for Charlotte's not-very-steady nerves. True, Delle was helping with mother, daughter, finances, and Charlotte's now-pending divorce. (Charlotte had filed for divorce in 1892 in Alameda County, California, on grounds of willful neglect, though it was not granted until April 1984.) Still, their own new relationship needed attention as well.

Although Charlotte was severing her relationship with a husband she continued to describe as loving and tender in order to be free to test herself, she remained encumbered not only with her mother but also with a young child. After all the public activities that are recorded in her diary—meetings and speeches and conventions and classes—Charlotte returned each night to a home and family for which she was responsible.

Not surprisingly, she fell victim to growing exhaustion. Dr. Kellogg "says I put myself back 3 weeks by my exhaustion of yesterday," she wrote on October 29. Two weeks later, in a paper with the title "Our Maternal Duties," she urged dutiful daughters not to allow obligations to elderly parents to swallow up their lives, yet she undoubtedly felt she was doing just that. On Christmas Day, she noted that she celebrated Christmas "by a fit of hysterics in the morning." The following day she reported that Dr. Kellogg "doubts if I can stand the strain of our present family arrangement much longer." She commemorated the event with a church sermon on pain.[7] On December 31 she wrote, "I have another hysterical attack."

In February 1892, the newly constituted family, Charlotte with her mother, her daughter, and Delle, moved into a new boardinghouse in Oakland. Soon after their arrival, the owner turned her business operation over to Charlotte, who began to keep house and cook for a household that included nine boarders. Although for a time her mother boarded with Dr. Kellogg when the strain on Charlotte was perilous, the three generations of women were together much of the time, the central burden resting on Charlotte. That burden grew more taxing when, in September 1892, it was acknowledged that Mary was mortally ill with cancer. Charlotte's response was a complex one, in which guilt and anger undoubtedly played an important part. She had reason to feel anger and frustration at her mother's intrusion into her life. Finally free from marital duties, she was beginning a new loving relationship with a friend with whom she hoped she would share her life. She was working with limitless energy at her writing and lecturing. Suddenly she found herself stuck with a sick mother for whom she had never felt much respect or love. She surely felt great pity and sorrow for her, but there is no reason to suggest her fondness for or closeness to Mary grew at this time. To acknowledge fully such limited feelings for one's mother comes very hard. On learning of Mary's illness, Charlotte chose, as much as possible, to fill her days and nights with feverish activity to block out the reality around her. References in her diary occasionally indicate "Mother very low again,"[8] but add not a word about how that made Charlotte feel. She used her journal to express feelings about Delle, about how she responded to receptions at public events, about money troubles, but when it came to her dying mother she would not let her feelings out, even in her diary.

At this time Charlotte took so much responsibility on herself that one can only wonder if she was trying to demonstrate to Mary, to herself, and to the world what a good and loving daughter she really was, how many sacrifices she was prepared to make, even to the point of risking her own health, just as her mother had made those sacrifices for her. She was unwilling for so long to share responsibilities with hired servants or nurses—partly, but not entirely, one suspects, because of financial considerations—that inevitably her friends began to hover over *her*, to worry about *her* health. Dr. Kellogg, she wrote, "says I had better break down honestly now than be bolstered up and break more extensively later. A wise physician."[9] By December Charlotte was forced to admit: "It appears that I am sicker than I thought."

Events relating to the divorce added greatly to the strain on her. Charlotte's reputation as an activist and reformer made her divorce case lively material for newspaper reporters. The *Boston Globe* ran a story, the *San Francisco Chronicle* followed, and then the Hearst-owned *San Francisco Examiner* sent a reporter to interview her. Unsophisticated as she was about the nature of the enterprise of creating newsworthy events, Charlotte spoke freely to the reporter, but asked him not to make much of her personal situation since her mother was then upstairs dying of cancer. The result was a full page in the paper, with interviews from various people on the topic "Should Literary Women Marry?" During the fall of 1892 her name became, she said, "a football for all the papers on the coast." Charlotte was devastated; from that moment on she refused ever to publish a word in any Hearst publication.

Walter was no more tactful in his interview published in the *San Francisco Examiner* on December 20, 1892. He was quoted as saying that their married life was "quite pleasant" for a year or two, until Charlotte "espoused the Bellamy doctrine and began contributing letters on dress reform, discarded corsets, heel boots and the like, and practiced daily in a public gymnasium. She thought it her duty to sacrifice the domestic and conjugal relations for what she felt she was called to do in the cause of women's rights, dress reform and nationalism." Walter's public comments did not do much to quiet the public flurry, which continued a good deal longer.

On Christmas Day, 1892, the *San Francisco Examiner* summed up the force of the editorial assault:

> There are not many women, fortunately for humanity, who agree with Mrs. Stetson that any "work," literary, philanthropic, or political, is higher than that of being a good wife and mother.

There it was. She had rejected woman's highest work in order to pursue, selfishly, her own interests.

As her mother's death drew closer, Charlotte continued to write feverishly. "Nothing seems to seriously affect my power to write," she said in her diary on March 3, 1893. She had just finished a "short powerful paper" with the title "The Sex Question Answered" for the upcoming World Congress. She wrote the paper, she said, "in short, laborious efforts during these wretched days, and finished last night by mother's deathbed. She is very low now—going fast." The next day's entry referred to a short paper she completed which ended with the words, "The essential indecency of the dependence of one sex upon the other for a living is in itself sexual immorality," words addressed, perhaps, to her dying mother, a statement about her life. Two days later, Mary "passed away at 2:10 very quietly." A small funeral was held, at the end of which Frederick Perkins took the body to Los Angeles for cremation. Within a few days Charlotte was back to writing and lecturing at her usual frantic pace. She never gave herself time to grieve.

The last months before Mary's death provided Charlotte with a rich opportunity finally to say goodbye to her mother, to sever, to acknowledge the reality and legitimacy of her own anger and then put it to rest, to forgive her mother or not, to understand Mary's limitations that so scarred and hurt her children, to comprehend the dimensions of her complicated feelings for this unhappy and embittered woman. But Charlotte could not let go. She held her breath, plunged ahead, and then in March of 1893 Mary died and it was too late.

During her California years, however, and particularly after her mother's death, Charlotte was more successful in sorting out her feelings for her father. When she had been settled in California for three years without any communication from him, he called on her in Pasadena on March 19, 1891—"in the morning, and meets his granddaughter for the first time. No emotion amongst us," she wrote in her journal. Later on somebody, probably Charlotte, scratched out that last entry with two dark parallel lines, and we can be sure that there was indeed emotion in that room, however firmly denied. The following day Charlotte recorded that he had called again; no comment is added. Two months later she was dropping in to see him. During this period Charlotte was beginning to proceed with the divorce action, and her own need to free herself from her mate may have contributed to a reassessment of her father's desertion of his family years before.

In her autobiography, Charlotte wrote with anger of her mother's sitting patiently by the window in Oakland, looking toward San Francisco, waiting in vain for her former husband to visit her as she lay dying. Still, he came to see his daughter the day after Mary died, and they began to keep in touch as they never had before. He continued to be in and out of her life, contributing a small monthly allowance to her for a while. Despite the lectures and the boardinghouse, Charlotte was unable to sustain herself without constant small loans, from Grace, from Dr. Channing, from Delle, from her father, and from many others. Charlotte was at last asking and Frederick was at last responding to the needs of his daughter, now an adult woman, in ways he had not been able to when she was a child. One can be fairly sure that they never talked much about their tensions, the distance he kept from his family, or Charlotte's suffering from that rejection, but in small

"Portrait of Mother (as a young girl) by Lincoln (in oval frame)" *(Photograph by Pearl Grace Loehr, 1915, Courtesy of the Schlesinger Library, Radcliffe College)*

ways they were able to mend their estrangement when Mary was no longer a presence between them.

Before long, Frederick married Frankie Johnson, the love of his youth, and it is possible that Mary's death freed both father and daughter to begin to reach out to each other and to others in ways they had felt unable to do while Mary lived.

Mary's illness and subsequent death inevitably affected Charlotte's relationship with Delle as well. Charlotte turned increasingly to her new, dear friend for help and support as the pressures brought on by Mary's sickness mounted, pressures heightened by the financial strain of new loans to float the boardinghouse and then by the coverage in the *San Francisco Chronicle* about the impending divorce. In the midst of these difficulties, Delle was sent on a lengthy assignment in Hawaii. Charlotte turned to another woman in their circle, Harriet Howe, who had taken a room in their house in mid-September. "Hattie moves in," Charlotte had written then. "Bless her heart. We all love her and wear her out with many services."[10] Delle was away when Charlotte's mother died, and Charlotte turned to Hattie for sustenance. On April 5 Charlotte noted Delle's return from Hawaii with joy: "I am absurdly glad to see her." Although they were living by then in separate rooms, they slept together the night of her return. But then we know she sometimes shared a bed with friends to obtain comfort in times of stress, and she had in fact slept with Hattie on and off during those difficult weeks.

Meantime, tension between Charlotte and Delle had begun to develop, perhaps exacerbated by Hattie's presence. Delle was a woman who worked hard at being ingratiating. She clung excessively and when she was rebuffed, she made scenes, humiliating public scenes. She was possessive and had difficulty sharing. If Charlotte was not an easy person to live with, neither was Delle. By early May Charlotte was writing in her diary of "trouble with Delle over the yard and other things." A few days later she recorded: "All along lately hard times with Delle." The following day: "Scene with Delle all the way up from ferry to house in the car." Two days later Delle "decides to leave the house. I have so desired since last August—and often asked her to."[11] Delle moved temporarily to Dr. Kellogg's, which seems to have been the stopping-off place for Charlotte's troublesome houseguests. Their connection continued with occasional picnics and dinners. But the tensions were not eliminated by their new living arrangements, for Delle moved back in, and troubles resumed. July 6: "Delle comes up and spoils the rest of my evening. She and her affection!" July 12: "General disturbance with Delle." July 13: "Much perturbation in the family owing to Delle." July 15: Delle's "behavior has been such as to gradually alienate my affection. . . . It is a great relief to have her go." A relief it may have been, but it did not happen so smoothly. August 7: "Delle calls early and is so offensive." August 16: "Go to Call office. Delle attaches herself to me there. Great difficulty in getting home alone—she sticks so!" By the fall Delle was still in and out of the house; Charlotte was unable to terminate their relationship.

In early 1893 Charlotte was finally able to force the permanent break she had sought for months but somehow had been unable to bring about. A signed and dated statement by Delle, which appears to be a part of a letter but is not clearly identified and was kept by Charlotte among her papers, describes the end of their relationship in vague and evasive terms:

> I left Mrs. Stetson's house for Mrs. Stetson's good. Very ill temper and unreasonable contact having rendered it impossible for her longer to endure it. I would have remained had not my remaining sense of decency driven me away.[12]

Alongside this written statement, in Charlotte's hand, in pencil, with no clue as to when they were written, are the words "She's dead."

It is not clear whose ill temper did what, but it is clear that Delle cast herself as the one making the noble sacrifice; her remaining sense of decency required her departure. Within a year she wrote again. She had a debt to another party which she could not repay; would Charlotte help? Her request has the insinuating tone that seems to have characterized her mode of dealing with Charlotte: "Any amount you may deem yourself owing me I shall consider more than cancelled if you can devise some way of lifting this responsibility." If Charlotte cannot "devise some way" of paying a debt that is not hers but that is related to the debt she owes Delle, although Delle pointedly does not ask for its repayment directly, then Delle will have to "let Pussie go for her keep," adding that "I need not tell you how hard that would be for me." In fact, Delle says, had she been able to sell her pet cat for the amount owed she would have done so, rather than "mention this matter to you, but I see nothing else to do."[13] It is a letter of emotional blackmail and indirection.

In her autobiography, written many years later, Charlotte gave vent to strong angry feelings concerning Adeline/Dora. Indeed, her reminiscence of that relationship is filled with straightforward fury:

> Harder than everything else to me was the utter loss of the friend with whom I had sincerely hoped to live continually . . . (but) later I learned that she was one of those literary vampires who fasten themselves on one author. . . . The kindest thing I can say of her character is that she had had an abcess at the base of her brain, and perhaps it affected her moral sense . . . she was malevolent. . . . She drank. . . . She swore freely. . . . She lifted her hand to strike me in one of her tempers. . . . What did matter was the subtle spreading of slanders about me . . . I do know of similar mischief-making from her in regard to others. At any rate that solace ended not only in pain but in shame that I should have been so gullible, so ignorant, as to love her dearly.[14]

While one can guess about whom she was writing, she did not even call this "malevolent" person by the pseudonym she had assigned; she was simply "the friend."

Charlotte's diary entries written at the time of the breakup adopt a very different tone. Her daily diary had reflected, if only with a few words or a phrase, the immense joy and growing tension of the love she had felt and then begun to lose with Delle. But when the end loomed, the emotions shut off: "Delle packs. I write 'A True Wife' "[15] Did she see the irony? Then on December 31, 1893—at Charlotte's yearly summing-up time—the diary tersely notes: "My last love proves even as others."[16]

What solution did she pose for these persistent unsatisfying and short-lived loves? "Out of it all I ought surely to learn final detachment from personal concern." She was still locking herself into the either/or world which she inhabited in her early twenties.

Why did Charlotte's relationship with Delle fail? One can only speculate. They rushed into it precipitately, the two of them, without adequate knowledge of each other and without giving themselves time to explore each other. And one never knows to what extent a failure in love is caused by bad timing, and the timing was certainly not favorable in this case. In this relationship Delle was the lesser-known person; it was Charlotte who was the public figure, the knowledgeable partner who taught her friend about politics and about socialism, as well as chess. It was Delle, the working journalist, who came up with needed money, who helped out at crucial moments with Kate and Mary. Charlotte seems to have enjoyed the role of mentor and she surely needed the emotional support Delle initially offered, but perhaps Delle did not like the role of the lesser partner, the helpmeet, the one who was expected to do the deferring. Both were needy women who required attention. It seems to have been a relationship in certain ways not unlike that with Walter, except that with Delle, Charlotte was the more powerful partner. Charlotte, as we have seen, was still probably too unsure of herself, too frightened and burdened by emotions she sought to brush away, to establish a solid, mutually giving relationship with anyone. But it also seems evident that a woman as difficult as Adeline Knapp, her Delle, was the right choice for a relationship that would not work, the right choice for a relationship that would only demonstrate again to Charlotte how unworthy she truly was and how the "home joys" were not meant for her.

Charlotte was also put off by Delle's unladylike ways, her rough language, her drinking, the kind of behavior Charlotte would have seen as somewhat vulgar. Charlotte was ultimately more comfortable with a very different kind of working woman, that represented by Helen Campbell, who was of an older generation, well-mannered, more restrained, more familiar to someone of Charlotte's background. Delle was independent but not well-bred. Time together, and Mary's death, brought to the surface all of the incompatibilities that had been hidden.

It was not necessarily by chance that the friendship with Delle ran concurrently with the last phase of Charlotte's engagement with her mother. In certain ways Charlotte projected onto Delle the unresolved ties that held her to Mary. Delle, like a parent, provided warmth and security and even financial assistance. She was, in the end, not a loving parent, any more than Mary had been; Delle too was rejecting. But Charlotte dealt with her with more direct anger than she had ever been able to muster with her mother. With Delle there was, eventually, closure. Just as Charlotte had earlier taken on her father in the person of Silas Weir Mitchell, so now, perhaps, she faced her mother through Adeline Knapp. In both cases the resolutions were incomplete because they were indirect and unclear, but they constituted another important step in Charlotte's life and growth, and in losing both her mother and Delle, Charlotte was freed from two more involvements, two more entanglements that had pulled at her, perhaps held her back.

There remained, of course, Kate. Early in 1893 Charlotte was able to write of her daughter's life: "Kate is doing well. Having just the uneventful ordinary emotionless childhood I wanted for her."[17] How revealing of Charlotte is her wish for an "emotionless childhood" for her daughter. One wonders how uneventful Kate's life could have been under the circumstances, with a mother who was an active public figure and was also running a boardinghouse; with a grandmother dying of cancer at home; with the turbulence Delle brought into her life; with her parents' private lives being publicly examined in a most scandalous way. True, Charlotte and her household did live on a safe and quiet street in Oakland, with a yard for Kate to play in, near a pleasant school for her to attend, but it seems more accurate to say that Kate was managing well her very eventful emotional childhood.

The only "eventful" occurrence Charlotte acknowledged in her autobiography was that Kate, as a girl of eight or nine, learned from some "unbelievable brute" that her mother and father were getting divorced and her father was immediately to marry again. Kate "came to me in tears," said Charlotte, but the smiles broke through, we are told, when she learned that her new stepmother was to be the Grace "she had known and loved since babyhood, loved as another mother."[18] What Charlotte did not examine was how traumatic it must have been to learn such news from an outside source, nor did she explain why she had not herself first told Kate.

Within a very short time afterwards life altered profoundly for Charlotte and Kate. Mary died. Charlotte ended the relationship with Delle. The divorce was granted in Alameda County, California, in April 1894, Charlotte Stetson plaintiff, Walter Stetson defendant, on grounds of willful neglect. The boardinghouse had always drained Charlotte's energies, limiting her ability to write and speak, but now it seemed unmanageable. Meanwhile, as she said in her autobiography:

> There was new work opening for me in San Francisco, but in a place unsuitable for a child. It was arranged that [Kate] should go to her father for a while, my father, going East, taking her with him.

Charlotte did not mention here that she hastily sent Kate off just before Grace and Walter's wedding, so that they had to welcome the child as they were about to be married and make arrangements for Grace's family to care for her during the honeymoon. It seems clear that Charlotte was uncertain as to how long she expected this separation to last. Her decision seems almost impulsive, spontaneous. Months later, on January 9, 1895, she wrote to Grace, "Some day I shall be with her again—God knows when," and while Charlotte probably hoped to share her home with Kate sooner rather than later, in fact she did not do so until Kate was into her teens. Despite the speed with which it was acted upon, the decision was equally agreeable to father, mother, and stepmother, and it was a wise one. Grace was clearly the more nurturing of the two women, the one who could better mother Katharine.

Charlotte continued the story in her autobiography:

> Since her second mother was fully as good as the first, better in some ways perhaps; since the father longed for his child . . . and since the child had a right to know and love her father—I did not mean her to suffer the losses of my youth— this seemed the right thing to do. No one suffered from it but myself.

Of course, many people suffered, probably Kate most of all. After all, Kate had not seen her father in years, and nobody had asked her what she wanted to do or explained to her why she had to do what she had to do. "I never once let her feel that it was pain, a break, anything unusual," wrote Charlotte, and off she went "happily enough." As Charlotte said of Kate, "she climbed gaily aboard. . . . We smiled and waved and threw kisses to each other."

All of them were involved in a conspiracy of silence, of withholding the feelings they harbored; everybody was behaving well. "That was thirty years ago," wrote Charlotte. "I have to stop typing and cry as I tell about it."[19]

Charlotte never stopped longing for Kate. "I find I grow more sensitive, rather than less," she wrote to Grace in the fall of 1895.[20] Someday "she will be with me again," said Charlotte, remembering the "five lovely years when I could read to her . . . one of the few things I could do." Two years later her mother's anguish was barely diminished:

> I *know* that she is in all ways better off with you than with me now. But sometimes it gets out . . . pure selfish longing. And one wakes up the others—as in lunatic wards they say and I ache a thousand ways at once.

Many of the ideas that later came to be worked out in *Herland*, Charlotte's feminist utopian fantasy, probably have their roots in this part of her life. In her utopian fiction she created worlds in which mothers such as she would not suffer the torments of hell, a world in which mothering was socialized and all mothers cared for all children. But the world in which she resided was no utopia. It felt more like a lunatic ward.

There was another side to Charlotte's decision to have Kate live with her father and new stepmother. Just before the separation from Kate, Charlotte wrote in her diary: "I am about to give up my home, send Kate to her father, and begin new: being now a free woman, legally and actually."[21] By parting from Katharine, Charlotte freed herself from domestic responsibilities, responsibilities she had great difficulty managing, and freed herself for the career and independent life she craved.

Charlotte did indeed give up her home in Oakland, as she said, but settled into another one, in San Francisco, in the summer of 1894. Oakland had been a failure, as she assessed it, leaving behind debts and unhappiness. In San Francisco, as we have seen, she began afresh with the *Impress*. As important, perhaps more important, was a new family constellation she gathered around her, one which consisted of her two new colleagues on the journal, who shared half a house with her. "I have a Home, a Mother, a Brother, am

loved and cared for, life sort of settled it would appear," she wrote.[22]
The "mother" was Helen Campbell, the first of several adopted
mothers for Charlotte, and "far nearer to me than my own dear
mother," she later said, and the "brother" was Paul Tyner. So she
traded in her biological family for a new one. Instead of heading a
household with a dying mother and a young daughter, she now
lived in one where a competent, loving woman, twenty-one years
her senior, was pleased to take charge and let Charlotte, even though
she was to edit the paper, be cast as daughter.

However, Charlotte's life soon changed again when the *Impress*
foundered after a mere five months under its new management. A
number of factors contributed to its demise. Little magazines in
general have a short life. This one had cut itself loose from the
official connection it had to the PCWPA, and tried to broaden itself
beyond strictly women's issues, with resulting political controversy
within the women's movement. But scandal also seriously weakened the position of the new journal. The entire Charlotte-Walter-
Grace relationship was a cause of malicious gossip; when the divorce
was finally over and Kate went to live with her father and Grace,
outrage erupted again.

The fiasco of the *Impress*, said Charlotte, "showed me my standing" in San Francisco. Helen Campbell, perplexed at the lack of
editorial and financial support the magazine was able to rally, was
told that "nothing that Mrs. Stetson does can succeed here." One
of the charges leveled against Charlotte was that she published a
poem of Grace's in the first issue.[23]

The situation in San Francisco, so attractive just a few months
before, was falling apart. When the *Impress* venture failed, Helen
Campbell decided to leave California, and Charlotte felt suddenly
very much alone, although several of her friends rallied to her
support.

Mary Austin wrote in her autobiography, *Earth Horizon*, that
she did what she could to defend Charlotte's "freedom from convention that left her the right to care for her child in what seemed
the best way to her."[24] Charles Lummis, editor of *Land of Sunshine*,
a prominent and successful regional journal, which published work
by both Charlotte Stetson and Grace Channing, stood by her. But
the "family" was gone. And the public, whose evaluation was so

important to her sense of self-worth, had turned its back on her—at least in San Francisco.

In the summer of 1895 she left San Francisco. "I had warm personal friends," she wrote, "but the public verdict was utter condemnation."[25] Not entirely. She had arrived in California in 1888 a broken and frightened woman. She had achieved a great deal in the following years. She had won the public endorsement and private support of William Dean Howells and Edward Bellamy. She had become a critic, published poet, lecturer, and writer, known and respected in radical and reform circles. She was under a great deal of public criticism when she left San Francisco, but the criticism itself testified to the public success she had achieved.

"I am going east," she decided.[26] She had a speaking engagement in Sacramento: that would get her out of San Francisco. She had an invitation from the social reformer Jane Addams, who had met and liked her, to come for an extended visit to Hull House, the famous Chicago settlement house she had founded—and that would get her to the Midwest, with a place to stay, to collect herself. It was time to take to the road.

Charlotte was now thirty-five years old and she had never lived without dependence upon a family—her own by birth or marriage or an adopted one—to define her, embrace her, often to smother her. Now, by setting out alone, truly alone for the first time, she continued her healing process. She had tested herself in California and had achieved a reputation as a respected and valued social critic. Now she was about to test herself as a person, a woman, alone. She was without structure in her life—without plans, money, family. She was free of responsibilities to others and obligations to others, but she was therefore also without supporting family and friends nearby. It was a frightening and lonely moment. But, she said, "I was alive and had my work to do."[27]

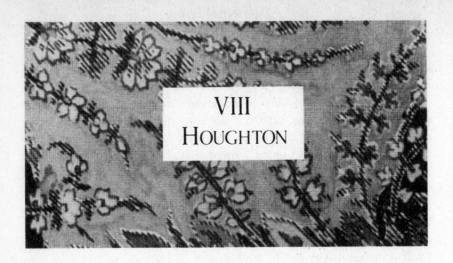

VIII
HOUGHTON

On her way to Chicago Charlotte was asked to write her name and address in a visitor's book in Los Angeles, her last stop before leaving California. She wrote: "Charlotte Perkins Stetson. At Large." For the next five years, from 1895 until her second marriage in 1900, that was her address.[1] She traveled back and forth across the nation, up and down from North to South, and across the ocean to England. There was, as she phrased it, no address to which to send her remains in case of accident.

The task she had set for herself was "to find out what ailed society, and how most easily and naturally to improve it." The task she achieved was to preach and lecture ceaselessly to hundreds of thousands of people in five years and to put her thoughts together in the book that gave her immediate international acclaim.

Charlotte left California in the summer of 1895, heading to Chicago, where she spent the fall and winter at Hull House. The decaying Hull mansion, located in Chicago's Nineteenth Ward, had become Hull House, the pioneer American settlement house, only six years before, in 1889, when Jane Addams and her close friend, Ellen Gates Starr, had founded it. By the time Charlotte arrived, Hull House already had a strong reputation for providing community service with its more than forty clubs, gymnasium, day nursery, and varieties of courses and lectures. More than two thousand residents from the neighborhood, most of them immigrants, passed through its doors weekly. Addams, who earned an international reputation as a social critic and peace activist, made Hull House her home until her death forty-six years later.

Jane Addams had called Charlotte her "one bright spot in San Francisco" in an earlier letter to Helen Campbell. Now it was to Hull House that Charlotte went, to the nurturing soil of that community of remarkable women residents, for one of Addams' skills was in attracting exceptional people, most of them women, who lived in Hull House for a period of time and contributed their talents to the institution and to the community. Jane Addams, said her biographer Allen Davis, created "a sense of unity, a sense of purpose among the residents,"[2] and if Charlotte already had a sense of purpose before she left California, she was in need of a community of people who shared her goals and who would take her in.

Hull House was, in the words of social critic Henry Demarest Lloyd, "the best club in Chicago."[3] Through it passed settlement-house workers from across the nation and beyond, Fabian intellectuals, labor leaders, professors from the University of Chicago, founded three years after Hull House, among them the sociologist Albion Small, the economist Robert T. Ely, the philosopher John Dewey—all frequent visitors. But it was the extraordinary group of women who gave Hull House its special stamp: women like Julia Lathrop, Florence Kelley, Grace Abbott, and Alice Hamilton. It was, said Davis, a "training ground for new professional careers as experts and administrators in government, industry, and the university."[4] For Charlotte it was a place to breathe, to take stock, to participate in a community with which she could identify and from whom she could gain support. Although each resident had a room, it was considered "in some way selfish" to stay in it; one was expected to participate in the communal life of the settlement house. Hull House stood for "common humanity and *social* democracy," wrote Charlotte to Grace, and Jane Addams "might be President of the United States to the great advantage of the country."[5]

Hull House gave Charlotte a chance to catch her breath and make her plans. It was, as she said to Grace, "meat and drink to me to be among people who *care*. . . . It is the kind of home I am most at home in," because she was a "small fish in a large pond— well stocked with bigger ones." Charlotte immediately assured Grace that she did not mean "that I believe any of these to be greater women or with greater work than I," but they were sufficiently important to "make no bones of me."[6] She decided to stay till the following summer (though, in fact, she left before that), then go East to visit friends, then head to New York or Boston to spend the winter with Helen Campbell, then on to London for a year, and then to Paris, after which she would "get back my pencil power," go home to Pasadena, and "build a house, with a career in lecturing, writing, teaching and preaching." This five-year plan did not include Katharine. Most of these plans were never realized, but the world of Hull House gave Charlotte a chance to dream while she planned her strategies for the time ahead.

Charlotte worked at Hull House, lectured a good deal, wrote some poems, talked, felt herself of value, but one among many. While she set herself on the margin of the women's movement, she nevertheless grew in its nourishing soil. She was formed, ideologically and politically, in the burgeoning reform activities of the 1880s and 1890s. She took what she needed and went off on her own, but it was the world in which she grew. It was, as she said, the kind of home in which she was at home, not a domestic setting but a social one. It gave her a place.

Throughout the five-year period that began with her stay at Hull House, she worked for the suffrage movement, though she did not see it as a panacea, and spoke for socialism, believing it to be a good system, "in spite of the mishandling of Marx."[7] She wrote frequently for and was contributing editor to the *American Fabian*, a journal espousing Fabian Socialism as it was developing in the United States. The Fabian Society had been founded in London in 1883, on the belief that capitalism had produced great inequity and that the remedy rested with socialism, or "cooperative collectivism," which was seen as inevitable and as emerging from the process of capitalist development. Unlike the Marxists, the Fabians did not aspire to be or expect to become a mass movement. They saw themselves as having primarily a middle-class constituency whose goal was slowly to educate the larger community. They believed in gradual change, rejecting the idea that revolutionary struggle was necessary or possible. By suggesting that socialism did not necessitate violence and that much of its program could be brought about piecemeal by elections, over time, it made the idea of socialism more generally acceptable. The Fabian movement, a force of considerable significance in the United Kingdom, had influence in the United States as well, where its ideological and political position was much like that developed by the Nationalist movement.

From the inception of their organization, the Fabians demanded universal suffrage, citing the cause of women's rights as foremost on their agenda. One of the most prominent Fabians, George Bernard Shaw, in particular argued that capitalism had to be transformed into socialism if women ever were to achieve legal and economic equality, because capitalism, he insisted, acted on women as a relentless pressure forcing them to enter into sexual relations for money, in marriage or out of it. Although Charlotte did not much like what she had heard about Shaw, his ideas were, in general, quite compatible with hers. The New York Fabians, in fact, believed that Charlotte "was a worthy female counterpart of G. B. Shaw."[8]

The *American Fabian* proclaimed that the principle of individualism and unrestricted competition, once believed to offer a solution to economic and social problems, had proved itself deficient and must be replaced by the principle of solidarity, the principle that recognized that the interest of each is inseparable from the interest of all. The Fabian movement saw progress being achieved through reason, not force. Charlotte wrote frequently for the journal, contributing to a long-term series called "First Class in Sociology," a brief exposition on the principles of collectivism.

Charlotte's speaking engagements during these five years took her around the nation; she was on the road most of the time in Milwaukee, Detroit, Chicago, Providence, Philadelphia, Kansas City, Rochester, Omaha, Washington, D.C., New York, Newark, Iowa City, Kalamazoo, St. Louis, Memphis, Atlanta, and Birmingham. She was paid $5, $25, $50 per lecture—$10 was about the average—and she boarded with friends and followers, who took her in, applauded her, fed her, and listened to her. Some of her lectures were "Collective Ethics," "Duties Domestic and Other," "America's Place Today," "Heroes We Need Now," "A New Way to Heaven," "The New Motherhood," "Woman Suffrage and Man's Sufferings," "How to Get Good and Stay So," and "The Social Organism." When she went over her papers many years later in the preparation of her autobiography, she penciled in the margin of the sheets that listed her lecture tours, "I was busy then," something of an understatement. She lectured on topics appropriate for sermons, for clubs and parlor meetings, for a series of courses.

Early in 1896 she was a delegate to a suffrage convention in Washington, D.C., where she addressed the Judiciary Committee of the House of Representatives, renewed her friendship with "Aunt Susan" (Susan B. Anthony), and most exciting of all, met sociologist Lester F. Ward, "quite the greatest man I have ever known." The Wards hosted a reception for Charlotte, having been fans of hers since the publication of her poem "Similar Cases," and she having been a follower of his since his article in the *Forum* of 1888 describing his gynocentric theory, which Charlotte called "the greatest single contribution to the world's thought since Evolution."[9]

Meanwhile, her personal duties, she said, were to Katharine, Walter, Grace, her brother Thomas, his wife Margaret, and their son Basil, as well as to her father and new stepmother and stepsisters. Frederick had finally married "the love of his youth, now his widowed aunt," Frankie Johnson, whose husband had shot himself. While in Washington, Charlotte had visited the home of her father, his wife, and her three adopted daughters. "It was literally the first time I had ever been in my father's house since infancy, and at that it was only a boarding-house, kept by my step-mother," she said. Her father was "probably trying to arrange for some employment."[10] Frederick Perkins suffered from deteriorating physical health during these years. Ultimately, he broke down completely and was placed in a sanitarium, where Charlotte visited him when her lectures brought her nearby. "He seemed to value my coming— so long as he knew me." He lingered until 1900. "Softening of the brain. It is not right that a brilliant intellect should be allowed to sink to idiocy, and to die hideously." Someday, she stated, "when we are more civilized, we shall not maintain such a horror."[11]

In her annual self-assessment on her first New Year's Day on her own, in 1896, she described her state of mind in these words:

> I am now thirty-five years and six months old. As far as I can judge my work lies mainly in public speaking, in writing for a purpose and in organizing. My personality still stands in my way somewhat. I must not forget to apply to myself the truth I preach to others.

While it is not certain what she meant by the words "My personality still stands in my way," my guess is that she was referring to her unsteady nerves, her sense of her own emotional instability.

During this period of continued activity, Charlotte's health followed its cyclical patterns, with periodic depressions, "the same old misery and exhaustion." Her busy activity in the winter of 1896, she reported to Grace, was "very profitable in living and has helped me in the world's esteem. But it has been very hard indeed on my health." The return of the "intense nervous weakness and depression" was sufficient to "make me feel that I can not live so for any length of time." So bad did she feel that her "mother"— Helen Campbell—sent her to see Dr. McCracken, the female half of a married couple, both physicians. Her health may have been bad, but it did not stop her from speaking four nights running on women's suffrage, "and the last was better than the first." Her diagnosis? "Health comes at once as I take the field again. I shall always have to keep moving I fancy."[12] Just as her mother's dying did not interfere with her writing, so her own depressions did not prevent her successful lecturing.

Her next year's summing-up, on January 5, 1897, described her life as "strangely quiet now. All the wants are gone, and all the pains." Her sole goal was to get well and work. "I can write an hour or two a day without breaking down," she wrote. As always, the diary includes details about money and lists: lists that cover money she hoped to make, money she had to use for living, money she needed to pay off debts, how many poems she had to write per week at how much apiece, how many novels per year, and how much in royalties and lectures she might earn, always figuring down to the smallest amounts, the entire year's calculation adding up to under $5,000 in income, a reasonable expectation at the time, although one she did not achieve. Her goal was to improve for three more years, during which time she should be able to earn $5,000 annually and know that she could have a "clear contented mind" with "steady quiet easy work." She must be sure she is whole and functioning, she must not too quickly reward herself.

I must come out forever from the feelings of shame and regret. Must leave off the past more fully than ever before. Must feel and be a strong brave happy useful honorable woman.

She must, she told herself, earn her happiness. "To be worthy, *worthy*." From today, "to live as I would wish my daughter—as I would wish all women to live."

In March of 1897, Charlotte Stetson dropped into the Wall Street office of her cousin, George Houghton Gilman, to solicit legal advice from him. They began a new friendship, their contact having lapsed for some years. This friendship, essentially carried out through the written word, was to culminate in their marriage three years later.

George Houghton Gilman was born on August 8, 1867, in Norwich, Connecticut, where he remained through his early years. He was the son of William Coit and Katherine Beecher (Perkins) Gilman. His mother was Charlotte's father's sister, so he and Charlotte were first cousins.

Houghton was educated first in the Norwich Free Academy. He entered Columbia University at the age of sixteen, and after graduation he studied law at the Johns Hopkins University, where his uncle, Daniel Coit Gilman, was president. Houghton had a reputation as a man of learning and culture. He loved music, particularly opera, and he owned a fine phonograph and listened often to his favorite symphonies on it. He was something of a Latin and Greek scholar, who also did calculus to entertain himself. His skills went as well in the direction of languages other than the classical ones. Katharine remembered her stepfather reading *The Three Musketeers* to her in English from a French edition and, she said, "no one would have guessed that he was not reading from an English translation." At the time he and Charlotte resumed their friendship, he was a member of Company B, 7th Regiment, New York, having enlisted in July 1888 as a member of the Guard. (He later resigned from the regiment, in 1906, said Katharine, because her mother hated the idea that he might be called upon to act as a strikebreaker.)[13]

Charlotte and Houghton had had a sweet and playful relationship as young cousins; for Charlotte that early connection proved important. To a thirteen-year-old boy the grown-up twenty-year-old cousin wrote:

O long suffering youth! Behold me on my knees! I did get your other letter and, wretch that I am! left it unanswered

George Houghton Gilman

till this late date. But I had good excuse after all, for the wild vortex of dissipation in which I have been plunged during my holidays was enough to stop any correspondence.

Charlotte wrote to "Oh guileless infant" of her festive trip to Boston, "that fairy city," where she recounted tales of sleighing, parties, theatergoing, and a variety of other joys and pleasures. Their regular exchange of letters during this period reflects a warm, comfortable set of feelings on Charlotte's side, including a slightly superior, more knowledgeable older-sister stance. She offered advice on the best method to learn Pitman shorthand. In mid-December of 1879 she mentioned a poem recently sent to her "Young Friend," as well as instructions on how to make a plaster cast of an object. "Write soon to your loving cousin," she admonished him in the fall of 1879.[14] To "Dear Ho" in March 1880[15] she wrote applauding his expert skill on the bicycle, "for I love the beast myself," she said, "and only wish 'we girls' could ride them." Bicycles were still not quite respectable. "I have seen them flitting dimly by at dusk," she wrote to him, "bestridden by a spectral Brown student, who feared derision by daylight." Her letters to Ho are also charmingly illustrated.

George Houghton Gilman, Charlotte's Ho, suffers from the invisibility ordinarily associated with the wives of famous men. Despite his prominent family, despite his solid credentials in the professional world, Ho did not make a mark in the usual ways that permit a biographer to trace his life. He was not an aggressive, ambitious, competitive attorney. He did not make much money, it seems clear, from his Wall Street practice, or later, when he moved to Norwich, from his practice there. What little can be gleaned about him from what others have said suggests a gentle, reserved, kind, and lovable man, who put the considerable strength and energy that he possessed into sustaining strong bonds of marriage and family rather than into advancing a career.

We know so little about Ho partly because Charlotte said virtually nothing about him in her autobiography, which has led to a great deal of speculation about the nature of their marriage. Indeed, there are only three brief references to Ho in her memoirs. The first described her arrival in Detroit in 1900, and being met "by my cousin G. H. Gilman of New York, and we were married—

and lived happily ever after. If this were a novel, now, here's the happy ending." The second reference was to a vegetable garden behind her home in Connecticut "which Mr. Gilman and I cultivate with our own hands."[16] The final reference dealt with her last illness and his death.

We do know something about the courtship because of its epistolary nature, although the record is incomplete. Ho kept Charlotte's letters; she did not keep his. She did not keep most of her letters, probably because of her nomadic life; her rootlessness, psychological and geographic, gave her a sense of impermanence that discouraged burdensome baggage. She was, until her marriage to Houghton, traveling light through life. She did make sure, however, to take care of her precious journals and diaries.

The letters are especially important because Ho and Charlotte seldom met, so that the courtship was essentially carried out through the mails. For three years she wrote to him often, usually every day, sometimes more than once a day. Most of the letters were somewhere between eight and ten pages long. She described what she did, what she wore, what she ate, what she said, what she read, what she saw, and, perhaps most important, how she felt. Charlotte was more self-examining in her letters to Houghton than she was in her diary, because in her letters she was purposefully trying to present herself to Ho as she was, to force him to accept her, if he was to accept her, without any deceptions or illusions. The entire range of concerns that she was able only to hint at with Walter, when she was an inarticulate, uncertain, untested young woman, she was able to explore and expose as a more worldly woman in her late thirties, having lived and suffered and tasted substantial personal and professional triumphs and defeats.

In these passionate, tormented, ecstatic, raging, self-demeaning, exuberant letters, one glimpses the Charlotte that resided under, alongside, the controlled, rational, disciplined person. In the course of presenting herself to Houghton with honesty and integrity, she was able to work through some of her fears and anxieties. In this way she was once again working things out through talking. I believe Charlotte said things to Houghton that she had never said to anyone else. He was not a stranger. He was the family she had never had.

It was natural for Charlotte to be herself, to share with a loved one, through the vehicle of a letter. She knew something had actually occurred when she wrote about it, when she explored an event she had experienced. Reality was confirmed when it was committed to a page. This concept clearly applied in her work. She took her woman's life, her experiences, and first talked about them in her lectures, and then wrote about them in her books, and so merged the world of her mother, the woman's world of experiencing and feeling, with the man's world, her father's, of thought and rationality, thereby demonstrating the necessary integration and dependence of the private and the public, the felt and the thought, the heart and the head, thereby also demonstrating the impossibility of separating either aspect of life from the other and the utter foolishness of assigning one to a particular sex. Her calling, as a woman in the Beecher clan, was to translate her life into words. Her famous male Beecher relatives, the best-known being Uncle Henry Ward, had achieved success through eloquent spoken words, but the best-known of the Beecher aunts, Harriet and Catharine, had done so through the written word. It was the vocation at which her father had failed.

The sizable collection of letters from Charlotte to Ho that began in 1897 and ended with their marriage have such force and intensity, even in the reading eight decades later, that it is tempting to draw some conclusions about the character of the man who was bombarded with these almost daily communications. However reserved his expression of feeling—and Charlotte periodically berated him for his reserve—Houghton must have had emotions that matched hers, as well as a reservoir of security in his loving feelings, to have accepted those cascading words, to have accepted them without retreating from them or being consumed by them.

This correspondence is crucial to an understanding of Charlotte because in these letters she struggled again with old issues, but this time she came closer to resolution. This time she had found someone she could trust, someone she believed would not abandon her, reject her, but would stay and understand and accept and love. And she was right. Charlotte, who had always felt comfortable and safe with words, communicating at a safe distance, took those three years to present herself to the man who became her husband in a way she would not have been able to before. Much of what remained bottled up and withheld from Walter Stetson was unleashed to Houghton in lengthy letters written while Charlotte toured the country, lectured extensively, wrote *Women and Economics*, and traveled to Europe to participate in international conferences. Charlotte's love for Houghton was created in these letters.

Very shortly after Charlotte and Houghton met again as adults, he began the correspondence, even while she was still in New York. "Pleasing and Desirable Cousin," she wrote in answer to the letter of his that "gives me a most disproportionate pleasure—same as you do!" She had "such a good time the other night" that he floats and hovers in her brain "in a changing cloud of delectable surroundings." She signs off with "your transient cousin-Charlotte Perkins Stetson."[17]

Within a month her letters began to show signs of the uninhibited exuberance and openness that characterize the correspondence as a whole. She was already expressing herself impulsively, not thinking out her ideas and offering them finished, but pouring out her feelings in such a way that he must have been aware of an underlying confusion and intensity, even this early in their new relationship. "Most Excellent Cousin," she wrote sometime in April, "Mostly these years, when I stop doing things and my mind settles and things come up into view, most of these things are of so painful a nature that I have to rush around and cram them back," but now, she continued, "when I'm quiet—there's a pleasant-sunlight sort of feeling—warm and cozy and safe—like sitting on the doorstep in the sun and eating bread and milk and huckleberries—a purring kind of feeling. Half the time I don't realize what it is till I see your eyes—and then I say, 'Why it's Houghton—bless him!' Truly, cousin, you are one of the pleasantest people I ever knew." As if she has suddenly caught herself being a bit forward, she immediately withdraws, saying that she wants him to have a lovely life, a beautiful home, and "one of the very *charmingest* of wives," whom Charlotte will love but "she won't love me." Charlotte conjures up a most unlovely picture of herself, "the image of an overgrown cuckoo, laboriously stepping out of one exhausted nest after another, and anxiously advising other possible nesters to get at it—so she can board with 'em!!'"—as she had once wished to board with a married Martha Luther. She moves immediately into a contrasting picture of Houghton as a man of "intense Beauty," true "Manhood—at its highest" for his "harmony, simplicity, re-

straint—the clear Greek quality of being." He is "such a deep comfort to me." And then she ends on a self-deprecatory note: "And
it won't surprise me in the least when you get over liking me as
they all do—nor alter my opinion either! Your affectionate cousin."
Here was the beginning of the exposure of the needy Charlotte,
finding comfort in the strength and calm of Cousin Ho, telling him
early on how important he is to her, warning him how important
she will make him be to her.

 Later in April she expressed her new sense of him in a poem
called "A Ballade of Relatives," written in high good humor, with
a significance neither one could really have fully understood at the
time.

> By Father and Mother the tale's begun,
>   High they stand when you are low;
> Grand- and Great-Grand-parents run
>   Out of sight in an aged row;
>   Always airing the things they know,
> Always large when you are small,
>   Always going where you can't go—
> An agreeable Cousin's the best of all

> Sisters are cold as saint or nun,
>   Or hot with mischief as coals aglow,
> Brothers are wild as Goth and Hun,
>   Or tame and dull as a lump of dough;
>   Uncles and Aunts are grave and slow,
> With words that weary and gifts that pall,
>   Trying to make you do just so—
> An agreeable Cousin's the best of all!

> Husbands and Wives we may not shun,
>   Part of the scheme of life below;
>   Over our children we boast and crow
> Saintly Sally and Perfect Paul—
>   But often they cause our tears to flow
> An agreeable Cousin's the best of all!

Cousin whose name begins with Ho!
    Man of Law, and Soldier tall!
I hope you feel as I've tried to show
    An agreeable Cousin's the best of all!

"Written on a train, April 25, 1897, by Charlotte Perkins Stetson," this was a prophetic poem, for indeed Charlotte had already rejected all her relatives, or been rejected by them, except for her agreeable Cousin Ho, "the best of all." He was the only family member with whom she could feel safe.

Writing from Chicago in early May, Charlotte began what became her characteristic lengthy, self-exploratory letters written to a person in whom she felt great trust. Offering an explanation for what she acknowledged as excessive emotionalism, she told him that "feeling this exuberance of joy and loving kindness as I mostly do, and your defenseless head having popped up within my range of late, I shower so much affection on you—quite passing the mild limits of cousinliness. Hasten, therefore, and supply me with some half a dozen other desirable cousins, male and female, that I may distribute my regard and give you a rest occasionally," she urged him, so as to diffuse any growing concern "that her life is inappropriate." Houghton had apparently balked at some of her earlier outbursts, for she referred to his talk of being threatened by her. But, she offered as explanation, her "lack of family ties—of near persons to consume some measure of my affection" lead to "rather strong" emotions when turned full onto "one unprotected young man."

He is thus, she said, a "scapegoat for all this bottled emotion." Representing all her relatives, he carries the weight of "all her family feeling, the undrawn bank account. Father-Mother-Brother-Sister—all comparatively untouched capital. Lover—an immense account here—scarcely opened. Husband—child even—why the whole lot are more or less thwarted and sealed up." And one unfortunate cousin innocently drifted within range, "and Presto! I charge down on him."

But, she assured him, the compensation is that this intensity "is not everlasting," as she had once told Martha. She will always be his affectionate cousin and glad to serve always as a close friend, but he need not fear being "saddled for life with a female relative" with the "unmeasured and delighted devotion" she now expressed.

Why, then, she asked of herself, does she not now moderate her behavior "to that of a rational and ordinary cousinliness?" Why, because "I don't want to," because he is the only person, save Katharine, to whom she can turn with comfort.

On page 7 of the letter, she turned to Houghton and his request that she tell him what she wants from him in their correspondence. "I am most interested in *you*—rather than in what you do." She wants him to "open the doors of your heart and mind to me—let me in where you live—but if that doesn't come easily, I don't want it at all." Perhaps he never will be "as near as that—just a perfectly pleasant friend and relative." She only wishes what shall evolve naturally.

She is "close as your own heart—far as the sun. I am near—thrillingly near—to the folks that I touch; but not near—anywhere as most people are near to each other—to live steadily at an equal distance. That kills me. That is why 'wife' is a word unknown to me, and must be always." Here Charlotte warned Houghton, describing the boundaries of her love, just as she had once warned Martha about her mercurial temperament. With Houghton she demonstrated it dramatically; she made no effort to restrain herself, for fear she would mislead him in some way so that he would become entangled with a woman who had withheld herself, deceived him, played a part.

Her determination to present herself as an older female relative was inconsistent, for later on in this same letter she "gets down to feminine ground" and asks at what point did he find her "startlingly beautiful . . . I'm ever so glad you find me pleasant to look at—it makes me feel good." She then adds that after a recent talk in a nearby church she asked the minister if "my purple gown struck him or the congregation wrong," and he assured her that, quite the contrary, they commented to him on how beautiful she was. And she was pleased.

After the first two months of correspondence, during which time they introduced themselves anew to one another, their friendship moved into a new phase, the beginnings of a recognizable courtship, which was to last until early in 1898. Throughout this phase, Charlotte maintained a frenetic pace, working hard and exceptionally fruitfully. Her extensive traveling continued with a lengthy lecture tour. She was, for example, in Kansas and Oklahoma in July of 1897, in Wyoming in early August and in Maine at the end of the month, in New Hampshire in September, in upstate New York in October, in New York City in early November, and she ended the year in Boston.

Her lectures were enormously successful. Jane Addams, hearing her talk—their lecture tours overlapped in Wyoming—was impressed with her ideas on economics. The acclaim which Charlotte met most of the time gave her, she said, "a deep steady overgrowing joy, to be so widely loved." Sometimes there were setbacks. A cooperative community in Greenacre, Maine, for instance, canceled her lecture on "The New Motherhood." The reason, extracted with difficulty from the woman in charge, was that she had left her child and thus could hardly be thought of as a model of motherhood. She objected, she wrote, to the word "left," insisting that Kate was living with her father, who also had rights and duties. "If I had put her at boarding school you wouldn't say I left her, would you?" she reported asking the woman, who admitted she would not. Besides, she asked, what have any of her private activities to do with the quality of her lecture? No one had said the lecture was bad; no one had heard it. It was thought "unbecoming."[18] She faced what she described as "some resistance" again to the same lecture the following week in Belmont, New Hampshire. But these were minor, if irksome, irritants in an otherwise successful tour.

Most important of all, during these months she was working vigorously on her first prose book, *Women and Economics*, which she began five months after her reacquaintance with Ho, on August 31, 1897. After years of thinking and teaching others, she said, it was time to put her views together. On the first day she wrote 1,700 words, on the second day, 2,400, on the third, 3,600, on the fourth, 4,000. In her autobiography she remarks:

> I well remember the 4000-word day, the smooth, swift, easy flow—it was done in about three hours and a half—the splendid joy of it—I went and ran, just raced along the country road, for sheer triumph.[19]

The first draft, more than 35,000 words, was accepted by the Boston publisher Small, Maynard, and Company. "It was done in seventeen days in five different houses."[20] It was entirely written in fifty-eight days. It was a book Charlotte had been writing all her life, for it dealt with the issues she had been grappling with all her life.

She referred to *Women and Economics* occasionally in her letters to Ho. "Wait till you see my book," she told him. Nobody had touched on the subject in this way before, "not even August Bebel," she said. Even her socialist friends, she went on, insisted that a woman always wants to be supported by the man she loves,[21] addressing a theme in her book that would soon be pertinent to her life. She would send him the book, she promised, only when it was finished and he was to read it before they met again, so that his attention to her work would not be divided—even divided with herself.

The courtship phase that coincided with this singularly productive period professionally was ushered in by flirtatiousness and professions of jealousy. "I wish I had been the girl you took," she said to Ho on May 11, 1897, in response to his report on an outing to the theater. As for the "military-electoral business, I am simply unable to grasp. Behold the limitations of the feminine mind!" she said later in the same letter. She ended on a pouting note: she had another poem to send him but since he did not mention receipt of the last, she concluded that her poems did not amuse. Although she signed the letter with the words "Your loving cousin," the cousin is being transformed into a slightly jealous woman who has a "feminine mind," and who is irked at her dear friend's indifference. Not long after, in mid-June, she was provoked by his reference to a dinner party to which he had been invited in order to be matched with a young woman. "I can't for the life of me see how a dinner—can 'bring people together' . . . I rejoice that you did not bite," she said, not one to sit on her feelings and brood.

Charlotte is remarkably open, and very quickly, about her growing feelings for Ho. In mid-June, less than three months after their meeting, she wrote to him:

One thing that makes me hold you very near is that you knew *me*—me before I died. Truly—wasn't I strong and of good promise? It is hard to keep faith in one's self through long years—when your brain goes back on you and there's *no one to corroborate your memory*. It comes horribly close sometimes—the feeling—"What's the use of fussing—*This* is you—and all you'll ever be!"[22]

At the end of the summer she wrote poignantly about how her feelings for him were different from any she had ever felt before. "I have loved many people, in various ways," she said, "mostly because they needed it—but as to men folks I have told you of my having taken them in chapters as it were—a serial story without, unfortunately, any connection to it—mere chapters begun and ended piecemeal."[23] In each of her intimate relationships, she said, there were disadvantages, something to bear with. "But the astonishing thing about you is that I don't have to 'bear' at all. . . . You seem to be all made as it were, and made to fit. . . . I expect it is the 'blood is thicker than water' theory."

Ordinarily, she said, what she did for a person was no measure of her liking for that person but only a sign of the person's need and her capacity. But "the way you make me feel" she told Houghton, "is different . . . the uppermost feeling is of pure personal gratification because you *are* so! I never felt that way about anyone before, and it does taste good!"

Within six months the nature of the relationship had dramatically altered, through their written words; Charlotte was comfortable in speaking openly about her deep feelings for her cousin Ho without resorting any longer to strategies of indirection and coyness. She could acknowledge the nature and intensity of her feelings for him, as in an October 1 letter, where she wrote, "The foreground is quite empty. You are at present the only figure in it." The following month Charlotte was in New York, and they spent time together. In a letter written while she was still in New York, she wrote of her "intense shame" the previous week when she "had really as good as asked you to kiss me." To offset the shame, she dismissed him the previous night "without my usual friendliness even," and so was writing to apologize.

The passage recalls the diary entry after her marriage to Walter in which she says she went off to bed crying because he accused her of being too "affectionately expressive" and admonished herself for not learning to curb this tendency. But this time she was able to tell Houghton about her feelings, to explain the initial outburst, the shameful recoiling and the desire to strike a more satisfactory balance.

She was also remarkably open about her life, her experiences, her demons. She told him of herself in her younger days. "As a girl I was unattractive, indeed repellent to men," she said, and was "a bit lonely." But within the last four years "I seem to have changed . . . and I can feel a difference in men's attitude toward me." Is she pleased at this new image? Of course not. "I don't think its very creditable. I have an uneasy feeling that perhaps I don't behave as I ought to. I never had 'an assured touch' on this ground anyhow, have always taken most comfort with women."

She occasionally referred to her marriage. "I told Walter once I wished he was a woman, and it seemed to hurt his feelings," she wrote. "I can see why now, but I didn't then," revealing much about the younger Charlotte and her first marriage.[24]

Several weeks after their reacquaintance, Charlotte began to discuss her depressions, and she continued to do so throughout their correspondence, making no effort to spare Houghton anything. "My brain is all mixed up with other internal machinery," she explained.[25] The depression she was referring to deepened. She warned him that she would berate him for not understanding her or caring about her, that she would tax his patience, and so on. If the burden gets too heavy, she said, she would just stop writing till it was over and she could return, "companionable and smiling, in the Fall." That was several months away.

"You see," she told him, "nobody *can* be near me when I've fallen through a hole: I *have* to be alone because I've gone there! and I have to be miserable because that is the condition." She had had six months of feeling well that year and perhaps next year would have seven or eight, "but just now it feels discouraging." The letter is signed "Your dilapidated cousin."[26]

True to her word, Charlotte did soon turn on Houghton. "Why do you persist in talking about 'dizziness' and 'vertigo' in connection with my not being well? Have you materialistically misconstrued my description of symptoms to that effect? So that when I say 'things grow dark to me' you think I mean chairs and tables? Let me explain more specifically that it is my mental atmosphere that darkens—not the scenery. . . . I am simply low-spirited and weak. . . . I feel most meatless—loveless—bloodless—

spiritless—a limp and shadowy thing." But still she must attend to "this book business," which was the writing of *Women and Economics*. She signed the letter, "Goodby. Yours in a fluctuating manner," and the shaking, slightly sprawling handwriting reflects her emotional state.[27] The following month brought little relief; she was pulled down by "that brain-sinking melancholy business . . . which I have carried off and on for fourteen years."

Some months later, in New York, she was still suffering from her downward spiral, although the tone of her letters, the quality of her handwriting, and the ability to assess herself accurately all attest to the beginnings of recovery. "Please bear in mind that I am not horrid when I feel well—and try and be patient with the drag and flop of my exhausted brain as you would, I know, be inexhaustibly tender and patient if it were an exhausted body." She would withdraw entirely if she did not know that he "would really be more grieved." She went on at length about the parallel with a sick body. Nobody "judges" a person sick in bed. But it is her brain that now is sick, with "the slowly retiring remnants of years of a terrible disease." It makes her want to "hide like a leper." All that is to be done is to bear it and "count the slow years of improvement." But however much Charlotte was willing to reveal of her illness, she did not want Houghton to flee. "You've had sensible and pleasant hours enough with me—and letters from me— to know how I feel toward you. Believe that and count on it— always. And don't mind my flopping on to you and turning away from you in these times any more than you would mind if I insisted on holding your hand by my sick bed, or turning my face to the wall."

Charlotte frequently berated herself for her "compelling desire to talk" about her need "to complain and explain—to whimper." But her "compelling desire to talk" was central to her ability to cope, and her urge to unload it all onto Houghton, so long as he was willing, was necessary. She knew in a general way what the source of her neediness was. She knew it at this time in her life more clearly than she had in the past.

You see all my life I haven't had what I wanted in the way of being loved. . . . From mother up. The whole way is lined with—not all gravestones, but some, and some kind of trap-

door-stones that keep things down. When the will-strength
or brain-strength, or whatever it is that keeps me happy and
steady and brave, gives out, up hop all these buried things,
dead and alive.

I want everything I haven't had—all at once—It isn't as
if I'd had 'em and lost 'em, you understand. I have never
had—save in the one girl friend—a satisfied love. The others
have all gone wrong somehow—like a stopped sneeze!

These were risky words for Charlotte to send. She was opening
herself to him at the same time that she was clutching at him and
testing him. She was suffering, she said, from a "choked, thwarted,
fiercely unreconciled feeling" and she needed to have all her needs
satisfied—"from Child to Mother-Sister-Brother-Father-Lover-
Husband-Friend." It was her "elegant and irreproachable" cousin's
misfortune to happen to be about. So she clutched at him, she said,
and immediately tried to break away. "Horrid I know, but I can't
seem to help it."[28]

In this budding relationship with Houghton, Charlotte inevitably addressed her sense of her sexuality. It was her humanness,
rather than her femaleness, that she long valued in herself, what
she called "the power to reach right across sex-distinction, and be
the dispassionate friend and confidante—of men," she wrote, in
language almost a paraphrase of what was to appear in *Women and
Economics*. She hoped not to lose that quality "for this other foolishness," as she wrote to Ho, who was the object of it, but who
was also valued as a "dispassionate friend."

Her dismissive tone about "the other foolishness" did not negate
Charlotte's desire to be found attractive or her concerns about her
womanly appeal. "It strikes me oddly and freshly," she wrote to
Ho, "—always does—when anybody calls me handsome." She recognized that she had "good points," but the face "I see in the glass,"
she wrote, "does not often give me an impression of beauty, and
the feeling I carry about with me—which is what counts most—is
so far removed from a sense of personal beauty that as I say I'm
always surprised when I give that impression."[29]

Charlotte was even able to acknowledge to Ho not only the
pain of the loss of Kate but the guilt and shame she felt at her failure
as a mother. The baby downstairs, she wrote to Ho on June 5,

"makes me think of Kate so, Kate when she was little and o so lovely! and I *knew* it, but couldn't *feel* it! And it aches and aches." Months later she contrasted how often Ho was in her thoughts with how little her daughter Katharine was. Thoughts of Kate, she wrote, would be, to one of her temperament, death. Hers was a mind unhinged, she reminded Ho, and thoughts of Kate were painful and she could not bear "any more leaks and losses and pains."[30]

Charlotte wrote to Ho about the books she remembered, enjoyed most, even with her "weakened memory," books by George Eliot and Charles Dickens. She wrote of the impact *Looking Backward* had had on her, about reading the famous Populist novel *Caesar's Column*, about dipping into Fabian literature and some of Richard Ely's economics, all the while admitting that for many years she had not been able to read systematically or in any sustained way, a condition exacerbated during the periods of depression. She wrote about George Bernard Shaw: "I do not love the man. He has an evil spirit." "Can you read Marx?" she asked Ho. "I can't now. Maybe never could."

Besides giving evidence of her growing love and trust, Charlotte was also testing the limits of Ho's commitment, expressing her worries and fears and reservations about their relationship. She had a recurring tendency to depict herself as unworthy and then apologize for her intensity and neediness and self-deprecation. "I'm an old nuisance anyhow. A tagging unavoidable elderly relative, open even to awful suspicions of being a Bore."[31] And again: "For all the invulnerable self-belief and self-reliance which I have to have to live at all, you've no idea how small potatoes I think of myself at heart. . . . Being so many times marked N.G. [no good] it has sort of struck in!"[32] She even turned situations in which she was the more knowledgable into occasions for self-deprecation. Houghton had never heard of Jane Addams, which appalled Charlotte. "Behold the deficiencies of a college education," she quipped, but then added, "How good it feels to know something you don't," followed with a paragraph about chess, and ended by expressing a plaintive hope that she, with her "strained and shattered mind—untrained entirely," might occasionally beat him at the game.[33] She criticized herself for pouring out letters to him that she knew he couldn't possibly welcome. She herself was "appalled at the voluminous character and merciless frequency of my letters to you."[34]

As Charlotte acknowledged her growing dependence on Houghton, her anxiety about that dependence rose, as did her fear of consuming him with her neediness: "It's as if you offered your hand to help me down from something and I fell all over you. . . . It's as if you said 'call and see me some day,' and I came and stayed six months." She senses that Ho is strong enough to carry her, but it is mortifying "to have to be carried." Perhaps, she went on, "it is better to have no close friends than to have one and make him pay for the absence of the others."[35] She returned to these fears often. "You touch me on my weak side—my defenseless side and my grievously injured side," she wrote some months later.

A state of vulnerability aroused inner turmoil in her, strain and tension that she gave voice to, perhaps as a warning to Houghton. "As soon as any one comes near me and takes hold," she told him, "I wobbly awfully." She admitted that she was getting "exceedingly fond" of him. "And I don't like it. . . . I can't afford to be fond of anybody in that sort of way—man, woman or child. I can't afford to want things." He is "undeservedly kind" to her "all the time." He is her "entire family," and brings out all "that is worst and weakest in me instead of what is best and strongest." "It makes me want," she blurts out, "to be petted and cared for—me!"

The warnings to him persisted: "I tell you truly Houghton I'm *not* a nice person to be close to. I do very well at long range." She told him again: "I *am* a wreck on that side of me: the inside, the personal side; and you come dreadfully close to it." To make herself even less endearing, she told him: "I shall probably behave worse." She warned ominously: "You'll find it a most trying occupation—getting along with such."[36] These were not idle words Charlotte sent him. She was protecting herself, and Houghton, by revealing the unlovely side of herself. She had hinted about it to Walter, but the reality, when it came, destroyed their marriage. Charlotte was terrified that Houghton, like Walter, would enter a relationship unaware of her inner nightmares. To make certain that he did not suffer from such a lack of knowledge, Charlotte barraged him with painful details. At the same time, she used the revelations as a way of binding him. Could he leave her under such circumstances? Her neediness made a claim on him, a claim he apparently found comforting and satisfying. One suspects that Houghton was not frightened away, that he stayed not in spite of her neediness but because of it. She had found a loved person who needed her dependence and need.

Charlotte had warned Ho that she would turn on him, and then she did, as we saw earlier. The seven-year age difference between them distressed and frightened her. Ordinarily she used the age issue to deprecate herself. In one letter she used it against Ho. "If you were only old and experienced and used to sick women!" It was a wail that both demeaned her by labeling her a "sick woman" and challenged his ability to care for her properly. But he was all she had.

She was sometimes condescending and boastful, as when she referred to herself as "spiritual advisor at large." She complained when Houghton did not comment upon her poems, but then she was "amused" when he criticized them.[37] In an obviously irritable mood, she wrote to him:

> I wish I had somebody—young, older, middleaged—male, female or neuter—to whom I could say *everything!* . . . you are just near enough to arouse all this foolishness and not near enough to—assuage it—as it were.[38]

But then she remembered her four years in California "with this kind of trouble inside and all kinds of real ones outside—and *nobody* to holler to!!!"[39]

Through all the issues they addressed in their letters, they were working their way closer to each other. Charlotte showed Ho all of herself, the good and what she perceived as what he would see as the bad, so that she could be sure they were on firm ground.

Whatever Ho's response was to her letters, if we can deduce something of it from Charlotte's, he did reassure her of his devotion, steadfastness, and concern. We know he asked her for a reading list so that he could better understand her work. We know that he told her he found her beautiful. It is true that just before their wedding, years later, she referred to a time when he had stated that he "did not love me 'that way'—did not wish to marry me."[40] There is no further information available to explain the circumstances surrounding such a moment, but whatever his earlier reservations, his feelings toward her changed. Within three months after their meeting as adults, she was able to write to him:

I mean to have such pretty clothes—and be so charming—I wish I could make men envy you. . . . I can't ever be what a better balanced woman could, but what I can I will.[41]

That she was able to think of herself as lovable and enviable attested to a great change in her sense of self, a change encouraged and supported by Ho. Six months later she described herself as "childishly happy," as "young—and pretty—and desirable." She feels, she wrote:

> like a child, tucked up and "put to bed" with all due nursery formalities—the right doll on the pillow—'a drink of water'— everything. The sense of wide empty darkness changes to a feeling of closeness and warmth and support.
> I guess it's "the eternal feminine" after all. Any how it's a comfort—you are—altogether.[42]

More than the "eternal feminine," it was the "eternal child." The soft comfort she needed was child-comfort. The safety of Houghton's love for her, the full trust she now allowed herself to feel for him, permitted the child in her to be satisfied so that the woman could develop. By February 1898, less than a year after their correspondence began, she was writing almost daily love letters, most of them with the character and language appropriate to a lover, not a needy child clutching an anchor, although the latter aspect never entirely disappeared.

Houghton and Charlotte passed the first stage. They declared their love for each other. By this time Houghton had proposed, although it is not clear when, most likely when Charlotte was in New York in February 1898. Charlotte was then thirty-eight years old; Houghton, thirty-one. At this crucial moment as they moved together more fully, began to plan how they would share their remaining years, at this moment Charlotte, clearly still frightened about such a commitment, pulled back and demanded two more years, two more years to work at her writing and her lecturing and to travel extensively. During this period, she told him, she would not "think or feel much personally." Still, she added that she would actually be glad when she left New York, where she was staying when she wrote this letter, because then she could bury him "way down deep" in her heart till it was "time to open the door and look if you come out."[43]

Was she still testing to make certain that he would not desert her, that she would not want to flee him, as she had Walter? Was she still afraid of commitment? Did she still feel herself undeserving of such goodness? In this same lengthy letter, she wrote of "the terror of this immense, unknown feeling you have aroused in me." She recalled "with bitter misgiving" every word and deed with which she "begged and demanded love" from him and worried that she had once more fabricated something, a "cloud castle" such as she had been building to comfort herself all her life. Would all this love too disappear? She needed time to be sure, so that they would be on "solid ground." Her best happiness had always been, she said, "the creation of my own mind," so that her happiness with Houghton "by its very intensity seems a phantom." Lovers often indulge in such words in the early days of exploration, but Charlotte really meant them deeply, so much so that she did indeed back away from marriage for an extended period. It was not a coy gesture, designed to elicit comforting words. It was a desperate act. She had for years yearned for this kind of love, one that allowed her to be open and trusting, but each time she thought she had found it, it had slipped away. She was right that she had always demanded love from others, created it out of her own need. She suspected that with Houghton it was different. But she was too frightened to take a chance without further testing.

She spoke truly of her fears. She must "go way back and get things straightened out—all the way. I've got to start new—all new. And mind you, all this is *done*, is mine, if you died tomorrow! It has come. It is in my life." And what will two years mean for such a life together—"if it is to be?" But she "must be surer than the past has ever been before I dare attempt it."

As she had with Walter, she cast her struggle as one between love and work. Charlotte Anna Perkins had believed it was necessary to opt for one or the other, not both. But even Charlotte Stetson, many years later, fell back on familiar language. If she had to choose, "I would choose the work, if I died next day, just *because* it means so much." Still, she now knew that she could have both and that her ambivalence about Houghton had to do with her fears of trusting, fears of losing, fears of not deserving, and could not be simply reduced to earlier issues that she had thought prevailed when she was in her early twenties. She knew his importance to her. "Look you! Something has come to me which I dare balance for a moment with my work!" It is because he is so important to her that she is afraid to make the commitment. She is much closer now to locating the source of her fears than she has ever been.

She bravely assured him that she put "no embargo" on him for the two-year waiting period. She urged him to be "most freely and naturally yourself in all ways." She would always be a loving cousin, "almost sister," to him. Did she really mean it? Do we ever? Yes and no. We want the loved person to be free to do what she/ he wants, but then hope that that person will do what we want. And so, having urged him to act in his own interest, she reminded him of her feelings. "But this unspeakable heavenly wonder, so utterly unknown, undreamed of in my life—as it grows and grows on my consciousness I am the more overwhelmed with new feelings as to it—to you—to myself—to life. I feel as if I had been only playing before—that *this* is life, and I am but just born!" So much for her "no embargo." He would be a cad to reject such total love.

Even so, in closing this love letter, she repeated that she wished to give him the chance to escape, to be "free, utterly free of the insistent pressure of my intense personality, to recover yourself." He must not try to hang on to feelings if he feels them passing. "What is *true* is right, and I do not want anything that is not mine. I think that is all. Yours, Charlotte."[44]

This must have been a difficult letter to write and a difficult one to receive. Charlotte and Houghton would now have two more years to discover whether their relationship would be sustained and deepened. She had put off Walter for two years, but it was different now. She and Ho did not have a relationship built on strain. She needed the time to be certain, and he accepted her decision. Unlike Walter, who pursued her relentlessly for two years, Houghton waited, using the time to continue their intense correspondence.

The proposed two-year wait actually became several months less than that, for they married on June 12, 1900. In this long period after the postponement, Charlotte continued her energetic lecturing and traveling. In the spring of 1898 she covered many Southern states, and finished the summer in Cold Spring Harbor, in New York State, where she often spent time with Kate, as she did now.

Summer Brook Farm in Essex County, also in New York, was another favorite place for Charlotte in the summer; it was a collective community where each of the residents performed some labor as part of their contribution. She was an occasional visitor at another cooperative community in Fairhope, Alabama. "A community life is evidently well-suited to my style of beauty," she wrote to Houghton,[45] indicating that she had abandoned her earlier opposition to the Swedenborgian community she had lived in as a child, and which she had, as an adult, generalized to apply to all such living arrangements.

Her 1899 lecture tour took her to Michigan, Illinois, Missouri, and California (where she spent time with Kate, who was living there because Grace was caring for her aged and ailing parents), Utah, Colorado, Georgia, and several stops in Tennessee, Alabama, and North Carolina. She returned to New York, where she saw Houghton, and then was off to England in May for an extended stay of five months, during part of which time Houghton came to visit, before she returned to New York for three weeks.

As is clear from the quantity of traveling she did, Charlotte was in great demand in 1898 and particularly in 1899, largely because of the publication of her first prose book in 1898. Her publishers named it *Women and Economics*, using her original title as a subtitle: *A Study of the Economic Relation Between Men and Women as a Factor in Social Evolution*. The immediate success of the book made her an internationally known figure, although her financial condition never improved much. She wrote for magazines, most of which paid little, if anything, and the lecturing covered expenses and a bit more. But it was not money Charlotte sought, it never was; it was the opportunity to have her message heard. By the time she returned to England in 1899 for a convention of the International Council of Women, a British edition of *Women and Economics*, published by Putnam, had arrived. "I became quite a lion," Charlotte admitted. A second printing of the book in the United States followed in 1899, adding an 18-page index to the original 340 pages. There was a third printing in 1900; a fourth in 1905, with G. P. Putnam's Sons in London; a fifth, jointly issued, in 1908; a sixth in 1910; a seventh in 1912; an eighth, by Putnam alone, in 1915; and a ninth, with a new introduction by Gilman, in 1920. Within five years of its appearance, *Women and Economics* was translated into Danish, Italian,

Dutch, German, and Russian. "It sold and sold and sold for about twenty-five years," Charlotte said.

The discrepancy between the success of the book "and its very meager returns" Charlotte said she never understood. She received no income at all from the translations, except for a gift of thirty dollars for the Italian version. What she did get that was of importance was a five-hundred-dollar advance from her publisher for what she thought would be her next book, *Human Work*. She wrote it and rewrote it many times, but was never satisfied with the result. It was soon clear to her that it would not be ready for publication when promised—it "was not to be reeled off like my usual stuff,"[46] so she began to work on another book, *Concerning Children*, which was published just after her marriage, in 1900, under her married name, Gilman. Her publishers were distressed at the change of name from Stetson to Gilman, fearing that she would lose her large and devoted following. She should have remained Perkins from the first, she later decided, adding that we are, happily, outgrowing "the nuisance" of changing women's names at marriage.[47]

For reasons not entirely clear, Charlotte wanted to keep her relationship to Houghton and their marital plans hidden, and Houghton complied. Their relationship remained a secret almost to their wedding day. She suspected—correctly, as it turned out—that the announcement would cause a stir among friends and family, some of it negative, and would give rise to considerable gossip about their age difference, their first-cousin relationship, her divorce, the kind of rootless life she led, and the early trauma with Kate; perhaps she wanted to postpone such unpleasantness as long as possible. Perhaps she wasn't certain their love would survive the test of the separation. Perhaps she enjoyed the intimate conspiracy and the private pleasure they shared thereby. The letters that continued to flow from Charlotte to Houghton attest to the increasing strength of their connection. Here is a typical one:

> You are my darling, my beloved, my comfort, my hope and strength and joy. . . . I'm so happy I can hardly see it any more. . . . It is somehow part of me now, and all of the universe—it is life and I'm in it, and what is there remarkable about that I'd like to know? Happy? Why not? This is the way things *are!* If this goes on I shall soon cease to write you

these little little lectures. Why write to myself? Don't I know? Are you not right here by me—with me—in me—not part of my life and I part of yours?

No need to say anything, only to look into your eyes— to reach out my hand and know you are there.

I am so thankful, my heart, for every hour—every moment—we have had together. . . . It was only a year and must last us over quite a long space.

And we have used the time well—building ourselves together.

"Letters aren't much good," she wrote him. "I want to be kissed!" A new, more assured woman has emerged. "You can't make me happier than by telling me just how unhappy you are without me." Doesn't he feel similarly? "Don't you like to know that I go to sleep missing you and wake up missing you and that when the people stop talking or the meals are done or whatever is going on stops and I wonder what it is that seems lacking—why its you that are lacking, Heart's Dearest, and I want you all the time!"[48] She spoke less with her former frantic desperation and more like a woman in love who misses her lover. Increasingly she came to have confidence in herself and in Houghton, and she moved on from there to address new issues, resolving conflicts and confronting the future with optimistic realism.

Charlotte was learning, for example, to be more realistic in regard to their respective characters and weaknesses. "Satisfied with you!" she wrote, apparently in answer to a previous question of his. "Why I will admit that you are not perfect, just to prove that I am coolheaded and reasonable." Then she listed his deficiencies, beginning interestingly with physical ones, and she did point to ones that were real. "You might have a better chin, a bigger chest, just as I might have a straighter nose, finer longer hair, a clearer complexion, better teeth, better health, stronger nerves, prettier hands—we are neither of us perfect." (Did Houghton begin to grow his beard just after her comment about his chin?) "You might have a more creative brain—I might have a better head for figures." He has told her he is sullen when angry, but she is implacable, "cold, immovable, cruel." He is obstinate and she is arrogant. But it all does not matter because, she tells him, "I love you dear—I love you more and more and more."[49]

Charlotte now addressed in a new and satisfying way the place of domesticity in her life and the tension she had long felt between her mother-side and her father-side. She was learning to identify what she needed and how to ask for it. She approached the tensions she had been so long struggling with in such a way as to integrate a life that had been so long fragmented. She resolutely explained to Houghton what he might expect of her in the way of housewifely duties, for this was the terrain that had triggered her collapse once before. "As you value my life, my sanity, my love. . . . You will have to give up a certain ideal of home . . . I *must not* focus on 'home duties' and entangle myself in them." However "vague and absurd" she may sound, she said, it is "a question of life and death with me."

She was now able to move beyond the failings of mother and father, taking from their example what was positive and moving on. It now seemed possible. "I would like a rose-covered cottage with you—there isn't any absurdity of romance I don't feel equal to. Such a tidal wave of grovelling abnegation I never dreamed myself capable of feeling." She reminded him of how her mother saved the hair from her husband's head and the parings from his nails—"She loved him absolutely." Ordinarily she spoke of this aspect of her mother with contempt or anger, but now she embraced this side of Mary. "It appears that I am her daughter." But, she added, "also—I am my father's child, and his nature, however perverted, was facing toward the larger right." It is true, she acknowledged, that "he failed and failed but he meant the biggest best things." Now she wants both, the best from her mother, "the rose-covered cottage," and the best from her father, his reaching out to the larger world. Now she knows that it is possible to have both, that she can merge these two sides of herself in a life with Houghton—so long as he does not demand of her that she engage in domestic work, even minimally.[50]

During the remaining months before marriage, Charlotte examined the place of work in her life and what it would mean for their life together. "You understand to the full," she wrote in May 1898, "that I am a world-worker and must be—that I simply give you the part that stays at home and that I shall go right on thinking, writing, lecturing and travelling when I must."

She ruminated on the nature of their relationship, now that she was able to free herself from the narrow focus of her own fears. "I think you will be better able to be content with the scrappy life I can give you than almost any man I ever saw." With jolting insensitivity she told him if she married "some kind of genius—as indeed I did, before," then he would need her and it would drain her. But with Houghton, so long as "we are clever enough to avoid housekeeping complications," there is nothing he needs from her except love, "and that crop seems coming on finely."

Because his life is "in a way, commonplace," she felt easier about him, she went on. Her work has forced her "into what has always been held a man's place." "As we have often noticed," she went on, indicating that this subject had been examined earlier, it is as if "you held the woman's place toward me." It was the male role she saw herself as filling, not a maleness about her person. "Surely my lover, my husband—you find no lack of womanliness in me—do you dear?"

She was aware that her kind of life demanded "an awful sacrifice" from him, for theirs would hardly be a traditional marriage. "I seem to be swallowing you." Still, she was reassured at the thought that "you are the kind of angel that only seeks to be swallowed." He is a free agent, he "frantically" insists on her being the swallower, "preferring to find pleasure" in the process. And so she accepts the "sacrifice of a good man's life," by which she means the conventional home he might have had, the children he might have had, the advantageous connections he might have had, "the good human happiness"—all of them given up so that he may devote himself to her. "Your fate is sealed," she told him. "I am going to marry you just because I love you and so I can't help it."[51]

Months later she pondered whether her work would suffer with marriage, any marriage, whether her growing devotion would sap her and thus weaken her work. She decided it would not, that she was a thinker, "a kind of social philosopher," whose expression would always be in writing and in "amateurish and inspirational sort of speaking." And so, she concluded, "there was nothing to prevent this work, and much to help it in our being together; that it would probably grow saner, rounder, sounder, more effective."[52] Early in 1899 she once more explored the tensions she had been voicing for twenty years between work and love, public and private life. She now knew she could have both and could say that "getting as near you as I am now does not in the least prevent this big sweep of work that follows close upon it." Her tour was going well, as was her writing. The success of *Women and Economics* strengthened her self-confidence enormously. "Finding that loving you does not at all interfere with loving all the rest, but seems to help it on, why *I shan't be afraid to love you!*"[53]

The issue of children remained, and it too Charlotte could now face realistically. It was tied to concerns about her age and her instability. "For your sake far more than mine," she wrote to Ho, "I want to lay a child in your arms—your child and mine; to fill and lighten your life, and to be with you when I must needs be gone. I shall hope for it—to the last chance."[54] A month later, still exploring, she wrote: "I hold that a well-born and well-loved baby is not wholly bereft even if his mother is not a good nurse. We'll see. Time enough." But still she worried: "if that thing happens it is a tremendous risk to my tottering nervous system and I mean to take prodigious precautions."

Her concern about her age was partly a matter of health. She reported to Ho about her visit to Alice Stone Blackwell, the activist and reformer, whose mother, the abolitionist Lucy Stone, had been past thirty-nine when her only child was born. Said Charlotte, "If I may have one child as good as she I should be more than content. But also I shall be more than content if I have you alone."[55] Charlotte may also have been embarrassed about the age difference. "Margaret Fuller married a man younger than she—Elizabeth Stuart Phelps [a popular writer]—Miss Blackwell told me several, as I artlessly talked about her mother and father this morning. Come now—why didn't you look up some precedents to comfort me with—that's right in your line."[56]

While Charlotte was addressing her issues, Houghton spoke to his; he was concerned about his limited financial resources. Charlotte was not concerned about finances, which additionally worried him. "The money part of it isn't anything," she assured him. She comforted him with the words: "If you were the kind of man that was pushing and successful and making money hand over fist—I should not love you—nor would you love me."[57]

Charlotte's old fears of abandonment, of not being worthy, did not disappear, but their hold on her seemed to lessen. "I would give so much if I could be sure I was really doing right by you," she wrote.[58] She spoke of a "painful sense of inadequacy and of owing" him so much. "I never was all I should be to mother or brother or child—to anyone I loved," she insisted, and now she felt the debtor again. If only he were "some poor ruined wretch" she could care for! But no, he is a "strong sweet noble man" who might be "a thousand times better off" without her. What did she want from him? Reassurance. "Please talk to me and make me feel better about it." And in a later letter she warned him that she "shall always feel apologetic before all your relatives and most of your friends . . . shall always be feeling contrite and deprecatory." Even at these moments of pain she has learned to turn to him for support. "Now, darling, what can you say to comfort your disagreeable lady and reassure her waggling faith in you."[59] She has learned not only to ask for help but to seek out the kind of person who wished to be asked.

The depressions never disappeared, but they eventually came less frequently, and more important, Charlotte's response to them changed in time. In June of 1898 she was vacationing in Cold Spring Harbor with Kate, with Houghton and Frederick not far away, and she felt herself slipping into a familiar downward spiral. Her letters to Houghton that followed were predictable. "Don't make me happy even to think of you! Except that I'm glad you're not legally bound to me yet. You shan't have any such wife as this I promise you." Again comes the self-flagellation. If this heavy fog comes on while she is with Katharine, has Houghton at hand, is living a pleasant country life, then "it must be a permanent condition . . . liable to come at any time." And so plans must be altered. "No motherhood is possible—it would be wrong."[60] What did not occur to her was that, of course, the terrors would strike at the very moment when everything seemed to be in place, for then the fear of loss was at its height. It was at the instant she could envision having it all that the loss of it all was most frightening.

Nonetheless, despite the pain—"it's very black and it hurts.

. . . I can really feel it—physically"—she was able to think of a time ahead, of plans for the coming winter, perhaps "that Christian Cooperative Colony in Georgia," where "in the flux and stir of such a place I dare say I may pick up some stimulus to start again." She was down but not out.

By the end of July she had come to a new calm resolution, and it gave her "the first partial peace of mind I have known this summer."[61] It came with the recognition that she would probably never recover entirely from her "genuine mental disease." She restated the theme of the earlier letter, but this time with some distance and calm. "Nothing touches it"—the depression—"not Love even." The summer "has shaken me to the very foundation." After a "year below level" and then "a heavy plunge at the end" in spite of "increasing fame," better finances, "personal freedom and comfort . . . and, above all, a new great happiness," came the acknowledgment that her emotional illness was not simply connected to external problems.

Not only did Charlotte finally acknowledge that her depressions were rooted in her, not in her surroundings, and that they would probably plague her permanently although not destroy her, but she had two other new and helpful reactions. First, she was calmed, not driven into frenzy, by this new insight. Second, acceptance of her emotional state did not cause her either to flee from Houghton or to clutch frantically at him, as she had with others in the past.

Her old dependency fear also persisted, but in an altered form. She wrote of the "ingrained terror that assaults" her as soon as she attaches herself to anything, of the need to break free, to remain untied, saying to herself, "I'm not tied—I can get away—I *can* get along without him." Her fear of being swallowed up had always kept her from leaning. Her dependence on others had traditionally been excessive and without sensible boundaries. In these letters through these years she was trying to work out a healthy dependency on Houghton that would help her and be good for her. For all the pulls and tears, she was "settling more and more."[62]

Charlotte came out of the depression in the summer of 1898 with new insights into her emotional state, but she plunged into another one in January of 1899, and for the next several weeks she suffered terribly. "Hoping that you can somehow catch and bring me back to life. . . . there is a queer dead spot," she wrote to him.

How did it come on? "As near as I can remember what hit me, it was a great sweeping recognition that I had gone too far—said too much—given more than was wanted—*from the first*. And then there was a tidal wave of shame . . . and I guess I was drowned or something, but I haven't *felt* anything since."

All through January Houghton was bombarded with letters saying that she knows she loves him but has no feeling of love for him, that he does not connect to her, that she has been writing letters for two years to him but that he still does not understand her, that they are emotionally incompatible. The letters, abusive in tone, pour out her pain and insecurities. She berates herself for having dragged him into the relationship, she is really unfit for him, why doesn't he write back to her with sympathy rather than simply ignoring her outbursts? On January 25, from St. Louis, came this letter, with no salutation, beginning abruptly: "I feel as if I did it all—that it was only my intense feeling which you courteously respond to. . . . that there is not in your heart a voluntary love—but only a response one. I have these terrible sinkings of the heart—my poor little hand-made heaven vanishes in thin air—I am again alone." And what is Houghton's response? "You preserve an attitude of masterly inactivity. You will wait, you say, till I come back. *Don't you see that this simply corroborates my worst fears,*" she railed at him. He was trapped in a situation where at that moment there was nothing he could do to comfort her. If he engaged with her, he risked losing that sense of self-mastery that ultimately was to provide her with the stability and anchor she sought. In the meantime her abuse continued: "You are only what I call for, it appears. If I am only a friend, you are a friend. If I am but a cousin you are a cousin. If I ardently love, you will then come forward and ardently love also. Sort of an echo."

Then came her own echo, the self-demeaning comments. "I am not in a position to dictate," she told him. "I am no blooming charmer, surrounded by suitors. . . . I ought to be thankful for any kind of love." As her panic deepened, she returned to the old rhetoric, another echo, this time of courting days with Walter. "I truly believe that I am too valuable a servant to the world just now to take any such chances. . . . I would rather love you and live on alone—the last great and final sacrifice—giving myself absolutely and forever to my work, than to feel that I am accepting in my life a risk like this. I must have peace, though it be in utter renunciation."

But Houghton was able to offer the comfort, apparently, that Walter could not or did not. By the end of a few weeks his letters had consoled her, she began to believe again that he did truly love her, and the climb upward began again. In the following weeks, letters from her poured in from Tennessee, Alabama, Georgia, North Carolina. "Things are going gorgeously. . . . The town is at my feet . . . what is best is the warm loving welcome of the folks here."[63] Success at lecturing, the warm and accepting response of the audiences, also contributed to a recovery, for the moment at least, of her self-love.

By early March Charlotte was feeling happy and cheerful again and able to provide some comfort to Houghton who, not only suffering from a prolonged cold, had also just returned from attending a funeral of a friend. Charlotte took some responsibility for his low spirits: "I fondly imagine that when I'm not loving you as much as usual maybe it does affect you a little," and so she offered him some "comfort and stimulus."

In this same letter Charlotte referred to the letters she had written long ago to Adeline Knapp, letters which would be harmful to her reputation if made public, she said, letters explored in an earlier chapter. In context, these remarks may be seen somewhat differently: "I loved her, trusted her, wrote her as freely as I write to you. I told you that I loved her that way." She asks him, "*Am* I a woman you ought to marry? Are you willing to give such a mother to your son—or Daughters? . . . I am not afraid to face the rest of life alone. . . . I have never been able fully to feel that the home joys were meant for me. . . . I shall make my world tour and, if I come home alone I shall come bravely and live on." Perhaps Charlotte was dredging up ways to demonstrate that she was unworthy and undeserving of normal private happiness; to test again and again Houghton's faithfulness and patience, which seem saintlike; to prepare herself for the possibility that Houghton will flee, as all the others had. She returned often to the theme of her emotional instability, she called upon her need for autonomous work and freedom from traditional housewifely responsibilities. Now she conjured up a scandal in the press over her past with Adeline. She also returned to the issue of children. Although she had often told

Houghton in the past that she wanted to lay a baby in his arms, here she raised again the question of whether she was fit to be the mother of his children. Charlotte was still running scared.[64]

Five days later she returned calmly to the question of their marriage and future children. For eight years of her life, she began, from ages fifteen to twenty-three, she had done "only what I thought right." But then she married "without that knowledge of right-doing. I did not have my own sanction." Assuring herself that her marriage to Houghton is different from that to Walter, she told him "you are more to me than my child—far more."

Glad as Charlotte said she was about her tour taking her East, she told Houghton in a letter in mid-March that she had written to the *Woman Journal* and the *Club Woman* that she was open for engagements the last two weeks in April, so that she feared she would not see as much of him as she would like.[65]

After spending time in Boston and New York, she sailed, in May 1899, for London, where she began her tour of England. As we have seen, Houghton visited England at this time to see her, although their engagement was still a secret. Although Charlotte met with great success in her public appearances, the trip abroad triggered another depression, in spite of, or maybe because of, Houghton's presence. Given the secrecy of their connection and the heavily subscribed schedule for Charlotte, the two saw little of each other, again communicating a good deal by letter. "Bad again," she reported to him on June 8, 1899. "Can't think of what I ought to do—and very anxious and guilty about it. . . . It's all mixed up and black, but—I'm hanging on to you like a sick octopus! Poor Houghton." Except that poor Houghton, unlike his predecessors, seemed to thrive on her need for him. And Charlotte, though she occasionally slipped back into hostility toward him, turned more and more to Houghton for support.

During this time of blackness and depression she was lecturing constantly. She heard that her English publisher, Maynard, had said that anything she wrote would "sell well enough to justify publishing." To which she added, "I'm *having* to respect my work more now that so many do." But along with her reports of success in lecturing came expressions of her yearning for safety, her anxiety about his love, of regression to childlike needs, combined with an occasional backhanded slap at him. For instance:

I wish you were somehow Bigger. Could take me right off the ground and say "Little Girl, Little Girl! Stop thinking. It is all right. You are mine and I've got you and I'll never let go—never. You shall rest and work and play—I won't let anything hurt you or bother you. Rest on me."

"I lean farther and farther toward you," she told him. She called to him: "Dearest—dearest—if you can carry me for Heavens sake *make me feel it*. If you can't—I must know before it is too late. I'm heavy. I always told you I was heavy and hard to carry. And I'm *so* tired. Please help me dear." It is signed from "your own poor wife." The words are reminiscent of her last words to Walter in her diary, but they are filled with yearning, not bitterness. The following day she cried out that "the affection and admiration of a vast and increasing multitude does not satisfy me. . . . I want to be *loved*—by you, more and more and more. . . . I want a man's love, big and deep and strong and fierce if you like." Two days later the love for him spilled over again into the wish for a child: "O Houghton—if we can have one! You don't know how I shall love it, a child of *yours*—that's what makes the difference." Another letter written the same day, from Kent, advised Ho about a visit to the doctor earlier that day, who said that she "might conscientiously have a child, that there was nothing hereditary the matter with me."

However often Charlotte regressed, she continued to move ahead. In July of 1899 she made a statement that would have been impossible for her earlier. What she must do, she said, was "to prove that a woman can love and work too. . . . To give up neither."

The next weeks brought letters bubbling with enthusiasm about future plans for a steady income from writing and lecturing. "I'll have an income of a thousand or two soon," she told him, "even if I'm sick!!!"[66] The marriage was now less than a year off—if they stuck to their schedule—and Charlotte began making elaborate plans about her income to be certain that she would not be financially dependent on Houghton. The issue was not finances—although Houghton was not well off—the issue was Charlotte's need for economic independence. By October she was back from England, and the following month she was lecturing in Denver, Colorado.

As the year ended, Charlotte's spirits began to dip once more. She planned her lecture tour to be in Pasadena near Kate, Grace, and Walter during the Christmas holidays. In Pasadena on Christmas Day she was accosted at a neighbor's home for being an unnatural mother and giving away her child. She ended her letter to Houghton with "You love me don't you dear. You don't think I'm an unnatural mother do you? You'd even trust me with a child!" Two days later she wrote to him. "I want a new baby so! I want to begin again and have a fairer chance."

She was becoming much concerned with children and babies. For instance, she showed great interest in her brother Thomas's son, Basil, for Charlotte did not approve of his "gaudy and flashy" mother. Basil needed home influences "of a higher sort," and so Charlotte took him with her to California. "I never coveted a child so much," she said of her young nephew.

As the new year began, the year she was to marry, her first letter was an accounting of her outstanding debts, which included $5 owed to the milkman, and which totaled $2,030. Charlotte expected to earn $4,000 that year, so she said, "I think I can clear these up and marry safely!"[67]

From Pasadena, while lecturing, writing, visiting, she wrote to "My Precious Sweetheart" that "Its all very well to sit on a hill and write great books––but I want to be *kissed!!!*"[68] They began to discuss daily living arrangements after their marriage. They will live in an apartment. "We would want a room apiece if possible. Everybody ought to. . . . Will not our rate of mortality decrease 50% if we have a room apiece?" she asked, although he can come to her "when you're good, as you say—and that is all the time."[69]

Thoughts of the coming marriage bring joy, finally, to Charlotte, although mixed with a little anxiety. "What an endless wealth of good times we can have together . . . even if I *am* a crone—I'm better fitted to have a good time with than a younger and more attractive woman!"[70]

The marriage plans were still a secret, but Charlotte decided it was desirable to inform at least Walter and Grace, which she did. She received, she wrote, "a very touching and sweet note" from Walter. "Isn't it funny," she mused, "how completely one outgrows an emotion," for she had not "the faintest flutter of consciousness with regard to him."[71] She was able to speak of Walter and his life with Grace with a "sense of warm goodwill." She was cleaning up all old business emotionally as she prepared for a new life. Grace had expressed some concern about whether Charlotte was going to be able to cope with marriage, since her explanation for the previous marital collapse had been the institution and not the man. "Well—circumstances alter cases, that's all I can say," was what she offered as an answer.[72]

Eventually the family was informed. Houghton's Aunt Emily and some cousins, with certain reservations in tone, did wish him well. His father was opposed to the marriage and remained so. His opposition pained both Houghton and Charlotte, but that was the only impact his reaction had.

By early March Charlotte was down again, but to each setback she responded with greater insight and strength. "Right across all my happiness this old sense of pressure and pain—and no work done," she wrote to Houghton, March 3, 1900. "I try to say to myself 'it is a headache—a toothache-neuralgia-indigestion! . . . I wouldn't make a fuss over those—I won't over this." She now turned without hesitation to Houghton, not away from him. "You'll steady me when I have little ones," she said, still planning a future with children, "and stand by waiting and being good to me when they are big. . . . Folks that will marry infirm old ladies ———" The humor is still self-deprecatory but she was trying not to take herself so seriously. "But I do love you, even in the dark."[73]

Within two weeks she was out of the dark and able to see patterns ever more clearly, in ways quite impossible two years before under similar circumstances. "My place in life is *mine* now, I have made it, all myself. My work is clear before me. A temporary depression will not make me think that marrying you has 'spoiled my life.' "

It is true, she said, that her life is thriving and "set" already and so they will not be able to build together, "woman fashion," in other words in a conventional way. But, she told him, "we can sustain a very beautiful married life—quite aside from the usual style of immersion of the wife in the husband."

As to his helping her when she is "down," she said, "I begin to think it is only a natural hallucination to think anyone can." The trouble was a "wilting brain tissue," so no one outside could help. She was finally able to acknowledge: "I think my reproachful attitude toward the innocent bystander is part of the disease."[74]

Charlotte had resolved many issues with Houghton in the course of their correspondence. She had learned to trust him, to see that he was loyal and would not abandon her. She had made clear what her professional and emotional needs were in ways that she probably never had been able to articulate in the past. She explained over time and in great detail exactly how she saw their life together as providing both autonomy and intimacy. The success of *Women and Economics* added to her self-confidence. Finally, she had freed Houghton from any responsibility for "curing" her depressions or even significantly affecting them. She was finally taking full responsibility for her emotional debilities as well. Whatever their buried causes, these depressions were hers now.

We may be slowly approaching a happy ending to this part of Charlotte Stetson's life, but it is not a simple happy ending. She was still able to plague her poor lover with new fears. "Now I am going to have a Cancer! I have no right to be married! Perhaps this thickness in my head is due to a physical cause—some awful disease in there!" But then she recovered from these anxieties and told Ho that he gave her everything to make her "personally as happy as a well-mothered baby, and to sweeten and soften and strengthen" her work. She wished she were beautiful for him, but "it's no use wishing. I am as I am . . . you know it all—and yet—love me."[75]

Less than two months before the wedding day, she commented that her early doubts about their bliss had slowly changed to a "growing sense of reality and permanence." "It is as if," she said, "I had always been pretending-aspiring-trying—and now I first begin to feel what I really *am*—namely your wife 'Mrs. Gilman, of New York—one of our literary women, very pleasant to know—you ought to make her acquaintance—husband a delightful man.' "[76]

They turned increasingly to wedding plans and their future together. She refused to be given to Ho by anyone, certainly not her brother, whom she had not seen for five years. She thinks formal announcements are absurd. Why not just tell the family and friends and the word will spread? If pushed, she will agree to a simple statement announcing the marriage. She apologizes endlessly for being so unconventional.[77] In looking for a minister to marry them, she has heard of a good one, but he's "a Presbyterian by trade—

and I'm afraid would want me to obey or something dreadful." So she leans toward the Reverend Jenkins Lloyd Jones, who is a Unitarian and "very progressive." As for the date, it seemed that the date they chose, June 11, was the same as Walter and Grace's wedding day. Grace laughed over it and Walter saw no objection. As for Charlotte, she said, "I don't mind—it seems rather poetic somehow." The original date chosen had been June 12, but she wanted to stay with the eleventh because "we shall be able to kiss each other one day sooner!"[78]

Anxieties fade as the time approaches. "Your letter that came last night gives me just the feeling that I so love, that I suppose all women love—the protecting strength of a husband." She thanks him for the comfort his letters have brought her, "the dear loving steady letters" that have "bridged the years and taught us to know each other better." She wants "to cuddle up to you and be so *small*—like a kitten—and have you wrap me all up *in* you somehow."[79]

A few issues were reopened for new exploration. She talked once more about her first marriage and why it did not last. "This time I'm going to be *married*. I was never married before. To plan for years of happiness in companionship—well tested and proven; with a deep sweet cousin love behind it; and a new rich wonderful man-and-woman love before—*quite* another relation!" This is the model she would use many times in her fiction—the ideal mate, selected on the basis of a deep and long and loving friendship that ripens slowly into love rather than a hot, passionate, sudden, impetuous attraction. Houghton looked again at her wish for two bedrooms and set forth his preference for one room and one bed, an idea that she said was agreeable to her as long as she was able to sleep comfortably, although they did ultimately have separate rooms.

She looked again at the pattern of her depressions and began "to feel more confidence" in her "nervous system." She was able to say something very new and different about herself. "I don't think I'm sick just because I feel pretty badly. To be so splendidly well all winter and then feel horrid under a few days' strain doesn't mean any 'illness'—merely touching my weak spoke. As if I had a broken bone somewhere."[80]

The baby question remained. Charlotte spoke with Mrs. Van Orden, an old friend and physician, who said it was important that she have unbroken rest and quiet while carrying a baby, that she have a "calm and happy spirit during the time of bearing." When Charlotte advised her of her crowded schedule during the first year of marriage, the doctor advised a postponement. "Then—if that blessing comes to us," Charlotte wrote Ho, "I shall simply give up lecturing for a while, and take it out in writing!"[81] Charlotte expressed sadness for Houghton as more members of his family expressed their disapproval of his marriage partner. She would do her best to give him a beautiful home, entertain his friends, even help him in advancing his career. "And if we *did* have a lovely child—that I scarce dare hope for. But if we did—and it was good and beautiful and clever—they might be sort of halfway reconciled."[82]

Charlotte expressed the desire to have Katharine live with them soon after their marriage. She suggested to Ho that "Mother" Helen Campbell also join their household to care for Kate while Charlotte was on the road, and to free Charlotte and Ho in the evenings when she was not, although this never happened. Ho expressed delight at having Katharine, even immediately after the wedding. This prompted Charlotte to respond that Kate's presence would be "both joy and duty," feeling that it would be easier for the two of them to be alone for a while.

Whatever Houghton was writing to Charlotte, he was saying the right and reassuring words. His words of love to Charlotte elicited the following response: "I'm not young and beautiful that a man should love me like that. But—but—it makes me feel like a little smiling girl again. All blushes and dimples and tossed curls. To be thousands of years old inside—and surely no chicken to look at—and then have you just naturally make love to me———well, I won't bother trying to understand."[83]

Just a few weeks before the wedding Charlotte reported on two medical check-ups she had undergone to determine the wisdom of trying to become pregnant. The first doctor, a woman, assured her that she had a good chance of producing a healthy offspring. But "she does not know me as well as Dr. McCracken," and he very strongly urged her against conception. They had, he said, only a bare chance of having an "exceptionally fine child." Their two highly developed Beecher brains, the close relationship of first cousins, and Charlotte's previous mental condition combined to present a dismal prognosis. Dr. McCracken thought that the marriage would do Charlotte good. A child might also do her good, but on the other hand might cause great harm. As for the child, he was quite certain that the odds were heavy against its health and well-being. He is only one doctor and they have thought of all this before, she says. But the risk seemed great and for Charlotte, as she put it, "the wreckage it would mean to my conscience if the thing went wrong" was terrible to contemplate. She urged Houghton to seek some medical advice. As it also happened, she was then suffering some unspecified malfunction that Dr. Low, a woman physician, told her meant that she was unlikely to become pregnant at least for a time. "Happy thought—take no precautions—take no treatment—all runs smoothly and naturally and nothing happens!!! There's an easy way out of the difficulty." Both Houghton and Charlotte agreed not to be devastated if there were no children "because of all these heavy chances against." Again Charlotte reiterated her desire to give her husband a child "because I love you so. And when a woman loves a man that's the kind of a present she wants to make him." But, she mused, "perhaps after all you'll have to take the will for the deed. It is a good will I assure you. But it does seem kind of Providential if this little disarrangement down there should obviate the danger without any strenuous measures on our part."[84]

It was Houghton, ultimately, who made the decision not to have children, a decision Charlotte evidently really did want to hear, though there is no reason to assume that his sense of her wishes determined his decision. His reason apparently had to do with their being first cousins. "Look here young man," she told him in that serious-playful way: "If you think I'm going to take the trouble and the risk and the pain and all the various chances of having a child in the face of a fond-parent-that-might-be's explicit declaration that he doesn't want any—you have an exalted idea of the maternal instinct in yours truly."

The different parts of Charlotte's life, once so separate, were finally coming together. "At first . . . the place that loved you was a little spot—by itself. Now it has spread over a great deal . . . and living and loving are becoming very much the same thing. A new depth—or height—of joy continually opens to me."

Charlotte was writing from Chicago, where the wedding was scheduled to take place on June 11. Houghton was due to arrive a few days before. "You mustn't make a spectacle of yourself," she

warned him. "Don't fling your grip to the winds and rush at me—
I might run." However, when they are duly married she will, she
says, be delighted to spend the following week "in a more or less
frequent exchange of kisses. Or a fortnight."[85] The woman of forty,
a world-famous writer and lecturer, was finally able to enjoy the
pleasures of the young bride.

The next day the soft sighs and whispers of the bride-to-be
continued:

> I remember that time . . . you put your hand out toward
> me—touched me softly and said "O my dear love!" as if you
> simply *couldn't help it* . . . a sort of passionate sigh of utter
> love—I can hear it yet. You are generally so restrained, so
> quiet. That little phrase has stayed with me more than many
> kisses and I remember kisses too. I remember the first time
> you asked for one . . . and then didn't take another for ever
> so long. . . . I remember . . . when you first taught me what
> kisses were.

She concluded the letter with "how proudly glad" she feels to have
the love pour from her, "to find that I *can* love after all. That
triumphant joy you have given me past recall."[86]

She summed it all up in a letter the following week:

> I just sit here and feel happy. Only two weeks. . . . And then
> I shall belong to him. And he will take care of me—and I
> shall not be alone and among strangers anymore.
>
> Born among strangers. Brought up among 'em. Looking
> with a child's large disapproving eyes on the way they be-
> haved . . . being very lonesome and married a stranger. Got
> out alive—barely. Then strangers—Strangers—Strangers.
> Now I'm coming home to My Family.[87]

At the last moment it appeared that a Chicago wedding was
not possible because of a law prohibiting marriages between first
cousins, and so the ceremony was moved to Detroit and postponed
one day. The last days of letters from Charlotte are filled with
making "swell" hats with pretty flowers, the right petticoat to go
with her elegant suit. "I never wanted such pretty things before. It

Charlotte in 1900 (Photograph by Chas. K. Lumius)

didn't matter. Now I want to shine."[88] It was almost a year since Charlotte and Houghton had seen each other.

On June 11, 1900, Charlotte spoke in Milwaukee at a meeting of the Women's Federation of Clubs. The next day she and Houghton were married in the home of friends in Detroit.

In her autobiography, Charlotte wrote: "we were married . . . and lived happily ever after. If this were a novel, now, here's the happy ending."[89] And so, I believe, it was.

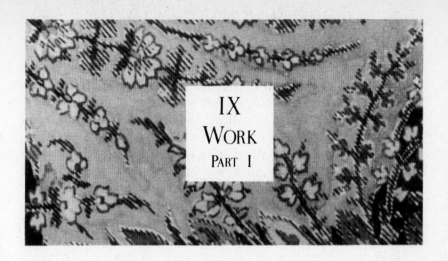

IX
WORK
PART I

Charlotte Perkins Gilman wrote *Women and Economics* during the period of her courtship with Houghton, an appropriate symbol of the successful resolution of the major tensions of her life. With the publication of that book and her marriage to Houghton, which occurred within two years of each other, Charlotte Gilman's life came together in new and important ways. She had learned to trust herself and others, she had overcome her fears of abandonment sufficiently to establish an intimate relationship with a loved person, and she had evolved new self-confidence and self-love in the triumph of a major and significant book. She had essentially resolved the struggle between the public and private selves that had plagued her all her life. As she settled into a satisfying and comfortable life with Houghton Gilman, the central focus of her energies became her work.

She wrote dozens of books and hundreds of articles and lectured to thousands of audiences. Her last speaking engagement occurred only weeks before her death in 1935. Her last published writing, her autobiography, was completed with her knowledge that it would appear after her death. From the earliest entries in her diary and the poems, letters, and short stories she wrote as a very young girl, to the final words she wrote as a dying woman of seventy-five, she used her energies and her gifts in an effort to understand the world and her place in it and to extend that knowledge and those insights to others. Her search for the meaning of human existence was in its deepest sense autobiographical, for she drew on the lessons of her own experience to help her understand the experience of others—indeed, of everyone.

She is known today as a feminist. She saw herself as a humanist. She was both. She was a nineteenth-century intellectual woman. Although she lived on the margin of intellectual life—she was never an accepted member of the intellectual establishment except through some personal contact with those who were—she was a part of the international currents and movements that shaped the new ideas of her time. Because she is less well known today than she was in her heyday, because the full range of her scope and vision and soaring imagination was inadequately understood even in her own time, it may seem preposterous to think of her in the company of Henry Adams, Charles Darwin, Max Weber, William Spencer, Karl Marx, Frederick Engels, and Sigmund Freud—thinkers, some preceding and some following her, whose goals were to create a unified world-view. That was also her goal: to draw upon anthropology, biology, history, sociology, ethics, and philosophy to comprehend the contours of human evolution and human society in order to create a humane social order. She, along with other intellectuals of her time, sought to understand the world in order to change it.

She suffered, as all outsiders do, from lack of engagement with the trained, critical intelligentsia of her day. She did not have access to the active, dynamic, exciting university world. She was denied the give-and-take it could have provided, the necessity of responding to serious challenges from the established intellectual world, the concern for rigor and intellectual discipline. Her poverty, her idiosyncratic radical politics, her gender, her own psychological needs—all joined to keep her on the margin of mainstream American cultural and intellectual life. She found no place in the center.

Nor was there a place for her even in the institutions on the margin: within socialist circles. Her radicalism was not theirs. She sharply rejected any notion of class struggle and class violence, which effectively removed her from all Marxist circles. The strength of the Fabian community that formed in the wake of Edward Bellamy's *Looking Backward* was already beginning to fade in America by the turn of the century. It never was able to create a cohesive political force as it did, for example, in England, where politically Gilman would have found a more congenial community. Moreover, she differed from traditional Marxism as well in this important respect: she took the restructuring of relations between men and women as a central focus of her new vision. Karl Marx and Frederick Engels assumed that a change in the means of production would eventually carry with it all the other necessary changes in social relations. Gilman asserted that attention needed to be paid initially to the ways in which people's lives had to be altered in their homes, in their families, in their intimate relations, and that no changes in social relationships could be expected to come about automatically. Issues of class were generally submerged for her in the overriding issue of gender. By placing women at the center of her intellectual inquiry, she separated herself from radical women within socialist circles. And despite Gilman's indebtedness to the thought of Lester Ward and ties to the Nationalist movement, she went beyond Ward's theories to envision a fully structured cooperative, socialized world.

She was also on the margin of the women's movement, where one might have thought she would find a home because of a shared belief that issues of gender take precedence over issues of class. But Charlotte did not quite fit with the women's movement either, although that world was probably closest to her. To the extent that the women in the complex of groups, clubs, and organizations called "the women's movement" were concerned primarily with contemporary aspects of politics, trade unions, social or literary activities, Charlotte's central interests were not theirs. Only rarely in our history have reform or radical communities, whose concerns are political and contemporary, seen the value of connection to intellectuals who share a comparable vision. Only rarely have intellectuals sought a place in a political community. Such a separation between intellectuals and activists has its roots in a distinctly American past, for in much of the rest of the world that separation, sometimes antagonism, does not exist in the same way. But here and at that time there was not a place in the women's movement for a person whose activity was primarily intellectual. The lecture circuit was Charlotte's place, if she had any, but the lecture circuit provided the mechanics of her endeavors, it did not provide a community.

When Charlotte insisted that she was not a feminist she was not entirely wrong. As she said, she was a humanist; the world was masculinist and she wished to restore an equitable balance. She saw the submergence of women as a critical handicap retarding the best development of society, and it was in this context that she spoke of the social need to emancipate women. Nor was her argument for women's freedom rooted in a natural-rights position, which asserted that basic rights are inviolable and inalienable because they are rooted, not in theology or history, but in human nature. She argued that women were narrowed by their position in society and that they therefore narrowed the lives of their men and their children. To improve society as a whole, it was necessary to free women from their domestic place. For Charlotte the emancipation of women was a step towards human emancipation, not an ultimate goal in itself. Socialist women, too, sought full human liberation, but in general, they felt that women's liberation would come as a product of a socialist triumph. A victory of the working class would carry with it the emancipation of women. To Charlotte, the opposite was true: the emancipation of women would lead to freedom for all.

There were benefits as well as losses involved in Charlotte's position as an outsider. The power of Gilman's ideas comes from their stark originality and jolting freshness. She sees with an uncontaminated eye and brain, because her ideas were never filtered through a conventional educational process, pounded and bludgeoned into a form acceptable to conventional wisdom. It is the very boldness of her ideas, their unconventionality, that is so valuable. One can only imagine how a college education might have dimmed her ability to perceive and convey shocking truths.

Charlotte Gilman took the disadvantages of her life and turned them into strengths. She suffered the pain and cultural deprivation poverty entailed, but that poverty gave her a perspective and a vision she might otherwise have lacked. She even, in a way, made use of her psychologically based inability to read for more than a short time. This reading debility denied Charlotte a thorough self-education, but also forced her to rely primarily upon herself. What she knew about the intellectual and political currents that surrounded her she knew partially from reading but largely from absorbing what she could from her cultural environment. She wanted to know about *her* roots, *her* evolution, *her* history, but history and science and sociology were not written about her, and so she wrote about them herself.

Since Gilman's articles and lectures provided the arena in which she examined and developed the ideas that eventually found their place in her books, my assessment of her work will focus on her full-length studies, because it was in the books, rather than in the many and varied lectures, that her ideas came together in a systematic and cogent way. The logical place to begin is with her first and most influential book, *Women and Economics*.

Women and Economics is what its subtitle claims it to be, an examination of the economic relationship between men and women as a factor in social evolution. Its central thesis is that the major influence in our lives is the way we earn a living, an assumption inherited from classical economics; Gilman extends that assumption beyond human society to all living creatures, reflecting the overriding influence of Darwinian evolutionary ideas on her thought. What makes us different from *all* other animals, she says, is that in the human species alone the female depends on the male for food, so that the sex relationship is also an economic relationship. This original formulation of Gilman's is fundamental to all her subsequent ideas.

Among some birds and animals, she admits, the male assists with the young, but in no case does the female depend on the male, with the sole exception of the hornbill, who, while she is nesting, is walled in with clay in a hollow tree, with only her beak projecting, and is fed by the male. But even the female hornbill is not fed at any other time. Nowhere in nature is the female supported by the male throughout her life, except among humans.

This is not to say that many women, most women, do not work hard. Peasant women, tribal women, poor women in industrial societies, all work hard, but the rewards they receive are not connected to the intensity or quality of their work. Hard work is not the same as economic independence. The economic rewards of women depend on the ability and whim of the men on whom they are dependent.

Men's work is more important to the social life of any community than is women's, Gilman continues, thereby separating herself from many nineteenth- and twentieth-century feminists who see women's culture as equal if not superior to men's. Gilman maintains that the collective activities surrounding trade, crafts, arts, manufactures, inventions, and political institutions, the values by which we judge the achievements of human society, the ways by which we measure the significance of activities, are almost exclusively masculine, since women are prevented from participation in society's public activities, except for the most primitive kind. If men were removed from a community, it would be much more seriously paralyzed than if women suddenly disappeared. "Women's work" could easily be performed by men; advanced workers would merely be reduced to much simpler tasks. "Men can cook, clean, and sew as well as women, but the making and managing of the great engines of modern industry, the threading of earth and sea in our vast systems of transportation, the handling of our elaborate machinery of trade, commerce, government—these things could not be done so well by women in their present degree of economic development."[1]

It is not that women lack the inherent ability to perform, says Gilman, but rather that their present condition prohibits them from performing. Women share in the world's activities and rewards more through their men than through their own labor.

True, Gilman says, some people argue that women earn a share of their husbands' wealth in their capacity as wives. Now in a large sense, a real sense, one could claim that all living things need each other and depend on each other, she goes on. But the assertion that a wife has a claim to a share of her husband's earnings presupposes something more specific: that she has earned it, works for it. Using a traditional labor theory of value, Gilman describes how we depend on a shoemaker or tailor for shoes or clothes and we pay for their skills with our own, as a farmer or builder. We retain our personal independence so long as the labor imbedded in the goods or services we offer is equivalent to the labor in what we receive. Such is not the case with most women, who consume but do not produce comparably.

To justify woman's position as consumer on the grounds that she is a marriage partner is to use the word "partner" improperly. Husband and wife are partners in their mutual responsibility to their children and they are partners in their shared love. A male doctor who marries a woman has not taken a partner in his wife, unless she too is a doctor. A woman who marries a composer is not thereby enabled to create music. A man's work is not destroyed when his wife dies, however much grief he feels, unless the grief itself impedes his work.

If the wife, then, is not a partner, in the sense of a business partner, how does she earn her keep? By service in the home, through the labor expended in carrying out household activity, some argue. It is surely true, counters Gilman, that the labor of a wife at home enables her husband to produce more outside it, which demonstrates that women are "economic factors." But then, so is a horse. Neither horse nor woman is independent.

It may prove impossible to determine the actual economic value of domestic work, but whatever it is, its rewards are not allocated justly among women, argues Gilman. The women who work the hardest get the least money, and those who have the most money do the least work. Even if women were paid fairly for their housework, their livelihood would be reduced to that of a servant, a fact neither women nor men are inclined to acknowledge.

It is often said that women are valued, receive their living, then, as mothers, Gilman notes. If this were true, then economic status would be connected in some way to the quantity and quality of children reared. It is perfectly obvious that women's economic prosperity has no relationship to their motherhood, or lack of motherhood.

What, then, remains to justify a woman's being supported by a man? It is the assertion that the very function of maternity makes a woman unfit for economic production so that she has the right to claim support by her husband. But what is demonstrably true is that it is not motherhood, not child service, but house service—cleaning, cooking, washing, mending—that keeps the housewife working unendingly. Thus we have a situation in which the housewife-mother works at nonmaternal duties sufficiently long hours to provide her with an independent living and then is denied an independent living on the grounds that her motherhood keeps her from working. Such a ludicrous notion is made even more ludicrous when we consider the years available for other work before women have children or after those children have reached adulthood.

Human life has always been sustained by the hard labor of the mother at work. But her work does not provide her with economic independence. Her living is unconnected to the production of wealth, to her housework, or to her motherhood. Her economic reward is related only to "the man she married, the man she depends on—to how much he has and how much he is willing to give her."[2] To a wife, her husband is her food supply.

This sexuo-economic relationship, as defined by Gilman, profoundly distorts human relations. She distinguishes between what she calls a "natural" process of social development and an "unnatural" process, one that advances the collective good of a species and one that retards it. Complex organisms gradually evolved from the earliest and least complex ones, she argues, and this evolution was accompanied by a gradual development of differentiation between male and female. As the distinction between male and female developed, attraction between the two increased, until now among all the higher creatures there are two markedly different sexes, "strongly drawn together by the attraction of sex, and fulfilling their use [function] in the reproduction of the species."[3] These are "natural" features, by which Gilman means they evolved in the best interest of the species. In the human race we have created an "unnatural," a "morbid excess in the exercise of this function." Excessive sex-indulgence is a distinctive feature of the human species, Gilman claims; we have carried the natural and normal distinctions of sex to such an extreme degree as to be "disadvantageous to our progress as individuals and as a race." (Calling some products of evolution "natural" and others "unnatural" and assuming that she could distinguish between them was Gilman's way of designating what she thought desirable in the human race and what she thought harmful: she thus embedded her own critical judgments in the language of evolutionary theory.)

Here she introduces some basic distinctions important to her analysis. For a species to thrive there must be a successful balance of self-preservation and what she calls "race-preservation," forces that are often in opposition. Self-preservation, which she defines as the development of qualities that help to maintain individual life, evolves through natural selection acting on the individual, which provides him or her with those qualities. Race-preservation, the development of qualities that are useful to the survival of the species but may be detrimental to individual needs, is produced by "sexual selection"—selection for specifically gendered traits—acting on the individual, which leads to profit ultimately for the offspring, directly or otherwise. Each species must create sexual differences sufficient to maintain reproduction but not so great as to threaten the species. The force of natural selection continues to produce identical "race-qualities," and these act as a check on sexual selection, which produces different sex qualities. As male and female, members of a species perform different functions and thus develop somewhat differently. As a species, both male and female perform identical functions and therefore develop equally. A balance is essential to sustain the life of the species.

To illustrate her point, Gilman turns to the tail of the male peacock. Its size and splendor are a secondary sex characteristic, crucial in attracting a mate, but were that tail to grow too huge, then the sexual distinction might jeopardize the survival of the individual, who would then die out, taking his overlarge tail with him. The male deer is larger and stronger than the female, but unless she is large enough and strong enough to keep pace with him, he flees foes, she does not, and so ends the future of the deer.

In general, she insists, the male and female of a species are more alike than different. Cow and bull, mare and stallion, are different as to sex but alike as to species, and the likeness in species is far greater than the sexual difference. Cow, mare, cat, and woman are all female mammals, but considerably more different than similar.

The balance of forces so necessary in any species is disrupted in the human race. The balance is shaken because the human female is economically dependent on the human male. As a result, natural selection not only does not check the action of sexual selection, it accelerates it. It operates this way: By supporting woman, man has defined himself as her economic environment. He is her food supply. Under natural selection each creature is shaped by its environment, developing qualities to enable it to feed itself. Under sexual selection, each creature is modified to the requirements of the mate. But when the mate is also the economic factor, then these two evolutionary forces move to the same end: to develop sex-distinction. Man is shaped by natural selection, woman by sexual selection, because the man is her economic environment and thus the major economic factor in her life. Sex-distinction is her way to win a mate, as it is with all creatures, but her mate is also her means of livelihood, as with no other creatures. The result is excessive sex-distinction. This "morbid" quality is then passed on to the offspring and so steadily ingrained in humans.

Gilman's definition of sex-distinction is as ingenious and as idiosyncratic as are many of her ideas. In her vocabulary, "over-sexed" refers to an excess of any distinction of sex, primary or secondary. She believed that such excesses occur in the area of secondary sex characteristics. Some sex-distinctions are physical, such as a deer's antlers or a lion's mane. Some, Gilman asserts, are behavioral. "Maternal passion" is as much a sex-distinction as antlers. The predisposition to "sit" is a sex-distinction of the hen, as strutting is of the cock. Males tend to fight, females in general to protect and nurture, Gilman claims. It is important to note that Gilman did *not* extend her belief in sex-distinctions to the mind. She said very emphatically: "There is no female mind. The brain is not an organ of sex. As well speak of a female liver."[4]

Whether these sex characteristics, particularly as they emerge in humans, are genetic or cultural and how they are passed on to subsequent generations is a complicated and controversial issue Gilman tends to sidestep.

In human society, she maintains, the "over-sexed" behavior of the male, consisting of sexual indulgence far beyond what procreation requires and leading to extramarital indulgence, is injurious. Our error, she tells us, lies in assuming that men are voluntarily behaving immorally, rather than recognizing that they are suffering from a "condition of morbid development" in the male of the human species.

However excessive the male human is, he is less "over-sexed" than the female of the species. Sexual life is but one part of his world. He has been largely responsible for the development of industry, commerce, science, manufacturing, government, art, and religion. Women, having been excluded from these arenas of public life, are confined primarily to domesticity. It is in woman that excessive sex-distinction is most exaggerated in ways physical, psychical, and social.

For dramatic illustration, Gilman this time looks to the cow, contrasting the wild cow with the domesticated milch cow. The wild cow has healthy calves for which she has adequate milk. That is her "femininity." Aside from the adaptations necessary for her maternal function, she is a bovine like any other. "She is a light, strong, swift, sinewy creature, able to run, jump and fight, if necessary." We have artificially exaggerated the cow's milk-producing capacity. We have made her into a walking milk machine, bred to that purpose. Since the secretion of milk is a maternal function—that is, a sex-function—the cow is "over-sexed."

So too is woman. Woman is a member of a healthy, vigorous, strong animal species. Permitted to develop freely and naturally she would be, and has been for brief periods in human history, a healthy, independent creature. Instead, she has been bred to sex-activity, by which Gilman means to activity in her female, rather than human, capacity. We can speak of a "feminine hand" or a "feminine foot," while it would make no sense to refer to a "feminine paw" or a "feminine hoof." Hand and foot are not designed to be secondary sex characteristics, but in the human race we have encouraged smallness and feebleness as a sex-distinction. Women are actually known as "the weaker sex." In no other advanced species is there such a startling difference between male and female.

Women are selected as mates for their feebleness and weakness but they transmit their physical debilities to their children, boys and girls, so that all human development is retarded. That much-sought-after feminine "delicacy," which is really physical weakness, makes a woman a less effective mother and wife as well.

The psychological manifestations of sex-distinction in women are no less apparent, says Gilman. Prominent among them is what we know as woman's intense, unreasoning emotionalism. It is desirable both for the individual and the race—that is, species—to have evolved such a degree of passion and love as to make for the happiness of individuals and the successful reproduction of the species. We have encouraged such passion beyond what is good for the race. Man has other outlets which temper his erotic passions; for woman, these represent the major part of her life.

From earliest childhood we accentuate sex differences between boys and girls. How proud we are when a little girl plays like a little mother; yet maternity and paternity are inappropriate in a child. These sex-distinctions should not be encouraged until adolescence, Gilman says. When they are encouraged too early, the boy is not as damaged as the girl because he is permitted a whole range of human activities. When a healthy girl shares in those activities, we call her a "tom-boy." As a result, we now believe that most human qualities are masculine, simply because we permit men to develop them but prohibit women from doing so.

All the varied activities of our complicated civilization are part of the process of self-preservation and they belong to all of us, to both sexes, says Gilman. Economic, cultural, religious, and scientific activities are not sex functions, they are race functions. Yet virtually the entire arena of human progress has been a masculine prerogative, a clear demonstration of just how extreme the excessive sex-distinction of the human race has been.

Gilman relied on what natural and social scientists in the nineteenth century defined as biological and sociological laws and on some rather simple evolutionary notions of that time to explain how it all came about. In the dawn of human evolution, she postulates, primitive man and woman were both nimble and ferocious. He, as a male, had the added belligerence required for the sex-competition needed for mating, she tells us. In those mating times, he, like other advanced animals, fought competitors, while the female mated with the winner. At all other times she remained an independent creature. At some point in history, she asserts, "this amiable savage," the male, understood that he was able to subordinate the female because of his own superior strength and the limits imposed by her childbearing capacities. The male then had to take responsibility for feeding the enslaved female and their offspring. The poet may extoll this lovely arrangement, says Gilman, but sociologically it was a disaster for the female, who now had no direct relationship to the natural environment. With the male as her environment, she began to respond to his demands and modify her behavior accordingly. Qualities of strength and speed were no longer desirable. The qualities that now were valuable for her survival were qualities that enhanced sex-attraction. Growing armies of employed women are now changing this demeaned status, says Gilman, but at the moment it is still unhappily true that "women's economic profit comes through the power of sex-attraction."[5]

This fact boldly confronted in the open market we call vice. The same economic relationship supported by law and religion and covered with flowers and sentiment we think wonderful. The biological effect is the same whether the trade is transient or permanent, Gilman reminds us.

Unlike the females of all other species, who have the full range of experience that their males have, the human female is confined to her home, denied access to the knowledge and experience of the world outside it. What we do changes us more than what is done to us, and the "ever-growing human impulse" to create, to make, to do, to have impact, has been denied to women. Even worse, women are forced to carry out their limited and narrow labor in private, alone.

Human progress has been achieved by specialization, by division of labor, says Gilman, asserting another tenet of classical economics. In earlier times working in the household was not so limiting because the household *was* the community, but as society developed and what had been household skills became professionalized, women were denied access to those new skills. A housewife and a baker both bake bread. She performs unpaid labor. His is a career for which he is paid and respected and whose skills he has the time and opportunity to develop to a high degree. In religion too, as civilization advances, women's position deteriorates. "In dim early time," she says, woman shared in mysteries and rites. As religion developed, her position was reduced, until Paul commanded her to be silent, and she is silent to this day. Only now, in the last years of the nineteenth century, are women beginning to make advances into the public world, Gilman asserts.

Fortunately, Gilman says, the demeaned position of the female has been countered genetically each generation because each boy and girl inherits from both parents. Thus heredity functions to equalize what environment and education have made so different. Here, Gilman looks to genetics to temper the abuses of environment and education. Most other reform Darwinists took the opposite position: that environment was crucial in ameliorating genetic differences. Gilman recognized the advantage in having each operate to check the other.

Since what she asserts is undeniably true, Gilman asks, how is it possible that so many deny it? The answer lies, first, with the "law of adaptation," whereby with ceaseless repetition the organism adapts to the environment. All manner of ghastly sounds become acceptable with repetition. The first time a healthy woman puts on a corset it is hideously painful, but the woman habituated to a confining corset does not feel the pain, although the body is not deceived. Adaptation by men to their stiff high collar is another instance of the force of habit. Cultural habits are developed similarly. We know how much easier it is to criticize customs other than our own, because ours seem so "natural." A custom which has existed for unrecorded ages, which exists everywhere, and to which the individual is exposed from the moment of birth will not even be noticed. Such a "habit" is the "sexuo-economic relationship."

There is another law that minimizes our perception of general truth: It is easier to personalize than to generalize. Slaveholders admitted the existence of abuses among some cruel or incompetent slaveholders. What the slaveholder did not see was that the very existence of chattel slavery inevitably led to such evils. The sex relation seems to be personal—it involves a man, his wife, and their children—and so it is easy to take a "personalized" and therefore distorted view of it.

Women, locked into a definition of themselves as sexual rather than human beings, a fact neither they nor their men are fully aware of, pass on that vision to their children. The messages about marriage passed from mother to daughter, and to son, are inherently hypocritical. While marriage is what a girl is trained for, what she is "exhibited for," what will become her means of livelihood, she is not permitted to look as if she is seeking it. She must sit passively by and be chosen. Since it is not honest employment, but rather economic beggary, no honest woman can ask for it directly. It is a strange denial of reality, Gilman reminds us, to denounce the girl who marries the rich old man, and we do denounce her. Why blame her for pursuing her vocation? After all, "the mercenary marriage is a perfectly natural consequence of the economic dependence of women."[6] We have forced woman into a "hideous paradox" whereby she is made to identify love and true loving feelings with gain and with self-interest.

Recently, says Gilman, a growing community of women have emerged who prefer what they call "their independence" to being confined to husband and children. These women arouse fear in the majority, who see them as threatening the sanctity of the home. The very admission that economically independent women may not want to marry is proof that only dependence has forced women into marriage. The independent woman's reaction to marriage is understandable, but such an attitude will cease to exist when marriage ceases to involve the loss of liberty.

Marriage to a dependent woman is unsatisfactory in many ways for men as well. The male farmer gets a working partner when he marries, but in our society most men are not farmers. The middle-class man marries a consumer, and he needs to be able to afford her before he can marry. The result is that the man seeks promiscuous and temporary sex relations, says Gilman, which are inherently wrong. Such behavior is wrong not because society holds such moral views but because such sexual liaisons violate natural laws. Gilman argues that in the long evolutionary process a lengthy infancy proved beneficial to the improvement of the species. "The best care" could only be provided by both parents, which in turn presupposed and encouraged a more permanent mating.

At this point in her analysis, Gilman moves from the economic relationship to the economic process, to the way we produce and distribute wealth. However we decide to distribute wealth or think it should be allocated, there is no question, she reminds us, that wealth is produced collectively. Society advances as human labor develops collectively. The more highly specialized our social organization and productive capacity, the greater is the wealth produced. The spirit that emanates from collective production should be a social spirit; we should acknowledge that personal interest must be submerged in the common interest. No individual interest should stand against the common good. But it does. We are burdened with an unreasonable commitment to individualism. The sexuoeconomic relation is the villain.

Woman's social spirit is never developed because of the economically dependent state in which she is confined. A group of young women at a summer resort hunting the limited supply of young men are locked into a competitive situation. Each woman obtains her livelihood, not by combining with others to mutual advantage, but by winning an individual victory against the others. Herein can be seen, Gilman tells us, the roots of the antagonism of the virtuous woman toward the prostitute. The woman of virtue clings to her economic goods—virginity—until she achieves her goal of marriage and economic support, and she has reason to view as her enemy any woman who offers similar goods at a far smaller price. The hatred engendered is comparable to that of the "trade unionist for 'scab labor.' "[7]

The economically dependent state in which women are locked, a condition of servitude, develops qualities of a servile personality. Women have been denied physical freedom, which is the basis of knowledge. Women are denied the mental freedom and moral freedom to be responsible for themselves and to learn the consequences of their actions. As a result, women have remained "undeveloped in the larger judgment of ethics."[8] Since they are always being blamed or praised for their conduct, they have an excessively developed moral sense. The virtues for which women are praised are faithfulness, submissiveness, and self-sacrifice, and thus we call women morally superior to men. But our complicated civilized world requires new moral virtues, and these women cannot develop because their economic dependence continually retards that progress.

Men are engaged in social activity by participating in the marketplace world where progress is regularly achieved by increasing specialization and thus increasing productivity. However, their tendency to individualism is exaggerated by contamination with the sexuo-economic relationship. "She gets her living by getting a husband. He gets his wife by getting a living." If it is disastrous to her that her individual economic advantage comes through securing a mate, it is no less disastrous to him that his economic gain is used to achieve individual sex-advantage. If sex-functions have been distorted in her to economic ends, then economic functions to him have become sex-functions.

We are accustomed to thinking it is a man's first duty to support *his* family, and this, Gilman argues, is a violation of the sociological law that requires the recognition of the superiority of the community. To a young man the dependence of a helpless creature whose food must come from his earnings does not stimulate courage or community activity, but compels timidity, conservatism, and submission. Legitimate sex-competition brings out the best in men, Gilman claims. To please the woman he cares for, a man does his best. But if her economic dependence on him is added to the equation, the man struggles not to do things to please her but to get things with which to purchase her.

Just as economic dependence in women fosters a servile personality, so do men suffer from their position of dominance, says Gilman. "The lust for power and conquest, natural to the male of any species, has been fostered in him to an enormous degree by this cheap and easy lordship." His dominance comes not because he is worthy of leadership. It is an accident of sex. Having a whole person catering to his needs develops his selfishness to an inordinate degree.

While sons are forced to accept the power of tyrannical fathers, no democracy can exist. So long as the family is the core of social life, no higher collectivity can develop. Speaking at a time when the family was an enshrined and revered institution, Gilman boldly insists that the family as it is constituted is a retrogressive institution. It is primarily the sexuo-economic relation, she says, which sustains and nurtures primitive individualism in a world where socio-economic progress lies in the direction of collective growth. Gilman predicts that when sexual relations between men and women no longer exist as an economic relationship, then a commitment to humanity will not be seen as an unnatural sacrifice, and a concern for collective prosperity will cease to be frightening. There is hope, she assures us, because women are increasingly demanding their freedom, economic and social freedom, and when that freedom is achieved, the sort of genuine union long sought between men and women will be possible.

The central force behind such sociological changes, "the crux of the whole matter,"[9] is to be found in changing economic relationships. The pressure of industrial development requires increasing specialization, which operates to break down the family as an economic unit. Women have been driven into public economic activity, often driven reluctantly, because many women still work only because they must. But with that public work has come a better spirit among young women who taste independence and then cherish it.

Many argue that the working mother is a threat to the family, to marriage, to parenting. It is true, Gilman concedes, that she does represent a challenge to the inviolability of the old way of doing things—but the old way is no longer appropriate. The family as a tightly knit unit is changing and should change.

Despite the economic reality that more women are entering the paid work force, we still cling to outdated notions of social relations,

Gilman argues. With larger opportunities opening up, women today feel all the more the personal limitations of being locked into
primitive individual home life and the outdated ideas that flow from
that condition. In the meantime "the very best and foremost women
suffer most," she comments, undoubtedly thinking partly of herself.[10]

Women are becoming masculine, it is said. Absurd, says Gilman. If it could be shown that the women of today were "growing
beards, were changing as to pelvic bones, were developing bass
voices, or that in their new activities they were manifesting destructive energy, the brutal combative instinct or the intense sex-
vanity of the male, then there would be cause for alarm." Here
Gilman has summed up what she sees as male qualities, physical
and psychological. The new woman will be no less female than the
old, she says, but she will be able to do more. The rapid changes
we are witnessing have nothing to do with masculine or feminine
traits but are simply products of advances in human development
of traits both sexes share.

These changes involve women's entry not only into the work
force but also into some sense of community of their own. Until
recently, Gilman notes, virtually the only place women could find
solidarity was in the church. Now, the entire country is "budding
into women's clubs."[11] To Gilman the women's club movement
was "one of the most important sociological phenomena of the
century—indeed, of all centuries—marking the first timid steps toward social organization of those so long unsocialized members of
our own race."[12] Women such as Elizabeth Cady Stanton, Susan
B. Anthony, Dr. Elizabeth Blackwell, all the others who have suffered and battled not for themselves alone but for one another and
all of us, have paid a price in their heroic activities, a lessening of
"soft charms and graces," but those who follow will be able to
keep much of what "these strenuous heroes had to lose."[13] One
wonders what price Gilman saw herself as paying for her efforts.

Great as these women are, Gilman says, we still have a long
way to go to undo the legacy of weak and little women "with the
aspirations of an affectionate guinea pig." Gilman had great hopes
for the future of womankind, but little respect or admiration for
most women as they were. And she certainly had a low opinion of
motherhood in its current state.

Motherhood is seen as so sacred, so binding, that we must acknowledge at the start how biased we all are, how deeply trained we are to accept the conventional notions of motherhood, warns Gilman, in language that continues to reverberate ninety years later. Our ingrained ideas of what motherhood means are so tied up with our notions of sexuality and religion that it is "well-nigh impossible" to think dispassionately on the subject, she says. But we must try. Although the powerful feelings we have about mother truly reflect the real power and place she has in our life, motherhood is a process and we must examine that process as we do any other.

Mother is the main agent in reproduction, the main agent in developing love, the initiator in times past of industry, and the first and final educator of the child, Gilman tells us. Why, then, do we leave such important work "to the methods of primitive instinct?"[14] In more primitive life forms motherhood is unconscious and functions by simple instinct. Motherhood among humans is a conscious and complex process and can best be judged by its results.

The purpose of "right motherhood" is to leave the offspring a person better than its parents, a theme that Gilman returns to persistently throughout her life, as well as a statement of her own personal determination to go beyond the limitations of both her mother and father. Humans are improved, generation after generation, first by the instinctive strong emotional bond that flows from the individual function of reproduction, and second, by the complex social function of the educational process, Gilman says. Thus the human child requires the love and care of the mother but, more important, the care and instruction of many others.

How well does the human mother succeed, compared with mothers in other species? "Human motherhood is more pathological than any other, more morbid, defective, irregular, diseased."[15] The more woman is segregated to sex-functions only, consequently tending to be soft, small, weak, and ill-proportioned, the more pathological does her mothering become and the more physically deficient are her children. The less a woman is confined to sex-functions alone, the better mother she is, Gilman argues, citing approvingly the example of the peasant woman and the "savage" woman, who produce physically superior children.

If human maternity does not produce a superior child physically, does it at least prove beneficial in the arena of education, Gilman asks? No other animal species must care for its young for so long a time and must teach it so much. "Ask yourselves honestly," she demands of her readers, how many of the mothers they see on the street, in shops, in their neighborhoods, do they regard as really good mothers? In reality, the human mother does less for her young, "both absolutely and proportionately, than any kind of mother on earth." She is not responsible for food, shelter, protection, or the defense of her young. She cannot give her offspring the necessary knowledge of the world because she does not have it. The poor man's wife has little time for her child. The rich man's wife usually hires someone else to care for her offspring.

We talk unendingly about the beauty of maternal sacrifice, but in no way do we prepare young women for it. The rearing and training of the young, which is the most important social function because it reproduces the race, is left in the hands of absolutely uneducated women. What most women have to offer their children intuitively is maternal love, but this love requires direction, and in this world as it is it does not receive it. "Simply to love the child does not serve him"[16] is a statement that applies as well to Gilman's own experience, as a daughter and as a mother, as to that of others.

Men are expected to study a trade before entering it. Women are given responsibility for the life or death of the human race and yet are given no instruction in how to go about fulfilling it. They rely on maternal instinct. "The record of untrained instinct is . . . to be read on the rows and rows of little gravestones which crowd our cemeteries." No, maternal sacrifice does not produce physical or mental progress in the young. When we genuinely respect motherhood as much as we say, we will then train women for that duty, not for acquiring a husband.

The home is considered as sacred as motherhood, Gilman continues. We love, revere, cling to the home, firmly convinced that "one whole woman" is required for each home, and usually more, and that we will vehemently oppose any efforts to strike at the foundations of this sanctified place. However, if women are to achieve their economic independence, which is necessary for *their* health and happiness and for their development as human, not female, beings, then the management of and relationship between home and family must be reformed. The present system of raising children by means of "millions of private servants" will have to be altered.

If we understand that marriage and "the family" are two different institutions, she goes on, it is easier to isolate what belongs to each. Marriage is a form of sex-union sanctioned by society. The family is a social group, once the central social unit, but now decreasing in significance. As the family is distinct from marriage, so is the home distinct from both.

Home is a permanent dwelling place, a place to be safe in, to eat in peace and sleep quietly in, a place of close familiar limits. But the highest goals of humanity are produced and achieved outside and apart from the home. We must live, think, feel, act, outside the home to become "humanly developed, civilized, socialized."[17] We need to extend the love generated in the home out into the life of the community.

Because we have restricted women to work at home, we have come to identify the work of the home—cleaning, washing, mending, preparing and serving food, that is, "the nutritive and excretive processes of the family"—as female functions, and we have assumed that such processes must take place in the home. But where "twenty women in twenty homes work all the time, and insufficiently accomplish their various duties, the same work in the hands of specialists could be done in less time by fewer people; and the others would be left free to do other work for which they were better fitted, thus increasing the productive power of the world," declares Charlotte Gilman.[18] The home would then cease to be a workplace in a stage of arrested industrial development, but would instead reflect the personal needs of its occupants for peace, rest, love, and privacy.

We see the flaws in the home and blame men for not staying in it. We blame women for being inadequate housekeepers. We blame children for being disobedient. "But we have never thought to blame the institution itself, and see whether it could not be improved."[19] Many fear the impact on the home of women's seeking larger social interests outside it. There is no cause to worry, Gilman assures her readers. We will lose the kitchens, as we lost the laundries and bakeries. The home will remain as a place to live in and to love in, to play and be together in. The home will be a place in which an economically free mother resides, a "world-servant instead of a house-servant," and she will make the world a better place for her child.

The children will be better off in other ways, too. What the baby must learn is that she or he is but one of many babies. The saying goes that an only child is apt to be selfish; "So is an only family."[20] A baby who spends the day with other babies would know that however much the mother loves the child specially, most of the day he or she is cared for by a trained child-care specialist exactly like other people of the same age. Our unfailing mother-nurse, says Gilman, gives us an absurdly exalted sense of our own personal importance—although her mother, of course, never did give her anything of the sort. Gilman's call for community child-care during the work day, which would permit women to seek full-time jobs, though heard frequently in our day, was scandalous in hers. It challenged the prevailing belief in the necessity of a full-time mother in the home.

In social evolution, as in all evolution, Gilman explains, the process of outgrowing the older form is accomplished only slowly and with great pain. We are only now growing aware that our notion that the family, not the individual, is the social unit is no longer valid. The residence hotel, the boardinghouse, the restaurant, the lodging house, all attest to the newly growing community of nonfamily individuals, she writes, referring to single men and women. "Broken sets," she called them, those who fall short of a traditional family unit or who are left over from it—people just like Charlotte, who do not fit into an ordinary mold.

Everybody needs a comfortable and beautiful home, she points out, not just people with families. Married people generally like to live together, but so may groups of men or women; others may wish to live permanently alone. These people must have the chance to fit comfortably into the social structure, as they do not quite yet. Such a need is particularly urgent for women, who must be assured that they can lead full and happy lives even if not married.

However much we change some family arrangements, we need not fear a threat to marriage as it exists, Gilman assures us, because it conforms to "a law of racial development which we can never escape," resting on the need for prolonged care of children by both parents.[21] Her belief in the central role of parents in rearing children exists alongside her belief that children, beginning in infancy, would benefit from spending their daytime hours under the care of a specialist. Once again Charlotte Gilman offers us an odd mixture of the radically new and the unchallenged old. It did not at this point occur to her to question the idea of the nuclear family or of heterosexual monogamous marriage, and she bolstered her own thinking in this respect with reference to biological and social "law." Whether Charlotte could not yet imagine questioning them or whether she did not want to startle and alienate an audience she was trying to win over is unclear; perhaps a little of each. She probably chose not to stretch her imagination beyond what she felt was an acceptable boundary for the time, for herself, and for her audience. For the moment she focused on the absolute necessity for women to earn their own living and on the changes society would need to make if that were to be done properly.

Women and Economics is an extraordinary and important book. It is original, provocative, subversive. It is not a book to which one can be indifferent. To strengthen an argument or illustrate an idea, Gilman took material from what others had said before her, but the essence of what she wrote and how she thought was boldly original.

Her issue is gender. She pays inadequate attention to class or race or ethnicity, and her argument is thereby weakened. But what she had to say about gender is still startling today, ninety years later.

Her major assertion that the "sexuo-economic" relationship is the central fact of human relationships is a brilliant formulation. She built on the labor theory of value, but extended it to the issue of gender. She did the same with evolutionary theory, giving new life to both widely held notions by that extension. Gilman used the accepted "scientific" wisdom of her time but infused it with a feminist angle of vision, and thereby transformed it profoundly, offering a view of gender relationships that appears obvious after she says it, but that is deeply original. Like other theorists committed to the theory of evolution, she used it to explain and insist on the desirability of change. What she wanted changed was hers alone: women's work, home, marriage, child-rearing.

Gilman locates the source of the subordination of women in the home, the most venerated institution in her society. The "sexuo-economic" relationship locks women into their homes and then identifies the work that is done in them as "natural" work for women. Gilman tears away that façade, exposing the reality of the institution as a limiting place, and she does it with a theoretical formulation that explains how it came about and why and how it must and will change.

She was a socialist, a collectivist. She endorsed an economic and social doctrine that acknowledged the cooperative nature of production and demanded that distribution be similarly collective. But at the same time she had a truer sense of individual rights and needs than the conservatives, who talked about individualism but clung to traditional notions of family as the core social unit, and the liberals, who spoke of unfettered individual rights. Gilman argued that the future lies with the growth of a collective spirit, but that the "sexuo-economic" relation sustains an outmoded primitive individualism. That individualism is bolstered by making the family the basic social unit. Gilman sought to replace the family with the community, for if this was done, she said, not only would the collectivity be enhanced but individuals as well, especially women who otherwise have their individuality submerged in the family system.

Unlike many women reformers and social critics of her time, Gilman acknowledged but did not seriously value the importance of a powerful female culture. She did not envision the domestic role as generating effective power for most women. She stressed, instead, the condition of servitude imposed on women and the servile personality that resulted from that condition. Gilman saw male contributions to civilization as superior. Feminist scholars in the last fifteen years have focused on how many nineteenth-century women gave their lives meaning by stressing the importance of female values and female community, finding strength and empowerment in a world they did not control. But Gilman's overriding concern was the pervasive, oppressive system that structured women's lives and not the creative responses some unusual women were able to develop. Although she underestimated the importance of women's culture, her words are an important reminder of the larger patriarchal world in which women have shaped their strategies for survival and of the negative impact of that patriarchal power on most women.

Her book is a stark indictment of a system built on women's dependence. She understood in a way different from *all* who preceded her how damaging that system was for all involved in it and how changing that basic relationship would change everything else. She understood that the changes she sought, and believed were coming, would enrich the lives not only of women but of men and children as well.

As we have seen, when *Women and Economics* first appeared it was widely reviewed and well received. Reviews appeared in a sizable number of prestigious magazines and journals which had an influential following, if not a mass readership. There were reviews in the *Outlook*, the *Sewanee Review*, the *Dial*, the *Independent*, the *American Fabian*, the *Nation*, the *Land of Sunshine*, the *Woman's Journal*, the *Conservator*, the *Poet-Lore*, the *Southern Educational Journal*, the *Arena*, the *Critic*, the *Bookman*, and the *Humanitarian*. It was also reviewed in the *New York Times Saturday Review of Books*, the *Boston Advertiser*, the *Denver Post*, and the *Political Science Quarterly*.[22]

Women and Economics had an immediate and enormous impact on radical and reform writers and critics. It was frequently quoted, and Gilman became an acclaimed figure, catapulted by world opinion into the position of a leading intellectual of the women's movement. But recognition of the importance of her ideas, especially those in *Women and Economics*, her best-known book, did not last beyond the first two decades of this century. This book did not have the kind of long-term impact on the world of ideas it deserves. Part of the explanation lies with the beginning of a retreat into conservatism in America in the period following World War I, when ideas about socialism and radical change of any kind were no longer tolerated as they had been earlier.

But even when *Women and Economics* was at the height of its influence, there was no serious effort within any part of the intellectual world, in the university or in the radical communities, to grapple with the kinds of issues Gilman addressed. Gender was too new a category. The many social critics and intellectuals who praised the book did not then go on to try to incorporate its ideas into their own work. It was too radical a project.

Women and Economics was reissued as a classic text in 1966 with an essentially positive assessment by the noted historian Carl Degler, who introduced it to a new generation of readers. It remains in print today. Perhaps it finally has a constituency.

Important as *Women and Economics* is, it is nevertheless only the first step in Gilman's construction of a complicated and ambitious historical and sociological analysis of men and women in history and society. After *Women and Economics* Charlotte turned to two central aspects of her thesis in that book, home and children, central not only to her analysis of gender in history but to the lives of women and, she would argue, therefore to men as well. In *Concerning Children*, a 298-page book published by Small, Maynard, and Company in 1900, and *The Home*, a book published by McClure, Phillips, and Company in 1903, she expands and refines the lines already drawn in *Women and Economics*. Thereafter she moved in quite new directions. Thus, to know only *Women and Economics* is to be familiar with only part of her ideas. It is to settle for a view of the ground floor and to neglect the enticing staircase that leads to more elaborate and intriguing rooms above.

In *Women and Economics* Charlotte addressed the overriding questions she faced in her own life: how to explain her mother, Mary Fitch Westcott, and her mother before her, how to explain the world that thwarted the gifts and blighted the possibilities of such women. In *Concerning Children* and *The Home*, this examination persists, now more pertinently, if indirectly, addressed to her own life, her life as daughter, and then her life as wife and mother.

Concerning Children, published just two years after *Women and Economics* and in the year Houghton and Charlotte were married, has one overriding theme: children are a part of any society, and a huge one. Individual children grow out of childhood but children are, as a category, a permanent class and a group larger than the adult population. Yet children are treated merely as parts of a family, not recognized as belonging to society. That personal view of children constitutes the greatest unfairness in the way we raise them.[23]

"We have the power to improve the species," is the way Gilman begins the book, quoting directly from Lester Ward. Improvement of the human race is transmitted through its youth, she declares. If we wish to raise the level of a group, we do not educate the older generation and let them die out; we educate the young, so they can pass on the advantages they have absorbed to their offspring. For the long-range interests of the human race, she goes on, it is better for a couple to be healthy and vigorous when of child-rearing age than to be "sick and vicious" before their children are born and saints afterwards. "The sowing of wild oats would be far less harmful if [they were] sowed in the autumn instead of in the spring," she says, indicating that somehow cultural and personal changes are passed as an inherited legacy to future generations. The real value of education is to change people before they become parents so that the improvement is passed on by birth as "an inbred racial progress."[24]

In this context she asserts that a "savage" baby, whatever the child's individual gifts, cannot have the "advanced" cultural qualities of a modern English infant. Such ideas reflect the racism that spilled out periodically in Gilman's work, particularly as she aged. She did unquestionably believe in the superiority of some races over others. Like her disturbing notion of using people as breeding stock to improve the species, this belief was grounded in her understanding of the latest "scientific" thought of the late nineteenth century, as well as in the attitudes of her class and time. She was not as free from the conventional views of her age as she liked to think. Although Gilman's racist, anti-Semitic, and ethnocentric ideas are most apparent in her personal writings, in her letters and journals, these biases inevitably limit and scar her theoretical work as well. The explanation for them must reside primarily in the psychological realm, because the nativist and racist views that she held did not fit with the vision she espoused of radical social and political transformation. Evidently she could not let go of the racism that accompanied an ideology which in large part she rejected. And so her racism, while always limiting and always inexcusable, has a quality of ambivalence and uncertainty about it. She did, for example, vigorously dissent from the newly revived eugenics movement, which was rooted in the belief that most human traits were irrevocably genetic in origin and therefore unchangeable. The most important and influential voice to challenge these assumptions was Franz Boas, whose book *The Mind of Primitive Man*, published in 1911, asserted that history and culture, not genetics, explain why different peoples went different ways, and that what is most striking about different races is their similarities, not their differences. Years before, Charlotte Gilman had argued similarly, but she extended her assertion only to the differences between men and women. On the issue of race and ethnicity she wavered, sometimes saying one thing and sometimes another, but always feeling, one senses, that all of these strange people with their odd customs and language and look were not quite as good as her people. Even so, despite her racist ideas, Charlotte's was the only voice raised at the 1903 convention of the National American Woman's Suffrage Association against a literacy requirement for the vote, the device commonly used to disenfranchise black citizens. Ten years later, in the April 1913 issue of her magazine, the *Forerunner*, she wrote: "That we have cheated the Indian, oppressed the African, robbed the Mexican . . . is ground for shame."

In arguing her point about the importance of educating and "improving" the young, Gilman decisively—and, again, erroneously—rejects August Weismann's theory that acquired traits are not transmissible by heredity. Weismann argued that however many generations of pigs have their legs amputated, each new generation has the original number. Her answer? There is a difference between a mutilation and an acquired trait. "An acquired trait is something that one uses and develops, not something one has lost." The shrunken feet of Chinese women are not transmitted, but Chinese habits are. The children of the soldier do not inherit his wooden leg, but they do inherit his courage and habit of obedience. Common sense tells us, she says, and parents and teachers know, that "as the twig is bent, the tree's inclined." She is fairly relaxed about the explanation: "Inherit we must to some degree; and whatever comes to us by that method must belong to the parent before he is a parent."[25] Gilman's idea of the inheritance of acquired characteristics was based on the work of Jean-Baptiste Lamarck, a pre-Darwinian scientist whose position on this question was already being challenged and was later discredited.

Gilman goes on to assert that, since parenting generally begins at about age twenty-five, and that age fifteen brings to most people a new sense of selfhood (as we know it did for Charlotte), these ten years are the important decade of a lifetime for the "race." But, she maintains, it is important that the first fifteen years of a child's life should develop the powers of judgment and will, in order to make the following ten years count most.

What are the virtues we instill in children, she asks, and do these virtues have value in and for the contemporary world?

Obedience is the quality we encourage most of all in children. In earlier times, Gilman's analysis continues, people lived in constant danger, so military service was universal, despotism was the common form of government, and slavery the common lot of nearly all men and women. Each of these institutions rests upon obedience to sustain it. And where men were slaves to others, their women were slaves to them. Subordinate to everyone else were always the vulnerable, defenseless children: "Naturally they were expected to obey." And since "our clouded brains" ascribed to the gods we created the habits of our earthly rulers, obedience to the gods was given first place in primitive religion.

Many changes have occurred since, Gilman argues, particularly in religion, where the Protestant Reformation established the idea of free thought. But The Home, still the stronghold of tradition, has been little affected by the idea of individual freedom. Women are just beginning to demand their freedom, but the child is still expected to obey.

However, since a child is only temporarily a child, it is an adult we are training and obedience is not a good quality to instill. The habit of obedience creates a habit of submission to authority, or else it has an equally injurious opposite effect, instilling a fierce determination to rebel.

The habit of obedience has, in Gilman's view, other serious disadvantages. From the beginning of time, she maintains, we have repeated the same mistake in educating our young: we have systematically forbidden our children acts that followed naturally from observation and inference, and insisted upon acts that, to the child's mind, made no sense. Thus we have trained generations to act without understanding and to understand without acting. Gilman stresses that we must teach children to learn, not to obey. They do learn in spite of us because "natural laws" cannot be entirely shut out. But, Gilman says, the brain is an organ like any other: it needs nourishment and stimulation to achieve its full growth.

The universal error is that we concern ourselves with what the child does, not with what the child feels and thinks. We stop the behavior that flows from feeling and thinking and then we substitute different behavior, that which we prefer. But this is a jolt to the child's brain; we make the body do something the brain has not authorized. And so the child cries "Why?" asking for some consistency. For most children, "don't" is the most common word in the mother's vocabulary. The child is trained to act on the basis of another person's feeling and thinking. We must change our system of child education, Gilman says, so that children learn that their conduct is their own, so that they understand the desirability of the behavior we wish produced, so that they can learn to practice sequential reasoning.

How then should a child be disciplined? The oldest and most common method is with physical pain; we hurt the child. We know that horses are better trained with gentleness than with severity. Still we justify the use of force with children by asserting, first, that it works, and second, that children are so depraved that it is necessary.

As a consequence, children learn that certain acts will cause a whipping—if they are caught—and so they either avoid the acts to avoid the whipping or they avoid being caught. But they are no wiser than before because they are confronted with arbitrary punishment rather than the knowledge of natural consequences. The worst result is the effect on their moral sense. We train people to avoid evil because they fear arbitrary punishment, so that we grow up afraid, "not of stealing, but of the policeman."[26]

We need to teach children right action, says Gilman, but we ourselves are still ignorant of ethics. Ethics is the science of social relations, she goes on; it is the examination of how people relate to each other. Distortion of a child's conception of morality starts early—for example, in the habit of lying to children, which we do often. What are the results of lying to a child? The child discovers it and learns that it is not wrong. The child accuses us of it and is punished. The child lies to us and is punished. We accuse the child of it and are not punished. If we articulate any principles, it is that God hates a liar and that to lie is a sin. The flexible human brain manages to absorb all these confusions, but "progress in ethics is hardly" to be expected.[27]

Since, says Gilman, the basis of human ethics is social, ethical behavior requires awareness of collective rights and duties. Years later she returned to this notion in a full-length study, but at this time she connected it primarily to the idea that a sense of belonging to a community should be instilled early in a child by parental example. If the parent would demonstrate to the child the importance of social duty, the correct learning process would be under way. As it is, most children think grown-ups do what they want.

Whatever idea of right and wrong the child succeeds in putting together, it is almost exclusively of a personal nature, based on interpersonal relations within the family. It is primarily the mother, Gilman says, who needs to be grounded in social ethics so that she can create a similar sense in her child. Here, again, Gilman extends her vision of child-rearing into a larger arena. We can only achieve genuine community, she is saying, when we raise our children to understand it and value it.

Gilman emphasizes that just as the family should be more involved in the larger society's concerns, so the community should be more involved in the family's. For instance, she argues that whatever the arguments for or against the physical punishment of children, to protect the helpless they should be made in open court. We are all fallible, and a private person should not be permitted to administer justice in secret and alone. As it is, the child is in the absolute power of the parent, without appeal, without a defense, and without witnesses. Gilman acknowledges that some parents seriously overindulge children, which also causes serious injury. Again, we need publicity and community action to examine standards of domestic justice.

Gilman takes her advocacy of community involvement in child care another, critical step further. A visitor from another planet would find little place in our modern society designed for children, she notes, not in the public community or even at home. We need large and beautiful public nurseries where children can stay during the day. But, she anticipates, to say so will lead to an outcry: "What, separate mother from child?" Her answer: Just as a private staff of college professors would not adequately replace the experience of going to college, so one mother at home cannot provide the kind of community every child should have, a community that has physical resources impossible at home and offers the company of a large group of children.

The isolation of a private nursery is damaging. We grow up selfish, "aborted in the social faculties," because each of us is for so long the focus of family attention at home. If we learned from infancy on to say "we" instead of "I" we would become more responsible adults, more responsible members of our societies. The mother's special place will never be taken from her, but "the terror of the mother lest her child should love some other person better than herself shows that she is afraid of comparison—that she visibly fears the greater gentleness and wisdom of some teacher will appeal to the young heart more than her arbitrary methods."[28] These ideas clearly expand upon parallel themes Gilman earlier addressed in *Women and Economics*.

The mother "loves much and serves endlessly, but reasons little," Gilman said many times in many ways. The child is preeminently "her" child, but she has no real understanding or respect for this complicated person because she herself is permitted to know so little. A human body three feet long deserves as much respect as a human body six feet long, Gilman tells us, and yet we handle the little ones with the "grossest familiarity." We tweak them, pull them, push them, kiss them, hold them, make jokes at their expense, peer at them, insist they smile at and kiss those they do not wish to.

A child needs kindness, love, and consideration, but the child also needs to learn justice. A too-self-sacrificing mother develops a selfish child. The child who "absorbs his mother as a natural victim"[29] is not helped to become a responsible adult. Maternal passion, "like all passions . . . needs conscientious and rational restraint."[30]

In an effort to visualize for the reader how to translate her vision into reality, Gilman conjured up architectural designs that incorporated her ideas. In doing so, she could call upon the work of a rich community of architects and urban designers who were at that time creating new ideas about urban space. Three generations of extraordinary women who lived and worked between the 1870s and the 1920s challenged, in their designs and blueprints, the physical separation of domestic household space (female) from public space (male) and the economic separation of the domestic economy (female) from the political economy (male). In an effort to abolish the idea and the reality of relegating women to a separate "woman's sphere," they conceived of new types of buildings and neighborhood organizations, including the kitchenless house, the day-care center, the public kitchen, and the community dining room. They also proposed and designed feminist cities. By focusing upon different kinds of housing needs for women and their families, they inspired some architects and urban planners, male and female, to reexamine the effect of design and architecture on family life. These "material feminists," as the historian and architect Dolores Hayden calls them, expounded one overriding idea: women must create feminist homes and feminist communities that incorporate socialized housework and child care before it will be possible for them to become truly equal members of society. Charlotte Gilman, by incorporating many of these ideas, is now the best-known representative of this vital and neglected tradition, one that nourished her greatly, even if she presented some of its ideas as if they were hers alone and never acknowledged her debt to it.[31]

Gilman notes that despite the then current interest in child study and the focus on exploring the psychology of child-rearing, most mothers continued to grapple with their individual problems alone. Rather than relying on the experts in the child-study movement, she urged mothers to establish a collective enterprise in an effort to break down the isolation of the private home and to provide the individual woman with a sense of her own empowerment.

Gilman was aware of and acknowledged the existence of mothers' clubs and congresses that existed in some major cities and communities, and that consisted of informal groups of mothers, often associated with local churches and schools, who met regularly to discuss parenting issues. However, she saw a need for national activity. "Our children suffer individually from bad social conditions, but cannot be saved individually," she reminds us, for a society includes all its members and cannot outstrip its own lesser parts.

The mother does her duty as best she can by her child, Gilman says, and the father does his. But we do not do our duty by any of our children when we concentrate on one child and neglect children in general. The advantage of living in a society rather than alone is that we are better taken care of by one another. We can use large resources to create libraries, schools, roads, and public peace and safety. The father, Gilman says, is better aware of his duties of "social parentage" because of his connection to the public world. The mother serves her children only personally. If each man had to build, fish, do blacksmith's work, make all his tools for himself and his family, this would immediately reduce his competence and increase his limitations. Women should not be "content to give their children only what they can do themselves alone," because they then deprive their children of the "rich possibilities of civilized motherhood, combined, collective, mutually helpful."[32]

Motherhood can be improved in two central ways, Gilman argues: by training young women to choose superior fathers for their children; and by improving the environment of children, physically and psychologically, by the intelligent coordination of mothers. Gilman recommended a year or two of instruction for each girl to allow her to decide if she wishes to be a specially trained mother-educator. Skill and training are necessary for the rearing of children, Gilman points out, but such gifts do not come "naturally" to mothers. Every mother may "naturally" love her children but not understand what is good for them.

Let us look, says Gilman, at what is called an "unnatural" mother—thinking, no doubt, of the time when she was wounded by that label. As a young girl such a person develops a strong character and a strong physique. She studies child-rearing but is disappointed to realize that her gifts lie elsewhere, in music or business or skilled labor. She considers the training of young children the highest work in a society but sadly acknowledges that she is not suited for it, so she works at a profession for which she is gifted. If she is attracted to a man who is "diseased or immoral or defective," she will not accept his offer of marriage, whatever her feelings for him, for the sake of her future children. She marries, has healthy children, and at an appropriate time resumes her work. She places her baby during the day in the care of a home that the child's mother, along with other mothers, has established and that is run by trained and talented women. This, in the world's view, is an "unnatural" mother.

The "natural" mother believes that her own care of her own child is better than anyone else's could possibly be. She has no evidence of this, and she will not be tested. She must squeeze caring for her child in between cooking and dusting and sewing and shopping.

"We have an urgent need of the unnatural mother," Gilman concludes.

The care of children belongs to women, she felt. It is women who bear the responsibility of improving their city, state, and country to provide the sort of environment in which our children can best grow, for the progressive education of a child should envelop the child's whole life, without sharp breaks between home and school. Thus, although Gilman challenged many conventional notions of her generation, the belief that women alone could and should nurture and nourish the young was not among them.

Concerning Children was reviewed positively but less widely than *Women and Economics* had been—reviews appeared in the *New York Times Saturday Review of Books*, the *Dial, Unity*, and the *Athenaeum*, and it was excerpted in the *Ladies' Home Journal*—and it achieved considerably less recognition, despite its originality and inherent interest.[33] However, it had a second printing in the United States in 1901, the year after its publication. It had been published in London the same time as it was published here, and was then excerpted and reprinted in 1907. It had a Dutch edition in 1904 and a German edition two years later.

Many of Gilman's ideas about child-rearing and children's needs came from the child-care movement and the progressive-education movement of her time, but she took those ideas and connected them to a larger conception of social organization, much as she did with the work of urban planners and social architects. She focuses on the deprivation to which children are subjected and the inadequate child-rearing of most mothers, again locating the source in the imprisonment of the mother in a private home and the privatization of mothering. As she did with marital partners in her first book, so here with mother-child relations, she argues that that personal relationship is really a social relationship, the reality of which is obscured because it is located in the privacy of the isolated home. At the same time she offers an alternative vision of how this seemingly personal and intimate relationship of mother to child could be fully humanized if we understood and acted upon the social nature embedded in it. Her words eight decades later have an uncanny prescient quality.

Both during and after the period when she was writing *Concerning Children*, Gilman continued to rewrite and rethink *Human Work*, the major book she intended to produce. Still unsatisfied with it, she turned instead to a subject which flowed naturally from her first book on male-female relations and from her second book on children. She wrote about the home. *The Home: Its Work and Influence* is a witty and wicked book. In it, Gilman subjects one of our most sacred institutions, venerated beyond imagining in her time, to merciless criticism. It is a very funny book, the more so because it is so true, then and now. She wrote the book, she said, to improve the home, not abolish it, for we all, single or coupled, need a home, a place of refuge and peace. A happy and beautiful home is essential to work. But the home is a human institution and as such is open to examination, criticism, and improvement. It is too important an institution to ignore.

Her central criticism of the home, the home as it has been and as it is, is this: the world has advanced and progressed, but the home has remained the same, with "the man free, the woman confined, the man specializing in a thousand industries, the woman still limited to her domestic functions."[34] The two overriding flaws in this system are, first, the maintenance of primitive industries in a contemporary world, and second, the confinement of women to those industries.

As a young woman, Charlotte Perkins had struggled to reconcile the seemingly irreconcilable tensions between a public life and a private life. In this book she suggests that the strain need not have existed had she been raised in a different home environment.

For many millions of years, she begins, life on earth has been rooted in a home. The beehive, the burrow of the prairie dog, a bird's nest—all are homes. This accounts "for the bottomless depths of our attachment to the idea." For humans, the care and shelter of the young is a much more serious and long-term task than it is for all other animals, and the home, as shelter for the family, is organized primarily for reproduction. Indeed, Gilman asserts again, it is the long period of immaturity and dependence that produced monogamous marriage and the permanent home.

Another unique feature of the human home is the position of women in it. The identification of woman and home, originally based on the prolonged infancy of human children, was strengthened when it came to be believed that woman belonged to man, as did the home. The man connected woman and home in his mind and forcibly held her there in body, while he removed himself as much as possible, thus turning the direction of social progress away from the home, leaving the "ultra-feminized woman to ultraconservatism therein."[35] Change, Gilman says, has come primarily from the progressive man and has been retarded by the stationary woman.

The impact of our ancestors has dominated the way we view the home more than any other institution, "and the influence of our ancestors is necessarily retroactive."[36] We like what we are used to, Gilman reminds us, but what we are used to may not be good for us. We still think of the home as a place of safety and as a sanctuary of mother-love. But it is not the home that provides these services, it is the community. Safety is maintained by social law and order. The home is essentially defenseless, protected only by social law. Our children are better guarded, provided for, and educated by social efforts than by private ones.

Gilman proceeds to take popular ideas about the home one by one and neatly expose their speciousness. First, *Privacy*. The home does provide privacy for the family "as a lump," but not privacy for the individual. What results from this conglomeration of people is a good deal of bickering, often controlled by the dominance of the strongest member. The poor have no space for privacy, the rich are surrounded by strangers—servants. The mother's privacy in particular is imposed upon by four kinds of invaders: children, servants, tradesmen, and callers. How, ultimately, does she achieve privacy at home from unwanted callers? By claiming to be out of it.

Then there is the *Sanctity of the Home*. Is the home sacred because it is the depository of reproductive functions, the place of maternity? Is maternity better than Liberty, Justice, Art, or Science? The "sacred duties of maternity" reproduce the race but do nothing to improve it. Our eyes grow moist when we speak of our mothers and the mothers of great men. Had John Wilkes Booth or Benedict Arnold no mothers? Who raises our large crop of vicious criminals? What percentage of our human young live to grow up at all? About half. In fact, we are so used to "infantile diseases" that our idea of a mother's duty is to nurse sick children, not raise healthy ones.

Perhaps, then, we should revere the home because it is such an ancient institution. Then let us have a pilgrimage to primordial rocks, let us prefer the hourglass to the clock, announces Gilman.

Is the reality of home anything like the ideal—comfortable house, happy family enjoying each other's society, father devoting himself to maintaining this little haven, mother happily wrapped up in her cheerful and happy children? No.

Homes are not healthful; they are filled with dust and grease and poor air and food odors. Homes are not beautiful. People in love, sharing aspirations and interests, marry only to find that they run a commissary and dormitory. We struggle so hard that we need to flee the home to get a rest. Father and mother are too much occupied in homemaking, are so overtaxed and worried that they spend little time caring for children or each other. The home is where we suffer most. Many men who must behave well outside are domineering and nasty at home. Many women, considerate and polite to the outside world, are greedy and demanding at home "and cruel as only the weak and ignorant can be."[37] In sum, our homes are damaged because long-outgrown conditions are still maintained there.

The Home as Workshop. All industry began at home, but most has long since left it. But "the primitive woman, in the primitive home, still toils at her primitive tasks."[38] All other industries have grown; why haven't domestic industries grown too?

Women provided the first systematic labor, says Gilman, meaning regular, consistent domestic, agricultural work, as opposed to what she envisaged as the sporadic and irregular nature of hunting and warfare for men. As mother, woman is the carrier of the constructive tendency. "Male energy tends to scatter and destroy, female to gather and construct." So for countless ages her human labor, derived from nature, that is, from the earth, from agricultural production, sustained human existence, "while the man could only hunt and fight." At some point in history, the male took control of the female's industry, probably because he realized that the pasture was more profitable than the hunting ground. The riches she produced drew him. In his hands industry developed. The woman is a "patient, submissive, inexhaustible labourer. The forces of maternity prompt her to work forever—for her young." But for the man, sustained work is a habit acquired late and he works reluctantly, preferring others to work for him. He is caught up in such activities as warfare, aggressive, competitive economic activity, and enslaving others. But with all the faults of "unbridled male energy," it has advanced the world: "Through it has come our splendid growth."[39]

What accounts for the limitations of the female worker today as she works in her home? First, her average capacity and skill. What would shoes be like if every man made his own? To confine any industry, including domestic work, to a universal average level is to reduce it.

Second, she works for her family only, as "servant to the family, instead of servant to the world." Men have moved to new heights; she remains in the same place.

Third, she lives in virtual isolation. In earlier periods, as women toiled at primitive tasks, they did so in community with others. Today, women are "let out to play—but not to work."

Fourth, she is limited by the number of occupations she is expected to master. She is responsible for the cooking, cleaning, sewing, mending, nursing, and child care. She spends half her working time in the preparation of food. Her work in caring for the home is exhausting, and there is no time left for the children. Yet the central purpose of the home is the care of children. The duties of the mother are not compatible with the duties of the housewife. How can child-culture develop in "this swarming heap of rudimentary trades"?[40]

"The home that is coming will not try to be a workshop, a nursery, or a school," she tells us. At the time she was writing there were few data on day nurseries, but what there were suggested to her a higher record of health and happiness. In *The Home*, for the first time, Gilman specifically addressed the work of other domestic reformers, in the United States and Europe, indicating that all the ideas in her book were not hers alone.

Imagine a man who built his own home for his family and provided them with their food by daily hunting. Try to suggest that he combine with others to exchange labor and specialize their work, and imagine that he responds: "What, ignore my duty to my family? I will not let another man hunt for them or build their home or make their garments. It is my duty, as a husband, to serve my wife." Should we not all agree that such a hypothetical home-husband is a fool? Women offer to their families the quality of service appropriate to the Stone Age.

"A house does not need a wife," Gilman declares, "any more than it does a husband. . . . There is nothing in the work of a house which requires marital or maternal affection."[41] What is required to run a house efficiently is skill and business sense, and this it generally does not get.

What is needed from women is not more work but a different kind of work.

For work to develop and grow, it must be performed for the world. "A private poet is necessarily ignoble. So is a private cook." A job that causes the worker simply to cater to the whims of her master demeans both parties. There is nothing private about food. There must be some personal choice involved, "but it no more has to be cooked for you than the books you love best have to be written for you."[42] Imagine untrained laborers making shoes or watches or glass. Why do we imagine they are competent to prepare food and take care of children?

The performance of all these domestic industries is an enormous waste of labor. We are so accustomed to thinking of cooking as a woman's duty that we do not think of it as a loss of her productive labor. We waste in purchasing small quantities. It is time to free the home from these industries, decrease expenses, and increase productive labor, to cease using women as a class of house-servants, to raise the preparation of food to a professional and scientific status and acknowledge that the care of children is the most valuable profession. It is time to end our homes as greasy, dusty workshops and make them centers of rest and peace, properly maintained by organized industries, enjoyed by men and women alike.

Although she does not say so, Gilman was striking out at the new field of domestic science by arguing that no genuine or lasting improvement in food preparation or distribution can occur while the structure of the home remains unchanged.

Domestic Arts. The woman, "confined to a primitive, a savage plane of occupation, continues to manifest an equally savage plane of aesthetic taste," Gilman declares.[43] Hers is a patchwork life that does not evoke a sense of unity, harmony, simplicity, truth, or restraint. As she has no aesthetic sense about her environment, so she has none about her person, and indeed makes a conventionalized ornament of her body. As women, however, increasingly enter the public world, Gilman predicts, such limitations will change; for the working woman, the business woman, the woman artist have no time or inclination for such frippery.

Domestic Ethics. Our society cherishes a belief that all our virtues begin at home, she says. Home life often does produce generous care and lovingkindness, flowing from the mother's care of her helpless infants. A mother's love is limited, however, because it is limited to her own children.

What, in general, are the virtues we admire, Gilman asks? Love, truth, courage, justice, self-control, and honor, she answers. But the weak and dependent cannot develop truth or courage. As for justice, it presupposes equality, but in the home there is neither freedom nor equality. "There is ownership throughout; the dominant father, the more-or-less subservient mother, the utterly dependent child." Love, gratitude, and kindness are possible, but not justice, because "justice is wholly social in its nature."[44]

The Child at Home. Most of the people on earth are children, Gilman says. Once again she argues that our most vital problem is how to make better people, and the swiftest and easiest method of achieving social progress is to improve children, so that they, as adults, can pass the progress along. The two issues to be explored are, first, is the home the best and only environment for the child, and second, is the home an environment that can be improved?

The home as it now exists is not designed for the baby or the child. It is a building for adults to cook in, sweep in, wash in, eat in, see friends in, dress in, undress in, and sleep in. In the "cracks and crevices of all these varied activities," children are brought up. Mothers are beginning to take the first step toward knowledge with the new science of child-culture, says Gilman, but still children are ill-fed and ill-clothed in the home and the home is the main site of disease, crime, fire, and accident.

Assuming that the child has managed to survive infancy and childhood, what has this child learned? The principal occupation in the home is food preparation. The child has also learned that the mother devotes her entire life to home activities, thus associating womanhood with house-service, and that the central concern of life is to be clean and well-dressed and to eat with proper manners. The child learns of social values in school, in church, in the street, and from the father.

The Girl at Home. The boy gets out of the home as much as he can, imitating his father's behavior. But there are thousands of girls who stay at home "helping mother," as Charlotte herself did until she left to marry Walter. "The home is not the whole of life,"

Gilman says again. "It is a very minor part of it—a mere place of preparation for living. To keep the girl at home is to cut her off from life."[45]

Most girls marry. "All girls ought to—unless there is something wrong with them," says Gilman, sharply reminding us how deeply rooted many of her own conventional ideas were at the very moment that she ridiculed those of others.

Home Influence on Men. The eternal misunderstanding between the home-bred woman and the world-bred man is rooted in his growth outside the home, which gives him a different perspective. We call a larger, better-balanced brain a "man's brain," and a more emotional and personal one "a woman's brain," but the difference is really between the world and the home.

"It is not that women are really smaller-minded, more timid and vacillating; but that whosoever, man or woman, lives always in a small dark place, is always guarded, protected, directed and restrained, will become inevitably narrowed and weakened by it."[46] The woman is narrowed by the home, says Gilman, and the man is narrowed by the woman.

Many men fear that their security in the love of their women would be weakened if the structure of the home were to change. Not so, says Gilman. Men and women will be drawn to each other as they always have been. The error lies in associating home labor with womanliness. It is rather the domestic duties that cause men to stray, for the "one-sided ownership wherein the wife becomes the private servant, cook, cleaner, mender of rents, valet, janitor and chambermaid" causes rifts.

The home burdens the man most through his need to finance it alone. The poorer a man is, the more he must pay for everything. If a poor man had a self-supporting wife, the daily household income would be doubled, and he would have a wife far fresher and more enthusiastic about returning home than one who is exhausted by remaining in it ceaselessly. Instead, he now finds an exhausted wife who provides no companionship for him. Off he goes to the cheerful environment of the saloon. The evil results we all know, but "we do not dream that it is the home which drives him there."[47]

There is no way the domestic wife can provide the social stimulation the man needs, for no man of any grade can get the social stimulus he needs by spending every evening with his cook! . . . Your cook may be "a treasure," she may cater to your needs most exquisitely, she may also be the mother of your children . . . but she is none the less your own personal servant, and as such not your social equal. You may love her dearly . . . but you are not satisfied with her conversation.[48]

The home of the poor, hard-working wife gives the males in it the impression that women are servants. The home of the idle wife gives husband and sons the picture of a rapacious and useless woman, a "dainty domestic vampire."[49]

We must change the system, says Gilman. We must set "the woman on her feet" as a free, active human being, a producer as well as consumer. Put the outdated "domestic industries" into the past and let efficient modern industries take their place. The wiser mother, free from home imprisonment, will be able to acknowledge child-culture "as an art and as a science." The man, relieved of some financial burdens, will have at his side a different kind of companion, and he will be able to work better in the service of his society. "The man and woman together, both relieved of most of their personal cares, will be better able to appreciate large social needs and to meet them." And then each generation of children, born better and reared better, will contribute to social progress.

Gilman was certainly aware of the growing numbers of exceptional women breaking out of their traditional places, and she applauded the success of each of these women. "From the harem to the forum is a long step, but she has taken it. From the ignorant housewife to the president of a college is a long step, but she has taken it. From the penniless dependent to . . . [the] wholly self-supporting [person] . . . is a long step, but she has taken it."[50]

Another fifty years, Gilman predicts, will show more advance than the past five hundred. It was to technology that she looked, rather than to reform agitation, again not understanding how technological changes could be harnessed to old ways and new kinds of chains instantly forged with new materials. Yet for all her optimism about the changes she expected the future to bring, she was aware of the significance of persistent clinging to tradition. We have had no difficulty, she says, in having water and light "fully social-ized," but why are we so shy in carrying out similar changes in the supply of food? Most of us still live in dread of losing our domestic privacy, fearful that "we shall lose our family dinner table; that woman will lose her 'charm;' that we shall lose our children; and the child will lose its mother. WE ARE MORTALLY AFRAID OF SEPA-RATION."[51] In this significant final sentence, she has wonderfully merged the personal and the public, for she has exposed the psychological root of what often creates the anger and fear in those who resist change, while at the same time laying bare her own psychological anguish. It is a brilliant insight, although she probably did not fully comprehend what she said.

Her final words on the subject of *The Home*, however, are reassuring ones. In the book's concluding pages, she says:

> The love of human beings for each other is not a dream of religion, it is a law of nature. It is bred of human contact, of human relation, of human service. . . . Must we then leave it—lose it—go without it? Never. The more broadly social-ized we become, the more we need our homes to rest in . . . we need to return to the dear old ties, to the great primal basis, that we may rise refreshed and strengthened. . . . Private, secluded, sweet, wholly our own; not invaded by any trade or work or business . . . ; the place of the one initial and undying group of father, mother, and child, will remain to us.[52]

The Home is the book most clearly derived from *Women and Economics*, and perhaps because it is so identified with her most successful work, it has had a greater appeal than any of her other books besides *Women and Economics*. It is also extremely funny, Gilman's acerbic skills being used to good effect.

After its initial publication in 1903, *The Home* had its first British edition the following year and its second American printing in 1910, as well as a Swedish and a German edition. It has had two recent editions, one in 1970 and the other in 1972. At the time of its appearance it was widely reviewed. Reviews appeared in all the magazines and journals that had reviewed her earlier books, but in addition she had substantial coverage in major newspapers, such as the *San Francisco Chronicle*, the *Boston Herald*, the *New York American*, the *Chicago Tribune*, the *Detroit Free Press, Frank Leslie's Illustrated Newspaper*, and the *New York Tribune*. The subject matter and the scandalous message combined to touch a raw nerve.[53]

In *The Home*, as in her two earlier books, Gilman refuses to accept the prevailing distinction between public space and private space, arguing that the "domestic" world is an integral part of the civic world. The home is an institution like any other, she asserts, and then proceeds to take it apart, piece by piece, exposing the power relations within it—the dominant father, the subservient mother, the utterly dependent children—and exposing the myths that surround it: it is not a private, healthful, restful place; it is where we suffer the most. It is an institution owned by man, in which wife and children are forcibly held, forcibly by virtue of economic dependence and ideological pressure.

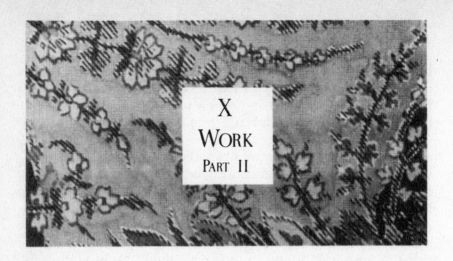

X
WORK
PART II

Gilman set out her major theses in these first three books, and while she continued to build on them in her subsequent work, which led to some repetitiveness, she isolated different specific issues in every subsequent book, offering quite different emphases and new insights with each. Major themes in her earlier work continue to play a central role later: the centrality of the economic subordination of women; a belief in human changeability and the inevitability of progress, subsumed under her devotion to evolutionary theory; a belief in human reason and rationality; opposition to behavior or ideas based on unexamined authority or blind obedience; the need to replace male power with what she called the female principle of nurturance and cooperation. Much of the repetition in her work has its source in her oral presentations. The books were often built on one of her mini-lecture series. But what appears to be simple repetition is often not that, because the ideas that are repeated are often marshaled for different purposes, just as, for example, she explored the implications of female subordination in economic terms in one book and the ethical ramifications in another. In addition, the overall direction of her work shifts over time. Her first works center on women's issues, then on concerns affecting men and women; her last books focus more on ideological issues, particularly ethical or religious ones.

Gilman described *Human Work*, published in 1904 by McClure, Phillips, and Company, as her best book, a judgment with which subsequent readers would probably not agree, nor did those at the time. It did not sell well—a great disappointment to Gilman. It was, she said modestly, a "treatise so large in scope as to cover all human life."[1] It took her an uncharacteristic four years to complete it, and she was still unsatisfied. Despite her own reservations, she was still distressed that *Human Work* made "practically no impression," but consoled herself with the notion that "neither did the work of Mendel, for some time."[2]

It is an ambitious book. Its focus is on the human, not female, community, in relation to the work we do, which she sees as "the most conspicuous feature of human life."[3] In her earlier work she located the home as the place of subordination. In *Human Work* she locates the source of "highest human duty", the key to our collectivity, in the work we do. The goal of *Human Work* is to demonstrate how the collective social relations that shape our economic life are not reflected in the individualistic way we think about the social and economic order, and what the implications are of that disjuncture between the reality and the way we see the reality. There is overwhelming evidence, she says, to demonstrate that our society is moved by collective action in the process of production, but we continue to maintain our "original animal theory of individualism—the Ego concept."[4] Indeed, she says, the parent of all the basic errors of the human mind is the Ego concept, valid at one time, at a prehuman point in evolution, but no longer so.

A second error that continues to haunt us, and one that flows from the Ego concept, is the belief that pleasure comes from accumulation; in reality, Gilman says, our pleasure comes from what we do as a part of collective humanity. A third error that we accept as truth, she says, is that pain and adversity are good for us, so we do nothing to remove them and everything to justify them. We operate on the wrong assumption, what she calls the Want Theory, thinking that people work only to satisfy desire, to produce for the purpose of consuming. Under slavery, it is true, she admits, people worked for fear of punishment, and similarly under the wage-labor system people work only for reward. "But both these systems are transient, superficial." But, she says, she is called utopian when she points out that though we live in a world dominated by interdependent social processes we are hampered by an ideology of individualism, and when she insists that we need to eradicate from our thinking this outmoded notion of individualism. It is the present system, she insists, that is ten thousand years behind the times, not she who is ahead. The idea that people could work for the pleasure of work is seen as unthinkable, but it is not. We cling to the basic error that what we get makes us happy rather than what we do, "and therefore consider our doing as a means of getting." Work is the expression of social energy for social use, and it has evolved from the first stage of mother-love, work for the production of the young, to slave labor, to serfdom, to the present wage-labor system. The last stage, which we are now discovering, she says, is working for humanity, not from coercion, "but from the action of social forces as natural as breathing."

Most people do not enjoy work because we have contempt for most work and because we have withheld from work love and pride in its value. We try to make people work at what they do not like and are not good at. But civilization is built on interdependent service, and we all can find a kind of work we like. The solution to tedious work is not to abolish the machine but to pay the worker well for doing it for a short time and to educate the worker to "see the ship in the rivet," to see the individual contribution to the whole. We need to educate our populations, she went on, to realize that the specialized worker, with a spade, an axe, a lever, or a pen, is obviously working for thousands of unknown people—and yet we continue to be restricted by the language of the Ego concept.

We believe in personal ownership and personal property. We hold these to be unshakeable principles, but they are, Gilman says, only reflections of a particular set of values at a particular time in history, now long outdated. Men once owned slaves, and it was then considered their right. That "right" was gradually withdrawn by society. Parents once "owned" children and could dispose of them at will. That "right" too has been withdrawn by society. In the present, she asserts, two other long-held principles are being challenged: property rights and the right to dominate women.

Our notion of the best way for a society to operate is by competitive struggle, which speaks to the prevailing doctrine of the survival of the fittest and the importance of competition. But, she says, if you wish to improve the egg-laying capacity of the hen—again she seeks illustrations within the animal kingdom—or the milk-giving capacity of the cow, you do not provoke combat within the community of hens or cows. If you wish to strengthen your horse, you do not withhold hay. The solution, though, is not to improve the stock by breeding, as the eugenics movement calls for—although she had earlier come close to that position herself—but to improve resources and opportunities for everyone.

What happens when there is a disparity between the reality that the economy operates on collective labor and our belief in the principles of individualism is that we get a social organism that does not work properly, as ours does not. Gilman often uses the analogy of the human body to illustrate her ideas: the social body has too much insufficiently nourished tissue, that is, poverty, and too much fatty tissue, that is, excessive wealth. Congestion is caused by arrested distribution in the arena of work.

But the process of evolution, she goes on, moves us inevitably toward acknowledging cooperation and altruism, toward learning that "human nature" is really "social nature." That cooperative tendency is felt in our impulse to work. Work is "what we are made for, what we are together for; that which constitutes the primal condition and line of development for human life."[5] And since "we make what makes us," and so can control our environment, purely physical evolution has given way to another kind, "psychical." In other words, the sort of society we make helps determine what we become, says Gilman, essentially paraphrasing Lester Ward on this point.

What we need to do to cure society's ills is not to punish wrongdoers, for they, and that includes the leisure class as much as the criminals or paupers, are the product of imperfect ideas. While these imperfect social ideas are rooted "in *all* our minds, not merely in the minds of the diseased portion," the "overconsuming rich" come in for special criticism. They pervert the social body, says Gilman; they are "a social disease," she argues, describing them with the phrase commonly applied to venereal disease. We need to understand our erroneous ideas and change them, beginning with the position of women.

Gilman proposed no specific mechanism to achieve her goals

beyond her own kind of education and persuasion. Does it all lead to her belief that private property should be abolished? Yes, especially if we include her utopian fiction as part of her developing world-view.

Human Work was reviewed in the journals that ordinarily reviewed Gilman's books: the *Outlook, Woman's Journal,* the *New York Times Saturday Review of Books,* the *Atlantic Monthly, Current Literature,* the *Independent,* the *Dial,* the *Literary Digest.* In general, positive comments were made about the book, but Gilman had the distinct sense that it was not understood in the way she wanted it to be and that its significance was not adequately appreciated. *Human Work* was never reprinted, an indication that its readership remained small.

Gilman's next books appeared in serial form in her monthly magazine, the *Forerunner,* which she founded in 1909 with "no capital except a mental one," and which ended in 1916 when she decided she had had enough. She wrote every line of the thirty-two-page magazine herself. Each issue contained editorials, comments and observations, critical essays, book reviews, poetry, and fiction. Each year two full-length books were serialized, ordinarily one fiction and one nonfiction. The full seven-year run of the *Forerunner* was the equivalent in length of twenty-eight books. The entire run was reprinted by the Greenwood Reprint Corporation in 1968 as part of its series of radical periodicals in the United States. Reading through these issues, one gets a sense of Gilman's virtuosity, of the range of her interests and attitudes. Gilman used humor, anger, irony, sentimentalism, and whimsy to speak to a variety of concerns. The overriding commitments reflected in the magazine were to the belief in the rights of women and to the superiority of a collective social order.

In 1909 Gilman serialized a book in the *Forerunner* which she published two years later under the title *The Man-Made World; or, Our Androcentric Culture.* It is a study, she said, of "excessive maleness," an analysis of the kind of mischief that occurs when one sex predominates over the other. As in most of her books, Gilman expresses her indebtedness to the work of Lester Ward. This book begins with a statement about his Gynaecentric Theory, about which she says, "nothing so important to humanity has been advanced since the Theory of Evolution, and nothing so important to women has ever been given to the world.''

Ward's theory, which she readily concedes is ''disputed by the majority of present-day biologists,'' asserts that the female is the ''race type,'' that is, that the female came before the male in the evolutionary process; she was the original human. The human male evolved later, first achieving equality with the female and then becoming her master.

We are so consumed, she says, by concepts of masculine and feminine that we do not know what *human* nature is. Aside from what relates to our separate roles as mothers and fathers, that is, aside from our part in the reproductive process, most of our nature is human nature, shared by men and women alike. She acknowledges that there are some specifically masculine and feminine traits, but these, originally related to our parenting roles, have been greatly exaggerated and distorted, with disastrous results.

Once again Gilman identifies male qualities as combativeness, desire, by which she means erotic energy, and display or self-expression, by which she means the presentation of sexuality that occurs in the process of wooing a mate. These basic masculine traits, ''all legitimate and right in proper use'' but ''mischievous when in excess or out of place,'' were once useful to humanity. But when man enslaved woman, beginning the long ''androcentric'' period, which has not yet ended, we entered into a stage in which masculine culture became dominant. The earliest government, Gilman speculates, was made up of a woman-centered group organized on what she describes as maternal lines of common love and nurturance. When men enslaved women, they formed a unit based on predatory activity, that is, organized hunting, followed by what Gilman describes as ''group belligerency,'' or organized warfare.

Ever since this ''androcentric'' period, and it begins with the written record, history has been made and written by men, and the ''male world'' has been accepted as the norm. What is masculine is believed, says Gilman, to represent the human, the natural, type, while women have been defined by their difference from this norm, as what Simone de Beauvoir many years later called ''the Other.''

Male dominance, she says, is clear even in our language. ''Effeminate" means too female, but there is no masculine counterpart. "Emasculate," not enough male, has no feminine analogue. "Virile," manly, has as its opposite, "puerile," or childish.

There are few great women artists, she declares—expressing little respect for or knowledge of folk art—because women are permitted only to be consumers, not producers. Women carry decoration on their bodies, but man is the decorator. Men also control literature, she says. Only slowly are women being permitted into the realm of literature, as readers or as creators. "It is but a little while," she reminds us, "since Harriet Martineau concealed her writing beneath her sewing when visitors came—writing was 'masculine'—sewing, 'feminine.' "[6]

Our masculinized literature has produced two predominant themes in fiction: desire and combat, love and war. The "humanizing of woman," she says, which is occurring for the first time in a substantial way in her lifetime, is opening up new fields of fiction in which the entire range of a woman's life is seen as a proper subject.

Sports, too, reflect the male combat ethic, and as such, she says, are in general alien to women. Those few sports that are of human, not just male, interest have been closed to women. There is something "inherently masculine," she insists, in the universal use of a projectile—the sending forth of something with violence by throwing, kicking, batting, or shooting. "The basic female impulse," on the other hand, is "to gather, to put together, to construct."[7]

As she did in her earlier work, especially *Human Work*, Gilman again points to the damaging results of the dominance of the "masculine" in our religious and ethical systems, how it has infected work and education with a system of competition and reward, which is not conducive to genuine learning, and produced coercive governments and economies based on competition and the violent struggle to win.

Male dominance has not only restricted women to the domestic sphere, with all the accompanying evils, which she had outlined in *Women and Economics*, but it has also fostered in women harmful, "feminine" traits designed to attract the hypermasculine male. As a result the woman is prized for her "innocence," which is another way of saying ignorance of masculine misdeeds. The "feminine" virtue for which she is most treasured is chastity, but this is a human, not a female, virtue. Women are criticized for their concern with fashion, although it is men who demand the trimmings and supply them as well. We might as well hold women responsible for harems, says Gilman, or prisoners for jails.

Her proposed solution is to make the man's world more truly human by making it more "feminine"—by bringing some of the qualities of motherly concern to education, government, the economy—and to make the woman's world more truly human by taking it out of its restricted place and, in some ways—for example, by specialization of labor—following a more masculine model. In this book she focuses on ways to end "excessive maleness," but it is useful to complete the equation with ways to reduce "excessive femaleness," as she did in *Women and Economics*.

Unhappy at how little impact *Human Work* had, Gilman decided that she had tried to do too much in one work, and so she undertook three separate studies to examine the issues presented in that 1904 study. *Our Brains and What Ails Them*, serialized monthly in the *Forerunner* in 1912, addresses the question: Why is the human being, who has vast superior knowledge, the most vicious, the most unhappy, the sickest beast alive? The book is about what she calls "mental mechanics"; it examines the brain as a physical organ that requires health and proper exercise.

The most important need of the brain is to develop the power to see things collectively. The social brain is lodged in the brains of separate humans, but it works collectively. A separate human being could want a hut, she says, could build a hut and live in it. A separate human being could not want a theater, for the very conception of theater presupposes community.

Our social spirit is embodied in buildings, clothing, tools, and implements of all kinds. The interaction of all of these social artifacts creates the way we act socially. Our collective conduct is modified by the use of the collective brain, and that brain, the brain of Humanity, is mainly on paper, in the written record. That written record is our external brain, a "vast secondary storage battery," a permanent and exchangeable brain. "Those who make books make the race mind," she says, and those records have been created by one sex throughout all history, and in each period that written record "bears the distinction of class interests" as well, says Gilman, one of her rare references to class.[8]

Is there any difference between the brain in a man and a woman, asks Gilman? Are a woman's mental processes and capabilities any different from those of a man? No, she answers emphatically; the brain, like all organs, is developed by use and most developed by most use, and therein lies the only difference. Restrictions placed on women and their education have checked the development of the women's brain. But since the brain is not a sex organ, it is inherited indiscriminately. "The daughter may inherit the brain of a line of scholars, as a Chinese woman may inherit the legs of a line of runners; but the 'female leg' in China has been sadly modified *by its environment*—and so has the 'female mind.'" The legs of a mare are as good to run with as are the legs of any horse, says Gilman, and so would the legs of a woman be as good as the legs of a man, if she were allowed to use them. (Recent work on male and female brains notwithstanding, it may be that Gilman's assertion that there is no significant difference will prevail.)

Women remain undeveloped human beings: that is what ails them. We have placed women in a morbid situation, we observe the morbid results, and then we say, "Woman is an enigma."

We must remember, Gilman advises us, that the whole measure of merit is masculine. The standard by which we judge excellence is masculine. When we one day come to honor constructive industry as much as warfare, she says in language that has the ring of prophecy, we shall have female heroes. When we learn to honor endurance as much as combativeness, when we understand the antisocial nature of ultra-male competitiveness and the positive value of the adaptable spirit of service that we have hitherto demeaned as "female," when that time comes we shall put up monuments not only to soldiers. "We shall have not only new achievements to measure, but new standards of measurement."[9]

Humanness, serialized in the 1913 *Forerunner*, builds on the central thesis of *Human Work*, namely, that it is our mutual service, our interdependence, that makes us human, that we have a developed social consciousness in our understanding of the church, the army, and our government, but we do not yet recognize the collective enterprise that shapes our economic institutions. When we learn, says Gilman, that the work we do is for others and the power we have comes from others, then our practice will fundamentally change. It is humanity that needs poetry, not the poet. The poet needs food, shelter, and clothing, but the poetry is created for others. That we understand, she says. What we do not yet understand is that this is equally true of anyone's product.

Only in very early human life, when tribal existence was undifferentiated and its members lived and thought in group terms, says Gilman, did humans understand the collective nature of their work. The successful hunt or the fruitful harvest engaged the entire community. (This 1913 account differs from earlier ones of hers in which she described the individual male hunter going off into the wilderness alone. She had probably read some anthropological literature between the publication of *Human Work* in 1904 and this more accurate description.)

What is especially new and significant in this study is Gilman's explicit discussion of sexuality and its role in the evolutionary process. Sex is for reproduction only, she says, and while we have continued to advance despite male sexual excesses, when we someday use this function "only for its natural purpose," our humanness will increase.

The excessive sexual activity in the human male, she says, "has no biological excuse" any longer. At one point in the past the male needed "desperate sexual desire" to drive him to mate because there was effort, danger, and pain involved. During this historic time, a polygamous male developed. But even this polygamous animal, she assures us, "is keyed a little higher in the matter of sex" than contemporary man, for although the polygamous creature serves many females, it is only during one season. "The rest of the year he is at peace," says Gilman.

In time, she says, monogamy emerged as a "natural" form of sex relation among the higher mammals, "and natural monogamy requires continence" because human energies are needed to procure food and shelter for the young. We have only recently become monogamous, she says, and so we are still hampered with the polygamous male. But we can breed this polygamous male out of our society by the process of female selection; that is, women will choose for husbands those men best calculated "to improve the race."

Love is not to be ignored, she assures us, "but the kind of person you 'love' depends on the kind of person you are." An ignorant, badly educated seventeen-year-old, for example, will "love" any man who is good-looking, polite, sexually appealing, "and able to furnish the usual bribes and tributes." The same woman ten years later will not be so easily attracted to such a man because she then better knows what life requires, the nature of marriage, and the present state of men "and the terrible dangers so many of them bring to matrimony."

Excessive male sexuality seriously threatens human happiness, Gilman insists, because it leads to men owning, hiring, or imprisoning women in order to make them sexually available. True manliness does not require excessive sexuality, she insists. "Manhood sufficient to father the necessary number of clean-bred children to the world is manhood enough." If we are to develop genuine monogamy, eliminate prostitution, and respect motherhood, then we need men who are "capable of health and happiness with continence for the great part of the time," says Gilman. There are such men today, she adds, but we need more of them. We have "grossly overestimated" the value of sexual pleasures, she says, because we suffer such poverty in the rich human development of which sexuality is but one small part.

Social Ethics, which appeared in serial form in the 1914 issues of the *Forerunner*, is the third part of the expanded *Human Work*. In this book for the first time Gilman addresses questions of ethics in a systematic way, the overarching theme being that the interests of the community, not the individual, are the proper basis of a human ethical system. Her ideas on this subject are more fully developed in her last book, *His Religion and Hers*.

What is of particular interest in *Social Ethics* is her continuing discussion of sexuality. She repeats her earlier assertion that the sexual function has one purpose, and that is reproduction, but then she continues in a quite different way. In the minds of many of us, she says, it has a further function, the expression of mutual love. "We will here grant both uses," she says, rejecting her statements the previous year in *Humanness* on the importance of continence. There is a general error, she goes on, held by half of us and taught to the other half, that this function "exists mainly for the pleasure and well-being of the male sex." For the first time she addresses the existence of female sexuality. There are very few people, she says, who object to the idea of sexuality as an expression of mutual love; only a "few earnest extremists who preach—and practice—

the theory of continence aside from reproduction, even in marriage," thereby dismissing a position she herself had held only the year before. It is only excess to which she now strenuously objects.

Her next two books, *The Dress of Women*, serialized in the *Forerunner* 1915, and *Growth and Combat*, serialized in the *Forerunner* in 1916, are not major works, but they are interesting illustrations of how Gilman takes one aspect of her general thesis and elaborates on it in a variety of ways. "Cloth is a social tissue," she begins *The Dress of Women*, "a sort of social skin." That men and women wear totally different costumes alone makes it clear that "we should never forget sex," that our common humanity is sacrificed to a culturally defined gender distinction. Chapter 6 of this small book is called "The Hat," and it immediately brings to mind her father's short story of the devil and the hat. The hat, more than any other article of dress, she says, is a reflection of distorted femininity, designed to please and hold the taste of the purchasing male. To judge the hat, put it on a man's head. Is it cute? Why does a grown woman want to look cute?

In *Growth and Combat* Gilman isolates the dominant, unconscious idea we hold that "the major process of life is resistance, struggle, combat, and that this process is good and helpful."[10] The truth of life is that life is growth, she says, not combat. We have often believed that which is not so, and while "opinions do not alter facts, they do alter conduct." Thus, wrong ideas have both great power and severe limitations.

> Once we thought the earth was flat—
>> What of that?
>> It was just as globos then
> Under believing men
>> As our later folks have found it,
> By success in running round it;
>> What we think may guide our acts,
>> But it does not alter facts.

His Religion and Hers: A Study of the Faith of Our Fathers and the Work of Our Mothers, published in 1923 by the Century Company of New York, was, except for her autobiography, the last book Charlotte Gilman wrote. This important volume deals with the power of ideas. Gilman's first book examined the economic relationship between men and women. At the end of her life—she was sixty-three years old when she published this book—she summed up her work with a study of ideology, isolating religion as a central part of the human ideological system. She has, here, not simply turned Aunt Catharine on her head by challenging the prevailing ideology of domesticity, as she did in *Women and Economics*, but has turned the entire Beecher clan on its collective head by asserting that religion, that which defined the life of her prominent ancestors, has done more disservice to humanity than any other institution or any other ideology, although it is capable, she concedes, if reconstructed, of providing new hope and new direction. By 1923 Gilman's influence and reputation had sharply declined from what they had been at the turn of the century when *Women and Economics* excited the British and American public. Although *His Religion and Hers* is not well known, it completes the intellectual journey begun when Gilman was a young woman demanding of the universe the recognition of her place in it and an understanding of how she came to be.

"Religion is the strongest modifying influence in our conscious behavior," she says, and it should therefore serve our best interests, but it does not. She returns to a contrast she made in *Social Ethics* between a true sense of ethics based on the living needs of society and a false one, derived from traditional religion, with its emphasis on reward and punishment in an afterlife, on blind obedience to authority, as well as on a belief in "fatalism"—the sense that we are fallen, that life is inherently evil and we cannot alter it—a theme she had begun to develop as early as 1904 in *Human Work*.

Religion can be a force for good, she argues, if it ceases to worry about putting souls in heaven and concerns itself instead with this life. That we suffer so much on earth is not God's fault or the devil's but our own, she says, as if she were in conversation with her kin.

Most religions are concerned with the beyond for each individual after death, not about the beyond of human life on earth after one generation is replaced by another. Think, she asks of her readers, of what is meant by a future life for Hebrews and Christians and Moslems and Mormons. It is one version or another of a happy hunting ground. It is a masculine vision. Certainly mothers, and fathers, too, she insists, should be more concerned about what will happen to their living children in the world we are making than about what may happen to themselves after they are dead. A life in heaven is appealing because it exists in the imagination as a fantasy about which we have no knowledge and feel no responsibility. The other future, that which we leave behind, has no "forgiveness" in the "transmission of sins from father to son."

The religion of Jesus is one of the few that teaches real improvement, for he preached love and service to humanity, says Gilman. But after twenty centuries Christianity has yet to establish a connection with life. The appeal is still to what is to happen after death, she says.

In tracing the origins of our religious misconceptions, she elaborates on ideas she expressed in *The Man-Made World*, identifying these misconceptions with the "androcentric" period and with masculine traits. She proposes that early men's hunting activities led to an obsession with death, particularly as expressed in nightmares and terrors. Medicine men, the predecessors of priests, interpreted these fears freely, since they were unhampered by facts. In this way religions developed at their core a confrontation with death, as interpreted by the priest. The sense of terror became the basis of priestly power, and to preserve that power, the idea of mystery emerged. "A mystery is not merely a thing you do not know; it is a thing you must not know."[11] Those who dare to question, who do not accept the word of the priest, are punished. And since ultimate punishment comes after death, who can contradict?

In addition to an obsession with death, we are also burdened with another aspect of dominant masculinity, "the guileless habit of blaming women for the sin and trouble of the world."[12] All the major philosophies share one common thread and that is a derogatory sense of women, says Gilman.

The universal requirement of all religions—belief—has the most disastrous effect on human conduct. To believe and to obey are the chief demands of religion. Even worse, belief and obedience are directed toward what is past. What "the fathers" saw and thought was probably the best they could manage at the time, but it is damaging to force their limited vision on those who come after.

These injurious restrictions imposed on all of us, Gilman points out, come from the minds of men alone. How did this happen? The explanation lies in the early and universal subjection of the female to the male. The male, left alone to carry on all important social activities, exaggerated beyond all reason his male qualities of combativeness, excessive sexual development, and competitiveness. Such is "his" religion.

Women, on the other hand, says Gilman, are oriented toward birth, not death, toward building—farming while men were hunting—and nurturing the young. "Her" religion, then, based on female principles of growth and nurturance, would be the ideal corrective to "his." A birth-based religion holds before us, she says, "the ceaseless visible re-creation of an undying race." She also expressed this lofty sentiment more prosaically: "We cannot improve a dead man; we can, a baby."[13] If religion had come to us through the minds of women, birth, not death, would have been the central issue, not a "posthumous egotism" of what will happen to me after I die, but an "immediate altruism": what must be done for the child who is born?

Gilman does admit, unhappily, that most contemporary women, having been created by ages of masculine selection, are not such as one would trust the world to now. As women achieve equality with men, she observes in 1923, it is "sickening" to see how many use their freedom in mere imitation of masculine vices. But, she goes on, "just that is to be expected from a subject class, suddenly released." These are hard times for men, she admits, for they are losing their servants. They are also hard for women, so long accustomed to dependence. The so-called free women, educated and independent, are just as much the slaves of fashion and the victims of license as they were before, no less in bondage than a harem prisoner, a victim of white slavery, or a kitchen drudge. Gilman's hopes, expressed in *Women and Economics*, that entrance into the public work force would liberate women, have not been realized, and she is deeply disappointed. Still, she says, every year there are more women working for world improvement, and every year there will be still more. A birth-based woman's religion will not bring an end to problems, says Gilman; "that only comes with an anaesthetic." But women have always tried to heal, to teach, and to help. When such women have as much power as men in the world, they will have an enormous impact on many social issues— on war, for example, Gilman predicts.

The new religion will bring new beliefs to replace the old:

evolution means growth, not combat; the human race is young and open to endless improvement; the human race lives immortally on earth, recreated through birth; social improvement is our chief duty; God is the Life within us. Her last book ends with a poem, which says, in part:

God is a force to give way to!
God is a thing you have to do!
God can never be caught by prayer,
Hid in your heart and fastened there—
    Let God through!

Gilman has taken the nineteenth-century notion of maternal service and made it the foundation of an ethical system and a guide for the conduct of everyone.

Gilman also wrote and published an enormous amount of fiction—short stories and novels—and poetry. Gary Scharnhorst's valuable bibliography, which he accurately describes as "reliable and virtually complete," provides, for the first time, substantiation of Gilman's claim that she was prolific. She published hundreds of poems—Scharnhorst identifies 490—and 186 pieces of fiction, mostly short stories but a number of them novels. Her verse and fiction appeared sporadically in such mainstream publications as *Cosmopolitan*, the *Saturday Review of Literature, Atlantic Monthly, Harper's Bazaar*, and the *New York Times*, but most of her work was published in periodicals and collections that primarily addressed the concerns of women, trade unionists, Fabians, socialists, Nationalists, Populists, reformers, and radicals of all kinds. In the months of 1894, while she edited the *Impress*, and in the period from November 1909 through December 1916, when she wrote the *Forerunner*, she published almost exclusively in these periodicals. She carefully selected both new and old pieces for the *Forerunner*. Three novels serialized in it were later published separately by Gilman: *What Diantha Did*, 1910; *The Crux*, 1911; and *Moving the Mountain*, also 1911, all published by the Charlton Company.

Gilman's fiction and poetry constitute part of her ideological world-view, and that, rather than their literary quality, is what primarily gives them their interest and their power.

In the nonfiction books, as we have seen, she analyzes the past and projects goals for the future on the basis of her particular feminist-humanist-socialist perspective. In the fiction Gilman dramatizes her vision of history, sociology, and ethics. "Until we can see what we are, we cannot take steps to become what we should be," she wrote, and she uses the fiction to show us what we are and then what we could be. She saw all her work, fiction and nonfiction, as intrinsic to her struggle to persuade her audience, primarily but not entirely women, of the value and possibility of her world-view.

Most of the problems Gilman addressed in her fiction are as relevant to our present day as they were to hers. Many of the themes she explored in her nonfiction reappear in the fiction. Socially useful and gratifying work is essential for all of us, men and women. Children are central, and it is by rearing them in a democratic and humane environment that permanent change will come about. Children are best reared in some kind of community and by women, although not necessarily their biological mothers. The prerequisite for genuine autonomy is economic independence, so that all citizens should leave their homes every day to do "world-work." Children of all ages do their "world-work" as well, that is, they go to "baby-gardens," or what we know as day-care centers.

Gilman's fiction belongs to one of two categories: realistic stories that deal with the everyday world with which her readers are familiar, and utopian stories, which reside in the realm of the imagination.

Until we decide to bring about the future world, which Gilman believes we can do, she suggests there are changes to be made in the meantime. Her fiction evokes "baby-gardens" as better environments for children that also permit mothers to seek work for which they are better fitted; unconventional marital arrangements that allow men and women work and cultural options so that they can do what is best for them, not what the world prescribes; children, young and adult, liberated from tyrannical fathers and passive mothers; seemingly hopeless situations resolved by the intervention of an older woman, frequently a doctor, who provides opportunities and knowledge; the young fleeing from their biological families and creating new families from among distant relatives, friends, or co-workers; middle-aged and older women finding creative possibilities for their lives after husbands die and children grow up, using their skills from the home in the public sphere. All her plots assert the need to break out of the traditions that bind us—men, women, and children.

And so Julia in "Making Change," a musician, unhappy at home with a young baby, conspires with her mother-in-law, a widow, to set up a "baby-garden" on the roof of an apartment house. The "baby-garden" is run by the older woman, who thereby finds useful, paid work. Julia returns to her music, and thus reduces the economic burdens on her husband, while doing the work for which she is trained. Mr. Peebles in "Mr. Peebles' Heart" is persuaded by his sister-in-law, a doctor and a "new woman," to turn his store over to his wife, who has the interest and talent to run it, which he never had, while he takes a year to travel, as he has always wanted. Vivian Lane in *The Crux* rejects the man she "loves," that is, the man who aroused her when she was a young woman, because he has venereal disease, and seeks instead a life filled with gratifying work. She founds a kindergarten, and slowly, over time, when she is twenty-seven, develops a deep friendship with another man, which evolves into mature love. Diantha, in *What Diantha Did*, flees from a smothering and oppressive but seemingly "loving" and protective family to go West and start a high-powered business. When she eventually marries, as all Gilman's young women do, she maintains a separate residence, with her child, for years, in order to maintain her business.

Gilman's realistic stories are splendid embodiments of her advice to those who feel trapped, for she offers a way out. But such a resolution necessitated creating problems that can be resolved by will, energy, and imagination, and so she avoided any situation which lacked that possibility. Her stories are peopled by middle- or lower-middle-class men and women, ordinarily of Northern European or English ancestry, who have some room in which to maneuver. Gilman's message resounds: We can get out of where we are if we use our skills and create new options. That might mean leaving the responsibilities for caring for elderly parents to hired nurses, rejecting a loved suitor who proves to be unsuitable, or going to Colorado with an elderly aunt. Even in Gilman's unpublished detective story, "Unpunished," written late in her life in bitterness and disappointment with a world that ignored her, the heroine, a disabled impoverished, disfigured, and abused woman, triumphs at the end.

But it is in the utopian fiction that Gilman's imagination soars most wondrously, and of the three utopian novels she wrote, *Herland*, serialized in 1915, is certainly the most successful, the most playful, the most appealing. It was preceded in 1911 by *Moving the Mountain*, a "baby Utopia," Gilman called it. In that book the world is, in its physical presence, familiar and recognizable. It is the people who are different, because in 1920 they voted for a socialist government, and in the next twenty years they moved beyond socialism to a New Religion, which Gilman calls "Living and Life."

Gilman wrote *Moving the Mountain* to show what possibilities exist in a world that is fundamentally recognizable. In this book she plays out in fictional form many of the ideas developed in *The Home* and *Concerning Children*, focusing on child-rearing as the key to developing a new kind of person; the collective nature of life in a world in which the profit motive is eliminated and social, not individual, goals are sought, but in which traditional monogamous marriage and the nuclear family are maintained.

There, a new social consciousness dominates, based on constructive industry, not warfare and aggression. The mothering and educating of the young, carried out by trained specialists, creates a new kind of generation quickly, and so the destructive, excessive male qualities inherited from a historic past are rapidly bred out. All these changes are achieved democratically, cooperatively, enthusiastically by virtually everybody. Those who resist are tolerated.

Moving the Mountain demonstrates how men and women can live together happily and productively in a feminist-humanist-socialist world. In *Herland*, women create a far more radical utopia without men at all. In this wonderful romp, three American men stumble on a community of women, initially convinced that such a superior society presupposes men, who they presume must be hiding. The narrator, the intelligence through whom we learn about Herland, is Vandyck Jennings, a sociologist, a man of reason. He is ultimately converted to a new consciousness when at the end he learns to see women "not as females, but as people." His comrades are Terry O. Nicholson, wealthy, arrogant, exploiter of women, and Jeff Margrave, who too uncritically and too easily accepts Herland.

Here, Gilman creates a world that values genuine privacy and genuine community by eliminating the family as a mediating agency. There are no men, no families, only individuals and community, and children are raised by a community of women. It is Gilman's radical, alternative vision of collective motherhood. The ideas she worked out in her nonfiction studies, all of them, are carried to fruition in this utopian world. For example, in *Concerning Children* she said that we narrow-mindedly think that to care for other children means to neglect our own, while in truth, unless we care for all, we neglect our own; in *Herland* she dramatizes that belief. All of her precepts, from *Women and Economics*, which calls for genuine autonomy for women, to *His Religion and Hers*, which envisions a birth-based woman-centered religious system, are imagined and dramatized in *Herland*.

The women of Herland have no knowledge of sexuality—reproduction is by parthenogenesis—or home or family or marriage or profit motive or sense of self apart from others. As they and their visitors learn about each other's worlds—and the men and the women do learn from each other—our culture is ridiculed; with wide-eyed innocence, common sense, and reason the Herlanders expose much that is ludicrous, oppressive, and unreasonable about the way we do things, about the way we work, define gender roles, and establish social expectations. Gilman's ideas are deeply serious, but in this playful book she offers her message with great good humor.

With Her in Ourland, the sequel to *Herland*, serialized in 1916, follows Van and his bride, the Herlander Ellador, as they tour our world just after the outbreak of World War I. Ellador, with her disarming questions, causes Van, and the reader as well, to see our world in a new and different way.

In the realistic short stories and novels, Gilman often warns young women of the dangers of rushing unthinkingly into hasty marriages, out of one's own desperate need or because of the pleasure in being sought and wooed. In her own life, in her own two marriages, she took years before she agreed to marry. It was her relationship to Delle that was hasty and unexamined. Yet never in her fiction did Gilman address woman-to-woman relationships that have anything like the intensity that she and Delle shared in reality. It is ordinarily mother-daughter issues that Gilman addresses in her fiction, not relationships of loving female partners. Partnerships in

Gilman's fiction are always heterosexual. Only in *Herland* does she create an all woman's community, but it is one without sexuality. Sexuality is introduced with the appearance of men, each of whom eventually marries a Herlander. Love between women was too dangerous for Gilman to confront publicly, and perhaps privately as well.

What, then, is Charlotte Gilman's intellectual legacy? Of her full and rich body of work, what remains of importance for us today? Should we continue to read the books her contemporaries read with enthusiasm and should we read the books her contemporaries slighted, and why?

It is easy to see her flaws: a simple, linear view of evolutionary progress; neglect of the role of class, race, and ethnicity and the way they intersect with gender; a belief in evolutionary stages of racial development that strikes a contemporary reader as racist and ethnocentric; acceptance of anthropological explanations that have long since been discarded and that cause her on occasion to invent a past to fit her theories. She relies on now unacceptable notions of biological and sociological "laws," which she sometimes invoked when they corroborated her ideas and which she tried to wiggle out of when they did not. It is worth noting, however, that her rigid acceptance of evolutionary "laws," and her racist and ethnocentric assumptions about stages of human development, were widely accepted ideas in the learned academies and universities of her day. Despite an extraordinary ability to transcend many of the limitations of the intellectual and cultural world she inhabited, she was nevertheless often imprisoned by others.

It is of course true that, as indicated in the Introduction, some thinkers of Gilman's era, such as Emile Durkheim, Max Weber, Sigmund Freud, and Thorstein Veblen, disavowed the prevailing belief that social sciences could be modeled on natural sciences. Their ideas were in most ways more compatible with Gilman's goals than the limiting natural-science model, but she was locked into nineteenth-century thinking because she had not the formal training and therefore the self-confidence to reject that which she had never studied systematically. Gilman read Veblen, but she seemed not to understand the ways in which he sought to replace the formalistic methodology of classical economics with empirical studies of actual behavior. Instead, she relied on stretching those formalistic structures, which upheld the idea of rigid laws of society, to create her own structures. She used what were then the conventional intellectual systems to challenge the prevailing ideas she opposed, rather than creating her own systems or utilizing those new modes of thought that were more congenial to her ideas but less compatible with currently established ways of thought.

Gilman's uncritical belief in the inevitability of progress and the moral lessons to be drawn from science—ideas that marred her work—continue to pervade present-day thinking. Stephen Jay Gould cautions contemporary readers that science is of value in describing how the world is constructed, but not in telling us how it ought to be or in assigning categories of "better" or "worse" or "higher" or "lower" or drawing moral implications. Many people today continue to hold to four invalid biases, all of which Gilman adhered to and which, according to Gould, have persisted: a belief in the concept of a ladder of progress in nature; a belief in determinism, that is, an ordered world, in which the random is rare; a belief in gradualism; and a belief in adaptationism, that is, that everything fits and everything works. There are no inherent moral messages in nature or in science, Gould tells us, words as appropriate to the nineteenth century as they are today.

Locked as Gilman was in an all-encompassing theoretical system, she occasionally was trapped into contradictions, although fewer than one might expect. In *Women and Economics*, for example, she spoke poignantly about the need to make room for single people, who hold a legitimate and deserved place in society. In *The Home*, she asserts that all girls should marry, and if they do not there is something wrong with them. If women initiated industry, as she says in *Women and Economics*, are the first educators of children and the main agent for developing love, then why does she so thoroughly denigrate women's contributions to civilization? An oversimplified evolutionary theory led her into these difficulties.

When Gilman described the initial subordination of women by men, she said that enslavement meant that women would no longer be able to care for themselves or their offspring, that responsibility now devolving onto men. She did not explain why, when women were enslaved, they could no longer feed themselves. Her neglect of class is at the core of this confusion. Her description of a group of women being fed and cared for by men is a description of a small, privileged class of women. Most women, in the nineteenth century as well as throughout history, were not removed from the process of production. Quite the contrary. They continued to produce, while at the same time they were subordinated, sexually and economically, to men. Gilman's analysis of the role of privileged women in industrial capitalist society remains insightful, but she oversimplified history and anthropology to make her point.

One can understand Gilman's general acceptance of Lamarckian principles that maintained acquired traits could be passed on by heredity, because such ideas were still considered somewhat viable in her day. She hedged on many questions having to do with the controversy surrounding heredity versus culture, which, given the state of knowledge at the time, may have been wise, but she was not always consistent. She assigned the virtues she associated with maternity to the innate, while the vices of women, she argued, were imposed by society, and while she made a case to defend that distinction, it was not always a strong one.

She was sufficiently free of social constraints to question many deeply held social values, but she was not fully free. What she approved of she called "natural," and saw as flowing inevitably and correctly from evolutionary principles, while what she did not approve of she called "unnatural," and in this way she could claim scientific validity for her own opinions. For example, she clung to conventional notions of the superiority of heterosexual, monogamous marriage and the nuclear family, and defended these ideas on the grounds of evolutionary "law," not as cultural creations.

If the flaws in her work are apparent, so are the strengths. She set out to forge a new world-view, a social philosophy whose central tenet was the social nature of life and whose major lens was gender. Nobody had done that before. She struggled to construct a feminist philosophy, and while she did not entirely succeed, her work provides continuing fruitful possibilities for further exploration by contemporary theorists.

She took the ordinary matters of everyday living for most women and put them in a larger context, making them appropriate subjects for intellectual inquiry. The central work assigned—still assigned—to women, the rearing of children, she saw as being of equal social importance to the public work of men, although she proposed doing it differently. She well understood that for most women a loving partnership and motherhood remain overriding goals. Her work addresses the issues still alive today of how to resolve the tension between love and work, intimacy and autonomy. She struggled to persuade others of the sweeping changes necessary to facilitate genuine participation of women in the work force. She called for the expanding of options for men and women, understanding the need for genuine egalitarian partnerships if we are to develop our gifts and talents.

Although she was concerned ultimately with the most profound and far-reaching changes in society, she never lost her interest in present possibilities. How do we get from here, where we are, to there, where we would like to be? Her advice was to start where we are, start the process with small but significant changes, so that those making the changes will learn how to take them further and everyone will see the benefits. She saw changes around her, and she had hope that these changes would bring long-term benefits, but then she confronted the reality that they did not bring the effects she had envisioned. By the early decades of this century, Gilman was writing about the vices of the "New Woman" who sought to emulate men's behavior, and she was dismayed. She had assumed that the limits that impede women's full expression would be largely removed as women moved out of the home and into the work force. Such was a belief she expressed in *Women and Economics*. It was a position she shared with most socialist critics on the subject of women's emancipation. But she underestimated the way in which women would be drawn into the marketplace without the accompanying social services she assumed would be developed. "Baby-gardens" did not proliferate to aid the growing numbers of working women. The result too often was that women were expected to work in the public arena and also maintain traditional domestic responsibilities. She seriously underestimated the cultural power that gender distinctions held over men and women, a cultural power that followed women as they left the home for factory or office. She did not realize how effectively the subordinate status that women suffered in the domestic sphere would be replicated in the public arena. She hoped that the various efforts to reduce housework would succeed, that the efforts to provide an alternative to the single-family residence, to private ownership of household tools, and to the allocation of housework to women would have lasting effects. She watched with delight the efforts to create, on a large scale, boardinghouses with public dining rooms and parlors, suitable for middle-class people, or the more elaborate apartment hotels, which offered various housekeeping services, or experiments with home-cooked delivery services—ways in which her theoretical ideas were being put into practice by others. She applauded these changes, which she saw as the beginning of a burgeoning mass movement. "This is the true line of advance," she wrote in *Harper's Bazaar* in 1907, "making a legitimate human business of housework."[14] But then all these efforts, including commercial housecleaning services, consumers' cooperatives, and cooperative kitchens, declined or disappeared by the end of the 1920s.[15] The promise held out in *Women and Economics* did not work out as Gilman had anticipated. Persuading the public was going to be a far more difficult task than she had originally envisioned, but she never lost her optimism about ultimately achieving her new and better world. Instead, she turned her attention increasingly to concerns of ideology, perhaps to try to comprehend why there was so much resistance.

Many of her words are uncannily prescient. She stripped the sentimentality from marriage and motherhood, a sentimentality that masked what she exposed: power relations that imprison women and children. She denied the distinction between public and private by subjecting all institutions to critical assessment and by demanding that all social relationships belong in the public sphere. By incorporating children, for example, into civic life, she would free them from the power of their parents. By locating women's oppression in the home and in their economic subservience to men, she would free women. In the process men, as husbands and as fathers, would be freed as well. She understood that the family claim and the social claim are often in conflict, and she argued for the superiority of the social claim. She did not push her ideas to the conclusions that many contemporary feminists have by calling for the abolition of the nuclear family, but she struck at the heart of exploitation with the call to abolish the work of the family, that is, the work of the mother in the home. She understood as did no critic before her that the home was the primary location of inequality for women. Dramatically illustrated in her fiction, her message was consistent: one must leave the family home in order to grow. The so-called individualistic concerns of conservative ideology define the family as the basic social unit, and then imprison women and children within it, Gilman asserts, denying those within the home free access to the public world of choices. Gilman spoke for the supreme social value involved in social, not individual, parenting. She socialized the domestic, privatized world of women by incorporating it into the public world of men, not by demeaning its importance, as traditional Marxism does by assigning it to a category called "unproductive labor," or by ignoring it entirely as most other social theorists do. In this way, by taking the individual mother out of the individual home, she simultaneously freed the imprisoned mother and enhanced the job of mothering. Although she did undervalue the strength and power of female community, her effort to bring child-rearing and housework into the public world ties her centrally to women's experience.

Gilman's ideas of woman as "Other," her discussions of the damaging effects of the masculinization of language, literature, history-writing, and sports—and of all the standards by which we measure excellence—are central to feminism today. Even two of the male thinkers to whom she expressed an intellectual debt, Charles Darwin and Thorstein Veblen, did not escape her criticism. Veblen condemns, and rightly, she says of *The Theory of the Leisure Class*, the power that the rich and powerful have kept for themselves in war, government, and sports. But he seems unaware, says Gilman, that the very ideas of mastery and ownership are male attributes. Gilman was especially critical of Darwin for taking evolutionary theory and masculinizing it, that is, stressing combat and struggle, male concepts, rather than growth, a female concept.

Gilman's insistence on women's full and genuine equality and autonomy and her repudiation of society's exaggeration of gender difference are echoed in today's feminism. So, paradoxically, is her belief that women are profoundly different from men—that, as mothers, they are more nurturing, less combative and less competitive, and that society would be more humane for having more of these "feminine" traits. Even some of the confusion as to what is innate and what is cultural that pervades Gilman's work persists today.

Gilman felt that her goal of a social transformation into a fully humane and just world could be brought about by changed consciousness. She came to realize, and wrote in words that could have been written today, that many newly emancipated women blindly and wrongly emulate men, but that such behavior must be expected and understood as belonging to a transitional and therefore temporary period.

Gilman's indictment of the sexism embedded in the history, ritual, and theology of world religions has a jolting contemporary ring. Her concern with an afterlife that she defined as our duty to our children, not a concern with our private fantasies of heaven, reverberates in today's feminist liberation theology, although the language remains uniquely hers. Her idea of a birth-based system of religious beliefs that stresses the nonsupernatural and focuses on ethical underpinnings provides a continuity with the past that we need to incorporate in the feminist present.

She raised all the questions to which she wanted answers, issues of sexual identity, male/female roles, work, education, child-rearing, the relationship between men and women, the limitations imposed by the institutions of home, family, and motherhood, the use of technology in bringing about change, the ways humans can change their circumstances, why it all was the way it was. Betty Friedan asked some of those questions again in 1963 in *The Feminine Mystique*.

Gilman asked, many times and in many different ways, but particularly in *Our Brains and What Ails Us*: since we know it all, since we know what we should do, how is it that we don't change? She never fully understood the answers to her question: first, that we do not know it all, that her ordinarily very simple resolutions often oversimplified complicated matters, and second, perhaps more important, that knowing the long-term goal does not easily or necessarily lead to the creation of strategies for change to achieve that goal. Her belief in human reason, her passionate, deep commitment to human reason, clouded her ability to comprehend psychological complexity and human irrationality. Her own unsettled relationship with Katharine, her daughter, illustrates on a personal level the limitations embodied in her social theory. Her need for rational, rigid, comprehensible order made it impossible for her to imagine the possibilities of a universe incorporating the random and arbitrary or a psychological theory incorporating the irrational and the unconscious.

But by making gender the center of her analysis, Gilman made the invisible visible, and that focus in itself greatly advanced social thought. Others before her had in a variety of ways addressed aspects of the issue of female subordination: Aphra Behn, Mary Astell, Mary Wollstonecraft, Margaret Fuller, Elizabeth Cady Stanton, Friedrich Engels, J. J. Bachofen, and Lester Ward. But Gilman made gender the core of her analysis, and thereby made the *idea* of gender, the *idea* of female subordination as a central fact of human reality, no longer hidden, no longer unseen. To deny the power of Gilman's extraordinary insight required the denial of the body of her work as serious or useful or worthy of attention, and so a new layer of invisibility was imposed in an effort to deny the discovery. That disowning of Gilman's work has until now been successful.

Gilman sought to create a general theory of men and women in history from the perspective of gender. Embedded in her effort are a variety of assumptions about the nature of society and human nature, assumptions which she, in general, shared with her contemporaries. But she used those shared ideas to create a world-view compatible with feminist ideology, despite the cultural and political biases that mar her work. The social sciences that emerged in the late nineteenth century accepted the model of the natural sciences, and as we have seen, Gilman remained uncritical of this notion. Society is a living organism, she repeated many times, and individual parts exist to serve the whole. Thus, individuals are intrinsically dependent upon each other and exist by nature as part of a larger community. Fundamental to her thinking is the centrality of the claims of community over the individual. The greatest possibilities for human happiness lie, not with the alleged autonomy of the individual, but in a collective world in which the individual has a unique place and functions reciprocally with all others in that collectivity. Individuals are not sacrificed for the greater social good, in Gilman's view, for there is no inherent conflict between the individual and the social body. Gilman, with her collectivist commitment, understood that the only way for the individual to flower is in a community in which each individual is valued separately.

The universal idea of individualism she regards as the "largest and falsest" concept by which we are burdened. The oldest, most pernicious error subsumed under that ego-centeredness is the subjection of women to the service of men, that is, the notion that woman's duty is to her private family and not to the social community. The central thesis of *Women and Economics*—that women's economic dependence on men came about through the combining of the sexual and economic functions into one sexuo-economic relationship for women—is the cornerstone of her ideology. For Gilman that one imbalance, that women are at the service of men, underlies all imbalance.

In her effort to accomplish "world-building," Gilman assumed that changed consciousness was the means to bring about social transformation, that the power of ideas to change thinking was the primary tool for changing behavior. False ideas have shaped us until now, the most pernicious being incorporated into religious ideology, but true ideas could replace the false, she said. Gilman was aware of the power of false ideas, because we modify our behavior to fit our ideas, to the extent we can, she argued. If we see ourselves as wicked, as religions tell us we are, then we will behave so, and become so. At the same time, she recognized that there is a real world which modifies our ideas. The first person to assert that the earth is round, she said, "had the opinion of all mankind against him, but he had the earth on his side." She has the earth on hers, but in the meantime, she works toward educating her audiences.

Thus Charlotte Perkins Gilman created, in rudimentary form, the beginnings of a theory of gender and gendering. Her effort was to degender the world by exposing its gendered reality, and we need to know of her work because it constitutes part of our intellectual legacy and we need to know of her work in order to build on it. Her angle of vision allows us to see more clearly the assumptions of gender in other social philosophies. "It is no easy matter to deny or reverse a universal assumption," said Gilman, in an uncharacteristic understatement. It is no easy matter, but she came very close to accomplishing just such a reversal. Her fresh look at our fundamental assumptions causes us to look again at the assumptions of others. Humanity lives and grows by the female principle, Gilman insisted, and while such language strikes a contemporary ear uncomfortably, we are accustomed to hearing the opposite without its sounding strange: that human beings are competitive and aggressive, that war is a natural state, that we are all motivated by narcissistic self-interest and a yearning for power over others. Claiming birth as a central experience for humanity, an experience that should be the core of a system of ethics and religious beliefs, sounds odd to us, but it is intrinsically no more odd than ethical beliefs and religious systems built upon death, fear of death, violence, adversarial struggle, and a notion of sin and evil.

Gilman tried to persuade her audiences of the need not only to socialize the private world, thereby making society as responsible for activities within the home as it is for those without, but also to humanize the public world, by infusing it with female values of cooperation and nurturance. She acknowledged instinctive male/female differences, more than we acknowledge them today, but these differences she located only in the distinct reproductive role. Otherwise we are more similar than different, she said persistently. She challenged the great stress on difference rather than similarity, although she did not much explore its origin.

Today's feminist commentators, such as Nancy Chodorow, Dorothy Dinnerstein, and Sandra Harding, offer psychoanalytic explanations to account for most gender distinctions. Using the lens of gender, Gilman understood the significance of that which we shared, rather than those qualities that divide us, although she did not have the tools to offer a satisfactory explanation. Gilman lived in a world defined by extreme gender distinctions, a world in which the different universes inhabited by men and women were described as natural, and yet she was able to understand that it was the immense plasticity and adaptability of the human species that made the cultural arrangements appear to be natural and inevitable. Although she did not have the scientific information to prove her case, she strongly suspected, and she was apparently right, that we cannot separate the genetic from the environmental causes of gender differences. Gilman was not fully free of the claims made by the scientific community, but she had a genuine respect for the flexibility of human beings, and so she sensed how most of what we call masculine and feminine is not innate but learned. By understanding how Gilman's categories were themselves contaminated by the reflections and replications of the very concepts she was criticizing, we can better appreciate how unable we are as well to free ourselves entirely from our own cultural limitations, even when we are certain that we are doing so.

Gilman's theorizing captures the feminist emphasis on contextual thinking, because she sought to put all the pieces together in one unifying and connecting universe. She struggled, and that is a great triumph, to understand the processes necessary for comprehending a world not of her own making, and a world she had little power to reshape. Jane Flax says: "Without adequate knowledge of the world and our history within it (and this includes knowing how to know), we cannot develop a more adequate social philosophy." Gilman did not know how to know and so she guessed a lot and imagined a lot, and some of it was sound and most of it was at least provocative.[16]

The feminist philosopher Sandra Harding reminds us that the great achievement of Archimedes was not his particular theory about how to create a unified perspective but his "inventiveness in creating a new kind of theorizing."[17] Harding's own work, a sophisticated and often brilliant analysis of feminism and science, itself demonstrates how much the work done by our foremothers remains unknown. She suggests that only now can we understand the ideas of eighteenth- and nineteenth-century feminists as "utopian," because although earlier feminists recognized the misery of woman's condition, "their diagnoses of its causes and their prescriptions for women's emancipation show a failure to grasp the complex and not always obvious mechanisms by which masculine dominance is created and maintained."[18] Gilman's work was not fully developed along these lines, but she certainly began the task of theory-building. If it is not possible even now to have a master theory, as Harding suggests, it was less possible for Gilman, but her contributions move us in the right direction—though only if we are familiar with them.

The philosophers Jane Martin and Evelyn Fox Keller have pointed to a serious flaw in Gilman's world-view—her inability to allow for intense emotions. "Nowhere in *Herland*," says Keller, "do we hear about the role of intimacy and its identification with the acquisition of science."[19] Martin suggests that it is not only science that suffers from her not joining together reason, feeling, and emotion in her ideal of mother-love and in her understanding of human personality in general.[20]

This criticism applies more to Herland, at which it is directed, than to the rest of Gilman's writing, but the weakness remains. Gilman was wedded to the construction of a fully rational human being. She urged women, who were designated as the nonrational, emotional sex, to use reason to understand the world in their own interest. She feared emotionalism in women because it was through appeals to emotions that women were often led to behave in ways and think in ways that were not in their interest. Rationality was the device she offered women as a way of breaking down the dichotomy between public/private, objective/subjective, active/passive, mind/body, rational/emotional. It was, to her, a force to unify men and women in their effort to achieve happiness. Gilman was wary of passion, although she did not deny it fully. *Herland* is a book about a woman's world without passion or intimacy. But both passion and intimacy appear with the introduction of sexual love in the form of the three male intruders, only one of whom, Van, sufficiently tempers his male sexuality to the requirements of human reason. Van learns from the Herlander Ellador about a universe he did not even have the language to imagine, and he teaches her about passion and sexuality. Together they achieve as much of their full humanity as they can, considering that they are living in a world not of their own creation. In much of her other fiction, Gilman accepted the reality and power of love and intimacy, but its greatest flowering always came within a context of calm reason. In her philosophical, historical, and sociological texts, the emotional ways of knowing, a subject of interest today, are a subtext. It is Gilman's experiences as a woman, as a mother, as a daughter, as a wife, as a friend, as a poet, as a lecturer, as a writer, that shape her inquiries. The emotional side of knowing the world is very much present in Gilman's work, as it was in her life; in her struggle to temper its seductions and its dangers, she denied more than she should have, but she did not entirely repudiate its importance.

Gilman healed herself by means of the work she did. It gave her a sense of self-worth, importance, goodness, intelligence—all the qualities she did not come to adulthood believing she possessed.

The content of the work was also significant in the healing process, for it made her understand her place in the world. That important intellectual, ideological, and political legacy is ours to use.

We have not sinned.
We are not damned.
We do not need to be saved.
Our business is To Learn and To Grow.
Social Ethics

XI
KATHARINE

Charlotte said many times during her lifetime, in lectures, in letters, in her autobiography, and in her books, in one form or another: merely to love the child does not serve the child. Being a loving mother is necessary but not sufficient; one must also be an intelligent mother, a wise mother. I think that Charlotte Gilman saw herself as a loving but not wise mother, who therefore could not provide her daughter, Katharine, with what she needed, just as she saw her mother, Mary Perkins, as one who could not fill her childhood needs. She said as much many times in her letters to Houghton, she alluded to her sense of herself as an inadequate mother many times in letters to Grace, she lectured about the institution of motherhood as a public issue and she wrote about it in her many books. But I believe she never fully confronted the issue to herself, for herself, and that she never, therefore, was able to communicate her feelings on the subject properly and fully to her daughter.

The decision she made to have Walter and Grace raise Katharine in those early years of the child's life was not only in the child's interest, it was virtually the only choice Charlotte could have made. For whatever reason, she felt, and probably correctly, that she could not adequately mother her daughter, and she knew that Grace Ellery Channing, soon to be Stetson, could and would. Still, she was never free of anguish or guilt about that decision. Public criticism made it all the more difficult to justify to herself, but the feeling of failure and of shame would likely have pursued her, though less seriously, even if the issue had not been made into a public one.

It would not have been easy under any circumstances for Katharine to free herself, as a child or even as an adult, from the sense of having been abandoned by a rejecting mother, as her mother felt abandoned by both of her parents. Mothers did not relinquish daily care of their children in the 1890s without severe social penalty, and the little girl was sure to be punished for her mother's decision. A scandal of national proportions made such a situation more painful. It was not inevitably an unhealable wound, for the child did live with a loving and nurturing mother-substitute, as well as with a father who loved her. She never lost contact with her mother, and as she grew up she learned of the sad circumstances surrounding her mother's decision. It was a dreadful trauma from which Katharine and Charlotte might have recovered better than they did. They did not because Charlotte could not let go of her guilt and could not let go of Katharine, and because Charlotte denied both to herself and to Katharine an opportunity to explore any painful emotions they felt about each other.

Although for years after the separation Charlotte spoke and wrote to Houghton and Grace about her feelings of loss and longing and ever-persistent mother-guilt, she dealt with all that intense emotion primarily by every possible means of denial. She sought to bury her own feelings. For example, in a letter to Grace in 1896, she wrote of Katharine:

> I said to myself the other night—"Now why not think about her—just think of her beauty and sweetness and all the lovely things that you can remember of her." And I opened the door a little and looked in. As well pluck an amputation. It began to bleed and ache and I hastened and shut it again.[1]

Two years later, again to Grace, she wrote about how, despite her efforts, her anguish about Kate "sometimes . . . gets out." And she commented: "This won't do. I can't afford to ache."[2]

Charlotte tried to manage Kate's feelings as well, to deny her the occasion or the chance to express them, as we can see in words she addressed, again, to Grace about Katharine. Can her friend please tell her what kinds of letters Katharine likes, she asks, for

Charlotte wants "to keep intimately and pleasantly in her mind" without too much intrusion. She runs on to the child, she says, about her lecture tours in order "to avoid such emotional touches as might make her grieve a little." This effort "to avoid such emotional touches as might make her grieve"—as if filling her letters with details of her tours could keep Katharine from grieving—was probably characteristic of the way in which Charlotte related to Katharine, as had Mary to Charlotte. Although Charlotte's letters to Grace continued to express her longing for her daughter and the pain of the loss of her, on the strength of the available evidence one can reasonably conclude that she did not write or speak of these feelings to Katharine.

Charlotte wrote often to her daughter. Those letters were filled with expressions of love and affection. They were rich in detailed information about the aspects of her life that a mother thought would interest a little girl, but the letters did not deal with the difficult issues between them. It was not until 1897 that Charlotte finally referred to their separation, but even then she preempted any complaint on Katharine's part by saying how glad she was for her daughter "that these years of your life are being passed with the best person I ever saw to guide a child—dear Grace."[3] Two years later she again spoke of their parting, but again not to explore Katharine's feelings but to present her own. "And all the time grows in my heart the love of you and the hope for the time when I can make your acquaintance personally again," she wrote in words that were evocative of a young Charlotte writing to her father and that could not have been reassuring to a twelve-year-old child. Nor would the words that followed have made Katharine feel very close to this odd mother: "You will be so different a person from my little gold hair of '84." She went on: "And I shall be a different person too from the sick feeble mother you had then, poor and shabby and struggling . . . ," language that would make any child who felt anger at such a mother certainly feel herself an ingrate.

Charlotte also cited the risk of her depressions to legitimize her decision to send Katharine to Grace, and often reminded herself, and Grace, in letters, how well her work was going, the work made possible by sending Katharine to Grace. Words of sadness about missing Katharine are often followed by words describing her own triumph, as if the separation was somehow justified thereby. After one such expression of loss, Charlotte described how reading about herself in a Topeka newspaper made her want to exclaim with Whitman: "O I am wonderful. I did not know I contained so much goodness!"[4]

Charlotte avoided thinking about the effect of her actions on Katharine or admitting that these actions might have caused pain. As we have seen, she offered a rosy account in her autobiography of the final separation of mother and child. It seemed "the right thing to do," she explained; after all Grace was as good a mother, perhaps a better one, and the father longed for his child. "No one suffered . . . but myself," Charlotte insisted, unwilling to acknowledge Kate's emotions. She glossed over the fact that no one had asked Kate what she wanted to do or explained to her why she had to do what she had to do. "I never once let her feel it was pain, a break, anything unusual," wrote Charlotte, and off Kate went "happily enough." Everybody behaved well, all involved in a conspiracy of silence, all withholding the feelings they harbored. "She climbed gaily aboard [the train]. . . . We smiled and waved and threw kisses to each other." Nobody was allowed to cry, to yell, to question, to demand. If there was going to be emotional damage for Kate, Charlotte did not want to know about it.

Despite Charlotte's efforts to deny the trauma of the separation, or perhaps in part because of them, Katharine suffered deep feelings of hurt and abandonment. Katharine was probably aware of her mother's feelings of guilt, which only added to the daughter's awareness that she had indeed been wronged. The pain the mother felt at the separation she spared her daughter, undoubtedly wishing to cause no more unhappiness. But because she did not share it with Katharine, then or later, she deprived her daughter of the chance ultimately to understand and to forgive her mother and made it impossible for the two of them to work their way free of the guilt and anger that tied them together. Katharine learned her mother's lesson well, and so refused to acknowledge her own pain and anger, which caused her to suffer and to rage even more.

I met Katharine Stetson Chamberlin in the summer of 1978. She was ninety-three years old and living in a nursing home in Pasadena. As a result of a fall and consequent broken hip, she was confined to a wheelchair. She had great difficulty hearing, which made conversation, especially in a busy nursing-home lounge, somewhat awkward, but she was alert, sharp-tongued, and intellectually alive and well. She looked startlingly like her mother, with her piercing blue eyes, sharply angled face, and attractive but biting manner, so unlike the soft roundness of her father and, particularly, Grace, with her gentle, self-effacing, large, full-bodied womanly presence. Like her mother, Katharine Chamberlin was rather tall—five feet, six-and-a-half inches—and slim.

She seemed unable to comprehend the point of my visit: why would I want to write a book about her mother? At that time I was preparing a collection of Gilman's fiction, having already contracted to publish an edition of *Herland*. I knew that Katharine had been in correspondence with the historian Carl Degler about her mother, and I knew that Mary Hill, who was writing a biography of Charlotte, had been to see the family in Pasadena. Since it was clear that Katharine Chamberlin had her wits about her, I concluded that her reluctance to understand my visit had to do with her reluctance to acknowledge the growing respect for her mother's work. For example, when we finally understood each other, she disparaged the merits of *Herland*, wondering why I had bothered to resurrect such an inferior piece of work.

"What is it that you want from me?" she asked, eventually conceding that she understood my mission—a very nimble-witted and artful woman. I told her that I wanted any recollections of her mother she would share with me, that she should start where she wished, talk till she wanted to stop, and let me come back as often as she would during the summer.

The first memory she spoke of was one of abandonment: "My mother abandoned me when I was nine years old. She put me on a train by myself to travel East." I knew enough of the family history to know that she had not been sent alone on the train, except metaphorically. You traveled with your grandfather, I reminded her. But, she countered, he sat with his cronies and played poker the entire time, and paid no attention to me. Then it was your grandfather who abandoned you, I suggested. She looked straight at me, hard, for several seconds, those strong, bright eyes flashing, and she said, "My mother abandoned me when I was nine years old."

Katharine's persistent anger at her mother became clearer as we continued to talk together in the following weeks, although I believe

Katharine would have denied any such statement had I made it to her. Nevertheless, the family habit of "behaving well" by denying hostile feelings, while it occasionally slipped during our personal conversations, was maintained in Katharine's unpublished autobiography, the final version of which had been finished five years before, in September of 1972, when she was eighty-seven years old. Entitled "My Life with Four Parents," it begins with her birth in 1885 and ends in 1911, the year her father, Charles Walter Stetson, died, and she uses her name at birth, Katharine Beecher Stetson, on the cover page.

Katharine depicts the trip East to join her stepmother and father in cheery terms, continuing the antiseptic family story her mother had presented more than thirty years before in her autobiography. Acknowledging, but without criticism, that her grandfather spent time with several men traveling with him, thus leaving her alone, Katharine described that time positively: "I was happy, however, watching the landscape flash by."[5] In the space between Katharine's determinedly rosy view of that separation and her spontaneous response to me in a nursing home lies her tragedy.

Even before the separation from Charlotte, Katharine had had much to cope with while her parents were together and in the few years she spent alone with her mother. Katharine's autobiography minimizes those strains as well. Despite its title, the focus of the book is on things and places rather than on people or connections among them. Each of the fourteen chapters is named after the city in which she lived at the time described, and the language and imagery, reflecting the gifts and training of an artist, which Katharine was, evoke places and things in rich and lush detail, recapturing smells and colors and angles of vision an untrained eye overlooks, but not much painful emotion is evoked in the brief descriptions of what were inevitably painful situations. For example, Katharine tells how after Mary Perkins's death her former husband, Grandfather Perkins, accompanied the body to Los Angeles, where it was cremated. "It must have been a hard trip for him—reliving the happiness of courtship and marriage and the births of their children,"[6] Katharine writes, conjuring up a memory of the couple as happily married and loving parents. The reality was starkly different, as she must have known from reading her mother's autobiography. Katharine glosses over not only her grand-parents' incompatibility but her parents' tensions during their court-ship and marriage, as well as her mother's breakdown. "My parents were an exceptionally beautiful and gifted pair," their daughter writes.

> After years of courtship, during which time Mama devised [*sic*] various "tests," such as no letters or visits for a certain period and so on (in reading their journals I wonder how my father stood it–!) Mama, at last, set the day.[7]

When her parents knew she was on the way, Katharine Stetson continues, "they were joyful—Mama wanted a baby, especially a baby girl. She was not very well during her pregnancy (who knows, maybe the fall she once had in the gymnasium, astride a chair back when trying to set the clock, may have made trouble)." The doctor, however, assured Walter that her condition was common and that "she would be all right after the baby was born." According to Mama, says Katharine, she was the best baby, but "in spite of that she grew more and more depressed." Katharine instantly moves from the subject of her mother's depression to say that her mother "had a bountiful supply of milk" and nursed her daughter for five months, then switched to baby food, "which I took readily from a cup. (The Doctor had said I must be weaned because of my mother's nervous condition.)"

> Grandmother Perkins, who loved little babies especially, was sent for and came to look after me and keep house for Papa, as Mama had accepted an invitation from the Channings to visit them in Pasadena. . . . She had a wonderful visit with the Channings and lost her heart completely to the country, the climate, the color and the flowers.[8]

This is a rather cleaned-up, tepid narrative of a woman's breakdown and flight from infant and husband, especially when that nightmare is so publicly documented. *The Living of Charlotte Perkins Gilman* had been reprinted only a few years before Katharine wrote her own autobiography, as Katharine knew, so she must also have known that what would be of interest to the reader would be, not essentially a narrative of the events of her mother's life, rosy or not, but an account of how those events affected a young child. Such sentiments Katharine did not share with readers, probably because she did not herself acknowledge them. She refers to a time when she found a bottle of her mother's white pills and consumed them all, but they fortunately proved not to be dangerous. "Who knows—may be the Doctor had given Mama a bottle of Placeboes!!" she writes, again indicating that she did not, could not, take her mother's breakdown seriously.[9] Her parents' divorce and her father's remarriage are passed over casually: the months in Pasadena convinced Walter "that there was nothing he could do to save this marriage and he found he had grown to love Grace Channing—which pleased my mother very much as she loved and admired them both."[10]

Katharine projects a somewhat idealized portrait of her father, who "always seemed a prince to me," while her sense of her mother, however careful she is to avoid direct criticism, comes through with considerable ambivalence. Katharine does praise her mother for one thing and another, but less often than she praises her father. Indeed, she speaks of her less often altogether. She occasionally hints at flaws in Charlotte's mothering but without ever criticizing her directly, just as Charlotte did in describing her mother in her autobiography. Katharine's portrait of Charlotte, Mama, describes a woman of sense and reason who was not sensitive to a child's emotional needs. For instance, Katharine recalls how she discovered a tiny inchworm in her shrimp salad and how Charlotte explained that the worm had been boiled and was therefore safe to eat, but how, consequently, Katharine never liked or ate shrimp again. Several other childhood memories evoked in the autobiography, unimportant in themselves, suggest a mother who saw herself as a wise and enlightened parent but did not know how to reach out to a child in just the right way, a picture reminiscent of the one Charlotte painted of Mary Perkins's educated mothering that lacked the nurturing qualities her daughter needed. Katharine remembers her grandmother trying to teach her to sew and to crochet. "Mama always said she did not sew as well as her Mother—but that I handled a needle like a crow-bar."[11]

Only occasionally does Katharine permit a sign of pain and unhappiness to emerge, but even then it is unacknowledged. She describes the long train ride from Providence to a new life in Pasadena, when her parents had separated and she was leaving behind the home she knew and the father she adored.

> One night on leaving the diner we stepped out on the car platform and there was nothing beyond but darkness. I stood in my dainty white pinafore holding my Mother's hand (she seemed very tall and far above me) wondering *what* had become of our car!!
>
> All I could think was, that in crossing some canyon a bridge had collapsed and the rest of our train had fallen in![12]

Katharine speaks of Grace as "as dear to me as my own mother,"[13] a phrase filled with layers of complexity and ambiguity. Whatever else it means, it suggests that Katharine was never able fully to embrace the love that Grace offered without a feeling that it was secondhand because it did not come from her biological mother. Katharine loved Grace deeply all her life, but she never truly forgave her mother for leaving her. Because she could not acknowledge those feelings, neither the love for Grace nor the anger at Charlotte could be expressed fully.

Katharine would never feel entitled to admit negative and angry feelings, any more than Charlotte could acknowledge to her daughter her own sense of guilt and longing or than Walter or Grace could acknowledge their role in a situation that inevitably confused and damaged Katharine.

In spite of the many childhood traumas she suffered, Katharine's subsequent life with Walter and Grace, which always included some connection with Charlotte, seems to have been a good and stable one. When Katharine arrived in New York in 1894, after the long train ride East with her grandfather and his friends, Grace met her, and took her back to her home in Boston until the wedding. She could not stay with her father until the wedding, Katharine explained in her autobiography, because "Papa was living in his studio and could not very well take care of a child and paint and without painting and selling, how was he to support me or himself?" It was a question she did not ask about her mother, or even about Grace, who, while the child was staying with her, was juggling an editorial job at a Boston magazine, *Youth's Companion*. Grace continued writing after her marriage, but it was on a free-lance basis, work far

Grace and Walter

more compatible with maintaining a home and caring for a child than a job that required her regular presence in an office. Although she never did stop writing, and did publish occasional pieces in magazines and journals, it is clear that after her marriage she saw her role as primarily that of wife to Walter and mother to Katharine. Soon after the marriage—about which Katharine was not informed until it was over, a fact which "grieved" her, although Grace assured her there was little to see—the family took rooms in a home in Old Norwich, Connecticut, and "Papa joined us as often as he could." Plans to travel to Europe were postponed when Grace's mother grew ill, and the family thereupon moved to Pasadena, where Kate celebrated her tenth birthday and, soon after, Mrs. Channing died.

Finally, in the summer of 1896, Grace and Walter made plans to make that long-desired trip to Europe. "It never occurred to either of them to see if I could be left with some relative," wrote Katharine, the unspoken remainder of that sentence probably being "as my mother did" or "as my mother would have." Referring to her family as "we . . . devout artists," she tells how the three traveled through Italy, Germany, France, and England during 1897 and 1898. Walter, Papa, was usually short of money, and struggled to show and sell his paintings, but he rarely managed to provide much comfort for his family. After their trip they returned to Pasadena, back to the Channing home, where they remained from 1898 to 1900. "We were now servantless," wrote Katharine, "and Grace tried to portion out housework so we would each do our share and she would get a few hours to write in."

It is difficult to know how much a part Charlotte played in Katharine's life during these years. She tried to schedule her lectures to allow for time with Kate, and they managed a vacation of several weeks most summers. During the first years after Katharine joined Grace and Walter, Charlotte was able to spend relatively small periods of time with her. As the years passed, the visiting times expanded, and eventually Katharine was living with both sets of parents.

In early 1900, when Katharine was almost sixteen, Charlotte went West on a lecture trip and stayed several weeks to visit with her daughter. The two hiked in the mountains, practiced target shooting with a pistol, and visited Susan B. Anthony. Anthony and Mama talked, "probably on the sufferage [sic] movement," something about which Katharine "neither knew nor cared," as she had about the galleries and churches she had loved when touring with Papa and Grace.

By 1900 Charlotte felt well enough to begin to vie more seriously for Katharine; perhaps Katharine's grown-up state made it easier for Charlotte to imagine caring for her, or perhaps Charlotte felt that Katharine's increasing age meant that her chance to mother a child was soon to end. Charlotte may have told Grace how lovely it was for Katharine to move between the old world—in her European travels with her father—and the new, with her mother, but by 1900 she expressed the hope that Katharine would stay with her and Houghton "for several years," at least until she was eighteen, two years hence, before she went again to Europe to study art. But—recognizing the inevitable when it came to a teenage daughter—she concluded that "it depends on how she feels, mostly."[14] Katharine decided to go to Europe for a while, during which time her mother and Houghton were married. Walter and Grace settled for a time in Boston, and Charlotte and Houghton found an apartment in New York City, on West Seventy-ninth Street, into which they moved in early September. When Kate returned from Europe, in 1898, she lived in Pasadena for two years. In 1900, she moved to New York City, where she lived with Mama and Houghton, establishing a comfortable relationship with both of them. They took their meals at "Mrs. Bartholemes's" (mother of Freddie Bartholomew of later movie fame, although the name is misspelled), which gave Charlotte time to write while Kate attended Miss Murphy's School. She saw her father and Grace periodically, and spent the summer with Mama and Houghton at Summer Brook Farm, founded by Prestonia Mann Martin, daughter of Horace Mann, who had been a member of the original Brook Farm. Each guest paid $3 a week and was allotted a portion of work. Who got what work was determined by lottery. The poet Edward Markham was there the second summer Kate visited and he had, she said, the unique distinction of being called by his last name. "I rather resented it, feeling my Mother was just as distinguished as he, and she was called 'Sister Charlotte' by everyone," she remarked, expressing a rare hint of pride in her mother's accomplishments.[15] At Summer Brook Farm Kate also met Clarence Darrow, John Graham Phelps Stokes, and Dr. Gilbert Murray, in whose honor a Greek pageant was put on, probably Mama's idea. The following year, back in New York, Kate contracted pneumonia, and she describes in great narrative detail how Mama nursed her, but when the pneumonia turned to scarlet fever, "Mama decided she must hire a nurse . . . so she could write articles and prepare lectures."[16] This language again suggests an implicit criticism of Charlotte's mothering, but Charlotte was supporting Kate and scarlet fever was a life-threatening illness, so on both medical and financial grounds Charlotte had reason to seek relief from her nursing duties.

Kate remained in the United States for two years, but in 1902 she returned to Rome, Grace and her father preceding her. It was during this time that Katharine decided to be an artist, initially choosing to be a sculptor but then switching to drawing. Her father was closely involved in her training and it was he who selected her teachers. In 1904 Charlotte, attending an International Congress of Women in Budapest, visited Kate, who showed her the sights, by which she meant the museums and galleries—"Just what she got out of it I don't know," wrote Kate[17]—and the two returned together to the United States. Kate, Charlotte, and Houghton spent the summer together in a cottage in the Catskill Mountains and then Kate returned again to Rome in the fall. She continued in art school, for a time the only woman in her class, remaining for two more years in Italy, until her father decided she should work with contemporaries in America. On his advice she entered the Pennsylvania Academy of Fine Arts in Philadelphia in 1906–1907. She began to sell a few paintings during this period. Katharine's strained identification with her mother went far enough to prompt her to tell a friend, who was studying at a woman's art school, that, "being my Mother's daughter," she felt she had to say that "I thought poor things of a woman's school—that it was better to study with men in that they were more serious. They planned to be artists, whereas most of the women were only working until they married."[18] Is this a comment on the mother who abandoned her home in order to work, or on the substitute mother who relinquished her work in order to mother?

Completing her studies in Philadelphia, Katharine moved to New York in 1907, summered with Mama and Houghton, and then, when they rented a house in New York on West Eighty-second Street, moved to a rear room on the top floor. Katharine continued to paint a good deal during these years, her particular interest being in portraits. She had, as she put it, a "one man show" in her mother's home and then traveled to Italy to see her father, whose health was failing. Walter Stetson died on July 20, 1911. Grace and Katharine returned together to the United States almost immediately, and moved together into an apartment on West 136th Street in New York. Soon after, Charlotte and Houghton moved uptown to the building next door, a kind of reuniting of the remaining family.

Katharine had met Frank Chamberlin in Rome, when he was a fellow at the American Academy. He returned to the United States in 1911, shortly before Katharine did. In 1918 they met again at the MacDowell Colony, where they were both guests, courted, and married. Their first child, Dorothy, was born later that year. Walter, their son, was born two years later, in 1920. The young couple lived for a time in a studio apartment in New York but moved, when Dorothy was fourteen months old, to Pasadena, where they spent the remainder of their lives. Katharine continued to work at her art, although she returned to her original work as a sculptor while continuing to paint. She occasionally sold a piece, primarily miniature portraits.

In their Pasadena home one could see something of the life of Katharine and Frank, two artists, two parents. Frank had a light and airy studio in the yard behind the house, where he could work undisturbed. Katharine worked on the dining-room table in wet clay, which, Dorothy Chamberlin explained, meant that she could always be available to her family when needed, and then return to the clay that did not harden. Dorothy and Walter Chamberlin speak of their parents' marriage as a happy and stable one, although Frank, who chose never to work at any job other than his art, was poor all his life. The family was on relief during the Depression of the 1930s and on welfare subsequently, and Charlotte, Houghton, and Grace made regular contributions to them for decades.

In their adult years, Charlotte and Katharine's relationship was carried on largely through their letters, since they rarely lived in the same city and visits and telephoning were expensive and only occasional. This epistolary connection conveys the closeness that bound them as well as some misunderstanding, insensitivity, and strain.

Evidently mother and daughter did more than just stay in touch, although how much more it is hard to say because the file of letters appears to be incomplete. They seem to have written often, at least Charlotte did, and through her words one can read the love between them, but also, predictably, the many problems.

Charlotte, for example, never lost her sense of herself as outsider in the triangular bond that held Grace-Charlotte-Katharine together. She was a necessary member of that small female community but she felt herself always to be its marginal member, an uncomfortable if familiar position. In a characteristic comment, Charlotte wrote to her then thirty-eight-year-old daughter: "When even Grace doesn't hear from you for a fortnight even I begin to worry a bit. Don't try to write a letter, but do drop me a post card now and then."[19]

Charlotte had a tendency to talk down to Katharine, at any age, to belittle her accomplishments in a competitive, critical, and sometimes even hostile way. For example, Katharine, a gifted sculptor, in 1923 sent her mother a bust she had done of her. Charlotte responded: "The 'bust' has come. I am very glad to have it. . . . I never congratulated you on that lovely linen smock you made for Frank." The lovely linen smock is praised more enthusiastically than the work of art.

A recurring issue which Charlotte regularly addressed was Katharine's sloppy housekeeping. It was exceedingly sloppy, if I can judge by the state of the home I entered in 1978 and by Charlotte's graphic descriptions. It was also none of her mother's business. Through the years, Charlotte, in a restrained but nonetheless intrusive way, chastised her daughter for her housekeeping failures. In July of 1922, in an unusual though no less intrusive letter, Charlotte congratulated her daughter on finally getting her home under control. Charlotte was particularly delighted because "I know it was a constant strain on Frank. He was wonderfully good about it, but that kind of visual chaos *is* trying."[20] An extraordinary note for Charlotte Gilman to sound: complaints about sloppy housekeeping that it is a woman's job to alter; complaints on behalf of the man of the house for whom it is unpleasant.

When Katharine began to write and to lecture, activities noticeably like those of her mother, Charlotte felt threatened and responded with direct criticism. "Why on earth should you write that gratuitous article for art and architecture?" she thundered at her daughter.[21] Two years later Charlotte had become sufficiently accustomed to Katharine's forays onto the lecture circuit to express willingness to read her speech, but the mother, the experienced lecturer, could not resist a jab. "It's funny to me that you feel nervous about speaking, but I know most people do. You seem to be doing a lot of it. Don't you get *anything?*"[22] This critical letter was followed two months later with Charlotte's report on a speech *she* was to give for nothing. Less than nothing, because Houghton covered her fare to Chicago. Charlotte justified her talk on the grounds that it was delivered to the World Fellowship of

Faith and even though she would receive no fee, she hoped to get an article out of the talk, and "failing that, it will rouse and stimulate my neglected powers and I'll be able to do better work afterward."[23]

When Katharine turned to her mother for help, Charlotte did try to support her, but Charlotte's insensitivity and self-centeredness often got in the way. When Katharine was strong and capable, her mother became competitive and critical. When Katharine was needy or vulnerable, Charlotte often treated her adult daughter like a child, a stance most evident in the arena of finances. By 1914, Charlotte's income began to drop significantly, but she and Ho continued to provide needed funds for Katharine and her family. In early 1923 the Chamberlins were in such financial trouble that it became necessary for Houghton to take over the mortgage of their Pasadena home, some $3,500. In subsequent years, particularly in the early days of the Depression, many mortgage payments were skipped. But though Charlotte gave financial help, she often did not give it graciously or supportively, perhaps because Katharine's need was a painful reminder of her own and her mother's situation in the past, of their having married men who did not provide adequately for them.

In the same letter that included a check for Katharine, Charlotte often complained about lacking funds herself. When Katharine responded that she would repay the debt, especially since Charlotte had pointedly said what a sacrifice she was making, Charlotte might reply in these words: "You don't have to pay back any of this 'mother money,' you know. It is the lovingest of free gifts. And who knows, I may come down on you in my old age and board it out," added Charlotte, thereby negating her claim that the gift was free.[24]

In a later letter Charlotte apologized for not sending more money: "I desperately wish I could do more for you—instead of having to pour my small earnings on Thomas"—Charlotte's brother. It "can't be helped," added Charlotte, although it is not clear why a brother had a greater claim than grandchildren.[25]

Sometimes Katharine's pleas were met with sharp refusal. "Your ideas as to Houghton's inheritance soar too high," Charlotte once said curtly.[26]

Most characteristic of Charlotte was her tendency to see Katharine's problems in terms of her own, which, in effect, belittled Katharine's troubles by reminding her that her mother had been through worse and survived. "I have at last arrived at a bearable attitude of mine regarding your difficulties; namely, that they are no worse than mine in past years," wrote Charlotte to Katharine in 1931, as if the central problem of Katharine's difficulties was how her mother would cope with them. "You have a comfortable home, a splendid boy, and a husband you love," wrote Charlotte to Katharine, who was then the mother of two children, only one of them a boy. "I was younger to be sure, but pretty much a wreck at that. So—as I pulled through I guess you will": such were Charlotte's words of encouragement.

Charlotte's tendency to refer Katharine's woes back to herself applied not only to finances. When Katharine tried to share with her mother her concerns about menopause, Charlotte again put herself in center stage.

> Mine had no "symptoms" that I remember, but I keenly remember what a blow it was for me—for I was hoping with all my heart for a baby for Houghton. To expect a child and then find it is the end of all hope—it hurt. I guess that is one reason you have been so "wuzzy" in the head on top of all the other troubles.[27]

What an extraordinarily insensitive letter, telling one child that "the end of all hope" resulted from an inability to have another child. It was also disingenuous of Charlotte, since she and Houghton had determined to have no children.

There were many other moments, however, when Charlotte broke through the barrier of her own ego to reach out to her daughter. In the following letter, quoted extensively but not fully, Charlotte moves back and forth from a public stance, reminiscent of her father's letters to her, to a truly motherly one, from a strong, loud voice speaking to a public audience, to a soft, intimate murmur to a daughter in trouble.

Dearest Daughter,

I wish—O how I wish! you and I were near enough for me to comfort you. This is the way I used to work it out, for myself and for the many who used to come to me for help:

A is the personal consciousness
B is the social consciousness

Pain is almost wholly in the personality. . . . As a gymnastic exercise, a life saver—stretch. Deliberately let yourself spread along the ages, backward & forward; and sideways among the millions. . . . Anything so to extend your consciousness that, temporarily, it "rests" you from the grinding pressure of personal distress. . . . If one can change the condition that hurts that is of course immediate wisdom. If one cannot—then comes one's undoubted power to change one's relation to that condition. . . . I'd no idea you were having it so hard, dear. I suppose you hate to tell me, knowing that I can no longer be of practical service. . . .

How children suffer from those who love them most! I did try so carefully not to hurt you, and to love and pet you as I so longed to be loved and petted and never was. But I suppose you were hurt in many ways I never knew. I've got a bit of verse you wrote me when you were about twelve, appreciative of the way I had brought you up. I can tell you I prize it. . . .

I can send you nothing but love and sympathy. . . . Yes, I can too! I can send honor and admiration for a brave strong life, for splendid talents, for magnificent motherhood, and wifehood and friendship. For duty done as far as you could reach. For a husband to your heart's desire, for two incredibly fine children. For the admiring love of many, many friends. You are a very noble woman, Katharine, my dear.[28]

Throughout Katharine's long life, the unresolved tensions between mother and daughter were central to the way Katharine viewed Charlotte. She never put to rest feelings of resentment and rejection. As we have seen, they colored her view of her childhood in her old age: she was eighty-seven when she finished her autobiography, and ninety-three when she told me so baldly, "My mother abandoned me when I was nine years old." They also colored her view of her mother's character and achievements. Indeed, many of the remarks she made in the last years of her life to those interested in studying her mother's life were disparaging, although she may not always have been conscious of the implications of her words.

To a written question about her mother's suffering from Carl Degler, who wrote the biographical entry on Gilman in *Notable American Women* and who brought *Woman and Economics* back to prominence with a new edition, Katharine responded:

> You speak of pain . . . and I don't know where you get that idea. She was remarkably free of physical pain or illness. Probably she suffered from the feeling that she was cut out to accomplish far more than she did. Most of us have that to some extent.[29]

Katharine Chamberlin was less veiled in assessing her mother's qualities in correspondence with the director of the Arthur and Elizabeth Schlesinger Library of Radcliffe College, Jeanette Cheek, at the time the library was negotiating with her for the purchase of her mother's papers. In describing her two mothers, Grace and Charlotte, she wrote:

> My mothers wrote and supported themselves thereby—both worked for "causes," both were "advanced." Perhaps the greatest difference—though generalizations are never felt—is that Mama saw Mankind as a whole and did not always understand the individual—whereas Grace understood the individual also.[30]

And later: "Though my mother was always the most honest and generous of people—I never felt she understood people very well."[31]

In an effort to persuade the Schlesinger Library to purchase not only her mother's papers but the letters of her father and stepmother, Katharine argued for the latter's greater merit: "On the bulk the Channing-Stetson papers are greater than my mother's and cover a wider range of subjects and are more interesting reading as a whole." The letters of Grace Channing "are for the most part far better reading than my mother's and deal with education, politics, art, literature, etc.," argued Katharine, unsuccessfully.

Katharine was so tangled up in mother-stepmother love and guilt that she often lost a sense of balance. For example, she knew that her mother wanted her letters "placed." But "Grace and Papa are an entirely different matter—both were shocked by the Browning Love-Letters (& burned a trunkful of theirs as instructed)."[32] Grace and Papa are preferred for their reticence and desire for privacy, and yet Katharine urged the Schlesinger Library to buy their papers. Katharine also took care to preserve the Stetson-Channing papers while some of her mother's missing diaries—the papers Charlotte made such a point of saving—may have been "so eaten by termites that I destroyed them."[33] Katharine failed to renew the copyright on *Human Work*, "which Mama felt was one of her most important books," although she admitted to feeling guilty.[34]

One of the most revealing of Katharine's letters to Jeanette Cheek reads in part:

My father died at the age of 53—three large paintings of his hanging on the walls of the Italian Building of the 1911 International Exposition (celebrating the reunion of Italy).

You must remember it is only recently that my mother has been sought after—She died in 1934 age 75 [she actually died in 1935]—and for years before that had hard work getting lecture engagements or placing books or articles. . . .

Though freely admitting the painter & writer cannot be compared, to my mind my father had the greater gifts and from an early age took care of himself and his father (my grandfather died in May, my father in July of the same year—)

My mother went to pieces over my birth—not a difficult birth—but a few months in Pasadena, acting in plays etc— she thought she was cured.

If you grant the premise or recognize the fact that I (and many others) consider my father a great artist you will understand why I do not feel any urge to have his papers with my mothers—as "her first husband"—and it would be of no great help to my mother—Personally it seems to me a man had to be an understanding sort of angel to have stood it all—[35]

Katharine even extended her sympathy to her mother's second husband. "Houghton gradually gave up things he loved—Stopped going to Ball Games—no longer went to the Opera because Mama did not care for it—and gave up the 75th Reg. because Reg. was used to put down strikes!"

Katharine also took great pains to make sure that her grandfather not be "made to appear too careless about his family," to say that he had not really abandoned his family while Charlotte was "not more than an infant," as the Schlesinger Library catalogue claimed, on the basis of information from Gilman sources, and that he not only could not be blamed for the miseries of her own traumatic trip back East as a little girl but that, instead, he had been imposed on by Charlotte, whose responsibility it was to take her to her father. Here again, Katharine shows sympathy for the men in her mother's life at her mother's expense.[36]

Years later, when I met Katharine Chamberlin, that train ride was the first memory she evoked; she no longer claimed that the trip was enjoyable, but she still did not criticize her grandfather for neglecting her. Her mother alone remained villain. An elderly Katharine still excused her grandfather in that long-ago memory.

It certainly showed a kind of self-sacrificing nature to do that for my mother. . . . It is obvious that my mother was not close to her parents—and I doubt if she really understood them—. . . . the longer I live the more impressed I am with the lack of understanding of people by people—and the readiness to condemn—especially the men in the case.[37]

Charlotte Gilman is blamed as a daughter for not understanding her parents, as a mother for not understanding and caring for her child, and as a woman for indicting men unfairly. Yet Katharine Chamberlin maintained, during the weeks I saw her often, that her relations with her mother remained good, that her mother, despite her flaws, was an extraordinary woman, and that her entire family, herself and her husband and their children, had only the fondest and most caring feelings toward their famous relative. "Her family has always thought of her as a great person," she wrote about her mother in 1960.[38]

Katharine Chamberlin was not purposely deceptive. So truly in conflict, torn between mother and stepmother, mother and father, genuine feelings and a sense of responsibility, the best she could manage to say were the conventional words, and probably much of the time she believed them.

Despite the many unresolved problems in their relationship, it was to Katharine that Charlotte turned in her last years. "I shall in all reason go before Houghton," Charlotte wrote her in 1931, referring to the age difference between herself and Houghton, "but if I don't—I'll be a very lonesome old lady. I can just see myself living on a little scrap of money, boarding somewhere near you and being a nuisance."[39] Katharine probably envisioned the same, and so it came to pass.

XII
CHARLOTTE

Charlotte and Houghton Gilman lived together for thirty-four years in contentment and satisfaction. They lived on the Upper West Side of Manhattan from 1900 to 1922, moving four times, each time farther uptown. Their last New York home was on West 136th Street, where they moved in 1911 and remained for eleven years. In the early years they lived in a building named the Avondale, on Seventy-sixth Street and Amsterdam Avenue, where, as we saw previously, Katharine lived with them on and off. Here they boarded out, eating their meals at a different building down the street. After six years they ended that arrangement and Charlotte did the cooking, a task she performed with proficiency if not enthusiasm.

They shared a love for the theater and went as often as they could, seeing, for example, Lionel Barrymore in *The Copperhead*, which made them both cry.[1] They attended Gilbert and Sullivan performances as often as funds permitted, and frequently saw a small group of friends, including reformers Martha and Robert Bruère and cousin Lyman Stowe and his wife. While she often forgot birthdays, as we know, Charlotte on occasion remembered Ho's, and was once especially pleased with herself because she had been able to buy him a splendid new briefcase.[2] She and Houghton occasionally had parties, entertaining themselves with shadow pantomimes of old ballads. Charlotte never tired of games and spent many evenings playing whist and bridge, as she had as a young woman.

She and Houghton extended themselves frequently to friends in need, among them Adele Liuville, who was dying of cancer and who stayed with them for a lengthy period, even at the cost of Charlotte having Ho sacrifice his room and move in with her.[3] Charlotte and Ho were particularly solicitous of Grace after Walter died, opening their home to her for an extended visit and urging that she ask them for funds if needed, a generous offer, considering their precarious financial situation.

In the summers she and Houghton vacationed happily at lakes and oceans. Both enjoyed long walks in the country. In the early years, their summer vacations were often taken with Katharine. In later years they occasionally went separate ways. In the summer of 1921, for instance, Houghton went off camping for two weeks while Charlotte visited with Inez Haynes Irwin in Scituate, Massachusetts.[4] During that visit Grace joined them and the two women tried again, though not successfully, to collaborate on another play. While they lived in New York Ho continued to work as an attorney, going regularly to his office on Wall Street, but he still did not achieve much financial success.

During the first fifteen years of their life together Charlotte continued to lecture widely and to publish poems, articles, and books. As we have seen, in 1900 she published *Concerning Children*; in 1903, *The Home: Its Work and Influence*; in 1904, *Human Work*; and in 1911, *The Man-Made World; or, Our Androcentric Culture*. Most of the 234 nonfiction articles and the 54 poems that she published between 1900 and 1909 appeared in the *Woman's Journal*, although occasionally she sold something to such mainstream publications as *Cosmopolitan*, the *Independent*, or *Harper's Bazaar*. But most of her energies from the end of 1909 through 1916 went into the publication of the *Forerunner*.

The lecture circuit continued to be the primary source of Gilman's income. While she was in great demand for the first fifteen years or so of the century, she had little difficulty realizing her plan of taking an extensive three-month tour each year and spending nine months at home with Ho. She used the talents of booking agents to promote her tours in given cities, she used national lecture agencies, and she herself wrote to supporters across the country to

Charlotte on the road, age about fifty

help set up speaking engagements. Publicity material often quoted authorities who described her as one of the three most outstanding feminists of her time, the other two being Olive Schreiner and Ellen Key, although Gilman continued to dissociate herself from the feminist label. Publicity material described her as having "taken a leaf from the book of the 'revivalist,' " by offering a course of lectures on six successive days, Gilman speaking for the first hour of each day and leading a discussion with the audience for the second.

The subjects she covered continued to reflect her cosmic view of culture and history. The themes remained surprisingly constant over time, but the specific focus altered with the years and with the subject she was primarily exploring at any given time. These later lectures were ultimately subsumed into the books she based on them, just as her early lectures in Pasadena had been. She used the lecture circuit as an opportunity to think out and talk out the

331

ideas that found their final voice in her printed books. She advertised a whole range of lecture topics, from "Assorted Sin" and "The Real Devil" to "Our Need for Beauty" and "Baby-Gardens." Staples among her offerings remained those that flowed from *Women and Economics*. As she developed the work that became *Concerning Children* and *The Home*, their themes were added to her lecture repertoire. The book that became serialized in the *Forerunner* as *Our Brains and What Ails Them* gave rise to a series of lectures on different aspects of that study. A series called "Studies in Masculism," which examined such topics as "Our Male Civilization—Its Influence on Women" and "Masculism and Ethics," ultimately found its way into *Man-Made World*. In the early 1920s, as she began work on *His Religion and Hers*, Gilman turned in her lectures to the ideology of male-female relations.

One year she experimented with a six-week summer-school lecture course that examined, each week, one of the following subjects: Ethics; Economics; Education; Men, Women, and People; Politics; and a concluding General Topics that covered such concerns as "Youth, Age, and Foolishness," and "What Life Might Be." In 1921 she took to the road with a series of six lectures, beginning with "The Fallacy of Freud," which addressed, the brochure stated, "his evil influence on the life of today." Gilman understood not only women's economic subjugation but the possibility that psychology could be used to oppress as well. Her opposition to Freud's ideas was likely rooted in a deep fear of the dangers of permitting anyone, but especially a man, a male doctor, free access to a woman's unconscious. She read little if anything of Freud's work. The very idea of the existence of an unconscious was enough to arouse her distrust and opposition.

Her lectures occasionally addressed topics of current interest. Thus, in the teens and twenties she examined concerns of government and democracy in such lectures as "Our Duty to Immigrant Citizens and to Invaders," as well as in "Americans and Non-Americans," which she described as a "timely and impressive discussion of nationalism and internationalism, of race mixtures desirable and undesirable, and of the practical problems before this nation today," her ethnocentricism persisting.

Although Gilman was by temperament a loner, she did lend her public voice to support policies and organizations with which she identified. For example, in the fall of 1905 Gilman joined with several other well-known socialist writers and critics such as Jack London, Upton Sinclair, and Clarence Darrow to form the Intercollegiate Socialist Society (ISS) and to publish a magazine called the *Intercollegiate Socialists*. The ISS would later change its name to the League for Industrial Democracy. In 1909 the American Socialists declared the last Sunday in February National Women's Day, and Charlotte participated in one of the many meetings held across the country to celebrate the event. To the congregation at the Parkside Church in Brooklyn she said, "It is true that a woman's duty is centered in her home and motherhood, but home should mean the whole country and not be confined to three or four rooms or a city or a state."[5] The following year at a rally again commemorating National Women's Day, Gilman spoke in Carnegie Hall.[6]

Gilman was also one of twenty-five women who formed a club in 1912 called Heterodoxy—a club for unorthodox women, Mabel Dodge Luhan called it in her autobiography, "women who did things and did them openly." It was a luncheon club located in Greenwich Village and it met every other week except in the summer. Its members embraced a wide range of political opinions and included married, heterosexual women, lesbians, free-love advocates, radicals, and reformers of all kinds. Its guiding spirit, the reformer Marie Howe, put together a group that shared the "pain and pleasures of being feminist women of accomplishments," as Judith Schwarz wrote in her essay on the group.[7] They talked about everything—their lives, international affairs, politics, feminism. They had speakers from within and outside the group. Everything was off the record. When Rheta Child Dorr resigned after the outbreak of World War I because so many members, particularly Elizabeth Gurley Flynn and Rose Pastor Stokes, opposed the war and refused to resign when asked, Gilman soon followed her out of the organization, although she renewed contact with the Heterodoxy group during the 1920s. Gilman, said George Middletown, "had little tolerance for those who opposed our entrance" into the war.[8]

In 1913 Alice Paul and Lucy Burns, impatient with the moderate program and style of the National American Woman Suffrage Association (NAWSA), formed the militant Congressional Union, which temporarily remained within the NAWSA but soon broke to form the Woman's Party in 1916, and shortly after, the National

Woman's Party. Gilman served on the National Advisory Council of the organization from 1916 to 1920, describing the party and its program in favorable terms in the August 1916 *Forerunner*.

By the beginning of the second decade of the century and accelerating rapidly with the outbreak of World War I, the political and cultural climate of the nation underwent a change, one which significantly reduced Gilman's success in reaching and wooing audiences. The hope and expectation of a future of social change, a vision sustained by the socialist movement and the women's movement, began to dim. Fear aroused at home in the wake of the Russian Revolution, violent and widespread industrial conflicts, and the shock of the Red Scare all contributed to dismantling the spirit of optimism that had prevailed. "Not just faith in the efficacy of political education," wrote the historian Mari Jo Buhle, "but confidence in an eventual triumph—the premises upon which the Socialist movement had been based—faded beyond recognition."[9]

The women's movement suffered similarly. It lost the militant stance and the vigor that had helped create a large and diverse community of women. With the passage in 1920 of the suffrage amendment, the struggle for which had shaped the women's movement for years and provided its cohesiveness, the community of women activists splintered. The National Women's Suffrage Association disbanded and, in 1920, a new organization, the League of Women Voters, was designated its successor. During the 1920s it focused on education, legal discrimination, and general social reform. Alice Paul's Woman's Party refused to endorse the league's program and instead committed itself to seeking an equal rights amendment, which said simply that "men and women shall have equal rights throughout the United States and every place subject to its jurisdiction." The League of Women Voters was never able to achieve the sense of urgency and unity that the suffrage societies had created, and the struggle to secure the ERA divided longtime activists permanently.

For most women the struggle for their rights came to mean efforts to enrich the individual aspirations of professional women. Young women sought very different goals from those who had preceded them. The nineteenth-century vision of productive citizens that had informed the spirit of the older generation of women had little appeal to many of those who came after them. They were drawn to a different promise of womanhood, one focusing on sexual and emotional satisfactions. Charlotte Gilman continued to hold to her socialist and communitarian commitment. The new world became increasingly an alien place for her and other old fighters.

Still, it did not occur to her to stop trying. She made a strong appeal to the executive committee of the National Woman's Party in 1920, for instance, to create policies designed to "appeal for the unity of women," and specifically to build "a great organization in the country which would represent mass power, not political power as we know it in existing parties."[10]

She also continued to lecture and to write as often as she could find audiences. If the audiences began to fall away, it was not for her lack of trying. She worked closely and persistently with booking agents and supplemented their activities with many of her own. To a Mrs. Rountree in Syracuse, New York, she wrote in 1920, offering the following suggestions: that if she asked a number of Syracuse women "What Mrs. Gilman Means to You," and if only "friendly ones were asked," it would "make good newspaper stuff"; that if she put together clever excerpts from Gilman's books and a selection of "Gilmanisms" from the *Forerunner*, such publicity might be used by the local press. "I am willing to do anything I can to help," Charlotte wrote to her, "except give interviews." Evidently she was still smarting from the press coverage she had received years before at the time of her divorce. She continued to make such overtures to friends in her own behalf, and did so more often as the demand for her appearances diminished, but she observed, "I'm not much good at this publicity stunt; if I were I should be richer."[11] Still, her Syracuse project with Mrs. Rountree was a great success. She spoke before the Women's Congress with "a whole lot of club presidents and such, was overwhelmingly successful, and a hundred of 'em signed up for a Gilman Week in early October," she wrote to Katharine.[12]

Charlotte's periodic depressions never entirely disappeared, but they diminished with the passing of time. "I am taking 'Thyroid' again," she wrote to her daughter in May 1922, "and begin to feel more capable. My contemptible below-par-ness has cost me half a lifetime's work." Two weeks later she was not yet able to work, "even letters—a long dull spell—I don't understand it. But it's no use driving—if I can't I can't." Her handwriting became sloppy

Charlotte, age about sixty

during these weeks, never as undecipherable as it had been in the early years, but it was a clear indication of her slipping. By the end of June she had "worked two days! That was hopeful. Then slumped again. Maybe my head won't get up any more!!!"[13]

During this period Charlotte and Houghton made a decision that, if it did not provoke her downward spiraling, did not do much to help. All through their years together in New York, Charlotte had clung to the dream of eventually relocating in Pasadena, a dream to which she periodically gave voice. "I so want that place next door," she wrote to Katharine just as her depression began, "where I could see you and them every day—and yet have my own place to hide in."[14] Her dream had a serious setback, for just at this time they decided to move to Norwich, Connecticut. In 1922 Houghton's Aunt Louisa, Louisa Gilman Lane, had died, leaving Houghton and his brother, Francis, each half her home in Norwich. Houghton and Charlotte were to share it with Francis and his wife Emily. Houghton's father had died earlier that year, in April, an event that did not cause Charlotte to grieve much. "He left no money and precious little in the way of 'effects.' " she wrote Katharine, but "Houghton is richer by two heavy overcoats . . . and several pair of old shoes"—although in fact he had bequeathed to Ho a sum of six thousand dollars.[15] Houghton's father had strongly opposed the marriage, and there is no sign that he softened much with the years. Francis was ill and unable to continue working in a local bookstore, and so Houghton was moved to go to Norwich, Charlotte thought, by his desire to help Francis and by her "urgent desire to get out of New York."

Charlotte was indeed pleased to leave New York, she wrote Katharine, to "escape, forever, this hideous city—and its Jews. The nervewearing noise—the dirt—the ugliness, the steaming masses in the subway."[16] Charlotte was no happier sharing a city with African-Americans. She was horrified to find "two negroes, grandmother and g-son" assigned a lower berth, under her, in a train, and she had herself transferred to "upper 8," with "an old, old lady under. She is a Prussian." She referred again to the incident the next day. "To have sat in the sun opposite those coons and their baggage–& their lunch—the boy squirming about and making all manner of noises—would have used me up pretty badly," she wrote to Katharine.[17] Still, much as Charlotte wished to flee the city, she could not have been much pleased at the prospect of sharing a home with a brother-in-law she disliked.

The depression that began in the spring lasted well into the fall. At the end of October 1922, having just moved to Norwich, she observed: "If the power to work comes back, as it seems to be, I shall soon be earning heaps!" The power to work did, indeed, eventually return, but the ability to earn heaps did not, alas, follow. When the couple first moved to Norwich, Houghton kept a room in New York while he wound up his practice there. He entered the Connecticut bar but never seemed to establish a practice of any significance, and their financial circumstances remained precarious. The Gilmans supplemented their income by raising some of their food; fortunately, gardening was an activity they both much enjoyed. "You should see your aged parent," wrote Charlotte to Katharine, "in her denim kneebreeches and green smock, hammering away with the hoe by the hour."[18] Charlotte estimated her personal annual expenses at approximately one hundred dollars. Since she did most of the gardening, she saw herself as substantially independent, despite the declining demand for her lectures and her articles.

Charlotte was happy in her home in Norwich. "I'm well and happy, very happy," she wrote to her daughter, "in the peaceful beauty of this lovely town. . . . Now if I get on well I can earn enough extra to really have that California place." She was now tailoring her Pasadena dream to a winter home. Several years later, still hoping she could earn more money, she was nevertheless able to say to her daughter, and mean it: "Meanwhile I live in peace and contentment with my garden."[19] She lived in peace and contentment with Houghton, too. In 1920, on their wedding anniversary, he wrote to her:

> Having been married to you for twenty years, I can only say that I'd like to go right out to Detroit and meet you there and begin all over again, but in default thereof we will start in to duplicate the record.

Her feelings for him also deepened with the years. Soon after her sixty-fifth birthday, having been married for twenty-five years, Charlotte, in her annual accounting of herself for herself, made this

Charlotte gardening, age about sixty

entry: "Make Houghton happy as I can. That means keep well, keep cheerful, keep on good terms with the rest of the family—love and encourage him." This was a time, too, of diminishing depressions, of continuing visits with dear, close friends who continued to bring pleasure and satisfaction to the Gilmans.

Peace and contentment with Houghton, her friends, and her garden, but not with Francis and Emily. Charlotte, who was herself not easy to live with, complained often about Francis and Emily, but Houghton, who was more tolerant and easy-going, also complained about the pettiness, nastiness, and anger that seemed to

Charlotte and Ho with her grandchildren, Dorothy and Walter Chamberlin

come without end from his brother and his brother's wife. Relations had been tense between the two families from the beginning, but they deteriorated seriously in the winter of 1930, when a battle between Charlotte and her sister-in-law resulted in Emily's accepting "the word of a colored cook against mine," complained Charlotte to her daughter.[20] Within two months after the open struggle broke out, Charlotte cheerfully reported that Francis and Emily planned to leave. Ho would be forced to buy Francis's share, which would be a financial burden, and the additional expense of running the house would be a strain, but both Gilmans were pleased with the decision.[21] For whatever reason, the desired departure never took place. Francis and Emily continued to live in the house with Houghton and Charlotte, with relations growing increasingly hostile.

Charlotte Gilman's last years in Norwich were spent happily with Houghton, but in her public life she faced more frustration and disappointment. Ultimately she reconciled herself to small successes in her lecturing. Still, many years she managed a tour that incorporated a visit to Katharine and her family in Pasadena. Despite her complaints about her lagging reputation, Charlotte had a nationwide tour in 1925, particularly important because her brother Thomas, living in California, was ill, and a lecture tour was the only way she could manage to see him. The following year she was on another lecture tour, this time with Houghton, who ordinarily did not accompany her. But in 1927 she did not see Katharine because of insufficient lecture engagements. Even when she could not sustain a nationwide tour, she often found speaking engagements closer to home. In 1930, for instance, she ran a small twice-a-month group sponsored by the League of Women Voters. She collected one hundred dollars at a luncheon for Carrie Chapman Catt, the suffragist and peace leader, who distributed a five-thousand-dollar award she had received among a sizable group of women she designated as equally deserving.[22] There was a "Gilman Week" in Hartford in 1933, which cleared one hundred dollars for six lectures. In the fall of 1933 there were two New York engagements, for which she received a small honorarium.

Charlotte became cranky and out of sorts with the generation of young women who ignored her. "The mass of women are 'the same old fools they always were.' " she barked in a letter to Katharine, and then added, "what an illtempered old lady I'm getting to be." At the age of seventy-one, she wrote, "I have small patience with them—painted, powdered, high-heeled, cigarette-smoking idiots. To deliberately take up an extra vice—or bad habit—just to show off—imbecile." Charlotte was ignored in her last years, and she was hurt. She saw herself as dated. "What I offer is 'old stuff,' " she said, "and ten years of almost unbroken repeated failures have dampened my enthusiasm."[23]

Charlotte never became wealthy on her words, written or spoken, but she did support herself throughout her life, without any organizational ties to any movement and while espousing controversial and unpopular ideas. It is more significant that she was able to support herself than that her income was on the meager side. She made enough money to provide substantial sums to her daughter and son-in-law, to her brother and two of his children. She never worked at anything other than her writing and lecturing, except for the brief time that she ran a boardinghouse. There was no family money behind her and no wealthy husband to provide a cushion. She supported herself and others even down through the 1920s and 1930s, when she was out of fashion and when lecturing as a genre had faded in popularity.

Her enthusiasm was dampened with her diminishing audiences, and she was irritable and irritated with a world that shunned her, but she continued to work in the one arena over which she had control—her writing. She wrote for the New York Tribune Syndicate, which meant that her published pieces appeared in a variety of places throughout the nation. During the teens and thereafter, she continued to publish. Some years, such as 1917, she published only three articles, and in other years, 1919, for instance, she managed a staggering 1,245 published items, although most of them were only a few pages. Throughout the 1920s she published at least a few pieces every year.[24]

In 1923 she published a major work, *His Religion and Hers: A Study of the Faith of Our Fathers and the Work of Our Mothers*. She was proud of and pleased with that book, as well she should have been. It is a significant piece of work, although it met with little public success. The following year, 1924, she asked herself in her diary: "Well then. What have I still to say?" Her answer was: "Nothing further that is new. I have made my discoveries and urged them with ability. Unless I manifest new abilities I can do no more."[25] Determined to keep going, she played with the idea of turning again to fiction. She continued to admonish herself to "get over being discouraged. If there are no more books of the first value give honest work to doing over," as she wrote to herself in her annual self-evaluation at the age of seventy-one. Then came efforts, in the form of notes and papers, to rewrite *Human Work, Social Ethics*, and *Our Brains and What Ails Us*. She also reminded herself that she had a "new avenue through League [of Women Voters]. Use it to the full." She did rework *Social Ethics*, but publishers consistently rejected it. Her own judgment was that on that book and on *Human Work* she would be willing to claim her service to the world.[26] Such ideas as those she developed in those two books, she insisted, were particularly important at the moment, in the depths of the Depression in 1934, "with the old bases of conduct wavering and new ones so weak."

Charlotte had begun to write her autobiography in 1926, and the following year it was in the hands of an agent, who tried, unsuccessfully, to serialize it and sell it in book form.[27] But two years later Charlotte wrote to a friend, the writer Zona Gale, that all the "book-vendors," her word for publishers, wanted from her now were her memoirs, probably a somewhat overstated claim. The Macmillan Company had expressed interest in her manuscript earlier that year. An editor at Macmillan, having read only the early portions of the manuscript, described it as a "deeply moving narrative; beautifully written." A week later, having completed the book, he changed his mind, recommending the kinds of revisions that suggest he found the autobiography seriously flawed and in need of major changes.[28] And so the manuscript remained untouched for several more years.

During this time Charlotte completed her last substantial piece of fiction and her only detective novel, *Unpunished*. The manuscript was finished in 1929 and placed with her agent, Charlotte A. Berbova, who worked for Putnam's, but despite Charlotte's efforts and desires, it was never published.[29] Never in any other piece of fiction did Gilman eliminate a villain with such direct violence. In this detective novel, Gilman triumphs over an evil male authority figure, not by persuasion or by gentle manipulation, but by destruction: she kills him off with a gun, a rope, a blunt instrument, and poison.

Perhaps in *Unpunished* Gilman gave in to the frustration she felt at having devoted a life to struggling for changes that did not occur. If she could not destroy patriarchy in reality, she could do it in literary fantasy.

All her life Charlotte made lists, lists of goals she wished to accomplish, lists of ways to achieve the goals, lists of how many lectures she would need to give at what fees to get a particular income, lists of ways to earn more, lists of ways to work more and harder. She was always trying to improve, to assess, to push herself. In 1924, for example, she listed these instructions to herself:

Re-educate myself in working.
Sit at my desk three hours, and
Do something daily.
Put some knitting work in place of solitaire.
It is absurd that I should not be able to launch out and earn far more than
I do.

By 1930 Charlotte was earning so little that it was Houghton who sent the monthly checks to Katharine, as well as to Thomas. Grace also sent Katharine fifty dollars a month. By this time the Gilmans were raising most of their own food. Ho had "a small trickle of business," Charlotte wrote to Katharine,[30] but monthly dividends in the amount of a few hundred dollars provided the mainstay of their joint incomes. In 1933 Houghton was appointed to a judgeship, with a "very small salary, but more than welcome," said Charlotte.[31] To save money, he decided to add lawn-mowing to his household chores, although he found the work burdensome, and in 1934 the Gilmans moved to a hotel in Norwich for the winter to save on the fuel costs involved in running their home. Charlotte was pleased to note that this was the third Christmas she had spent not a penny on gifts except for postage, as all of hers were home-made. The Gilmans were not in financial danger, but they managed on a small budget.

It was not an easy or reassuring old age that Charlotte Gilman entered. She had been respected, admired, and widely acclaimed, and now she was none of these. She must have hoped and longed to spend her declining years in comfort; if not in material comfort, which she never had nor much coveted, then in spiritual comfort, a sense of having accomplished much and having been heard and understood.

Although, as we have seen, she wrote a good deal of trenchant criticism of the "new woman" of the twentieth century, the hedonistic, self-centered, shallow woman who sought individual successes, in her private writing, her diary, she held herself responsible for her public repudiation. If only she could write with the old fire, she would chide herself, then surely everyone would listen! In her public writings Charlotte understood that she was out of harmony with the aspirations of many women of the 1920s and that it was more the failing of the times than hers, but in her scribblings to herself she held herself accountable, just as in "The Yellow Wallpaper" she spoke, if only indirectly, of the social context of women's illness, while in her diary she exposed the underlying sentiments of personal shame and guilt. Holding herself responsible for her diminishing success did, however, motivate her to strive harder.

Although the younger generation did not know or love Charlotte, she was remembered and admired by many. "Please, for the love of—everything, don't get tired like everybody else in the world. . . . May you live a thousand years," a dear friend had written to her many years before.[32] Charlotte did not seem to get tired like everybody else, at any rate not often when she was well, but she did not live a thousand years. In January 1932, she learned that she had breast cancer. "My only distress," she later wrote, "was for Houghton."[33] When Charlotte learned that she had cancer, that it was inoperable, that it was terminal, she determined to end her life when she decided it was senseless to continue to live. Till then she continued to live much as before, gardening, sewing, walking, writing, and lecturing.

She began a new kind of reexamination. She began to assess the situation of a woman facing flagging powers, old age, and death. She did it with the kind of straightforward, no-nonsense determination characteristic of her, and with the inevitable lists that accompanied her self-study. She would try to revive her former energy, provided she was "given opportunity, the same power to reach and stir, amuse and stimulate, convey ideas." Despite all her doubts, she recognized that "what I have written of late has been good—a few small things."

Then came the acceptance of her impending death, although how far off it was she did not know. "What I must face is lessening power. What I MUST do is get my papers in order, to use—or destroy." In April of 1932 she went into a downward swing, but she was up a few weeks later. By May 5 she could report "A feeling of 'life'—thank goodness. There may be some years of good work yet. Get at it. Write something, as often as possible, as well as I can. . . . Concentrate on arranging papers." At the end of the year her spirits were still up.

> For Heaven's sake look forward a little!
> This is splendidly worth doing
> Nobody else can do it!!!
> Poor thought it is its [*sic*] the best offering: ought to stir some women.

And then she gave herself the ultimate comfort, the ultimate reward for a life well lived. She wrote:

> One girl.
> One girl reads this and takes fire!
> Her life is changed. She becomes a power—a mover of others—
> I write for her.[34]

In 1933, at the age of seventy-three, she hoped for seven more years of active life, listing a series of strenuous work schedules for those remaining years, which included working on revisions of earlier works, new articles, "something novel, arresting, rousing new controversy." But she also created a contingency plan for a smaller time span: "If I live a year."

Shortly before Charlotte learned of her illness she had given her husband for Christmas a hand-drawn calendar with a poem she had written inside.

> Thirty-three years to remember
>   From the June I took your name

And in this remote December
   I love you just the same

Courteous, kind and tender
   Patient, loving and gay
You scattered a gentle splendor
   On every step of the way

We've been happy together
   For all our pleasant past
And we're going to have pleasant weather
   And love to the very last

Charlotte worried about Houghton's loneliness after her death, but he did not survive her. Houghton Gilman died suddenly on May 4, 1934. "Fell in the street—cerebral hemorrhage, a very good way to go. . . . I shall break up as soon as I can, and come to Pasadena," she wrote to Katharine the following day.[35] She had been at home reading, waiting for him to return from an evening of bridge at his club. She received word that he had fallen unconscious. "I stood at attention as I always do in sudden danger," Charlotte wrote later to Zona Gale, "went downtown calmly to a little office opening on the street—he lay on the floor at my feet, dead." She described herself two weeks later as "holding out very well." His death was unencumbered by the unresolved guilt and anger, the unspoken words, that had accompanied the deaths of her mother, Mary Perkins, and her father, Frederick Beecher Perkins. It was a dreadful grief, but it was "clean pain." "You see," she went on, "there's no one to be sorry for but me—and I'm not going to make much of that. All my Human life is untouched; only the personal life is injured; and I live mostly outside personality." She went back to the old compartmentalizing, this time to give herself protection.[36] Still, she did admit, "But my head's pretty thick." Her life with Houghton had been a good one. She said that and it was true. "After marrying Houghton there was peace and happiness," she wrote to Zona Gale soon after Ho's death.

Did she swallow him up as many people, then and now, believe? I do not think so. Very little is known about George Houghton Gilman, Charlotte's Ho, except through her words. His grandchildren remember him as a lovable and kind grandfather. Katharine, his stepdaughter, focused her attention primarily on Charlotte and Grace and Walter, her two mothers and her father, but when she spoke of Houghton it was with fondness.

Ho did seem to understand Charlotte's needs and he seemed to wish to make himself available to her emotionally, a quality she sought unsuccessfully in many others. Whether or not Ho would have assessed his own life as a successful one we can never know, but it seems fair to suggest that the marriage satisfied them both.

The sociologist Jessie Bernard suggests that marriage is a very different institution for men than for women. If one were to write a history of marriage, the chapter on very happy ones would likely be confined primarily to those in each epoch who were not the seekers, the doers, the driven. Those people who wish to have a significant impact on their world tend to be those who need to dominate, to be center stage, to use their vital force and energy in their personal relations as well as in their public lives. Men like this ordinarily seek traditional wives who will care for them, literally as well as emotionally, but will not challenge or confront them. Marriages of two strong, active personalities are less likely to work, or to succeed only if considerable distance is allowed for in the marital system. Unconventional women frequently seek to create unconventional relationships, incorporating their public worldview into their private relations. Unconventional men are likely to be less concerned with achieving that kind of integration. Thus, the radical woman is often let down by her radical man, who treats her the way conventional men treat their wives, while she has sought to break intimate and sexual conventions. Mary Wollstonecraft and many others like her, who tried to defy all social conventions at once, have rarely thrived, because society exacts enormous cost from women whose personal conduct is seen as unacceptable. One thinks of the Grimké sisters, one who chose a life without an intimate lover, and the other who married and then withdrew from public life. Elizabeth Cady Stanton raised her seven children but settled for an estranged marriage. Margaret Sanger married a radical man who wanted a traditional wife and left him in order to sustain her own personal mode of behavior, then ultimately married a considerably older man who accepted her unconventionality. Victoria Woodhull, espousing publicly a belief in her right to sequential lovers, caused endless scandal, but eventually threw over her wicked life to marry a titled Englishman. Thus, heterosexual women whose public lives challenge conventions by virtue of the work they do and the ideas they promulgate are wise to choose men, if they do so at all, who are supportive and have no competing or distracting ambitions of their own. The effort required for these kinds of women to sustain a relationship with comparably vital men often drains them of the energy they need to advance their own public goals.

Seen in this light, Charlotte was wise to leave Walter and later marry Houghton. It is difficult for anyone, man or woman, to accomplish it all at once. Some aspects of one's life must be kept out of the battle. It was a good marriage for Charlotte. It seems to have been a good one for Houghton as well, although it is not possible to know what sacrifices he may have made to provide his wife with the emotional nourishment she craved.

Charlotte's life and aspects of her work often evoke the question of how to define her life in its sexual dimension. Her ferocious commitment to heterosexual monogamy as the highest, the best, and the only acceptable form of intimacy is upheld with such inflexibility, determination, and rigor that it inevitably arouses one's suspicions, especially given her deep and loving feelings for several women in her lifetime. Martha Luther was her first love, Grace Channing was her longest love, in certain ways Adeline Knapp was her most intense love. Still, she is reported to have said to E. A. Ross, "I am altogether heterosexual and cannot do my best work unless in love and loved," a statement which is confirmed by her life's work. As a young woman she was drawn to a young, handsome, and sexual man, an artist, with whom she lived for years unhappily. But she lived for more than thirty years with Ho, who was home and comfort and familiarity and contentment.

After Houghton's death, Charlotte's relations with her brother-in-law Francis Gilman, already close to open conflict, deteriorated still further. He objected strongly to what he described as Charlotte's unconventional methods of dealing with Ho's death, referring primarily to the absence of traditional religious ritual and to the cremation. His terrible outbursts made it clear to Charlotte that she could not long remain in the home they had shared, even if she had wanted to, which she did not. Forced by family agreement to sell her share to Francis only, she realized a small amount in the sale. She inherited a few thousand dollars from Houghton's estate and began to make plans to move to Pasadena. Charlotte assured her daughter that she would not be a burden. Perhaps she remembered how her mother had come to her to die at a time when she was struggling to earn a living and to rear a child alone. "There will be enough to maintain an economical old lady, I think, and I may be able to do some work yet," Charlotte wrote to Katharine.[37] Her plan was to take a room near Katharine and board out.

Charlotte Gilman sold whatever she could and headed West once more, for the last time, to live near her daughter. The old toughness remained. "I tell you frankly that I do not intend to grow much older, with no work and no income!" she let Katharine know.[38] She did not let Katharine know that she was terminally ill. In August 1934, Charlotte set off for Pasadena with sixteen pieces of baggage, including one victrola, three boxes of records, six trunks, one box of pictures, and the rest boxes of books and manuscripts. She took no furniture.

Within a short time Charlotte was in her new home, in a rooming house in Pasadena, in a studio apartment on the third floor on a quiet and beautiful street, at a monthly rent of twelve dollars. Money remained a constant problem, but by dining with Katharine three times a week, she was able to keep her food expenses down "to about $7.00 a month."[39] She saw her daughter and grandchildren daily, visited regularly with her brother Thomas, wished that Houghton had been able to share these pleasures with her, and now urged Grace to join her.[40]

Dorothy and Walter Chamberlin, Charlotte's teenage grandchildren, remember their grandmother as a cheerful and playful visitor in those last months. They were unaware of her illness. Their memory is of a forceful old woman who spent a good deal of time lying in a hammock in the back yard, a woman filled with spirit and zest and still a formidable presence. She played games with them after school, even from the hammock or a lounge chair, and the games they played ranged from ball games to word games. She taught them dominoes, checkers, and chess. They enjoyed her presence and her interest in them, although she was a little more demanding than they would have liked.[41]

Katharine's domestic situation remained a source of distress to her mother. Frank is rarely with his family, wailed Charlotte to her confidante, Grace, spending all his waking time in his studio. "Katharine is a shadowy wreck." The family is having an "unusually hard time; and some one must help," wrote Charlotte, distraught that her help could only be meager. "Frank's many disappointments have not improved his disposition—nor added to his popularity," Charlotte noted. "It looks pretty dark all around."[42] Mired in this misery, Katharine was strained and ill and the result was a household in disorder and chaos.

In these difficult circumstances, Charlotte felt she could not share her dreadful news with Katharine. "I don't doubt she loves him . . . but Frank is—apparently—a dead weight. No 'life'—no stimulating current." Katharine had been holding the family together by borrowing small amounts of money wherever she could. "My poor little scrap," wrote her anguished mother, "the most she can get will be, say $4,000—will be lost in the shuffle" (a reference to the money Katharine would inherit at her death).

In other ways Charlotte continued with life as usual. She gardened and she read, keeping up with the outside world as best she could. She reported on reading John Chamberlin's *Russia's Iron Age* and "murmuring 'I told you so!' " She was one of the public figures who had never expressed any enthusiasm for the Russian Revolution. The games continued. She played word games with Katharine after the children went to bed. Even Grace kept her busy by sending puzzles for her entertainment.[43]

And she kept working. She engaged a speaker's bureau in Beverly Hills to manage her lectures.[44] She set up a few speaking engagements herself. She spoke several times, for instance, to congregations in the Pasadena Congregationalist Church. She addressed the Girls' Friendly Society. "That was easy," she wrote. "I discoursed cheerfully and read some verses." A little work now and then would enable her to give a "little more for Katharine & my poor brother," she wrote Grace.[45] Other work dribbled in. She taught a chapel class, "most old folks of negligible importance," but then she addressed a Wednesday evening church supper, with some young folks present: "I reached em!" Apparently it was age that determined whether people were more or less negligible. She also addressed "a club of colored young people! . . . They seemed to enjoy it."[46]

In December 1934, she ran a six-lecture series under the general title "Great Issues of Today." It began with "Socialism?—or Socialization," a discussion of the "essential errors of Marxian Socialism," with an emphasis on "the inevitable socialization of our economic functions." The second lecture, "Races, Nations and Our World," explored "the relative value of different races and nations measured by their contributions to social development" and ended with a call for a Federation of Nations. The third lecture, which she called "Males, Females, and Human Beings," looked at "our absurd Sexolatry" flowing from the "illogical assertions of Sigmund Freud." In "Our Brains and What Ails Them," the fourth lecture, she addressed the question why "the most powerful intellect on earth has failed to manage its life as well as do the lower animals." In "Personal Religion and Social Ethics," she discussed the "main errors and deficiencies of previous religions" and how and why humanity has outgrown them. Having essentially summarized the central themes of her life's work, this seventy-four-year-old woman, mortally ill, delivered her final lecture, which she called "The Glorious Game of Living." At least one class of twelve was convened for this final series.

Charlotte also continued to rework her earlier manuscripts. But most important, she went back to her autobiography. In 1934, aware that her death was not long off, and believing that her manuscript had serious shortcomings, Charlotte turned to her friend Zona Gale and asked her to write her biography. Gale, an old friend, was a prolific and well-known novelist and playwright, as well as an activist in the Women's Trade Union League and a former vice-president both of the Wisconsin Peace Party and the Wisconsin Woman Suffrage Association. Thus, she had the right combination of personal ties, literary skill, and social conscience to be the appropriate person for Charlotte to select. "A few years ago I did undertake to write my life," she wrote to Zona Gale, "and very poor stuff it is. The opening chapters are good, while I was alive, very strongly alive. Then came that mismarriage and the blank years." She asked her friend Zona: "Will you write my life?" All of her books were out of print, she said. A biography of her life would renew interest in her work, she was sure. "I'll send you the one I wrote, for facts and dates. I'll tell you anything you want to know," she pleaded. "I think you have seen better than any one else what I have tried to do, and measure better than any one else what I have done." For the sake of the "imperfect, desperately earnest work I have done, I hope you'll do this for me."

But Zona Gale was not to be persuaded to undertake the story of Charlotte Gilman's life, and so Charlotte turned again to extending and refining her memoirs. D. Appleton-Century offered her an advance of $250, which she accepted. The publisher was not happy with Charlotte's title, *The Living of Charlotte Perkins Gilman*, but Charlotte wanted that title and she got it.

Charlotte had so much wanted Zona Gale to write her story that she virtually convinced herself it would happen. Letters to Lyman Beecher Stowe in 1935 as much as say Gale has agreed to write the book. To emphasize the necessity of her doing so, Charlotte stressed the flaws in the autobiography. But the autobiography is not as poor as its author said it was. When it was completed and ready for publication, Lyman Stowe indicated that he might have been "unduly influenced" by Charlotte's "own low estimate of it," because upon rereading it he liked it considerably more than he had previously.[47]

In important ways, Charlotte's critical judgment of her autobiography has some validity. The final version is not significantly different from the original manuscript. The opening chapters evoke hideous memories of childhood, but then the book becomes a heroic story of overcoming obstacles to achieve success in doing one's duty to society. The book devolves into lists of activities, triumphs, impersonal descriptions of a busy, dedicated life. It is a manuscript designed to challenge the individualist ethos of the day, designed to evoke the older vision of community as a goal around which to organize a life. It is a statement of how to overcome the struggles of the private life in order to achieve public good. It is in many ways her mask.

There is much in the book as in all autobiographies, of fiction, of self-deception, of purposeful misleading, of a refashioned and recrafted life, of a persona created for the occasion, but its greatest disappointment is that it is a book that does not have the author's heart in it. A believer always in the future and not the past, she had little interest in writing about what she had already experienced.

The Living of Charlotte Perkins Gilman has come to be seen as a major part of her legacy, but she much preferred to be represented by *Human Work* and *Social Ethics*. She wrote her story, but she withheld much material that would have made it every woman's story. She does not explore the social causes of her breakdown; there is nothing about the anguish she endured over her struggle to learn to achieve intimacy and autonomy in a loving relationship, and nothing about the fears of loss she felt during that learning process. The book has an unfinished quality.

Still, the autobiography does have many strengths, quite aside from the fact that her life had such intrinsic drama that even a disappointing autobiography is a significant event. The book does not rely upon a simple happy ending; it is a story of struggle, of overcoming handicaps. There is little innocence in this book. No heroine like Jane Addams emerges, pure and saintlike. Despite the list of triumphs, there is much of the sordid here. The early descriptions of Charlotte's young life, her breakdown, her hospitalization, the homeless lecturing, the poverty, the struggles, create a portrait that is unbending, not soft, but strong, hard, and sharp. To her credit, a flawed woman emerges, whether or not she meant herself to appear so.

In the mid-1920s, when she first wrote most of the book, Charlotte was suffering from public neglect and general feelings of disaffection. It was as if she did not love the public enough, since it no longer loved her, to want to be generous with herself. She would lecture enthusiastically on almost any subject. But she did not want to make herself, her personal life, into her subject, a trait she shared with many public figures of her generation. When she returned to that cold manuscript in the mid-1930s, unable to persuade a biographer to do the job, she was probably too caught up with her imminent death to pay much mind to recapturing the past. She lived in the present, and the present meant preparation for dying.

Charlotte's illness continued to progress and increasingly sapped her strength. By the end of 1934, a series of X-ray treatments just finished, Charlotte decided that instead of struggling against the creeping exhaustion, she would submit to it and try to gain some comfort from it. "I am beginning to understand how women spend their lives consistently without doing anything!" she wrote to Grace. "I'm so glad to end my days in sunlight and moonlight too. . . . If I did not know of this lurking enemy I should say I was perfectly well. I feel so, I act so, and I do not think about the enemy at all!"[48] But she did confide in a letter to a doctor friend, Edmund P. Shelby, about her discomfort. She suffered from side-effects of the X-ray treatment she had undergone. Some months later he was distressed at a medical report which said that the cancer had spread into her lungs. "The involvement of your lungs is one of the complications I hoped you might escape," he wrote to her. He was also concerned about the effect of her dying and her death on friends and family, and he urged her to spend her last months under his care in Florida at the Florida Medical Center in Tampa, where he could "stand by you to the end and carry out your wishes." When Charlotte explained to him her determination to spend her last days in California with her daughter, rather than in Florida in a hospital, Dr. Shelby was enormously supportive. He kept in contact with her doctor in California. The diseased lungs made breathing more difficult and coughing became more painful. Charlotte described her accelerating exhaustion to him. "The increasing weakness is due to the spread of the cancer which consumes most of the nourishment which would otherwise give strength," he explained in a letter to her in March 1935. He was a doctor but also a friend. "We both love you and want to help all we can."[49] A few months later, the pain increasing, Charlotte reluctantly resorted to medication. "It is perfectly safe," Dr. Shelby assured her, "and not habit forming." He told her that she was entitled to relief from pain, words she probably needed to hear, and that she should take morphine if necessary.[50]

As she approached her final months, Charlotte carried out activities that amounted to a virtual orchestration of her death. She told friends and family, in person or through letters, that she was entering the last stages of cancer and that she would soon end her life. "My time and strength get shorter," she wrote to Grace, but she still had not told Katharine.[51] Grace urged Charlotte to tell her. "Yes, I'd better tell her. I do hate to, she is so pale and frail and overburdened," Charlotte answered, and now to add to her burdens, "I've got to tell her that I'm going to leave her soon." Charlotte wrote this on March 3, 1935. By the end of the month she had told Katharine. "The dear brave child [who was then fifty years old] took it as quietly as I knew she would." Having Katharine in close attendance, nursing her in her last months, Charlotte could write Grace: "I'm having a lovely time!"[52] A month later Charlotte reported to Grace that she was "enjoying being an invalid." She went on to say: "It's part of the beneficent process of departure, doubtless. My amiable and cheerful submission to being nursed and tended would surprise you." And Katharine "seems no worse for her added cares."[53] Perhaps Katharine was even better for this added care. She was finally able to offer her mother something as an adult, something other than the endless child-dependence that characterized their relationship.

Katharine pressed her mother to move in with her, to get into bed and stay there, if only "for a little while," and Charlotte complied. She described her daughter as "brave, patient, sweet," and if it were not for her "I should not wait any longer—I'm so tired of coughing." She reported to Grace that there was still no pain, "not a bit from first to last, but I'm TIRED."[54]

Charlotte reached out more and more to Grace. From the first she had confided in her about her illness and her decision to end her life. All along she had urged her to come to Pasadena. Her letters were filled with intensity and devotion.

> Just a word of loving remembrance, in lieu of the thousand
> things I'd like to give! . . . You've been a Giver all your life,
> bless your boundless heart. . . . It is still, beautifully still.
> And sweet aired. I just ache to have you here too.[55]

Whatever remained of any underlying tensions, the deep love and affection between the two women were real and present. "Dear Girl———I want you. I want . . . to have you near," she wrote in September 1934. Months later: "I love you as always, and can keep telling you for a while yet." A month later: "It's been an honor to be your friend, dear Grace. And I have loved you a long time!— some 56 or 7 years isn't it?" The following month, in April 1935, she again begged Grace to hurry up and come out. It is clear that Grace lacked funds for the trip. "Mama is full of plans of how nice it will be to have you in her little house," Katharine wrote to Grace in late April. "Present indications are that there is still some time ahead."[56] Grace did manage to raise the money to go West to be at Charlotte's side during her last several weeks.

As Charlotte reached out to many loved ones for support and nourishment, it came, providing her, one hopes, with the affection, love, attention, and respect she had craved all her life and which seemed to make her last months peaceful. Charlotte became observer as well as participant in her decision to end her life and to inform people some time in advance about her decision. She could watch the event unfold as she shaped it. Her strategy allowed her to know the eulogies that would come. "I find people I've mentioned it to are not shocked by my proposed exit," she wrote to her cousin Lyman. "The world does move. Its [sic] only that we are timid about openly facing it." And so she decided not to be timid.

Family support meant much to her. She told her brother; Thomas, she said, "is wholly of one mind with me. How nice it is to have folks understanding and reasonable." Loving concern from Lyman Beecher Stowe also meant a great deal. He wrote her:

> I think of you constantly, dear cousin Charlotte, and with pleasure in spite of your physical condition because your mind and soul and contribution to our common wellfare [sic] seems to dwarf even your physical limitations—I think of you not as old and ill but as a vibrant, radiant, unconquerable and deathless spirit.[57]

A few months later, in his last letter to her, he wrote:

> It's heartbreaking to have you speak of your final ceremony as due this coming month but as you know I agree that you should not stay beyond your possibility of giving or receiving pleasure. It is very hard—the thought of never seeing you again but thank heaven I cannot lose the inspiration of your stimulating ideas and your beautiful gallant character.[58]

Her nephew Basil Perkins, Thomas's oldest son, wrote to his aunt Charlotte from Vermont in May 1935 in a stiff style that echoes his father's, but the feelings are genuine.

> Your letter shocked and sobered me. I have delayed writing, not from thoughtlessness, but because I hardly know what to say, or how to say it. . . . You may feel that, because he is so lax . . . in correspondence, your eldest nephew does not

love and appreciate you, but such is truly not the case. The few times we have been together, I have enjoyed and bene-fitted from more than I can tell. Your generosity to me as a small boy afforded the most ecstatic happiness on Xmas and birthdays that I can remember; and your comfort and advice have given me an optimistic philosophy that has made life seem very much worth while. It hurts me that I have not written you oftener, and that you are suffering from this villainous affliction.[59]

Charlotte's old friend Martha Bruère, when told of the suicide plan, wrote: "How I feel about it—about you—you must know. . . . What I say to myself is 'Thank god I too have had her in my life!'—But what's the use of this—I just go to pieces." She ended a long letter with the words: "My dear Charlotte, you cannot die—too much of you has become part of this lovely world—too many of us have made your work ours."[60]

Martha Bruère's husband, Robert, offered his love in a different but no less loving and perhaps more meaningful way. As an en-gineer working for the National Recovery Administration during Franklin Roosevelt's presidency, he was seeking a strategy to utilize the resources of the nation in a new and socially constructive way, and in this context he was rereading the major books that had been milestones in his mental development. His way of saying goodbye to his friend was to tell her how he had been "reading you straight through" from *Women and Economics* to *His Religion and Hers,* and how again and again he went back to chapter 5 of *Human Work,* "with steadily increasing wonder and gratitude." I doubt that Char-lotte valued any farewell more than this one.

Her friends Alexander and Edith Black wrote to tell her of the place she held in their lives. Said Edith to her: "You are a great woman, Charlotte, and whatever tedious stupidities you may have had to encounter in life your place is safe and high in the history of civilization."[61] Edith's last words to her friend were: "My thought of you has always been as of a flame." Alexander, an older and closer friend, wrote of her autobiography, which had not yet appeared, and of the life it represented. "I look to it to complete the triumph not only of all you have *done* but of all you have *been.*"[62]

Dr. Shelby expressed some worry about the effect on her reputation of her decision to end her life. "Please don't misunderstand me," he wrote, "I do not think it wrong and I do not blame you for making such a decision or for carrying it out." He "regretted the law would not permit me to lend a hand" in similar cases when a patient wished to end great suffering. "Only a brave heart can carry out such a plan. I am sorry you do not realize how much credit I have given you for the huge courageous fight you made against depression and melancholia."[63]

During her last days the only terrible pain Charlotte said she suffered was from shingles. That agony she complained of frequently and loudly. "I've had the best behaved cancer you ever saw—no pain at all," she wrote to Edward A. Ross shortly before she died. "But in June I had shingles, which is a devilish disease, and now 'complications' have set in . . . so I'm going to go peacefully to sleep with my beloved chloroform. I'm getting fed up with sheer weakness. . . . Well—Goodby."[64]

Doctors had told Charlotte in March that she would probably live no more than six months; she thought it would be less. By early August 1935, she had completed the revisions of her autobiography, finished the proofreading, selected the photographs and the cover. No one else could have done it so well, said Grace, "though it taxed her tremendously." Grace recognized that the manuscript needed revisions and more data on the last ten years of Charlotte's life, "but it did not seem that she had an ounce more of strength to expend," she wrote to the publisher.[65]

She had also written her will. Her 1924 will gave her brain to the Cornell Brain Association and directed that her ashes be strewn in a garden "where it will do some good." She wrote another will in 1934, again calling for cremation, the ashes to be disposed of as was convenient to the heir, who was her daughter Katharine. Charlotte stipulated that there was to be no funeral service of any kind.

Publication of the autobiography was scheduled for October 4, 1935, although the publisher told Katharine that he would rush a special copy to Charlotte. "Do you think this will be time enough?" he asked on August 12.[66] It was not. On August 16 Charlotte called her fifteen-year-old grandson, Walter Chamberlin, to her side, and told him what she was planning to do, how she would do it, and why.

On August 17, 1935, Charlotte took the chloroform she had

long been accumulating, placed it in a washbasin, put a lampshade in the basin, placed her head on the opening of the lampshade, covered her head with a towel, released the chloroform, and died quickly and painlessly.

Many years before, she had written a wry piece in the 1912 *Forerunner* called "Good and Bad Taste in Suicide." Bad taste described those who threw themselves beneath the train in the New York subway, thus adding to the "debris of a battlefield," or the mean-spirited young man who blew his brains out in the presence "of the girl who had refused him," thus forcing upon a decent family the labor of cleaning him up. The "neatest suicide" was that of a well-bred New England woman who cleaned her home, dressed herself in a fresh nightgown, calmly went to bed, and then poured a bottle of chloroform into a crumpled towel and inverted it over her face, causing no trouble to anyone.

By an extraordinary and somewhat chilling coincidence, shortly before her death Charlotte had been approached by an unknowing editor soliciting from her an essay on the issue of the right of the state to permit euthanasia. The Reverend John Haynes Holmes, minister of the Community Church, had been an active supporter of the cause of euthanasia and had agreed to participate in such a symposium, as had H. L. Mencken, Lincoln Steffens, the liberal social commentator Horace Kallen, and the Marxist literary critic V. F. Calverton. Charlotte's article appeared after her death, in the November 1935 issue of *Forum*, the distinguished and liberal monthly magazine of social commentary. It was then condensed for the *Reader's Digest* the following month.

In the article she developed her views concerning suicide—her own suicide, although she did not say so. Each of us "owes to others the best service of a lifetime," she wrote, and thus any suicide that occurs early in life is "timid, feeble, foolish because it is desertion, not in the face of the enemy but before imagined enemies." But there are times, she conceded, when "surrender is justifiable. If persons are beyond usefulness, of no service or comfort to anyone," and above all, if they suffer hopelessly, "they have a right to leave." It is "the record of a previously noble life" that makes it "sheer insult to allow death in pitiful degradation."

Ever practical, she admitted that no such power to end another's life should rest with an individual, but said there should be "suitable legal methods" established by a civilized society so that when a sufferer "begs for release" or the attending physician acknowledges that there is no hope, then a committee might be established which, if it recommends euthanasia, could receive from the board of health a permit to bring "merciful sleep" to "end hopeless misery." Although she recognized that even with the most careful precautions there would still be a "small percentage of error," she said this consideration was too small to weigh equally with "the mass of misery to be able to be relieved." A committee decision, she concluded, is only to be used when the individual cannot make a reasoned decision.

What Charlotte Gilman proposed was a change in the cultural context in which we view death. Instead of calmly enduring suffering and waste, as we do now, we should shrink with horror from it and end it. "Death is not an evil when it comes in the course of nature," she concluded.[67]

The Living of Charlotte Perkins Gilman, published on October 4 as scheduled, sold at three dollars a copy. Zona Gale wrote the foreword, in which she described Gilman as having "flamed like a torch." The book was dedicated:

> To My Dear Daughter, whose ceaseless devotion and good cheer made me happy to the end; and to my beloved grandchildren, Dorothy S. Chamberlin, making me poems and pictures, and Walter S. Chamberlin, whose loving companionship and genuine interest in my work have been so deep a comfort.

In the first six months it sold 808 copies. It sold so poorly thereafter that in 1942 Lyman Stowe wrote to Katharine asking her if she wished to buy the plates, since it was unlikely there would be another printing.[68]

Despite its small initial sales, *The Living* was widely noticed when it first appeared. It received a sizable review in the *New York Times Book Review*, as well as in the daily and the Sunday *Herald Tribune*.

Perhaps because the reviews appeared within months of Charlotte's death, they tend to read like eulogies. "There is no denying to Mrs. Gilman and her life work the quality of greatness," said the *Times*. "She won world-wide attention and exercised a strong influence on social growth and trends." Charlotte Gilman was little known in 1935, but those of mature age remembered her earlier international reputation and wrote of that time in the reviews. Reviewers often simply summarized the autobiography, especially the early sections, skipping over most of her adult life, then focusing on her death. Clara Stillman in the Sunday *Tribune* was one of the few to confront directly the rise and fall of Charlotte Gilman's reputation.

> Thirty years ago Charlotte Perkins Gilman was a beacon light to girls and women struggling to find a place for themselves in a changing world in which all the taboos were pulling them back while all the necessities were forcing them forward. Since Mary Wollstonecraft's "Vindication" no book had spoken to women—and to men, on women's problems—so clearly, so authoritatively, with such revolutionary fervor and common sense as her famous "Women and Economics." She was an unforgettable figure.[69]

Lewis Gannett, in a daily *Tribune* review, wrote of her as a pioneer; "it is the tragedy of the pioneers that they seldom live to be thanked."[70] Dorothy Canfield, in perhaps the most sophisticated review, described Charlotte's humor as "tempering and mellowing the vigorous radicalism which in her younger days seemed shocking and by the time she was an old woman seemed only what any intelligent person believes as a matter of course."

Lyman Stowe was wrong when he said there would likely not be another printing, but it did not come for a long time, until, in fact, 1972, and then again in 1975. Once more out of print, *The Living of Charlotte Perkins Gilman* will once more be reissued soon, a testimony to her enduring significance.

APPENDIX

SIMILAR CASES

THERE was once a little animal,
  No bigger than a fox,
And on five toes he scampered
  Over Tertiary rocks.
They called him Eohippus,
  And they called him very small,
And they thought him of no value—
  When they thought of him at all;
For the lumpish old Dinoceras
  And Coryphodon so slow
Were the heavy aristocracy
  In days of long ago.

Said the little Eohippus,
  "I am going to be a horse!
And on my middle finger-nails
  To run my earthly course!
I'm going to have a flowing tail!
  I'm going to have a mane!
I'm going to stand fourteen hands high
  On the psychozoic plain!"

The Coryphodon was horrified,
  The Dinoceras was shocked;
And they chased young Eohippus,
  But he skipped away and mocked.
Then they laughed enormous laughter,
  And they groaned enormous groans,

And they bade young Eohippus
  Go view his father's bones.
Said they, "You always were as small
  And mean as now we see,
And that's conclusive evidence
  That you're always going to be.
What! Be a great, tall, handsome beast,
  With hoofs to gallop on?
Why! You'd have to change your nature!"
  Said the Loxolophodon.
They considered him disposed of,
  And retired with gait serene;
That was the way they argued
  In "the early Eocene."

There was once an Anthropoidal Ape,
  Far smarter than the rest,
And everything that they could do
  He always did the best;
So they naturally disliked him,
  And they gave him shoulders cool,
And when they had to mention him
  They said he was a fool.

Cried this pretentious Ape one day,
  "I'm going to be a Man!
And stand upright, and hunt, and fight,
  And conquer all I can!

From Charlotte Perkins Gilman, *In This Our World* (Oakland, Calif.: McCombs & Vaughn, 1893), pp. 95–100.

I'm going to cut down forest trees,
  To make my houses higher!
I'm going to kill the Mastodon!
  I'm going to make a fire!"

Loud screamed the Anthropoidal Apes
  With laughter wild and gay;
They tried to catch that boastful one,
  But he always got away.
So they yelled at him in chorus,
  Which he minded not a whit;
And they pelted him with cocoanuts,
  Which didn't seem to hit.
And then they gave him reasons
  Which they thought of much avail,
To prove how his preposterous
  Attempt was sure to fail.
Said the sages, "In the first place,
  The thing cannot be done!
And, second, if it *could* be,
  It would not be any fun!
And, third, and most conclusive,
  And admitting no reply,
You would have to change your nature!
  We should like to see you try!"
They chuckled then triumphantly,
  These lean and hairy shapes,
For these things passed as arguments
  With the Anthropoidal Apes.

There was once a Neolithic Man,
  An enterprising wight,
Who made his chopping implements
  Unusually bright.
Unusually clever he,
  Unusually brave,

And he drew delightful Mammoths
  On the borders of his cave.
To his Neolithic neighbors,
  Who were startled and surprised,
Said he, "My friends, in course of time,
  We shall be civilized!
We are going to live in cities!
  We are going to fight in wars!
We are going to eat three times a day
  Without the natural cause!
We are going to turn life upside down
  About a thing called gold!
We are going to want the earth, and take
  As much as we can hold!
We are going to wear great piles of stuff
  Outside our proper skins!
We are going to have Diseases!
  And Accomplishments!! And Sins!!!"

Then they all rose up in fury
  Against their boastful friend,
For prehistoric patience
  Cometh quickly to an end.
Said one, "This is chimerical!
  Utopian! Absurd!"
Said another, "What a stupid life!
  Too dull, upon my word!"
Cried all, "Before such things can come,
  You idiotic child,
You must alter Human Nature!"
  And they all sat back and smiled.
Thought they, "An answer to that last
  It will be hard to find!"
It was a clinching argument
  To the Neolithic Mind!

NOTES

The following abbreviations will be used:

CPG   Charlotte Perkins Gilman

GECS   Grace Ellery Channing Stetson

GHG   George Houghton Gilman

KBSC   Katharine Beecher Stetson Chamberlin

RIHS   Rhode Island Historical Society

BL   Bancroft Library

SL   Arthur and Elizabeth Schlesinger Library

Since most of the Gilman papers are in the Arthur and Elizabeth
Schlesinger Library, references will be to that collection unless
otherwise specified.

INTRODUCTION

1. Susan Ware, "Charlotte Perkins Gilman: The Early Lectures,
   1890–1893," unpublished paper, May 29, 1973.
2. Perry Miller, ed., *American Thought: Civil War to World War I*

(New York: Rinehart & Company, 1954), introduction, p. xxx.

3. This is a major theme in Gabriel Kolko's book *The Triumph of Conservatism: A Reinterpretation of American History, 1900–1916* (New York: Free Press of Glencoe, 1963).

4. See James Weinstein, *The Corporate Ideal in the Liberal State, 1900–1918* (Boston: Beacon Press, 1968).

5. See Barbara Sicherman, "Career Patterns of the Progressive Generation of Women," paper delivered to the Women's History Institute, Princeton University, July 23, 1980.

6. Barbara Sicherman, "Women's Contribution to Social Reform," paper read at the Cambridge Forum, October 14, 1981.

7. See Richard Weiss, "Racism in the Era of Industrialization," in *The Great Fear: Race in the Mind of America*, ed. Gary B. Nash and Richard Weiss (New York: Holt, Rinehart & Winston, 1970), pp. 121–43.

I

FATHER

1. Lyman Beecher Stowe, *Saints, Sinners, and Beechers* (Indianapolis: Bobbs-Merrill Co., 1934), p. 26.

2. Ibid., p. 58.

3. Ibid., p. 28.

4. Marie Caskey, *Chariot of Fire: Religion and the Beecher Family* (New Haven: Yale University Press, 1978), p. 152.

5. Kathryn Kish Sklar, *Catherine Beecher: A Study in American Domesticity* (New Haven: Yale University Press, 1973), p. 135.

6. Stowe, *Saints*, p. 152.

7. Charlotte Perkins Gilman (CPG), *The Living of Charlotte Perkins Gilman: An Autobiography* (1935; reprint, New York: Harper & Row, 1975), p. 4.

8. Ibid., p. 4.

9. Ibid., p. 6.

10. Ibid., p. 5.

11. February 18, 1876.

12. CPG to George Houghton Gilman (GHG), February 1, 1899.

13. CPG, *The Living*, p. 6.

14. Frederick B. Perkins, *Devil-Puzzlers and Other Stories* (New York: G. P. Putnam's Sons, 1877), p. 79.
15. Ibid., p. 140.
16. Ibid., p. 176.
17. Ibid., p. 215.
18. Frederick B. Perkins to Charlotte Perkins, October 15, 1878.
19. CPG, *The Living*, p. 5.
20. Katharine Beecher Stetson Chamberlin (KBSC), August 26, 1935.

II

MOTHER

1. CPG, *The Living*, p. 7.
2. Ibid., p. 8.
3. Ibid., p. 9.
4. Ibid., pp. 10, 11.
5. Ibid., p. 13.
6. CPG to Grace Ellery Channing Stetson (GECS), January 23, 1893.
7. CPG to GECS, January 11, 1897.
8. Unpublished autobiography, p. 30.
9. January 1876.
10. CPG, *The Living*, p. 92.
11. Thomas A. Perkins to CPG, October 17, 1926.
12. Ellen Moers, *Literary Women: The Great Women Writers* (Garden City, N.Y.: Doubleday & Co., 1976), p. 261.
13. CPG, *The Living*, p. 14.
14. Ibid., p. 31.
15. April 8, 1923.
16. November 23, 1878.
17. April 8, 1923.
18. CPG, *The Living*, p. 12.
19. Ibid., pp. 12, 15–16.
20. Ibid., pp. 20, 22–23.
21. Stories are in handscript in Gilman papers, 1870–1871.
22. Bruno Bettelheim, *The Uses of Enchantment: The Meaning and*

Importance of Fairy Tales (New York: Alfred A. Knopf, 1976), p. 39.

23. CPG, *The Living*, pp. 26–27, 23. Note that if fantasy had been her "chief happiness for 5 years," she begins that activity at age eight. Elsewhere in her autobiography, as quoted earlier, she described how she turned inward at age ten.

24. Moers, *Literary Women*, pp. 261–62.

25. CPG, *The Living*, pp. 24, 30.

26. Ibid., p. 34.

27. February 7, 1876.

28. CPG, *The Living*, pp. 35–36.

29. Ibid., pp. 56, 67.

30. Ibid., 64.

31. February 24, 1881.

32. Diary entry, March 30, 1880.

33. P. 50.

34. Diary entry, March 6, 1876.

35. CPG, *The Living*, p. 51.

36. Diary entry, January 1, 1880.

37. Diary entry, June 27, 1879.

38. Diary entry, June 1, 1880.

39. Diary entry, June 18, 1878.

40. CPG, *The Living*, p. 49.

41. Ibid., p. 46.

42. Diary entry, January 1, 1879.

43. CPG, *The Living*, p. 64.

44. Diary entry, January 1, 1879.

45. April 10, 1881.

46. June 18, 1882.

III

MARTHA

1. CPG, *The Living* , p. 26.

2. May 14, 1881.

3. CPG, *The Living*, p. 48.

4. May 14, 1881.

5. January 20, 1890.

6. Henry James, *Notebooks*, ed. F. O. Matthiessen and K. B. Murdock (New York: Oxford University Press, 1961), pp. 40–41; quoted in Jean Strouse, *Alice James: A Biography* (Boston: Houghton Mifflin Co., 1980), pp. 26–27.
7. July 29, 1881.
8. July 3, 1881.
9. August 10, 1881.
10. August 2, 1881.
11. August 15, 1881.
12. August 29, 1881.
13. July 20, 1881.
14. July 24, 1881.
15. August 2, 1881.
16. August 13, 1881.
17. August 15, 1881.
18. July 29, 1881.
19. August 16, 1881.
20. August 23, 1881.
21. August 29, 1881.
22. September 4, 1881.
23. October 31, 1881.
24. CPG, *The Living*, pp. 78, 80, 81.

IV
WALTER

1. Much of the material in this chapter comes from Mary A. Hill, ed., *Endure: The Diaries of Charles Walter Stetson* (Philadelphia: Temple University Press, 1985), Stetson's diaries, letters, and journals not being available to me.
2. Quoted in Charles C. Eldredge, *Charles Walter Stetson: Color and Fantasy* (Lawrence: Spencer Museum of Art/University of Kansas, 1982), p. 18.
3. July 10, 1883, Hill, *Endure*, p. xxi.
4. October 6, 1882, *Endure*, p. 5.
5. August 1883, *Endure*, p. 4.
6. August 6, 1883, *Endure*, p. 219.
7. June 23, 1883, *Endure*, p. 201.

8. November 15, 1881, *Endure*, p. 14.

9. CPG, *The Living*, pp. 80–81.

10. CPG diary entries, August 13, 1882; October 5, 1882; November 20, 1882.

11. February 13, 1882; February 20, 1882; February 21, 1882; March 6, 1882; March 26, 1882.

12. February 17, 1882, *Endure*, p. 48.

13. May 20, 1883.

14. CPG, *The Living*, pp. 82–83.

15. May 22, 1883, *Endure*, p. 190.

16. CPG, *The Living*, pp. 82–83.

17. "Word to Myself," November 3, 1883.

18. October 6, 1883.

19. January 1, 1883, my emphasis.

20. February 28, 1884.

21. March 25, 1884; April 28, 1884.

22. March 13, 1882, *Endure*, p. 58; March 20, 1882, *Endure*, p. 60; May 1, 1882, *Endure*, p. 69.

23. August 1882, *Endure*, p. 80; May 20, 1882, *Endure*, p. 75; November 25, 1881, *Endure*, p. 116; January 19, 1883, *Endure*, pp. 129–30; March 12, 1883, *Endure*, p. 139; March 19, 1883, *Endure*, p. 83.

24. April 27, 1883, *Endure*, p. 167; November 26, 1883, *Endure*, p. 246.

25. CPG, *The Living*, p. 85.

26. Diary entry, May 2, 1884.

27. May 9, 1884; June 15, 1884; June 25, 1884; June 26, 1884.

28. August 18, 1884, *Endure*, p. 264, original emphasis.

29. CPG, *The Living*, pp. 87–89.

30. August 30, 1885.

31. Quoted in CPG, *The Living*, p. 91.

32. January 25, 1885, *Endure*, p. 276; August 27, 1885, *Endure*, p. 282.

33. CPG, *The Living*, pp. 92, 94.

34. March 13, 1886.

35. March 20, 1887; March 22, 1887; March 27, 1887; January 16, 1887; January 8, 1887.

36. July 19, 1887, *Endure*, p. 343; July 20, 1887, *Endure*, p. 344.

37. October 1887, *Endure*, p. 357; February 9, 1887, *Endure*, pp. 331–32.
38. January 1, 1887.
39. March 28, 1887; April 4, 1887; April 5, 1887; April 10, 1887.

V

SILAS WEIR MITCHELL

1. Stowe, *Saints*, p. 116.
2. Sklar, *Catharine Beecher*, p. 184.
3. Noel Bertram Gerson, *Harriet Beecher Stowe: A Biography* (New York: Praeger Publishers, 1976), pp. 40, 76.
4. David Rein, *S. Weir Mitchell as a Psychiatric Novelist* (New York: International Universities Press, 1952), p. 37.
5. Ernest Penney Earnest, *S. Weir Mitchell, Novelist and Physician* (Philadelphia: University of Pennsylvania Press, 1950), introduction, p. v.
6. Ibid., p. 74.
7. Quoted in Barbara Sicherman, "The Uses of a Diagnosis: Doctors, Patients, and Neurasthenia," *Journal of the History of Medicine and Allied Science* 32, no. 2 (January 1977): 34.
8. See Franklin H. Martin, M.D., "Hystero-Neurasthenia, or Nervous Exhaustion of Women, Treated by the S. Weir Mitchell Method," *Journal of the American Medical Association* 8, no. 14 (April 2, 1887): 365.
9. See Rein, *Mitchell*, p. 46.
10. From Mitchell's *Lectures on Diseases of the Nervous System, Especially in Women*, quoted in Rein, *Mitchell*, pp. 270–71.
11. Ibid., p. 39.
12. S. Weir Mitchell, *Fat and Blood: An Essay on the Treatment of Certain Forms of Neurasthenia and Hysteria* (Philadelphia: J. B. Lippincott & Co., 1877), pp. 40–41.
13. Ibid., p. 62.
14. Jeffrey Berman, "Charlotte Perkins Gilman and 'The Yellow Wallpaper,'" unpublished paper, p. 27. See Berman, *The Talking Cure: Literary Representations of Psychoanalysis* (New York: New York University Press, 1985).

15. S. Weir Mitchell, "The True and False Palsies of Hysteria," *Medical News and Abstracts*, February 1880, p. 65, quoted in Rein, *Mitchell*, p. 36.
16. Quoted in Earnest, *Mitchell*, p. 151.
17. S. Weir Mitchell, *Wear and Tear; or, Hints for the Overworked* (Philadelphia: J. B. Lippincott & Co., 1886), p. 32.
18. Ana Robeson Burr, *Weir Mitchell: His Life and Letters* (New York: Duffield & Co., 1929), pp. 373–74.
19. Earnest, *Mitchell*, p. 227.
20. See, for example, the chapter "The Physician" in S. Weir Mitchell, *Doctor and Patient* (Philadelphia: J. B. Lippincott & Co., 1886).
21. Earnest, *Mitchell*, p. 245.
22. Ibid., p. 227.
23. Berman, "Charlotte Perkins Gilman," p. 27.
24. S. Weir Mitchell, "General Considerations," *A Text-book on Nervous Diseases, by American Authors*, ed. F. X. Dercum (Philadelphia: Lea Brothers & Co., 1895), p. 19.
25. Earnest, *Mitchell*, p. 180.
26. CPG, *The Living*, p. 96.
27. CPG to GECS.
28. CPG, *The Living*, pp. 97–98.
29. *Forerunner*, 1913, p. 271.
30. CPG, *The Living*, p. 97.
31. January 1, 1885, quoted by CPG in *The Living*, p. 88.
32. CPG, *The Living*, p. 120.
33. Original letter in Gilman papers, reference in CPG, *The Living*, p. 121.

VI
GRACE

1. November 21, 1887.
2. CPG, *The Living*, p. 97.
3. June 15, 1988, *Endure*, p. 363.
4. Alexandra Symonds, M.D., "Phobias After Marriage: Women's Declaration of Dependence," in *Psychoanalysis and Women*, ed. Jean Baker Miller (Baltimore and Middlesex, England: Pen-

guin Books, 1973), pp. 288–304. Alfred Adler, "Sex," ibid., p. 49.

5. CPG, *The Living*, p. 49.
6. Ibid., p. 106.
7. Ibid., pp. 115, 110.
8. June 7, 1890; July 27, 1890.
9. July 11, 1894; March 21, 1897; October 7, 1919; July 11, 1894.
10. CPG to GECS, July 9, 1929.
11. CPG to Martha Luther Lane, March 16, 1889, RIHS.
12. CPG to Martha Luther Lane, January 20, 1890, RIHS.
13. CPG to Martha Luther Lane, August 15, 1889, RIHS.
14. August 20, 1889; November 10, 1890.
15. See Lillian Faderman, *Surpassing the Love of Men: Romantic Friendship and Love Between Women from the Renaissance to the Present* (New York: William Morrow & Co., 1981).
16. September 16, 1895; February 25, 1896; June 1895.
17. March 1935.
18. Charles Walter Stetson to Rebecca Stetson, July 12, 1889, BL.

VII

ADELINE/DORA

1. F. I. Vassault, "Nationalism in California," *Overland Monthly* (published in San Francisco) 15 (December 1875): 659–61.
2. Mari Jo Buhle, *Women and American Socialism, 1870–1920* (Urbana: University of Illinois Press, 1981), p. 80.
3. See Susan Ware, "Charlotte Perkins Gilman: The Early Lectures."
4. CPG to GHG, March 7, 1899.
5. Diary entry, July 27, 1891.
6. Diary entry, October 14, 1891.
7. Diary entries, November 14; December 25, December 26, 1891.
8. September 3, 1892.
9. Diary entry, September 14, 1892.
10. Diary entry, September 16, 1892.
11. May 3; May 11; May 12; May 14, 1893.
12. May 1893.
13. March 10, 1894.

14. CPG, *The Living*, pp. 143–44.
15. July 14, 1893.
16. Quoted in CPG, *The Living*, p. 141.
17. CPG to GECS, January 23, 1893.
18. CPG, *The Living*, p. 162.
19. Ibid., pp. 162–63.
20. September 16.
21. May 9, 1894.
22. Diary entry, November 30, 1894.
23. CPG, *The Living*, p. 173.
24. Ibid., p. 293.
25. Ibid., p. 176.
26. Ibid., p. 177.
27. Ibid., p. 180.

VIII
HOUGHTON

1. CPG, *The Living*, p. 181.
2. Allen Davis, *American Heroine: The Life and Legend of Jane Addams* (New York: Oxford University Press, 1973), p. 75.
3. Ibid., p. 75.
4. Ibid., p. 80.
5. September 16, 1895.
6. June 16, 1895.
7. CPG, *The Living*, p. 187.
8. Howard E. Quint, *The Forging of American Socialism* (Indianapolis: Bobbs-Merrill Co., 1953), p. 123.
9. CPG, *The Living*, p. 187.
10. Ibid., p. 191.
11. Ibid., p. 215.
12. CPG to GECS, May 3, 1896.
13. KBSC to Carl Degler, July 24, 1960.
14. November 23.
15. March 11.
16. CPG, *The Living*, pp. 281, 326.
17. March 18, 1897.
18. CPG to GHG, August 1; August 23, 1897.

19. CPG, *The Living*, p. 235.
20. Ibid., p. 237.
21. July 27, 1897.
22. June 16, 1897.
23. September 1, 1897.
24. September 11, 1897.
25. June 4, 1897.
26. June 22, 1897.
27. June 29, 1897.
28. No date (November ?) 1897.
29. October 1, 1897.
30. October 1, 1897.
31. May 2, 1897.
32. March 2?, 1897.
33. July 27, 1897.
34. May 3, 1897.
35. July 15, 1897.
36. October 15, 1897.
37. June 16, 1897.
38. July 22, 1897.
39. November 3, 1897.
40. May 18, 1900.
41. May 1897.
42. November 10, 1897.
43. February 20, 1898.
44. February 20, 1898.
45. August 8, 1897.
46. CPG, *The Living*, p. 285.
47. Ibid., p. 284.
48. May 6, 1898.
49. May 25, 1898.
50. September 15, 1898.
51. May 22, 1898.
52. September 1, 1898.
53. January 1899.
54. October 11, 1898.
55. October 11, 1898.
56. October 7, 1898.
57. December 20, 1898.

58. May 6, 1898.
59. June 20, 1898.
60. July 14, 1898.
61. July 29, 1898.
62. September 1, 1898.
63. February 24, 1899.
64. March 7, 1899.
65. March 15, 1899.
66. July 15; July 26; July 28; July 26; September 26, 1899.
67. January 1, 1900.
68. February 1, 1900.
69. February 4, 1900.
70. February 22, 1900.
71. February 23, 1900.
72. February 27, 1900.
73. March 3, 1900.
74. March 14, 1900.
75. March 15; March 17; March 20, 1900.
76. April 3, 1900.
77. March 7, 1900.
78. April 11, 1900.
79. April 9; April 19, 1900.
80. April 16, 1900.
81. April 19, 1900.
82. May 6, 1900.
83. May 15, 1900.
84. May 16, 1900.
85. May 17, 1900.
86. May 18, 1900.
87. May 25, 1900.
88. June 1, 1900.
89. CPG, *The Living*, p. 281.

IX
WORK: PART I

1. Pp. 8–9. In order to avoid burdensome numbers of footnotes in this chapter and the next, I will footnote only sparingly or when the context is not clear.
2. P. 21.
3. P. 29.
4. P. 149.
5. P. 63.
6. P. 93.
7. P. 110.
8. P. 315.
9. P. 151.
10. P. 156.
11. P. 166.
12. P. 164.
13. P. 167.
14. P. 178.
15. P. 181.
16. P. 196.
17. P. 222.
18. P. 245.
19. P. 267.
20. P. 281.
21. P. 301.
22. See Gary Scharnhorst, *Charlotte Perkins Gilman: A Bibliography* (Metuchen, N.J.: Scarecrow Press, 1985), pp. 99–102. This bibliography is enormously useful. All Gilman scholars are indebted to Scharnhorst for the prodigious research and creative investigation embodied in this volume.
23. P. 119.
24. P. 9.
25. P. 14.
26. P. 34.
27. P. 103.
28. Pp. 135–36.
29. P. 195.

30. P. 197.
31. See Dolores Hayden, *The Great Domestic Revolution: A History of Feminist Designs for American Homes, Neighborhoods, and Cities* (Cambridge: MIT Press, 1981); and Polly Wynn Allen, *Building Domestic Liberty: Charlotte Perkins Gilman's Architectural Feminism* (Amherst: University of Massachusetts Press, 1988).
32. P. 284.
33. Scharnhorst, *Bibliography*, p. 105.
34. P. 6.
35. P. 29.
36. P. 25.
37. P. 78.
38. P. 83.
39. P. 90.
40. P. 97.
41. P. 101.
42. P. 115.
43. P. 155.
44. Pp. 171–72.
45. P. 267.
46. P. 277.
47. P. 294.
48. P. 295.
49. P. 297.
50. P. 324.
51. P. 335, my emphasis.
52. Pp. 345–47.
53. Scharnhorst, *Bibliography*, pp. 106–7.

X
WORK: PART II

1. CPG, *The Living*, p. 285.
2. Ibid., p. 275.
3. P. 13.
4. P. 54.
5. P. 153.
6. P. 88.

7. P. 114.
8. P. 136.
9. P. 249.
10. P. 246.
11. P. 110.
12. P. 43.
13. P. 53.
14. "Why Cooperative Housekeeping Fails," *Harper's Bazaar*, July 1907, p. 629.
15. See Ruth Schwartz Cowan, "The Roads Not Taken: Alternative Social and Technical Approaches to Housework," chap. 5 in *More Work for Mother: The Ironies of Household Technology from Open Hearth to the Microwave* (New York: Basic Books, 1983), pp. 103–54.
16. Jane Flax, "Political Philosophy and the Patriarchal Unconscious: A Psychoanalytic Perspective on Epistemology and Metaphysics," in *Discovering Reality: Feminist Perspectives on Epistemology, Metaphysics, Methodology and Philosophy of Science*, ed. Merrill Hintikka and Sandra Harding (Dordrecht, Holland, and Boston: D. Reidel, 1983), p. 289. Sold and distributed in the United States and Canada by Kluwer Academic Publishers, Hingham, Mass.
17. Sandra Harding, *The Science Question in Feminism* (Ithaca, N.Y.: Cornell University Press, 1986), p. 249.
18. Ibid., p. 159.
19. Evelyn Fox Keller, "Science and Power for What?" in *Science Between Utopia and Dystopia*, Sociology of the Sciences Yearbook no. 8, ed. Everett Mendelsohn and Helga Nowotny (Dordrecht, Holland, and Boston: D. Reidel, 1984), p. 67.
20. Jane Roland Martin, *Reclaiming a Conversation: The Ideal of the Educated Woman* (New Haven: Yale University Press, 1985). See chap. 6, "Gilman's Mothers," pp. 139–70, for an astute analysis in general and p. 166 for specific reference.

XI
KATHARINE

1. May 3, 1896.
2. October 13, 1898.
3. February or March 1897.
4. CPG to GECS, June 8, 1896.
5. P. 54.
6. P. 43.
7. P. 5.
8. Pp. 7–8.
9. P. 15.
10. P. 27.
11. P. 42.
12. P. 14.
13. P. 11.
14. CPG to GHG, May 17, 1900.
15. Chap. 8, pp. 13–14.
16. Chap. 9, p. 23.
17. Chap. 10, p. 10.
18. Chap. 12, p. 8.
19. April 15, 1922.
20. July 18, 1922.
21. July 21, 1931.
22. June 5, 1933.
23. August 26, 1933.
24. March 21, 1921.
25. June 28, 1926.
26. July 9, 1926.
27. September 10, 1931.
28. May 2, 1933.
29. July 24, 1960.
30. January 12, 1972. S.L. office file.
31. April 8, 1973. S.L. office file.
32. January 12, 1972. S.L. office file.
33. September 13, 1972. S.L. office file.
34. June 22, 1972. S.L. office file.
35. December 30, 1972. S.L. office file.

36. April 8, 1973. S.L. office file.
37. April 8, 1972. S.L. office file.
38. KBSC to Carl Degler, July 24, 1960.
39. September 23, 1931.

XII
CHARLOTTE

1. CPG to KBSC, March 23, 1920.
2. CPG to KBSC, August 9, 1920.
3. CPG to KBSC, June 13, 1921.
4. CPG to KBSC, August 15, 1921.
5. "The Suffragists and Socialists Demand Votes for Women," *Call*, March 1, 1909, p. 1, quoted in Temma Kaplan, "Commentary on the Socialist Origins of International Women's Day," *Feminist Studies* 11, no. 1 (Spring 1985): 163–72.
6. "A.B.C.: A Day of Anticipation," *Call*, February 27, 1910, p. 13, quoted in Temma Kaplan, "Commentary on the Socialist Origins of International Women's Day," *Feminist Studies* 11, no. 1 (Spring 1985): 163–72.
7. Judith Schwarz, *Radical Feminists of Heterodoxy: Greenwich Village, 1912–1940* (Lebanon, N.H.: New Victoria Publishers, 1982).
8. Ibid., p. 34.
9. Buhle, *Women and American Socialism*, p. 318.
10. National Woman's Party Papers, Reel 144, Minutes of the Executive Committee, September 10, 1920. Thanks to Katharine Anderson for bringing this to my attention.
11. "Biographical Sketch of C. P. Gilman," with letter attached, dated May 24, 1920.
12. May 26, 1920.
13. CPG to KBSC May 2, 1922; May 17, 1922; June 24, 1922.
14. May 2, 1922.
15. April 3, 1922.
16. August 5, 1922.
17. March 22, 1923; March 23, 1923.
18. July 10, 1924.
19. October 10, 1923; August 11, 1930.

20. February 14, 1930.
21. CPG to KBSC, April 24, 1930.
22. CPG to KBSC, November 21, 1930.
23. CPG to KBSC, August 19, 1931; December 19, 1931; May 2, 1933.
24. See Scharnhorst, *Bibliography*.
25. July 25, 1924.
26. CPG to Zona Gale, no date, written from Pasadena soon after she arrived.
27. CPG to KBSC, May 19, 1927.
28. From Robert Tapley, Macmillan Co., October 1, 1929; October 8, 1929.
29. The complete typescript is in the Gilman papers in the Schlesinger Library. An excerpt can be found in *The Charlotte Perkins Gilman Reader*, ed. Ann J. Lane (New York: Pantheon Books, 1980), pp. 170–77.
30. December 15, 1930.
31. CPG to GECS, March 13, 1933.
32. Rose Cecil O'Neill Wilson to CPG, November 18, 1910.
33. CPG, *The Living*, p. 333.
34. December 26, 1932.
35. May 5, 1934.
36. CPG to KBSC, May 5, 1934.
37. May 5, 1934.
38. June 4, 1934.
39. CPG to GECS, December 7, 1934.
40. CPG to GECS, September 5, 1934.
41. Conversations with Dorothy and Walter Chamberlin in Pasadena in 1978.
42. CPG to GECS, no date, after November 1934.
43. CPG to GECS, March 3, 1935.
44. Letter to Mrs. Boyle Workman, director of Speaker's Bureau in Pasadena, January 11, 1935.
45. November 4, 1935.
46. CPG to GECS, December 7, 1934.
47. June 24, 1935.
48. December 7, 1934.
49. March 26, 1935.
50. August 7, 1935.

51. February 20, 1935.
52. March 20, 1935.
53. April 17, 1935.
54. March 29, 1935.
55. December 21, 1934.
56. February 20; March 3; April 24, 1935.
57. May 19, 1935.
58. July 30, 1935.
59. May 1, 1935.
60. June 9, 1935.
61. May 7, 1935.
62. July 25, 1935.
63. March 26, 1935.
64. August 15, 1935. See E. A. Ross, *Seventy Years of It: An Autobiography of Edward Alsworth Ross* (1936: reprint, New York: Arno Press, 1977), p. 60.
65. No date.
66. August 12, 1935.
67. CPG, "The Right to Die," *Forum* 94 (November 1935): 197–300. Excerpted in *Reader's Digest*, September 18, 1937, p. 22.
68. Lyman Beecher Stowe to KBSC, May 12, 1936.
69. *New York Herald Tribune Books*, Sunday, October 20, 1935.
70. October 14, 1935, p. 14.

BIBLIOGRAPHY

MANUSCRIPT COLLECTIONS

Arthur and Elizabeth Schlesinger Library on the History of
Women in America, Radcliffe College, Cambridge, Mass.
The Charlotte Perkins Gilman Collection.

Bancroft Library, University of California, Berkeley, Calif.
The Charles Walter Stetson correspondence.

John Hay Library, Brown University, Providence, R.I.
Charlotte Gilman–Lester Ward correspondence.

Rhode Island Historical Society, Providence, R.I. Charlotte
Gilman's correspondence with Martha Luther (Lane).

Stowe Day Foundation, Hartford, Conn. Correspondence of
Mary Westcott Perkins and Isabella Beecher Hooker.

Vassar College Library, Vassar College, Poughkeepsie, N.Y.
Charlotte Gilman's correspondence with Marian Whitney.

UNPUBLISHED WORKS

Allen-Robinson, Polly Wynn. "The Social Ethics of Charlotte Perkins Gilman." Ph.D. diss., Harvard University,
1978.

Barker-Benfield, G. J. "S. Weir Mitchell and the 'Woman
Question': Gender, Therapy, and Social History," 1981.

Doyle, William. "Charlotte Gilman and the Cycle of Feminist
Reform." Ph.D. diss., University of California, Berkeley,
1960.

Potts, Helen Jo. "Charlotte Perkins Gilman: A Humanist Approach to Feminism." Ph.D. diss., North Texas State University, 1975.

Rothschild, Joan A. "Lester Frank Ward and the American Theory of Political Observation: A Test Case." Ph.D. diss., New York University, 1970.

Sicherman, Barbara. "Career Patterns of the Progressive Generations of Women." Paper delivered to the Women's History Institute, Princeton University, July 23, 1980.

Sicherman, Barbara. "Women's Contributions to Social Reform." Paper read at the Cambridge Forum, October 14, 1981. Mimeographed.

Thie, Marilyn. "Charlotte Perkins Gilman's Social Philosophy: A Resource for Feminist Theory." Colgate University, Hamilton, N.Y., 1989. Mimeographed.

Ware, Susan. "Charlotte Perkins Gilman: The Early Lectures, 1890–1893." Unpublished paper, May 29, 1973.

WORKS OF CHARLOTTE PERKINS GILMAN

Verse

In This Our World. Oakland, Calif.: McCombs & Vaughn, 1893; London: T. Fisher Unwin, 1895. 2nd ed. San Francisco: Press of James H. Barry, 1895.

Fiction

The Charlotte Perkins Gilman Reader. Edited with introduction by Ann J. Lane. New York: Pantheon Books, 1980.

The Crux. New York: Charlton Co., 1911.

Herland. With introduction by Ann J. Lane. New York: Pantheon Books, 1979.

Moving the Mountain. New York: Charlton Co., 1911.

What Diantha Did. New York: Charlton Co., 1910; London: T. Fisher Unwin, 1912.

"The Yellow Wallpaper." *New England Magazine* 5 (January 1892): 647–46.

The Yellow Wallpaper. Boston: Small, Maynard & Co., 1899. Reprint, with an afterword by Elaine Hedges. Old Westbury, N.Y.: Feminist Press, 1973.

Nonfiction

Concerning Children. Boston: Small, Maynard & Co., 1900, 1901; London: G. P. Putnam's Sons, 1900.
His Religion and Hers: A Study of the Faith of Our Fathers and the Work of Our Mothers. New York and London: Century Co., 1923; London: T. Fisher Unwin, 1924. Reprint. Westport, Conn.: Hyperion Press, 1976.
The Home: Its Work and Influence. New York: McClure, Phillips & Co., 1903; London: William Heinemann, 1904. Reprint. New York: Source Book Press, 1970.
Human Work. New York: McClure, Phillips & Co., 1904.
The Labor Movement. Paper read before the trade and labor unions of Alameda County, Calif., September 2, 1892. Oakland: Alameda County Federation of Trades, 1893.
The Living of Charlotte Perkins Gilman: An Autobiography. New York and London: D. Appleton-Century Co., 1935. Reprint. New York: Arno Press, 1972, and Harper & Row, 1975.
The Man-Made World; or, Our Androcentric Culture. New York: Charlton Co., 1911. Reprint. New York: Source Book Press, 1970.
Women and Economics: A Study of the Economic Relation Between Men and Women as a Factor in Social Evolution. Boston: Small, Maynard & Co., 1898. Reprint, edited with introduction by Carl N. Degler. New York: Harper & Row, 1966, and Source Book Press, 1970.

PUBLISHED WORKS

Addams, Jane. *Democracy and Social Ethics.* New York: Macmillan Co., 1902.
Allen, Polly Wynn. *Building Domestic Liberty: Charlotte Perkins*

Gilman's Architectural Feminism. Amherst: University of Massachusetts Press, 1988.

Allen, Robert, and Pamela P. Allen. *Reluctant Reformers: Racism and Social Reform Movements in the United States*. Washington, D.C.: Howard University Press, 1983.

Austin, Mary. *Earth Horizon: An Autobiography*. Boston: Houghton Mifflin Co., 1932.

Bader, Julia. "The Dissolving Vision: Realism in Jewett, Freeman, and Gilman." In *American Realism: New Essays*, edited by Eric J. Sundquist, pp. 176–98. Baltimore: Johns Hopkins University Press, 1982.

Baker, Elizabeth. *Technology and Woman's Work*. New York: Columbia University Press, 1964.

Bardwick, Judith M., ed. *Readings on the Psychology of Women*. New York: Harper & Row, 1972.

Bartlett, Richard A., ed. *The Gilded Age: America, 1865–1900*. Reading, Mass.: Addison-Wesley Co., 1969.

Bassuk, Ellen L. "The Rest Cure: Repetition or Resolution of Victorian Women's Conflicts?" In *The Female Body in Western Culture: Contemporary Perspectives*. Edited by Susan Rubin Suleiman, pp. 139–51. Cambridge: Harvard University Press, 1986.

Beecher, Henry Ward. *Norwood; or, Village Life in New England*. 1867. Reprint. Philadelphia: Richard West, 1978.

Bell, Daniel. *Marxian Socialism in the United States*. Princeton: Princeton University Press, 1952.

Bellamy, Edward. *Looking Backward: 2000–1887*. Boston: Ticknor & Fields, 1887.

Benstock, Shari, ed. *Feminist Issues in Literary Scholarship*. Bloomington: Indiana University Press, 1987.

Berkin, Carol Ruth. "Private Woman, Public Woman: The Contradictions of Charlotte Perkins Gilman." In *Women in America: A History*. Edited by Carol Ruth Berkin and Mary Beth Norton, pp. 150–73. Boston: Houghton Mifflin Co., 1979.

Berman, Jeffrey. *The Talking Cure: Literary Representations of Psychoanalysis*. New York: New York University Press, 1985.

Bettelheim, Bruno. *The Uses of Enchantment: The Meaning and*

Importance of Fairy Tales. New York: Alfred A. Knopf, 1976.

Bingham, Edwin. *Charles F. Lummis: Editor of the Southwest.* San Marino, Calif.: Huntington Library, 1955.

Birken, Lawrence. *Consuming Desire: Sexual Science and the Emergence of a Culture of Abundance, 1871–1914.* Ithaca, N.Y.: Cornell University Press, 1988.

Bowen, Catherine Drinker. *The Writing of Biography.* Boston: The Writer, Inc., 1950.

Boydston, Jeanne. "To Earn Her Daily Bread: Housework and Antebellum Working-Class Subsistence." *Radical History Review* 35 (1986): 7–25.

Boydston, Jeanne, Mary Kelley, and Anne Margolis, eds. *The Limits of Sisterhood: The Beecher Sisters on Women's Rights and Woman's Sphere.* Chapel Hill and London: University of North Carolina Press, 1988.

Buhle, Mari Jo. *Women and American Socialism, 1870–1920.* Urbana: University of Illinois Press, 1981.

Burr, Ana Robeson (Brown). *Weir Mitchell: His Life and Letters.* New York: Duffield & Co., 1929.

Campbell, Helen. *The Easiest Way in Housekeeping and Cooking.* New York: Fords, Howard & Hulbert, 1881.

———. *Household Economics.* New York: G. P. Putnam's Son's, 1897.

———. *Prisoners of Poverty.* Boston: Roberts Brothers, 1887.

———. *Prisoners of Poverty Abroad.* Boston: Roberts Brothers, 1889.

———. *The Problems of the Poor.* New York: Fords, Howard & Hulbert, 1882.

Cape, Emily Palmer. *Lester Ward.* New York: G. P. Putnam's Sons, 1922.

Carter, Paul A. *Another Part of the Twenties.* New York: Columbia University Press, 1977.

Caskey, Marie. *Chariot of Fire: Religion and the Beecher Family.* New Haven: Yale University Press, 1978.

Catalogue of the Exhibition of Paintings by Charles Walter Stetson: December 28, 1912, to January 19, 1913. Philadelphia: Pennsylvania Academy of the Fine Arts, 1912.

Channing, Grace Ellery, ed. *Dr. Channing's Notebooks: Pas-*

sages from the Unpublished Manuscripts of William Ellery Channing. Boston: Houghton Mifflin Co., 1887.

———. *Sister of a Saint and Other Stories.* Chicago: Stone & Kimball, 1905.

Chugerman, Samuel. *Lester Ward, The American Aristotle: A Summary and Interpretation of His Sociology.* 1939. Reprint. New York: Octagon Books, 1965.

Cochran, Thomas, and William Miller. *Age of Enterprise: A Social History of Industrial America.* New York: Harper & Row, 1968.

Cole, G. D. H. *Socialist Thought.* Vol. 3, *The Second International.* New York: St. Martin's Press, 1956. 5 vols., 1953–58.

Cole, Margaret. *The Story of Fabian Socialism.* Rev. ed. New York: John Wiley & Sons, 1961.

Conway, Jill. "Women Reformers and American Culture, 1870–1930." *Journal of Social History* 5 (Winter 1971–72): 164–77.

Cowan, Ruth Schwartz. *More Work for Mother: The Ironies of Household Technology from Open Hearth to the Microwave.* New York: Basic Books, 1983.

Daniels, George, ed. *Darwinism Comes to America.* Waltham, Mass.: Blaisdell Publishing Co., 1968.

Davis, Allen. *American Heroine: The Life and Legend of Jane Addams.* New York: Oxford University Press, 1973.

Degler, Carl. "Charlotte Perkins Gilman on the Theory and Practice of Feminism." *American Quarterly* 8 (Spring 1956): 21–39.

Delamont, Sara, and Lorna Duffin, eds. *The Nineteenth-Century Woman: Her Cultural and Physical World.* New York: Barnes & Noble, 1978.

D'Emilio, John, and Estelle B. Freedman. *Intimate Matters: A History of Sexuality in America.* New York: Harper & Row, 1988.

Dorfman, Joseph. *Thorstein Veblen and His America.* New York: Augustus M. Kelley, 1934.

DuPlessis, Rachel Blau. *Writing Beyond the Ending: Narrative Strategies of Twentieth-Century Women Writers.* Bloomington: Indiana University Press, 1985.

389

Dyer, Thomas G. *Theodore Roosevelt and the Idea of Race.* Baton Rouge; Louisiana State University Press, 1980.

Earnest, Ernest Penney. *S. Weir Mitchell, Novelist and Physician.* Philadelphia: University of Pennsylvania Press, 1950.

Edel, Leon. *Writing Lives: Principia Biographica.* 1959. New York: W. W. Norton & Co., 1984.

Edward Bellamy Speaks Again! Kansas City, Mo.: Peerage Press, 1937.

Ehrenreich, Barbara, and Deirdre English. *Complaints and Disorders: The Sexual Politics of Sickness.* Old Westbury, N.Y.: Feminist Press, 1973.

————. *For Her Own Good: 150 Years of Experts' Advice to Women.* Garden City, N.Y.: Doubleday & Co., 1978.

Eldredge, Charles C. *Charles Walter Stetson: Color and Fantasy.* Lawrence: Spencer Museum of Art / University of Kansas, 1982.

Faderman, Lillian. *Surpassing the Love of Men: Romantic Friendship and Love between Women from the Renaissance to the Present.* New York: William Morrow & Co., 1981.

Feldstein, Richard. "Reader, Text and Ambiguous Referentiality in 'The Yellow Wallpaper.' " In *Feminism and Psychoanalysis,* edited by Richard Feldstein and Judith Roof, pp. 269–79. Ithaca, N.Y.: Cornell University Press, 1989.

Fellman, Anita Clair. "Hapless Housewives in Havenless Homes." *Canadian Review of American Studies* 14 (1983): 297–308.

Fellman, Anita Clair, and Michael Fellman. *Making Sense of Self: Medical Advice Literature in Late Nineteenth Century America.* Philadelphia: University of Pennsylvania Press, 1981.

Filler, Louis. *The Unknown Edwin Markham: His Mystery and Its Significance.* Yellow Springs, Ohio: Antioch Press, 1966.

Flexner, Eleanor. *Century of Struggle: The Women's Rights Movement in the United States.* 1959. Reprint. New York: Atheneum Publishers, 1971.

Ford, Karen. " 'The Yellow Wallpaper' and Women's Discourse." *Tulsa Studies in Women's Literature* 4, no. 2 (1985): 309–14.

Gallop, Jane. *The Daughter's Seduction: Feminism and Psychoanalysis*. Ithaca, N.Y.: Cornell University Press, 1982.

Gardiner, Judith. "The Heroine as Her Author's Daughter." In *Feminist Criticism: Essays on Theory, Poetry, and Prose*, edited by Cheryl L. Brown and Karen Olson, pp. 244–53. Metuchen, N.J.: Scarecrow Press, 1978.

Gerson, Noel Bertram. *Harriet Beecher Stowe: A Biography*. New York: Praeger Publishers, 1976.

Ginger, Ray. *Age of Excess: The United States from 1877 to 1914*. 2nd ed. New York: Macmillan Co., 1975.

Glazer, Penina Migdal, and Miriam Slater. *Unequal Colleagues: The Entrance of Women into the Professions, 1890–1940*. New Brunswick, N.J.: Rutgers University Press, 1987.

Gosling, F. G. *Before Freud: Neurasthenia and the American Medical Community, 1870–1910*. Champaign: University of Illinois Press, 1987.

Gould, Stephen Jay. *Ever Since Darwin: Reflections in Natural History*. New York: W. W. Norton & Co., 1979.

Green, Harvey. *Fit For America: Health, Fitness, Sport, and American Society*. New York: Pantheon Books, 1986.

————. *The Light of the Home: An Intimate View of the Lives of Women in Victorian America*. New York: Pantheon Books, 1983.

Hale, Nathan G., Jr. *Freud and the Americans: The Beginnings of Psychoanalysis in the United States, 1876–1917*. Vol. 1 of *Freud in America*. New York: Oxford University Press, 1971.

Haller, J. S., and Robin M. Haller. *The Physician and Sexuality in Victorian America*. Urbana: University of Illinois Press, 1974.

Haller, Mark H. *Eugenics: Hereditarian Attitudes in American Thought*. New Brunswick, N.J.: Rutgers University Press, 1963.

Hamilton, Mary A. *Sidney and Beatrice Webb: A Study in Contemporary Biography*. Boston: Houghton Mifflin Co., 1933.

Harding, Sandra. *The Science Question in Feminism*. Ithaca, N.Y.: Cornell University Press, 1986.

Hayden, Dolores. *The Great Domestic Revolution: A History*

of Feminist Designs for American Homes, Neighborhoods, and Cities. Cambridge: MIT Press, 1981.

Hazard, Caroline. *Some Ideals in the Education of Women.* New York: Thomas Y. Crowell, 1900.

Heidbreder, Edna. *Seven Psychologies.* New York: D. Appleton-Century Co., 1933.

Hill, Mary Armfield. *Charlotte Perkins Gilman: The Making of a Radical Feminist, 1860–1896.* Philadelphia: Temple University Press, 1980.

———, ed. *Endure: The Diaries of Charles Walter Stetson.* Philadelphia; Temple University Press, 1985.

Himmelfarb, Gertrude. *Darwin and the Darwinian Revolution.* New York: W. W. Norton & Co., 1959.

Hintikka, Merrill, and Sandra Harding, eds. *Discovering Reality: Feminist Perspectives on Epistemology, Metaphysics, Methodology and Philosophy of Science.* Dordrecht, Holland, and Boston: D. Reidel, 1983.

Hofstader, Richard. *Social Darwinism in American Thought.* 1944. Reprint. Boston: Beacon Press, 1964.

Horney, Karen, M.D. *Feminine Psychology.* New York: W. W. Norton & Co., 1967.

———. *Neurosis and Human Growth.* New York: W. W. Norton & Co., 1950.

———. *New Ways in Psychoanalysis.* New York: W. W. Norton & Co., 1939.

———. *Our Inner Conflicts: A Constructive Theory of Neurosis.* New York: W. W. Norton & Co., 1945.

Howe, Harriet. "Charlotte Perkins Gilman—As I Knew Her." *Equal Rights: Independent Feminist Weekly* 5 (September 1936): 211–16.

Hubbard, Ruth, and Marian Lowe, eds. *Genes and Gender II: Pitfalls in Research on Sex and Gender.* New York: Gordian Press, 1979.

Irwin, Inez Hayes. *Angels and Amazons: A Hundred Years of American Women.* Garden City, N.Y.: Doubleday, Doran & Co., 1933.

Jaggar, Alison M. *Feminist Politics and Human Nature.* Totowa, N.J.: Rowman & Littlefield, 1983.

Jeffreys, Sheila. *The Spinster and Her Enemies: Feminism and Sexuality, 1880–1930.* New York: Methuen, 1985.

Karpinski, Joanne B. "When the Marriage of True Minds Admits Impediments: Charlotte Perkins Gilman and William Dean Howells." In *Patrons and Protegees: Gender, Friendship, and Writing in Nineteenth-Century America,* edited by Shirley Marchalonis, pp. 212–34. New Brunswick, N.J.: Rutgers University Press, 1988.

Keller, Evelyn Fox. "Science and Power for What?" In *Science Between Utopia and Dystopia,* Sociology of the Sciences Yearbook no. 8, edited by Everett Mendelsohn and Helga Nowotny, pp. 261–72. Dordrecht, Holland, and Boston: D. Reidel, 1984.

Kennedy, David M., and Paul A. Robinson, eds. *Social Thought in America and Europe: Readings in Comparative Intellectual History.* Boston: Little, Brown & Co., 1970.

Kipnis, Ira. *The American Socialist Movement: 1897–1912.* New York: Columbia University Press, 1952.

Knapp, Adeline. *An Open Letter to Carrie Chapman Catt.* Berkeley, Calif.: New York State Association Opposed to the Extension of Suffrage to Women, Nov. 10, 1899.

———. *One Thousand Dollars a Day: Studies in Practical Economics.* Boston: Arena Publishing Co., 1984.

Kolko, Gabriel. *The Triumph of Conservatism: A Reinterpretation of American History, 1900–1916.* New York: Free Press of Glencoe, 1963.

Lears, Jackson. T. J. *No Place of Grace: Antimodernism and the Transformation of American Culture, 1880–1920.* New York: Pantheon Books, 1981.

Leavitt, Judith Walzer, ed. *Women and Health in America.* Madison: University of Wisconsin Press, 1984.

Liddington, Jill, and Jill Norris. *One Hand Tied Behind Us: The Rise of the Woman's Suffrage Movement.* London: Virago Press, 1978.

Lifton, Norma. "Representing History: From Public Event to Private Meaning." *Art Journal,* Winter 1984, pp. 345–51.

MacKenzie, Norman, and Jeanne MacKenzie. *The Fabians.* New York: Simon & Schuster, 1977.

Martin, Jane Roland. *Reclaiming a Conversation: The Ideal of the Educated Woman*. New Haven: Yale University Press, 1985.

McGovern, Constance M. *Masters of Madness: Social Origins of the American Psychiatric Profession*. Hanover, N.H.: University Press of New England, 1985.

Merchant, Carolyn. *The Death of Nature: Women, Ecology, and the Scientific Revolution*. San Francisco: Harper & Row, 1980.

Miller, Jean Baker, M.D., ed. *Psychoanalysis and Women*. Baltimore and Middlesex, England: Penguin Books, 1973.

————. *Toward a New Psychology of Women*. Boston: Beacon Press, 1976.

Miller, Perry, ed. *American Thought: Civil War to World War I*. New York: Rinehart & Co., 1954.

Mitchell, S. Weir, M.D. *Doctor and Patient*. Philadelphia: J. B. Lippincott & Co., 1886. 4 editions.

————. *Fat and Blood: An Essay on the Treatment of Certain Forms of Neurasthenia and Hysteria*. Philadelphia: J. B. Lippincott & Co., 1877. 8 editions.

————. *Lectures on Diseases of the Nervous System, Especially in Women*. Philadelphia: H. C. Leas' Son & Co., 1881.

————. *Wear and Tear; or, Hints for the Overworked*. 4th ed. Philadelphia: J. B. Lippincott & Co., 1872.

Moers, Ellen. *Literary Women: The Great Women Writers*. Garden City, N.Y.: Doubleday & Co., 1976.

Morgan, Arthur. *Edward Bellamy*. New York: Columbia University Press, 1944.

Moseley, Eva. *Charlotte Perkins Gilman Papers, 1846–1961*. Arthur and Elizabeth Schlesinger Library on the History of Women in America, Radcliffe College, Cambridge, Mass., 1972.

Nash, Gary B., and Richard Weiss. *The Great Fear: Race in the Mind of America*. New York: Holt, Rinehart & Winston, 1970.

Neely, Carol Thomas. "Alternative Women's Discourse," *Tulsa Studies in Women's Literature* 4, no. 2 (1985): 315–22.

Nies, Judith. "Charlotte Perkins Gilman." In *Seven Women:*

Portraits from the American Radical Tradition. New York: Viking Press, 1977.

Noble, David. *The Paradox of Progressive Thought*. Minneapolis: University of Minnesota Press, 1958.

Oakley, Ann. *Woman's Work: The Housewife Past and Present*. New York: Random House, 1976.

Perkins, Frederick Beecher. *Devil-Puzzlers and Other Stories*. New York: G. P. Putnam's Sons, 1877.

————. *My Three Conversations with Miss Chester*. New York: G. P. Putnam's Sons, 1877.

————. *The Station and Duty of American Teachers as Citizens, in View of The Materialism of the Age*. Hartford: Association of the Alumni of Connecticut State Normal School, October 7, 1857.

Pivar, David J. *Purity Crusade: Sexual Morality and Social Control, 1868–1900*. Westport, Conn.: Greenwood Press, 1973.

Porterfield, Amanda. *Feminine Spirituality in America: From Sarah Edwards to Martha Graham*. Philadelphia: Temple University Press, 1980.

Quint, Howard E. *The Forging of American Socialism: Origins of the Modern Movement*. Indianapolis: Bobbs-Merrill Co., 1953.

Rein, David. *S. Weir Mitchell as a Psychiatric Novelist*. New York: International Universities Press, 1952.

Reisman, David. *Thorstein Veblen: A Critical Interpretation*. New York: Charles Scribner's Sons, 1953.

Rosenberg, Charles E. "Sexuality, Class, and Role in Nineteenth-Century America." *American Quarterly* 25, no. 2 (May 1973): 131–53.

Rosenberg, Rosalind. *Beyond Separate Spheres: Intellectual Roots of Modern Feminism*. New Haven: Yale University Press, 1982.

Ross, Edward Alsworth. *Seventy Years of It: An Autobiography of Edward Alsworth Ross*. New York: D. Appleton-Century Co., 1936. Reprint. New York: Arno Press, 1977.

Scharnhorst, Gary. *Charlotte Perkins Gilman: A Bibliography*. Metuchen, N.J.: Scarecrow Press, 1985.

————. "Making Her Fame: Charlotte Perkins Gilman in

California." *California History* 64 (Summer 1985): 192–201.

Schwarz, Judith. *Radical Feminists of Heterodoxy: Greenwich Village, 1912–1940*. Lebanon, N.H.: New Victoria Publishers, 1982.

Scott, Clifford. *Lester Frank Ward*. Boston: Twayne Publishers, 1976.

Scott, John A. *Woman Against Slavery: The Story of Harriet Beecher Stowe*. New York: Thomas Y. Crowell, 1978.

Scull, Andrew, ed. *Madhouses, Mad-Doctors, and Madmen: The Social History of Psychiatry in the Victorian Era*. Philadelphia; University of Pennsylvania Press, 1981.

Showalter, Elaine. *The Female Malady: Women, Madness, and English Culture, 1830–1980*. New York: Pantheon Books, 1985.

Sicherman, Barbara. "American History: A Review Essay." *Signs* 1, no. 2 (Winter 1975): 461–85.

————. "The New Psychiatry: Medical and Behavioral Science, 1895–1921." In *American Psychoanalysis: Origins and Development: The Adolph Meyers Seminars*, edited by Jacques M. Quen, M.D., and Eric T. Calhoun, M.D., pp. 20–37. New York: Brunner/Mazel, 1978.

————. "The Paradox of Prudence: Mental Health in the Gilded Age." *Journal of American History* 62 (1976): 890–912.

————. "The Uses of a Diagnosis: Doctors, Patients, and Neurasthenia." *Journal of the History of Medicine and Allied Sciences* 32, no. 2 (January 1977): 33–54.

Sklar, Kathryn Kish. *Catharine Beecher: A Study in American Domesticity*. New Haven: Yale University Press, 1973.

Smith, Sidonie. *A Poetics of Women's Autobiography: Marginality and the Fictions of Self-Representation*. Bloomington: Indiana University Press, 1987.

Smith-Rosenberg, Carroll. "The Hysterical Woman: Sex Roles and Role Conflict in Nineteenth-Century America." *Social Research* 34 (Winter 1972): 652–78.

Snitow, Ann, Christine Stansell, and Sharon Thompson, eds. *Powers of Desire: The Politics of Sexuality*. New York: Monthly Review Press, 1983.

Spacks, Patricia Meyer. *The Female Imagination*. New York: Alfred A. Knopf, 1972.

Starr, Harris E. *William Graham Sumner*. New York: Henry Holt & Co., 1925.

Stowe, Lyman Beecher. *Saints, Sinners, and Beechers*. Indianapolis: Bobbs-Merrill Co., 1934.

Strouse, Jean. *Alice James: A Biography*. Boston: Houghton Mifflin Co., 1980.

————, ed. *Women and Analysis: Dialogues on Psychoanalytic Views of Femininity*. 1974. Boston: G. K. Hall & Co., 1988.

Symonds, Alexandria, M.D. "Phobias After Marriage: Women's Declaration of Dependence." In *Psychoanalysis and Women*, edited by Jean Baker Miller, M.D., pp. 288–304. Baltimore and Middlesex, England: Penguin Books, 1973.

Thomas, John L. *Alternative America: Henry George, Edward Bellamy, Henry Demarest Lloyd, and the Adversary Tradition*. Cambridge: Harvard University Press, 1983.

Treichler, Paula A. "Escaping the Sentence: Diagnosis and Discourse in 'The Yellow Wallpaper.'" *Tulsa Studies in Women's Literature* 3, nos. 1–2 (Spring–Fall 1984): 61–77.

Treichler, Paula A. "The Wall Behind the Yellow Wallpaper: Response to Carol Neely and Karen Ford." *Tulsa Studies in Women's Literature* 4, no. 2 (Fall 1985): 323–30.

Vicinus, Martha. *Independent Women: Work and Community for Single Women, 1850–1920*. Chicago: University of Chicago Press, 1985.

Walker, Franklin D. *The Literary History of Southern California*. Berkeley: University of California Press, 1950.

————. *San Francisco's Literary Frontier*. New York: Alfred A. Knopf, 1939.

Ward, Lester. *Dynamic Sociology*. New York: D. Appleton & Co., 1883.

————. *Glimpses of the Cosmos*. New York: G. P. Putnam's Sons, 1917.

————. "Our Better Halves." *Forum* 6 (1888): 266–75.

Weinstein, James. *The Corporate Ideal in the Liberal State, 1900–1918*. Boston: Beacon Press, 1968.

Weintraub, Rochelle, ed. *Fabian Feminism: Bernard Shaw and Women*. University Park: Pennsylvania State University Press, 1977.

Williams, Juanita H., ed. *Psychology of Women: Selected Readings*. London: W. W. Norton & Co., 1979.

Wilson, Edward O. *On Human Nature*. Cambridge: Harvard University Press, 1978.

Wilson, R. J. *Darwinism and the American Intellectual*. Homewood, Ill.: Dorsey Press, 1967.

Winkler, Barbara Scott. *Victorian Daughters: The Lives and Feminism of Charlotte Perkins Gilman and Olive Schreiner*. Occasional Paper in Women's Studies, no. 13, American Culture Program. Ann Arbor: University of Michigan, 1980.

Permissions Acknowledgments

Grateful acknowledgment is made to the following for permission to reprint previously published material:

The Schlesinger Library, Radcliffe College: Excerpts from *The Living of Charlotte Perkins Gilman: An Autobiography*, by Charlotte Perkins Gilman (Harper and Row, 1975). Reprinted by permission of The Schlesinger Library, Radcliffe College.

Temple University Press: Excerpts from *Endure: The Diaries of Charles Walter Stetson*, edited by Mary A. Hill. Copyright © 1985 by Temple University. Reprinted by permission of Temple University Press.

Grateful acknowledgment is made to the following for permission to reprint previously unpublished material:

Dorothy S. Chamberlin and Walter S. Chamberlin: Excerpts from the unpublished writings of Charlotte Perkins Gilman. Reprinted by permission.

Dorothy S. Chamberlin, Walter S. Chamberlin, and The Bancroft Library, University of California, Berkeley: Excerpt from a letter by Charles Walter Stetson dated July 12, 1889, from the Charles Walter Stetson Correspondence, The Bancroft Library, University of California, Berkeley. Reprinted by permission.

Dorothy Chamberlin, Walter S. Chamberlin, and The Schlesinger Library, Radcliffe College: Excerpts from unpublished letters, diaries, manuscripts, and other unpublished material from the Gilman papers housed at The Schlesinger Library, Radcliffe College. Reprinted by permission.

Grateful acknowledgment is made to The College of Physicians of Philadelphia for permission to reproduce the portrait of S. Weir Mitchell by Robert W. Vonnoh. All other photographs are reproduced by permission of Dorothy S. Chamberlin. The photograph of Charlotte Perkins Gilman with the portrait of her mother is housed at The Schlesinger Library, Radcliffe College.

INDEX

Page numbers in *italics* refer to illustrations.